El pato mascota

por Patricia Abello
ilustrado por Phyllis Pollema-Cahill

Scott Foresman
is an imprint of

PEARSON

Glenview, Illinois • Boston, Massachusetts • Chandler, Arizona
Upper Saddle River, New Jersey

Every effort has been made to secure permission and provide appropriate credit for photographic material. The publisher deeply regrets any omission and pledges to correct errors called to its attention in subsequent editions.

Unless otherwise acknowledged, all photographs are the property of Pearson.

Photo locations denoted as follows: Top (T), Center (C), Bottom (B), Left (L), Right (R), Background (Bkgd)

Illustrations by Phyllis Pollema-Cahill

Photograph 8 ©Dorling Kindersley

ISBN 13: 978-0-328-61579-7
ISBN 10:   0-328-61579-X

Copyright © by Pearson Education, Inc., or its affiliates. All rights reserved. Printed in the United States of America. This publication is protected by copyright, and permission should be obtained from the publisher prior to any prohibited reproduction, storage in a retrieval system, or transmission in any form or by any means, electronic, mechanical, photocopying, recording, or likewise. For information regarding permissions, write to Pearson Curriculum Rights & Permissions, One Lake Street, Upper Saddle River, New Jersey 07458.

Pearson® is a trademark, in the U.S. and/or other countries, of Pearson plc or its affiliates.

Scott Foresman® is a trademark, in the U.S. and/or other countries, of Pearson Education, Inc., or its affiliates.

2 3 4 5 6 7 8 9 10 V0N4 13 12 11 10

Mira mi pato mascota.

Sí, mi pato Pepe me sigue.

Mi pato va a la tina de mami.

Mi pato Pepe nada muy bien.

Mi pato come de mi mano.

Así son los patos

Leamos juntos

Los patos son seres vivos. Necesitan comida y agua para vivir. Hay muchos tipos de patos. Viven en distintas partes del mundo.

Merrimack College

Library

DISCARD

North Andover, Massachusetts

LUTHER'S WORKS

LUTHER'S WORKS

VOLUME 5

LECTURES ON GENESIS
Chapters 26—30

JAROSLAV PELIKAN
Editor

WALTER A. HANSEN
Associate Editor

CONCORDIA PUBLISHING HOUSE · SAINT LOUIS

Copyright 1968 by
CONCORDIA PUBLISHING HOUSE
Saint Louis, Missouri

Library of Congress Catalog Card No. 55-9893

MANUFACTURED IN THE UNITED STATES OF AMERICA

Contents

General Introduction	vii
Introduction to Volume 5	ix
CHAPTER TWENTY-SIX	3
CHAPTER TWENTY-SEVEN	99
CHAPTER TWENTY-EIGHT	188
CHAPTER TWENTY-NINE	266
CHAPTER THIRTY	322
Indexes	387

General Introduction

The first editions of Luther's collected works appeared in the sixteenth century, and so did the first efforts to make him "speak English." In America serious attempts in these directions were made for the first time in the nineteenth century. The Saint Louis edition of Luther was the first endeavor on American soil to publish a collected edition of his works, and the Henkel Press in Newmarket, Virginia, was the first to publish some of Luther's writings in an English translation. During the first decade of the twentieth century, J. N. Lenker produced translations of Luther's sermons and commentaries in thirteen volumes. A few years later the first of the six volumes in the Philadelphia (or Holman) edition of the *Works of Martin Luther* appeared. Miscellaneous other works were published at one time or another. But a growing recognition of the need for more of Luther's works in English has resulted in this American edition of Luther's works.

The edition is intended primarily for the reader whose knowledge of late medieval Latin and sixteenth-century German is too small to permit him to work with Luther in the original languages. Those who can, will continue to read Luther in his original words as these have been assembled in the monumental Weimar edition (*D. Martin Luthers Werke. Kritische Gesamtausgabe*; Weimar, 1883 ff.). Its texts and helps have formed a basis for this edition, though in certain places we have felt constrained to depart from its readings and findings. We have tried throughout to translate Luther as he thought translating should be done. That is, we have striven for faithfulness on the basis of the best lexicographical materials available. But where literal accuracy and clarity have conflicted, it is clarity that we have preferred, so that sometimes paraphrase seemed more faithful than literal fidelity. We have proceeded in a similar way in the matter of Bible versions, translating Luther's translations. Where this could be done by the use of an existing English version — King James, Douay, or Revised Standard — we have done so. Where it could not, we have supplied our own. To indicate this in each specific instance would have been pedantic; to adopt a uniform procedure would have been artificial — especially in view of Luther's own inconsistency in this regard. In each volume the translator will be responsible primarily for matters of text and language, while the responsibility of the editor will extend principally to the historical and theological matters reflected in the introductions and notes.

Although the edition as planned will include fifty-five volumes, Luther's writings are not being translated in their entirety. Nor should they be. As he was the first to insist, much of what he wrote and said was not that important. Thus the edition is a selection of works that have proved their importance for the faith, life, and history of the Christian Church. The first thirty volumes contain Luther's expositions of various Biblical books, while the remaining volumes include what are usually called his "Reformation writings" and other occasional pieces. The final volume of the set will be an index volume; in addition to an index of quotations, proper names, and topics, and a list of corrections and changes, it will contain a glossary of many of the technical terms that recur in Luther's works and that cannot be defined each time they appear. Obviously Luther cannot be forced into any neat set of rubrics. He can provide his reader with bits of autobiography or with political observations as he expounds a psalm, and he can speak tenderly about the meaning of the faith in the midst of polemics against his opponents. It is the hope of publishers, editors, and translators that through this edition the message of Luther's faith will speak more clearly to the modern church.

J. P.
H. L.

Introduction to Volume 5

MOST of the lectures presented in this volume (Weimar, XLIII, 431–695; St. Louis, II, 122–609) are devoted to Luther's exposition of what he calls "the fourth book of Genesis" (cf. p. 200, note 11), covering the accounts of the latter part of the life of Isaac and the life of Jacob until just before his separation from Laban. It includes the birth of 11 of the 12 eponymous patriarchs of the tribes of Israel—of course, with the exception of Benjamin (cf. Gen. 35:16-20).

The chronological data about the actual lectures themselves are sparse and difficult to harmonize. Some of them come from the printed version of the lectures, some from the work of various scholars, notably Peter Meinhold. In part they are contained in external sources; in part they have been ferreted out of the text itself by our investigations. Arranged in the order of the chapters on which the lectures are based, these data present the following information:

26:1: On December 10, 1541, Jerome Besold wrote to Veit Dietrich (then in Nürnberg): "By the kindness of God, Doctor Martin is continuing with the exposition of Genesis, and a few days ago he began to expound chapter 26." Peter Meinhold suggests that December 5, 1541, a Monday, be taken as the day when Luther resumed his lectures, following an absence from the classroom that lasted a year or so.

26:9: Student notes indicate that Luther was lecturing on Gen. 26:9 on February 18, 1542. This was a Saturday, but it has been conjectured that he was making up for lectures he had missed, perhaps during his travels of the preceding month with Melanchthon.

26:24 and 30:30: Twice in these lectures Luther is represented as describing himself as "60 years old." The first such reference occurs in the context of some reflection about the mystery of human consciousness (p. 75). The other appears in the course of a discussion about many people whom Luther had known who had resembled the greedy Laban (p. 370). If both of these references were to be taken literally, this would mean that Luther traversed the ground from the end of Gen. 26 to the end of Gen. 30 between November 10, 1543, and November 9, 1544. Even apart from the other evidence, however, it should be pointed out that Luther often used round numbers when citing dates, even the dates of his own life; moreover, certain evidence suggests some confusion both in his own mind and in that of his relatives about the exact date of his birth.

27:11-22: In the eighth of his sermons, delivered from 1562 to 1565, on the life of Luther, John Mathesius reports: "When the Doctor was lecturing on Rebecca, Gen. 27, during the year [15]41 . . . I heard these words from him." It is evident from other sources that Mathesius was in Wittenberg until about April 12, 1542. Therefore Meinhold has proposed, quite plausibly, that the reference to "[15]41" be corrected to "1542" to bring it into harmony with the other information we have about the chronological sequence of Luther's lectures.

28: On June 29, 1542, John Forster wrote to John Schradin to inform him that Luther was still lecturing on the twenty-eighth chapter of Genesis.

28:20-22: In his exposition of this passage (p. 260), Luther speaks of Henry, who had become Duke of Saxony after the death of his brother, Duke George. Now Duke George had died on April 17, 1539. During 1541, Henry, who was feeling his advanced age, had turned over many of his administrative duties to his son, Maurice. Later in that year, on August 18, 1541, Henry had died, leaving the title to Maurice. When he succeeded to that title, Maurice was still a partisan of the Reformation and continued to be one during the time that these lectures were being delivered. Eventually, however, he switched sides and earned from the Lutherans the title "the Judas of Meissen"; this he had done by the time these lectures were edited for publication. Yet there is no reference at all to Maurice in the comment on p. 260; nor is Duke Henry spoken of as having died or as "of blessed memory," as Luther referred to him in an undated letter to Maurice, presumably written late in 1541 or early in 1542. Were it not for all the other evidence just cited, this internal testimony would suggest that Duke Henry was still living when this was spoken and therefore that Luther was lecturing on Gen. 28:20—22 sometime before August 18, 1541.

30:30: In connection with comments on the "sack of Rome," which took place on May 6, 1527, the lectures refer to the compact drawn up at Wurzen (p. 369). One of the parties to it was Maurice of Saxony. Luther was engaged in correspondence about Wurzen during April 1542. (The proximity of this reference on p. 369 to the second of the allusions to Luther's being "60 years old" must qualify any conclusions drawn from that allusion.) The comments on Wurzen here in the lectures suggest that Luther spoke these words a good while after the event.

As the introduction to Volume 6 will point out, there is at least some reason to believe that the materials on Gen. 31—37 contained there fall into the period from the latter part of 1542, through most or all of 1543, and perhaps even into sometime in 1544. The introduction to Volume 7 suggests that most of the lectures on Gen. 38—44 presented there were delivered during 1544, with some possibility that the earliest ones come from 1543. Greater precision of dating than this seems unattainable.

Collating these data, some of which cannot be harmonized with the rest, we would conclude that Luther seems to have lectured on Gen. 26—30 from the end of 1541 until the summer or early autumn of 1542. Nevertheless, some of the information does indeed seem difficult to square with such a conclusion, and we are compelled to take the text prepared by Luther's editors as it stands, without being able to determine either the precise date or the precise form of the actual lectures as Luther delivered them.

So far as the form of the lectures is concerned, that text manifests, in this volume as in the other seven volumes of the *Lectures on Genesis,* repeated evidence of editorial liberties which Luther's students took far beyond anything permitted by modern literary convention. Luther's quotations from the Latin and even from the Greek classics are extensive and almost always letter-perfect; his memory was, to be sure, phenomenal, but it was not infallible. The occasional outbursts of colloquial German are indeed sufficient to season the lecture, but they are much less frequent than they are in verbatim transcripts of other lectures. Various statements purportedly delivered in a classroom lecture are nevertheless (cf. p. 271, note 6) addressed to "the reader." Theological comments on various issues, including original sin (cf. p. 49) and the immortality of the soul (cf. p. 73), are cast in a form that arouses the suspicion of editorial manipulation and censorship. These and similar touches appear in the present volume too, alongside expositions which, both in form and in content, are so obviously Luther's own that we must accept them at face value, even though much of the text cannot be regarded as a presentation of Luther's *ipsissima verba*.

We have once more followed the practice of calling attention only to those typographical errors in the Weimar text which, if permitted to stand, would yield another Latin word; other errors we have simply corrected without comment. In most instances such corrections were justified by the text of earlier editions. Therefore unless the Weimar editors had access to manuscript evidence for the text beyond what they have listed, these divergences of the Weimar text from earlier editions must be taken as errors. In a few instances we have, either with or without the lead of the Weimar editors, adopted conjectural emendations that seem to be demanded by the context (e. g., p. 91, note 73; p. 100, note 2; p. 158, note 52; p. 178, note 64).

(During the translation of this volume Dr. George V. Schick died, having brought his work to nearly the end of chapter 27 [cf. p. 182]. Thus more than half of the American edition of these *Lectures on Genesis* stands as a monument to this learned Hebraist and classicist.)

J. P.

LECTURES ON GENESIS

Chapters 26–30

Translated by
GEORGE V. SCHICK and PAUL D. PAHL
Revised by the Editors

CHAPTER TWENTY-SIX

1. *Now there was a famine in the land, besides the former famine that was in the days of Abraham. And Isaac went to Gerar, to Abimelech, king of the Philistines.*

IT has often been stated that in this entire book the accounts of the fathers are described in a very ordinary covering, as it were, and are presented without any splendor or display of their religion, righteousness, and wisdom, yes, in accordance with the most inglorious aspect of their household management and their physical life. For what else does Moses relate about Isaac than that he was born to his father Abraham, begot children, tended cattle, and wandered about in various regions? Little or nothing is taught there about prayer and about the monstrous religious practices of the monks. But what is it to me that he was a husband and that he slept with his wife? Are these things to be taught in the church? For this is how the flesh clings to that external and very ordinary aspect when it looks at the life of the fathers and sees nothing that edifies but is only displeased. Later, however, it thinks about becoming acquainted with the life of St. Bernard, St. Antony, and men like them, where there are amazing and unbelievable works in the matter of abstinence, fastings, and vigils, and where there is no familiarity with women and servants, much less with cattle. It laughs at these ordinary and inglorious works in the household of Abraham, Isaac, or Jacob and devotes its attention to those that are splendid and magnificent. Or if these accounts are read at times in the churches, no one admires them; for no one observes the true worth and the true ornaments of these accounts.

Accordingly, we teach—and this should be diligently and frequently impressed—that in the examples of the saintly fathers it should be looked upon as the main thing and the highest commendation that God spoke with them and that they had the Word of God. This is the point that elucidates these accounts and gives a true understanding of what and how great these dregs and seemingly contemptible outward appearances of the greatest saints are. For where the Word of God is, there one also finds true faith and true works; for everything is done in the Word and under the Word. The other things, which are apart from the Word and without the Word, are performed only in accordance with our own will. Actually they are nothing else than dregs and dung before God.

For this reason all the lives of all the monks, no matter how showy they may be in the eyes of the flesh, are nevertheless altogether nothing. The outward appearance of sanctity was great in Antony, in Hilarion,[1] and in many others. Some of these men spent their life in fastings, and some in unnatural vigils, until they were 70 years old. The flesh, the heart, and the eye of man are taken in by these remarkable feats. But see whether there is a connection here with the Word of God. Ask Antony whether he has a word by which he has been commanded to go into the desert and to torture his flesh. He will say: "No, but to me this seemed good and pleasing to God." But that is the main thing that should be conspicuous in your works, Antony. Without it this entire life of yours is death and only the choice of your flesh; it is your own decision and nothing but ostentation and madness on the part of carnal men.

Consequently, Holy Scripture, in its accounts of the fathers, gives praise primarily to faith in the Word; for the Word of God sanctifies everything, inasmuch as it is holy, yes, holiness, truth, and wisdom itself. And the life that is governed by the Word is the true, righteous, wise, and eternal life. But if it lacks the Word, it also lacks truth, light, and wisdom before God, and all its doings are works of darkness.

Thus although marriage is an unclean kind of life because the copulation of the man and the woman cannot take place without carnal uncleanness, tending cattle is a filthy business, and the life of the government and of subjects is highly impure and abounds in vices — many sins flock together there, excesses of individuals as well as personal vices in addition to those that are general — nevertheless God has richly honored all this and has ordained it in His Word. And if you hold fast to the Word, you have already been cleansed of all your uncleanness.

---

[1] The names of these two hermits are frequently linked in the polemics of these lectures against monasticism; see, for example, *Luther's Works*, 4, p. 109.

Finally nobody lives without sins. But so great is the power of the Word that it devours all these, so that you can say: "I live my married life with my wife and children in peace, in fear of and trust in Thee; and thus I know that all is well." For in 1 Tim. 2:15 Paul says about the life of spouses that "woman will be saved through bearing children." How? "If they continue in faith." This is the first power of the Word.

Next the Word not only brings it about that the kind of life itself is saintly and pleases God but also stirs you up to all kinds of virtues and highly praiseworthy works; for it is not idle, provided that it is in your heart according to its true meaning and understanding. But it will remind you to think about calling upon and praising God. It will make you a priest and prophet of God, one whose sacrifices will be most pleasing to God because His eyes have regard for faith. The horrible monks do not see this effect either.

In the third place, if the devil notices that you have the Word and are confident that your life is pleasing and acceptable to God on account of the Word, he will not rest but will put in your way trials and afflictions of every kind even in the most trivial matters. You will experience faithlessness on the part of the household, the hatred of your neighbors, and the death of your children or of your wife.[2] All these things will happen in order that your faith may be exercised. But if the Word is not there, impatience and displeasure follow because of such an irksome and miserable kind of life, just as we hear many who exclaim that they entered into marriage not because God led them but because the devil urged them to do so.

The same thing happens to the magistrates. When they see the unrestrained wickedness of their subjects, the usurious practices, the greed and the lusts and endeavor to correct or punish these things in conformity with their duty, they incur the hatred and enmity of the people. Then grumbling and cursing arise no less than in marriage. And if such people are papists without any knowledge of the Word of God, they will flee and will abandon their marriage or the government and withdraw into solitude in order to serve God there in peace and quiet, but without the grace

---

[2] Luther's daughter Elizabeth died on August 3, 1528; his daughter Magdalena on September 20, 1542.

and the will of God. For God has declared His Word to all and has commanded everyone to attend to his calling.

Hence in order that you may overcome those difficulties and annoyances, whether in marriage or in the government, take care first of all that you have meditated well on the Word of God, in which the government is richly established, as we see in Rom. 12:8 and 13:1-4. Likewise in marriage, whether one is a manservant or a maidservant, whether a teacher or a pupil, they are sure of their station and the will of God. Just take hold of the Word, and bring forth fruits worthy of the Word, and you will see that affliction and trials follow at once. But prayer follows these. Deliverance follows prayer. The sacrifice of praise follows deliverance. Thus at the same time you will be able to bear your cross and to offer a sacrifice of praise, which the monks neither want nor are able to do. They are interested only in peace, the belly, and pleasure.

This is how Moses describes the life of this saintly father in accordance with this one chief point, namely, that he spent his life in many tribulations. He does not write about those speculations and contemplations and the hypocrisy of self-chosen works; he writes about the most excellent virtues of faith and godliness which those who are godless and carnal do not see. And this contrast must be carefully noted. The hypocrites choose outward and showy works, abstain from wine and meat, walk along with drooping heads, differ from others in dress, and avoid the inconvenience of life in the household and in the state. The fathers, on the other hand, live in the household with their children, wives, demestics, and cattle. Here there is no outward show of religion, but there is only one coarse sack of household life. The hypocrites put on gilded garments with which they shine before the world when they withdraw from the common life and from association with others. But under that sack of household life in the case of the fathers the sun, the moon, and the stars, that is, the most excellent virtues, shine. Under the most gorgeous dress of the hypocrites, however, the monstrosities of unbelief, spiritual pride, envy, and filth lie hidden. Nevertheless, it has the name and the outward appearance of a spiritual life.

But let us open our spiritual eyes and judge their spiritual vileness according to the rule and analogy of these accounts. For Moses makes no mention of their fasts or vigils and the like. You hear only that Isaac travels from Hebron to Gerar, suffers hunger, and seeks a dwelling place. But what great faith one sees there! What inestimable patience! What unbelievable forbearance, goodness, and kindness one sees! All these virtues shine like the sun and the moon. For me indeed it would be impossible to show such remarkable obedience. If I had two sons, a wife, domestics, such a great multitude of cattle and servants and did not have a footbreadth of ground to set my foot on, what would I do there? I would surely give up the control and management of the household and run away. For to be so unsettled and uncertain and yet to stay with wife, children, domestics, and cattle is a sign of an amazing faith that could [3] make bread out of stones. This the godless do not see.

But it was certainly a severe trial to change one's place daily and to look for new quarters. For this means living in the world and being an exile in the world. And Isaac could have sung with Christ (Luke 9:58): "The Son of Man has nowhere to lay His head." Consequently, it is not apparent to anyone who reads this only in passing what great faith is given praise in the case of the patriarch Isaac. In comparison with this faith the cowls, orders, and works of all the papists vanish completely. For there is no one of them who would want to be without a bed, a dwelling place, or food for a single day. But what an excellent religion, please the gods! Yet the condition of the patriarch Isaac is all the more difficult because he is not alone but is tied to his wife, children, and domestics for whose support he was compelled to provide in a foreign land. There indeed his faith was tried and severely exercised.

Therefore let us learn to enlarge upon and elucidate the accounts of the patriarchs in opposition to the monstrosities of the hypocrites and the monks, who maintain that to have a wife and children is a voluptuous life, and that for this reason it cannot be devout or saintly. For consider whether all opportunities for joy and physical pleasure have not been cut off for Isaac, since he was uncertain every hour where to set his foot. No one of the monks will imitate this. Indeed, they live a truly blessed life in this world, a life that abounds in pleasures; they have excellent houses, are under the protection of the pope, and rule over the world.

Therefore this wandering of Isaac puts to shame all the religious practices of the papists, and in him the highest form of wor-

---

[3] The Weimar edition reads *esset* here, but we have preferred the reading *posset*, which appears in the Erlangen edition.

ship shines; this is faith in God. He travels about with his entire household and has no fixed dwelling place, no pasture lands, and not a droplet of water. Someone else would say: "Where am I to get them?" Answer: "I believe in God the Father." For Isaac thought like this: "God will provide for me a dwelling place as I travel about. He will give pasture lands for my cattle and will provide food and drink for my domestics." Thus Isaac makes the highest sacrifice of faith every day of his life and lives in the world without the world and outside the world.

About this faith, which is very great in the fathers, the godless are not concerned; they look only at the little wife, the domestics, and the cattle. The faith which supports and preserves all this they do not see. If in our time someone were to roam about in this manner, he would not be able to have manservants or maidservants who would follow him as he traveled about. But faith works wonders; it brings it about that the domestics endure such great misfortunes, trials, and poverty with equanimity and show themselves obedient in all things. I certainly would be unable to acquire such upright servants, for I do not have such great faith. Nor can anyone of the saints in the New Testament [4] achieve this greatness of the virtues in these fathers. In comparison with them they are simply little children and infants. They have no sanctity whatever except their celibacy. But Isaac's wandering surpasses this too. Indeed, his marriage is far more excellent than all the celibacy of the monks, just as the light of the sun is brighter than any candle.

Therefore their entire life abounds in miracles, for they live simply from the hand of God and on almost nothing. They are dependent on the kindness and the promise of God and hold firmly to this hope: "If I have nothing today and do not see what I shall live on, I shall surely get it tomorrow or on the day after tomorrow." Virtues of this kind should be carefully taken into consideration in the account of Isaac, but above all the fact that he is filled with faith in God, who cherishes and supports him.

Then he undoubtedly accustomed his heart to patience, gentleness, and kindness toward his neighbor. He learned to bear wrongs, whether done to himself or to his household. He did not quarrel out of hatred and a desire for vengeance. For the saintly fathers

---

[4] From the context it is evident that by "the New Testament" Luther means the entire era since Christ.

were hospitable, compassionate, and kind toward friends and enemies alike, because in them there shone an outstanding faith, which produces such excellent virtues. About these virtues the sophists dispute ineptly and in a godless manner whether they are commandments or counsels, and they conclude that they are only counsels.[5] The Sorbonnists say that people can be saved even though they have shown no kindesss toward one another.[6] And the monastic life is indeed of that kind, namely, only an outward hypocrisy, which disregards these virtues, as though they were merely counsels.

But these examples teach that the highest forms of worship and those that are necessary in the highest degree are dependent on the promise and providence of God, who has promised that He will be our Father, and that one should hope and look for help from Him. This a monk does not do insofar as he is a monk. But after faith there follow, as fruits from a good tree, love toward the good and the evil, kindness toward the grateful and the ungrateful.

Furthermore, Moses tells about an outstanding occasion on which the faith of this most saintly man is proved. For a famine arises in the land—a famine which affects not only Isaac, along with his two sons, his wife, and his whole household, but the entire land round about Hebron. In this great and general disaster his faith is exercised, and is praised to such an extent that we can all marvel at it but cannot easily imitate it.

But one should note first of all that commonly, when the Word is flourishing and the Lord gives an abundance of spiritual food, physical hunger soon threatens; for the devil takes away the sustenance of the church and wants to kill it off with hunger. And this surely must have been an extraordinary famine, because Moses compares it to the earlier famine, which occurred at the time of Abraham and had now almost disappeared from memory; for meanwhile approximately a hundred or more years had elapsed. Therefore Moses recalls the earlier famine and compares it to the present one in order to point out the extreme scarcity and the distress.

But how does it come that such saintly people did not obtain

---

[5] On this distinction see Luther's comments, *Luther's Works*, 21, p. 4, and throughout the commentary on the Sermon on the Mount.

[6] In the course of these *Lectures on Genesis* Luther took several occasions to respond to the attacks of the theologians at Paris; see, for example, *Luther's Works*, 8, p. 284.

from God the food that was necessary for themselves and for others? For not only Abraham and Isaac but also other very eminent patriarchs and prophets—Jacob, Joseph, Elijah, Elisha, and eventually even Paul and other godly men—had to endure the general disaster of famine together with others. My answer is that God sends famine, wars, pestilence, and similar disasters in the first place to try and to test the godly, in order that they may learn to maintain with assurance that they will be nourished even in a time of famine, even though they are forced to experience various difficulties and, in addition, to look for unknown and uncertain dwelling places. In the second place, He does so in order to offend and punish the ungodly. For when the Word has been abundantly revealed, people become ungrateful, yes, persecute and hate the Word. The others, who seem to accept it, become disgusted with and sick of this very unimportant food; they despise and harass its ministers. With this contempt and hatred they provoke the wrath of God, so that He says: "If you do not want to be satisfied with spiritual food and life, I will take away from you even this physical life and will kill you with famine." Consequently, through neglect of the incalculable treasure they lose the advantages even of the present life. And just as the godly are preserved, so the godless are overwhelmed by misfortunes and despair; and, since they are without the Word, they are slain.

But then Satan, who is delighted by this offense, seizes upon this as a reason for slandering and disparaging the Word of God and turns it to his own advantage in order to alienate the hearts of men from the Word. For what else shall we suppose the Canaanites thought? Before Abraham's arrival, they enjoyed rich blessings of every kind, and now they were being compelled to endure hunger with him. What else shall we suppose they thought than that this Chaldean was the cause of all the evils and disasters? The second reason is this, that the devil and the godless may have an opportunity to blaspheme the Gospel, so that they become progressively worse just as today we are compelled everywhere to hear and bear similar complaints that in former times there were most abundant yields of everything and amazing good fortune, but that now grain is costlier and everything is in a far worse condition.[7]

---

[7] This was apparently a frequent complaint; cf. *Luther's Works*, 8, pp. 108 to 109.

Yet to me at least this does not seem to result from a scarcity of products but rather from the greed and wickedness of the people who arbitrarily increase the prices of things. Nevertheless, it is not a light misfortune with which the poor and the ministers of the Word are being hard pressed. The others, who have an abundance of wealth, have less trouble. Consequently, many long for the former state of affairs with its previous prosperity, and they add the blasphemy that nothing good has come from this doctrine of the Gospel and that, in addition, both the inclinations of the people and their morals are far more corrupt than in times past.

Thus the doctrine of the Gospel is blamed for every evil. When the Goths were laying Italy waste at the time of Augustine, in Rome the entire blame was put on the apostles Peter and Paul.[8] For wicked people remove from their eyes the sins of the world, and the Word of God, which is completely pure and holy, unjustly bears the blame for all crimes; for it does not teach usurious practices, greed, luxury, and the other misdeeds and frauds of the world, but it cries out and fights against all these sins. Why, then, is the Gospel burdened with such atrocious slanders? Because the wickedness of Satan, in which he delights, consists in blaspheming the Gospel and heaping up abuses against it from all sides.

It is altogether horrible and deplorable that people are so wicked and unrestrained while this light is shining. But you should have been taught this way from the Word, namely, that the Gospel does not grant a license for usurious practices, acts of rapine, luxury, gambling, etc. Yet if you attach this blame to the Gospel, you are now convicted out of your own mouth of being possessed of the devil, who is the author of these blasphemies. For you see that the opposite is being taught and that those who obey the doctrine acknowledge and are aware of salvation, yes, even live in a manner that is godly and pure. Nor can you deny that it is the truth. Yet whatever wicked deeds there are among the Epicureans and godless, you, because of sheer malice on the part of the devil, attribute to the doctrine, with the result that you and all who hate the truth are judged.

Augustine tells of many horrible crimes and wicked deeds of

---

[8] Luther is summarizing the early chapters of Augustine's *City of God*, which he had annotated more than 30 years earlier (W, IX, 24—27).

the Romans: murder, lustful deeds, usurious practices, etc.[9] Do those things not deserve to be punished by God? Consequently, this is altogether devilish, and the fact that people forget it all and attribute the cause of the evils as well as of the punishments to the Word cannot even be thought of without horrible wickedness.

These things have been written for our instruction (cf. Rom. 15:4), lest we be offended by blasphemies of this kind. For in this manner all the godly at all times have endured famine and the slanders of the godless; and the saintlier they were, the more punishments and disasters there were in the world, not that they themselves caused them and disturbed the world, but because the world spurned the light of the Word and engaged in idolatry. Thus Elijah answers King Ahab (1 Kings 18:18): "I have not troubled Israel; but you have, and your father's house, because you have forsaken the commandments of the Lord and followed the Baals."

Today we shall answer blasphemous complaints in the same way and say: "While the Gospel is shining and showing the way of salvation, you are ungrateful despisers and persecutors. For this reason punishments come, the Turk comes, and misfortunes of every kind begin."

Meanwhile, however, the godly, too, are afflicted, just as Isaac endured want and famine in his time. He was a stranger and an exile, and he thought that he should bear the current misfortune calmly. But the purpose of these afflictions should be carefully noted. Although public misfortunes affect the saints and the prophets, this does not happen as a punishment or because of anger, as in the case of the godless and the ungrateful; it happens for their salvation and to test and prove their faith, love, and patience, in order that the godly may learn to bear the hand of God in the management of their households. For God has promised that He wants to support them in the time of famine, as it is written (Ps. 37:25): "I have not seen the righteous forsaken." Likewise (Ps. 37:19): "In the days of famine they have abundance." God confirms these promises with such examples of the saints, and by means of this tribulation in the household He instructs the godly in the Word, in faith, in humility of spirit, in love, and in other virtues. But the godless are tormented to punish and offend them, so that they are hardened and become worse; for they are not improved by what is

---

[9] Apparently a reference to Book III of Augustine's *City of God*.

[W, XLIII, 437]

good but become worse by what is evil. For this reason one accomplishes nothing, whether joyful or sad songs are sung to them, as Matt. 11:17 says.

Now look at and consider that most ordinary outward appearance of household management, and compare it with all the works of the monks, of Antony or Hilarion. For what are all the fasts and all the exceedingly severe castigations of the monks in comparison with that one famine? It appears to be an insignificant and unimportant trial if you look at it only outwardly and in passing. But imagine that you are in the house of Isaac, who has a wife and children, likewise a large number of servants and cattle, when there is such a great scarcity of food and fodder. Imagine that you are hearing the complaints of the domestics, who are demanding either that bread be given to them or that hay be given to the cattle. If you answer: "I do not have any; I shall run away and forsake my household," yet the command of God stands in the way. He wants you to remain in your station.

You will say: "From what source, then, shall I provide food?" Learn to understand what kind of fasting this is when a poor head of a household is compelled not only to endure hunger himself but sees both his wife and his very dear children almost killed by hunger. Add to this the fact that Isaac was an exile and a foreigner and had no fixed abode. Undoubtedly he would have been glad to remain in Hebron; but since the people there were also plagued by the famine, they ordered him to leave. For they were unable to feed him along with such a large household, and they themselves were barely able to support themselves and their cattle.

Consequently, Isaac is compelled to depart, and the misfortune becomes twice as great; for exile is added to the famine. Then Isaac's heart surely throbbed and cried out; for in accordance with God's command in 1 Tim. 5:8 he could not give up or cast aside the concern for his household, and he had nothing to live on.

Now give me an example that would be like this patience. Surely you will not find one among the Carthusians or among the other hypocrites. They would simply say that these things are impossible. Why, then, do they say that it is vile and filthy to sleep with one's wife and to govern one's household? Indeed, consider how we behave in perils of this kind and how dejected we are if at some time an abundance of grain or money is not at hand, and how easily we lapse into despair or impatience. Here Isaac was in the height of anxiety and in the utmost peril. Yet he did not run away. Nor did he give up faith and hope.

And from this it is clear what it means to be a godly husband. Isaac struggles not only with famine and want but also with despair and impatience. But his firm and invincible faith shines forth; for he remains the head of the household, does not abandon his wife, and does not forsake his household but sets out for another place in order to seek provisions there. Although he, too, was not without perils and troubles, he nevertheless takes heart and sustains himself with this comfort: "God has ordered me to be a husband and has given me two sons. I know that this is His work. Therefore He will not forsake me."

Thus these domestic works do not teach pleasure and delight of the flesh but present examples of the battles and struggles of the saints against unbelief, distrust, and contempt for and murmuring against God. Of these conflicts the monks have no knowledge. They seek only full bellies. They are neither willing nor able to trust in God when misfortune comes.

But here there is an outstanding example of faith that struggles and cries out to God; for where the Word is, there prayer follows. And the journey through Palestine to Egypt which Isaac is undertaking shows how great this struggle was. This is why God has compassion on him and comforts him with a new statement. But the Word of God is not wont to come, especially not anew, except to those who are sorely afflicted and are in need of comfort. It does not come to those who are satiated, for it has no place among them.

Moreover, Isaac's two sons and his wife Rebecca increased his distress. At that time Esau and Jacob were about 18 years old, and amid such great difficulties the journey to an unknown land undoubtedly displeased them, and they said to their father: "Dear father, to what place do you intend to depart?" Thus Rebecca also said: "Dear Isaac, consider what you are doing." Thus Job's wife reproaches her husband with his misfortune (cf. Job 2:9). For they are saintly women, but they are not without trials. Therefore their hearts had to be comforted, in order that they might wait a little while and bear this cross with patience. And this famine led to many excellent sermons which Isaac delivered at that time in order to keep the domestics, and also his wife and children, in the faith. But at that very moment, when his children, his wife, and his domestics are almost overcome by their tribulation and begin to murmur or to think of running away, heaven opens, and a new and magnificent promise comes. While Isaac is thinking of entering Egypt through Palestine and is about to go into exile in the name of the Lord, and God permits him to gird himself for the journey, and the cord, which has been stretched exceedingly tight, is almost torn, then the necessary and excellent comfort is sent down from heaven: "Do not go down to Egypt, etc."

2. *And the Lord appeared to him and said: Do not go down to Egypt; dwell in the land of which I shall tell you.*

3. *Sojourn in this land, and I will be with you, and will bless you; for to you and to your descendants I will give all these lands, and I will fulfill the oath which I swore to Abraham your father.*

4. *I will multiply your descendants as the stars of heaven, and will give to your descendants all these lands; and by your descendants all the nations of the earth shall be blessed,*

5. *because Abraham obeyed My voice and kept My charge, My commandments, My statutes, and My laws.*

That this was a truly great tribulation is evident in particular from the fact that Isaac was not able to be satisfied with the earlier promises he had from his father Abraham and from Shem:[10] "The elder shall serve the younger, etc." (Gen. 25:23). For his heart is still throbbing, and his faith is in trouble, so that God is compelled to buoy him up with a new comfort. Accordingly, this example has been presented not only to us but also to the apostles and the saints themselves, in order that we may learn to make our hearts strong for patience and may not murmur against God in any trial, no matter in what kind of life we shall have to live. The condition of the church, of household management, and of the state is wretched, especially if you want to be a godly person; for all who want to live a godly life in Christ will suffer persecution. In household management there are constant quarrels and disputes with the domestics. In the government honor and power stand out, and for this reason it seems to be a life full of pleasure. But if you get to be a godly judge, a godly magistrate, you will find out what a great

---

[10] This reflects Luther's chronological computation; cf. *Luther the Expositor,* p. 104.

burden that outward appearance of honor, glory, and wealth brings with it. If you get to be a godly preacher, even among godly and grateful hearers, you will nevertheless be compelled to endure the utmost ingratitude of the heretics, likewise the hatred and the countless snares of the devil.

Consequently, you should not be dissatisfied with your station, which, as you know, has been assigned to you by God, no matter how despised and low it may be. But glory in God, who calls, directs, and is also present with His Word. For in Rom. 8:31 we read: "If God is for us, who is against us?" If some bitterness or difficulty occurs, pour on Falernian wine,[11] namely, the Word of God, and wash that bitterness away, in order that your faith may grow and be strengthened and you may be able to say: "I am sure concerning the godly and Christian kind of life in which I am living, and I shall continue in it in order that I may praise and extol God and teach others."

Moreover, we see that here nearly all the promises which God had given to Abraham in various places are repeated and brought together. All those promises are summed up here. For God spoke with Abraham rather often. But with Isaac He spoke barely two or three times. And this is also enough, for here, in a kind of summary, He confirms all His promises, lest the very saintly patriarch begin to have doubts about God's will when the devil tempts him. For the devil does not cease to harass even the saintliest and most perfect men with his fiery and poisonous darts (cf. Eph. 6:16).

Furthermore, this promise has two parts. The first is temporal. It deals with the possession of these lands. God says: "I will be with you. Do not be afraid. You will be driven into exile and be afflicted with famine. But there will be no danger. You will not perish from hunger. Nor will an enemy harm you in a foreign land."

In this manner God comforts him in the very serious trial in order to strengthen the hearts of his wife, his children, and his domestics, to whom Isaac set forth this comfort: "The Lord God is with me and has promised deliverance from all evils. Therefore I shall have peace, protection, and bread in the midst of enemies and famine." For to this promise he gave his firm assent, even though previously he was tempted to be in doubt. Later on, how-

---

[11] Falernian wine was celebrated in Roman literature for its taste (cf. Horace, *Carmina*, II, 11, 19).

ever, we shall hear how he was afraid of dying and denied that he had a wife. For those saintly men had flesh and blood, just as we have. Therefore they were sometimes troubled with weakness of faith, just as we are.

But God repeats what He stated previously, namely, "To you and to your descendants I will give these lands," and omits the little phrase "to you"; for He says only: "I will give to your descendants these lands" when explaining the promise. For neither Abraham nor Isaac nor Jacob possessed any part of this land. Thus it has been stated above that Abraham purchased with his own money a field as a burial place for Sarah (Gen. 23:16). Nevertheless, God did not give him even a footbreadth of the Promised Land until his descendants were brought into it. And the first promise of this land was made to Abraham on account of the glorious Seed in whom all nations were to be blessed, in order that there might be a land and a definite place from which Christ, who blesses the whole world and all nations, would have to be expected, in order that the Gospel might not go forth into the world without testimony, but that the whole world might be assured that He who had been born in this land in accordance with the promise is the true Savior and Blesser.

Yet by means of that earlier connection of Abraham himself and the Seed, eternal life and the resurrection are pointed out to believers, namely, that Abraham, Isaac, and Jacob are the possessors of this land, even though they did not own even a footbreadth. For even though they died, yet they live. Therefore this possession pertains to them, since Abraham is not dead but lives. Furthermore, when God says: "To you and to your descendants," it is also pointed out that the descendants would not have possessed the land if the fathers had not received the promise. And in the faith of the fathers the descendants got possession of the land.

The second part of the promise is spiritual, and because of this spiritual promise the physical promise was given, as has already been stated. Moreover, the words and the meaning are identical, as above in chapter 22:18. And whatever can be said here to explain it has been said above, just as the force of the verb "to bless" has also been explained.[12] It belongs to the fourth class, and the

---

[12] This is a reference to the earlier discussion, *Luther's Works*, 4, pp. 152 to 154.

Latins give the meaning with expressions like *gloriari in Domino, laudari in Domino* ("to pride oneself in the Lord," "to praise oneself in the Lord"). When I bless myself in the Lord, I do not cause you to bless, that is, to bless others; but I extol and praise myself, not in myself but in the Seed of ABRAHAM. For I am lost and cursed in Adam, delivered into the power of SATAN, who keeps me bound under the yoke of sin, death, and damnation. There no one can bless or glory; but there is sighing, crying, and boundless misery.

But when the Seed of Abraham is about to come, then all nations will become other men. To be sure, they will not have anything in themselves to glory in; but concerning themselves they will proclaim their condemnation and their wretched state. Yet they are destined to rule and, joyful and saved, to triumph, not in themselves but in that Seed. And this is done today by all who believe in Christ. In this way Scripture has been fulfilled. For all Christians feel and speak like this: "If I have been condemned in myself through Adam, yet I am righteous and holy in the Lord Jesus Christ, the Son of God. He is my life, my righteousness, sanctification, and redemption" (cf. 1 Cor. 1:30). Thus I bless myself on account of something else and through someone else, not with my own blessing but with the blessing of the Seed of Abraham. And when I take hold of Him through the Word and believe, I can glory, as it is written in Ps. 34:1-2: "In the Lord do I bless myself, and my soul glories" namely, that I have life over against death, salvation over against perdition, and God as my Father over against the devil, who is a tyrant and my enemy.

These are grand and glorious things, and they cannot be repeated and impressed enough; for they are words of comfort and eternal life. Thus Christ impresses the same things on His disciples often and diligently, as in John 14:1: "Let not your hearts be troubled; believe in God, believe also in Me." Likewise (John 14:19): "Because I live, you will live also." Likewise (John 16:33): "Be of good cheer; I have overcome the world and the devil." How? "Through My victory, which is yours." This passage concerning Abraham's promise and faith is the chief and foremost passage in all Holy Scripture. Thus Christ praises this faith in John 8:56 when He says: "Abraham saw My day and was glad." For Abraham understood that this blessing would be the one through which all nations in the whole world would be blessed, namely, that his glorying pertained not only to the descendants of his flesh but to all nations in the whole world. This is a memorable word which the prophets and apostles took pains to teach.

What these words contain in addition to this has been explained above,[13] namely, the resurrection of the dead; the victory over sin, death, and the devil; and the eternal kingdom. Likewise that the Seed is the Son of God and a man. For if He were not God, He would not be able to bless us accursed men; if He were not a man, the blessing would not come to us.

This little statement, "Because Abraham obeyed My voice, etc.," has also been explained above at chapter 22.[14] For this blessing was not given to Abraham in order that he might be made righteous through it; but since he was already righteous through faith, he received this blessing as a very excellent reward. He is righteous, obedient, and saintly. And because he is so obedient, he will be exalted to such an extent that Christ will put on flesh from his seed, as Romans 9:5 says. It it indeed a great honor that He who is the Son of God, the Destroyer of hell, the Victor over death, the Abrogator of the Law, and the Restorer of eternal life comes from the seed of Abraham.

But in the text there are four words which we shall explain, for the Jews want to conclude from this that the Law of Moses existed even before Moses. And it is true that almost everything in Moses was taken from the fathers and their books.[15] Yet there is a difference. מִשְׁמַר, that is, "charge," is a general noun frequently used in Leviticus; for the Levites are said to keep the charges of the Lord, just as we say in German: *wart, was ich dich heissen werde.* I am commanding someone to be ready and to wait for my commands. Thus the Levites stood in the tabernacle and waited for the command of the high priest in case he ordered them to do something. In the same way it is stated here: "Abraham kept My charge." *Er wartet auff mich, thet, was ich jhn hiess.* This means that when he was commanded to sacrifice his son, he obeyed My voice, etc.

---

[13] "Abraham understood the doctrine of the resurrection of the dead," *Luther's Works,* 4, p. 96.

[14] Cf. *Luther's Works,* 4, pp. 133—134.

[15] This suggestion recurs in these lectures; cf. *Luther's Works,* 2, p. 116, note 27.

Strictly speaking, מִצְוָה denotes commandments and a constant charge, as the Decalog is.

חֹק is the regulation of the rites that have to do with the divine worship, when God ordains something for the worship. It is not a command; it is an established form of worship. Ps. 2:7 says: "I will tell of the decree," that is, the form of worship. God will establish another form of worship through His Son.

תּוֹרָה is that which is beneficial for shaping morals. To this מִשְׁמַר [16] and the rites also pertain. Thus Abraham was observant and waited for the commands of the Lord, also for the commands that pertained to morals. At the same time he observed the Decalog, the rite of the Sabbath, and the law of circumcision.

But the difference between the Law of Moses and that of the fathers is this: Moses had a definite command to establish the Levitical priesthood, which pertained to a definite people, definite persons, a definite place, and to a definite time up to Christ. This is the principal part of the Law of Moses. Then he decreed a kingdom and 12 princes in the state. Strictly speaking, however, the Decalog and other laws that originated with the fathers are not Mosaic. Only those ceremonials that pertain to definite persons are Mosaic. But when the time appointed for all these things came to an end, the sacrifices and all the Mosaic regulations came to an end. The priesthood, with its sacrifices, no longer had any validity. Nor did the kingdom, for Moses had come to an end. But the kingdom and the priesthood of Christ followed, without a place, time, or person, and "without any outward sign," as Christ says in Luke 17:20.

Finally something must be said about the divine appearance. There is a twofold appearance in the Holy Scriptures: in dreams and in the outward aspect, or in a visible form or figure. God is also said to appear if He spoke through Shem or Eber, who were living at that time and were high priests. Yet because nothing is added here, but it is clearly stated that He appeared, it is understood that the appearance did not take place in dreams but in a visible form; that is, it was an angel who appeared in the outward aspect of a human being, just as the angels came to the Blessed Virgin, to Peter, and above, in chapter 18, to Abraham. And surely this appearance was an outstanding honor to Isaac; for although

---

[16] We are following here the conjecture of the Weimar editors.

he had heard his father's sermons about the promises, yet his heart trembled in this tribulation. Accordingly, God comes with a new confirmation of the promises.

And it is surely a great thing for God to appear to a human being and to fit His promises to a particular individual. For this reason many consider the saintly fathers far more blessed in this respect than we are, since they had such definite and individual comforts and appearances from God through the ministry of the angels. Someone will say: "If He were to appear to me, too, in a human form, what great joy this would bring to my heart! Then I would surely not be reluctant to undergo any peril or misfortunes for God's sake. But this has been denied me. I only hear sermons, read Scripture, and make use of the sacraments. I have no appearances of angels."

I answer: You have no reason to complain that you have been visited less than Abraham or Isaac. You, too, have appearances, and in a way they are stronger, clearer, and more numerous than those they had, provided that you open your eyes and heart and take hold of them. You have Baptism. You have the Sacrament of the Eucharist, where bread and wine are the species, figures, and forms in which and under which God in person speaks and works into your ears, eyes, and heart. Besides, you have the ministry of the Word and teachers through whom God speaks with you. You have the ministry of the Keys, through which He absolves and comforts you. "Fear not," He says, "I am with you." He appears to you in Baptism. He baptizes you Himself and addresses you Himself. He not only says: "I am with you," but: "I forgive you your sins. I offer you salvation from death, deliverance from all fear and from the power of the devil and hell. And not only I am with you, but all the angels with Me." What more will you desire? Everything is full of divine appearances and conversations.

But here we should complain and sob against our flesh, which is poisoned and sunk in sin and does not let us believe and accept such great blessings. Over and above this, it tells us to argue and to question whether these things are true. I am speaking about us, who are truly Christians, who teach and believe these things. I not only believe in Christ, but I know that He is sitting at the right hand of the Father to be our Mediator and to intercede for us. I know that the bread and the wine in the Lord's Supper are the body and blood of Christ and that the word of the pastor, whether he preaches or absolves, is the Word of God. Yet the flesh is weighed down by doubt, so that it does not believe these things. This is great wretchedness and is bitterer than death itself. Indeed, the reason why death is bitter is that the hindrances of the flesh prevent us from believing. Otherwise affliction would be a joy, and death would be a sleep for us who believe.

We should deplore these evils, which are implanted in us through Adam as a result of original sin, and we should pray God to increase and strengthen faith in us and to sustain us under the heaven of the forgiveness of sins, as Christ taught us to pray (Matt. 6:12): "Forgive us our debts." For it is a great evil that we, overwhelmed as we are with so many and such great appearances, conversations, and forms, still do not believe. And we are right in saying with St. Paul (Rom. 7:22-23): "I delight in the Law of God, in my inmost self; but I see in my members another law at war with the law of my mind." Likewise (Rom. 7:19): "For I do not do the good I want, but the evil I do not want is what I do." I would be glad to believe what is true, and to believe it as it actually is. I would want my faith to be as sure and strong as the fact itself. But the sin in my flesh resists the Spirit, so that I am unable to believe so firmly. He, however, who could regard Baptism with the wonder it deserves and could esteem it highly would laugh at death and demons, and to him the Turk would be כְּמֹץ, in accordance with Ps. 1:4, that is, husks or chaff.

Consequently, this should be read and meditated on constantly, and we should pray that our faith may increase from day to day. The thing is sure and unfailing. Therefore we should not long wonderingly for the special visions of the fathers. On the Last Day Abraham will say: "If I had been a Christian, I would have believed these things with a far stronger faith. I believed one single promise. I was the example and the first. You have countless examples; you have your parents; you have brothers who absolve you and offer you these visible species." Therefore it is disgraceful for us to be weaker in faith than the patriarchs themselves were. In consequence of one promise they overcame kings and kingdoms. They believed one word; but as for us, who have been helped by so many examples of past and present saints, the longer we preach, the more sluggish we become. And it is clear that the same thing is happening to us that Pythagoras told about the movement of the heavenly spheres, whether he had this from himself or from the fathers, namely, that these movements constantly produce the most delightful music, but that because of this constant repetition the minds and ears of mortals have become so numb that they no longer hear them.[17]

Thus we see God baptizing, absolving, comforting, and administering the Lord's Supper. But who hears this or wonders at it? We are moved either not at all or too little by His threat, promise, comfort, and sacraments. Therefore we deserve to be blamed, we who do not concern ourselves about that most delightful music of the kingdom of heaven. Even if we heard the angels preaching in their majesty, we would be affected no more than we are now when we hear a pastor or ministers. If we actually concluded that it is the Word of God that we are hearing, we would not snore this way. But because we think that human beings are speaking and that it is a human word, we are getting to be altogether like brutes. Here we should sob and grieve that original sin is so powerful even in the regenerate. Otherwise there are enough and more than enough of those who blaspheme and persecute the Word. Although we, too, are not good — as Christ says in Luke 11:13: "You, who are evil" — yet we should take pains that we do not persecute it and that we acknowledge that wickedness of our flesh. Thus Paul exclaims (Rom. 7:24): "Wretched man that I am! Who will deliver me from this body of death?" The body is mortal, filled with poison, corrupt, and wholly hellish. When the times are good, we readily glory, and we bless ourselves in the Lord, as is stated in Ps. 30:6: "As for me, I said in my prosperity: 'I shall never be moved.'" And again (Ps. 30:7): "Thou didst hide Thy face; I was dismayed." Then the flesh returns and drives out all joy.

Hence these things are written to instruct us, so that we are able not only to disprove and refute the arguments of our adversaries but also to resist our flesh, which depresses us with the weight of sin and fear, so that we do not say: "In the Seed of Abraham I am righteous, saved, and lord over death, the devil, and the Turks." Therefore we should learn and love the Word, in which it is taught that one should believe in the Promised Seed. But then the flesh must be subdued — the flesh which opposes the law of the mind and takes us captive. And wherever we have been overcome,

---

[17] This theory of Pythagoras had been the subject of comment in the exposition of the creation story (*Luther's Works*, 1, p. 126).

our faith should immediately take courage and become strong, lest the flesh completely suppress the spirit. But if we cannot suddenly attain perfection, so that we are without an awareness of sin, death, and hell; if we cannot become perfect dialecticians and rhetoricians, let us meanwhile be abecedarians and pupils of Donatus[18] until we come to dialectics and rhetoric. For this life is one of first fruits, not of tithes.[19] Therefore Paul himself complains, as has been stated before: "I see another law at war, making me captive" (cf. Rom. 7:23). I would want what is good and would gladly do it. I would gladly be the kind of person who would have no doubt at all and would not be distressed at all by any tribulation. The thing itself is certain, and Scripture is true; but the flesh stands in the way. What, then, shall I do? If I cannot take hold of it with such firm assent of my heart, I am angry with my flesh and say (Rom. 7:24): "Who will deliver me from this body of death?" For this body and flesh makes death bitter and terrible; but life, which is exceedingly bitter in sins and many thorns, becomes sweet through faith. And Holy Scripture everywhere concerns itself with teaching us how to acknowledge the Seed of God and ourselves, namely, to acknowledge the old and inborn curse of Adam and the blessing begun through Christ.

6. *So Isaac dwelt in Gerar.*

7. *When the men of the place asked him about his wife, he said: She is my sister; for he feared to say: My wife, thinking, lest the men of the place kill me for the sake of Rebecca; because she was fair to look upon.*

Here one can ask again why the Holy Spirit records these trifles. What purpose does it serve to relate such absurd and foolish things to the church of God? The people of God are not to be instructed by the fact that Rebecca said that she was Isaac's sister and not his wife, are they? I answer: In this way God makes a fool of the whole world with all its wisdom. If some Greek or Roman

---

[18] *Donatistae* does not refer to the schismatics combatted by Augustine (cf. *Luther's Works*, 13, p. 89, note 22) but to those who, like Luther, learned Latin from the textbooks of "Donatus" (cf. *Luther's Works*, 45, p. 370, note 45).

[19] An echo of Luther's familiar distinction; cf. *Luther's Works*, 13, p. 90, note 24.

were to read this, he would laugh at it as something altogether unworthy of being listened to. But God wants to make it clear that human wisdom is foolishness and that it is put to shame in this way. Up to this point He has related that Isaac had a conversation with God, and a heavenly promise, and has made him strong and altogether invincible over against the gates of hell (cf. Matt. 16:18) and all evils. Here such great weakness is apparent in him, such shameful helplessness, that one can think of nothing more disgraceful. For is it not a shameful example that he denies that Rebecca is his wife?

The theologians argue about whether he did not sin by denying his wife and by making the false statement that she was his sister.[20] His helplessness is surely disgraceful. For this is why he says: "I shall say that she is my sister, because they could kill me." It is as though he were saying: "Let anyone who wants to do so seize my wife and defile her, provided that I stay alive. If I say that she is my wife, they will think that they cannot take her from me without killing me." Is this not foolish, silly, and unworthy of so great a man? Should he not have said: "She is my wife, whether you kill me or not"? The text says that Isaac feared. Such a great man falls into such shameful fear that he is afraid of death. Thus Elijah had killed the 800 prophets with great courage (1 Kings 19:1-3), and no one's power was so great that he feared it; but when Jezebel threatened him, he is struck with such fear that he flees. Before this he was not afraid of the king; now he runs away from a woman.

Accordingly, all this seems to be foolish; but it shows great understanding and is very helpful, because it is recorded for the comfort of the churches, in order that we may know how merciful God is. We may indeed be evil and weak, provided that we are not found among those who persecute, hate, and blaspheme God. God wants to have patience with our weakness.

I am neither able nor willing to excuse the fathers, as others do. Indeed, I am glad to hear about the failings and the weaknesses of the saints. But I do not praise these failings and weaknesses as good deeds or virtues. Thus I do not excuse the apostles when they flee from Christ, and I do not excuse Peter when he denies Him. Nor do I excuse other weaknesses in them and other foolish and silly things they do. Nor are these things recorded for the sake of

---

[20] Cf. the opinions listed in Lyra *ad* Gen. 26:6-7.

the hard, the proud, and the obstinate. No, they are recorded in order that the nature of the kingdom of Christ may be pointed out. In His small flock He has poor and weak consciences that are easily hurt and are not easily comforted. He is a King of the strong and the weak alike; He hates the proud and declares war on the strong. He rebukes the Pharisees and those who are smug. But He does not want to break or confound the fearful, the fainthearted, the sorrowful, and the perplexed. He does not want to quench a dimly burning wick (Is. 42:3; Matt. 12:20). This is His way and constant practice.

Thus He has acted from the beginning of the world to the end. He is strong and almighty, but He will not quench a dimly burning wick. And He also commands us to receive him who is weak in faith, for it is a great thing to believe that for Christians there is a passing through death to life. The flesh is greatly terrified at the sight or mention of death, judgment, and eternal fire. Otherwise it is brave and undaunted if it is not assaulted or there is no adverse wind. Consequently, the kingdom of Christ is of such a kind that it has both those who are weak and those who are courageous, either constantly or for a time. Nevertheless, those who are always strong are rare. But those who are weaker than these should not be dealt with too harshly; for this is a kingdom of comfort, of the poor, and of the afflicted. It has been established to give orders to and to frighten only those who are inflexible. But to those who are terrified comfort should be dispensed, and they should be told: "You are a dimly burning wick, and God does not want me to quench you; for Christ is a King of the poor and the weak."

Here belong the examples of Holy Scripture, namely, of Abraham and Isaac, who were very great and saintly men. Scripture presents them as victors over death, the devil, and hell. It makes them friends of God (cf. Is. 41:8) and prophets, according to Ps. 105. Nevertheless, it describes them as very weak because of their completely disgraceful fear. Thus David says of himself in Ps. 30:6-7: "I said in my prosperity: 'I shall never be moved.' Death and the devil are as nothing in my sight; for 'by Thy favor, O Lord, Thou hadst established me as a strong mountain; Thou didst hide Thy face, I was dismayed.'" When God gives strength and adds courage, it is easy to be strong and immovable. But He lets us sink, lest we become haughty and attribute this strength to our own power. The same thing happened to the patriarch Isaac.

Accordingly, these things are useful for teaching the church, namely, that very great and very saintly men who have the promises of God and who triumph over sin and death fall so wretchedly and then become children and deserters. Fear of death is in itself an evil and a sin; but if it is coupled with danger to the chastity of one's wife, the evil is twofold. And the Holy Spirit presents this doctrine under such ordinary forms. Therefore we should apply this to ourselves. For today, too, we are strengthening the godly in their perils from the Turks in this manner: "Even if the Turk kills and devours you, what is he achieving? What more can he do than kill you? 'Do not fear those,' says Christ (Matt. 10:28), 'who kill the body.' If he seizes the body, house, and other things, what of it? These things have to be left behind in any case." And I would think that I had been treated well if I were to be killed by the devil for the sake of the Son of God. Surely this[21] is how we feel when we are courageous and the Holy Spirit adds strength to our hearts. But in another hour the same thing that happened to Isaac can befall me or anyone else.

Accordingly, this has been written for our instruction in order that through patience and the comfort of the Scriptures we might have hope (Rom. 15:4), lest we think: "I am not so saintly or so strong in faith as Isaac was or Jacob was." To be sure, those men were strong and steadfast when God was supporting them and was providing strength for their mountains (cf. Ps. 65:6); but when He turned His face away, they were dismayed (Ps. 30:7). And we can say the same thing about them that Peter said about himself to Cornelius (Acts 10:26): "I, too, am a man." For neither Peter nor Paul, even though they were saintly men, had better flesh than we have. They, too, were children of Adam, just as we are. Paul sometimes glories and boasts as if he were already victorious over all evils. Sometimes he complains pitiably about fears within and fightings without (cf. 2 Cor. 7:5). Where was that completely invincible hero, that victor over all hell, then?

Therefore we should not cast hope aside in evil days. Nor should we be proud in good days. For Abraham and Isaac, who were very mighty in faith, fell into that disgraceful weakness as a hope and comfort for us, in order that we might learn the condition and the

---

[21] We have followed the Erlangen edition and read *sic* here rather than *si*, which appears in the Weimar text.

ways of this kingdom and King; for there one sees invincible strength and, if I may say so, highly vincible weakness. All this serves the purpose of glorifying God alone. For we do not glory in our own power; but because our King is sitting at the right hand of the Father, we glory in Him and richly exalt ourselves. His power is made perfect through our weakness (cf. 2 Cor. 12:9), as can be seen again and again in all the examples of the fathers.

But of this wisdom the world has no knowledge. The Holy Spirit alone has it, and He presents it to the church under a very ordinary cover. And we should read the accounts of the fathers in such a manner that the examples of faith strengthen us and give us courage. But the examples of weakness should comfort us, lest we despair or become proud. And we should also comfort others. If you have been frightened, do not add evil to evil, do not flee from or deny Christ. For although I am weak, yet I would not want Christ to be blasphemed or abused. No, I want His glory to be unimpaired and His kingdom to be immovable. It is true that I have fallen. What shall I do? Shall I despair on this account? Not at all. After all, the same thing happened to the greatest fathers and to the ancestors of Christ.

Moses has carefully described Isaac's fear of death. He says that Isaac answered: "She is my sister." Why? "Because the men will kill me for the sake of Rebecca." Because of his fear of death he prostituted his wife's chastity, in order that he might be unharmed and safe. Consequently, he who would want to magnify and aggravate Isaac's sin will find many arguments. "For by denying that Rebecca is your wife you are denying God, who joined her to you and blessed you with two sons. Furthermore, over and above the sin of lying, you are endangering and betraying the chastity of your wife." This is the rhetoric of the devil. But let us abide by the rhetoric of the Holy Spirit. Nevertheless, that weakness on Isaac's part would have brought about the defilement of his wife, adultery, and many other evils if God had not prevented it. But God permits the saints to fall in this manner in order that He may preserve them in spite of this.

What the morals of the Palestinians were I do not know; nor do I understand the circumstance with which Moses deals, namely, that Abimelech was pious and forbade adultery on pain of death. Why, then, does Isaac fear him? Above, in the example of Abraham (Gen. 12:11 ff.; 20:2), he had to see how they abducted one another's wives. If someone had a wife who was a little more beautiful, he had her in common, as they say. If he could not tolerate this, he was killed by the adulterers. This usually happens in some places in Italy.[22] Therefore it is a surprising description of this region. It is likely that he had previously seen examples of this crime or had heard about them from others. But if the morals of these people were different, and if Isaac, without having an example, feared that they were people of the other kind, one can surely conclude from this that he was unbelievably weak. Perhaps he thought or imagined this way: "The inhabitants of this region are godless and are not concerned about God. Hence they also hold the people in contempt and treat them shamefully."

Moreover, this anxiety stemmed from the fact that Rebecca was beautiful. This is what the text says, and to the irreligious it seems decidedly ridiculous. For Isaac was at least 80 or 90 years old. When he was 60 years old, two sons were born to him, and 15 years later his father Abraham died. Rebecca herself was about 70 years old, because the women were 10 years younger than their husbands, as was stated above (Gen. 17:17) about Sarah, who herself, although she was 90 years old, nevertheless also excelled in beauty. Consequently, the people of that time were superior not only in beauty but also in physical vigor, inasmuch as they were able to beget children and to conceive at an age at which no hope of fruitfulness is left among us. But Rebecca, an old woman 70 years of age, is so beautiful that she surpasses the others, and on account of her beauty her chastity is imperiled. These are commendations of that age, namely, that people were more temperate and that their bodies were hardier than they are today. Now Isaac's exceedingly silly fun with Rebecca follows.

8. *When he had been there a long time, Abimelech king of the Philistines looked out of a window and saw Isaac fondling Rebecca his wife.*

Does a man who is so great and is almost 80 years of age have fun with his 70-year-old wife? Does the Holy Spirit take such delight in recording these trifles and in stooping to the lowest fooleries of married couples? Why does He not tell about 40-day fasts,

---

[22] Cf. also *Luther's Works,* 2, pp. 252, 254.

as has been related about Elijah (1 Kings 19:8)? But first we shall reject the completely cynical notion of the Jews.[23] For the very filthy swine say that Isaac had intercourse with Rebecca in public while Abimelech was looking on, as though the very saintly father had been a Cynic or a Diogenes who lay with his wife in the street.[24] The Holy Spirit is wont to cover and dignify marital intercourse. He does not bring it out into the open. Besides, Isaac and Rebecca had too much modesty to commit so extraordinarily shameful an act. For they were brought up in the fear and reverence of God, and they had a knowledge of original sin, by which the work of procreation has been marred. Therefore God wanted this to be hidden, and He adorned it with clothing and nuptials. But He detests bestial filthiness.

But the text hints that if you carefully consider the circumstances, this fun resulted from sadness of heart and some disturbance rather than from lewdness, especially in the case of Rebecca, who was almost broken down by so many misfortunes and disasters and may have said to her husband: "Alas, dear Isaac, consider into what a predicament we have been brought, how wretchedly we are wandering about in the land." Thus Job's wife reproaches her husband with his misfortune and says: "Curse God, and die" (Job 2:9). "Behold, we have two sons," Rebecca may have said, "likewise sheep, beasts of burden, and domestics. We are foreigners and exiles. In addition, we are forbidden to enter Egypt. Now I am losing even the name 'wife.'" These thoughts could surely have come into the mind of the woman who was not very courageous and was struggling with indignation and impatience in these misfortunes. For who could bear these things without sighing? Therefore in order to encourage her, Isaac may have embraced her, kissed her, and told her to be of good courage. "Dear Rebecca," he may have said, "do bear this misfortune patiently. God has appeared to me and has promised us deliverance and protection." In this manner we could defend or excuse Isaac, lest we, along with those Jewish swine, make him a Cynic or a Diogenes.

But I am undecided about these thoughts. I shall neither urge nor completely reject them. Nevertheless, they seem decidedly

---

[23] The source of this information is Lyra *ad* Gen. 26:8.

[24] This seems to be derived from Augustine, *City of God*, Book XIV, ch. 20.

probable; for in general it is not very pleasant to embrace one's wife in a hostile country. But comfort was needed, and an indication of God's presence and promise; and this could be achieved by embracing and jesting. This is honorable fun with one's wife; it is becoming to an honorable husband. Toward a sister or domestics it would not be proper. There authority and dignity are required, even when comforting. But with the woman who has been joined to me by God I may jest, have fun, and converse more pleasantly, in order that I may live with her with understanding and according to knowledge. Thus Peter admonishes when he says: "Bestowing honor on the woman as the weaker sex, since you are joint heirs of the same grace" (cf. 1 Peter 3:7). Women are mothers and the other part of the human race, even though they are the weaker part so far as the body is concerned. We are stronger, and for this reason greater duties have been entrusted to us. Yet in these duties we often display the character of a woman. But there is a difference between the character of a man and that of a woman. Women are burdened with household duties, childbirth, the rearing of children, and the care of the house. But we see well enough how we conduct ourselves in the church and in the state. In the government by men no smaller amount of weakness is often detected.

Consequently, I shall follow these thoughts and grant that Isaac embraced her not so much for the sake of giving comfort as to show that conjugal attitude which an honorable husband is wont to adopt toward his honorable wife — a playful and friendly attitude, such as can often be observed in the case of husbands who have a rather friendly disposition. The king was not so astute that he understood the very serious reasons for the embrace — the reasons I mentioned before; but he knew about the conjugal embraces which it is proper to show in public. And it is very fine when a husband also lets his affection for his wife be seen in his conduct. On the other hand, it is shameful and shocking if some show themselves surly, peevish, and harsh toward their wives and give no indication of love and affection either in word or in deed. Such seriousness should be adopted toward strangers or toward domestics. Thus we often hear words of warm praise and expressions of joy from women whenever they see a husband living pleasantly and harmoniously with his wife. "Oh, that is a good marriage! Oh, what a happy and auspicious marriage!" Here there is mutual love and the most blissful harmony. Husbands also praise the same thing. But from what source would they know this unless they had seen that such conjugal play is decidedly rare among many spouses?

But no disagreement and discord is bitterer and more horrible than that between spouses or between brothers. On the other hand, if there is mutual love, mutual play and friendliness, that marriage is loved and is praised everywhere by all; for it is rare because of the devil, who is its perpetual enemy, trying to disturb the divine union in whatever ways he can. Yet the world does not understand this but dreams that marriage is nothing else than sexual intercourse, kisses, and embraces. But it is a lawful union not only of bodies but also of hearts, and it makes itself known by definite indications and signs, which, although they are silly and laughable, yet are proper and fitting for a good marriage. I myself have often heard this from most honorable matrons when they praised other husbands on account of their affability, courtesy, and moderation, and praised it as a special miracle if such an obliging husband or wife had fallen to someone's lot.

Consequently, I shall explain this fun Isaac had in accordance with this opinion, although I do not reject or defend the earlier thoughts, except in opposition to the completely dishonorable Jews. But these are sound and pious thoughts, namely, that in praise of marriage a husband should conduct himself in a friendly and gentle manner toward his wife, not only in the bedroom but also in public. He should not be capricious, irascible, and surly; for examples of dissensions and offenses are easy to see and cause great displeasure, especially if jealousy is added. Then there is hell itself. Consequently, it is useful if there are such examples of friendliness and amiability among spouses, so that others become accustomed to being pleasant, affable, and patient if any offense or trouble occurs. For marriage is a divine institution, and concerning the wife it was said: "Let Us make him a helper fit for him" (cf. Gen. 2:18). Accordingly, there must also be an outward indication of kindness for the sake of others, especially since we have highly distinguished saints, such as Isaac is, in our society. For this life is full of countless offenses, as can be observed above all in domestic affairs. Therefore they should be ready to forgive each other and to forget offences, no matter how great they may be; and they should return to their customary friendliness, also to their outward friendliness.

For the Holy Spirit does not disdain to tell about trifles of this kind because, in the first place, it is His purpose to oppose those swine who seek only the pleasure of the flesh but in other respects show themselves peevish and harsh toward their wives. In the second place, it is His purpose to oppose the enemies of marriage, that is, the papists, who have forbidden marriage as though it had been condemned by God. He wants us to have an example to show that even a little frivolity does not displease God in marriage, which otherwise has been marred by the impurity of original sin, which is the source of that familiar mad passion for sex. But God makes use of this to unite the man with the woman, and He calls the woman a help fit for the man. Therefore it is a divine union, as Christ says (Matt. 19:6): "What God has joined together, let no man put asunder."

And it is a great comfort for us to know that the separation of spouses displeases God and that He wants amiability and mutual friendliness, embraces, kisses, and fun to spite the devil, who is the author of all dissensions. But those impure celibates will object and say: "It is well for a man not to touch a woman (1 Cor. 7:1).[25] Marriage is an unclean kind of life, etc." And others will say: "Should I be agreeable to a woman and put up with her disagreeable ways? I want to be feared by her and to rule with authority, in order that she may realize that I am a man." You will surely gain great praise if you crush the weak vessel and burden your conscience with excessive bitterness toward a sister and joint heir of the kingdom of God, one who is in the same fellowship of Baptism, of all the kindnesses of God, and of the entire church. Consider what a wife is and who you are. Or if you want to fight, why do you not fight with someone who is your equal? What praise are you going to get from it if you vent your rage on a weak vessel? This is surely unbecoming to any human being, much more to a Christian. And there is very little glory, yes, no glory at all, in subduing a sex so weak. Therefore I strongly detest those men who are full of courage toward women and, as the saying goes, are lions at home and rabbits outside the home. I am not talking about godless and vile women who cannot be corrected by any procedure.

But we should give thanks to God that we are sure that marriage

---

[25] The use of 1 Cor. 7:1 ff. to support the argument for celibacy and asceticism had been sufficiently important to call forth a commentary from Luther on that chapter in 1523; cf. W, XII, 92—142, and *Luther's Works*, Vol. 28.

has been instituted by God, that it pleases God, the angels, and all creatures. It pleases God that I am courteous to my wife. But peevishness and harshness displease Him. Much less do those who forbid and condemn marriage please Him. And that prohibition was horribly punished when the devil introduced promiscuity and the unspeakable crimes of Sodom in place of the divine institution. This happened through God's just judgment, because they disparaged a most saintly kind of life instituted and blessed by God. To be sure, marriage is not without its own imperfection and uncleanness; but God tolerates and overlooks this. If the natural order of procreating offspring is preserved, then God overlooks and forgives, or, as Luke expresses it in Acts (13:18) with a fine word, τροποφορεῖ, He bears with them. He says: "I shall bear with this way for the sake of the preservation of the human race. I know that you were conceived in sins; but I forgive you, and I permit you to have your wife as a help. In her alone you should take delight, and you should bear it patiently, even if something sad or irksome happens. I, too, shall have patience, whether you embrace her during the night, when she is naked, or during the day, when she is clothed."

If God, out of extraordinary kindness, had not instituted this union of one man and one woman, with what great desire the whole world would long for it, so that it could be freed from lust and defilement through this remedy! But now we scorn this lawful union He has sanctioned in a perpetual and firm law by which he forbids fornication and promiscuity. He commands you to choose for yourself one woman who pleases you and with whom you should spend your life. Of course, there is sin. "But I leave it to you," says God, "to play and laugh with your own wife and to keep away from the wives of others." Thus it is written in Prov. 5:18-19: "Rejoice in the wife of your youth, a lovely hind, a graceful doe. Let her affection fill you at all times with delight; be infatuated always with her love."

Thus this passage comforts us. Here it is recorded that Isaac, in his old age, had fun with his beloved Rebecca, not only for the sake of necessity and comfort but also because of some conjugal silliness, which is becoming to this kind of life, in order to point out their love for each other by means of outward friendliness. It is also recorded to comfort spouses and to spite, scorn, and refute the reprobates and the fanatics who condemn marriage. I recall that before these times of the revival of the Gospel husbands at confession frequently deplored this conjugal fun as a most serious sin. Indeed, what is most disgraceful and an affront to the Creator, if at any time some honorable matron or virgin had crossed the cemetery of the Franciscans, the monks immediately cleaned it with brooms and purified the sacred place with fire.[26] Yet they are our mothers. Nor can the flame of lust that results from original sin be purged out with brooms or fire; but it is kindled more and stirred up in this way, and a woman who has been denied increases the madness. But these hypocrites had no understanding of original sin. Therefore they had no knowledge of the remedies which God had pointed out. In the first place, Christ wants us to be baptized, in order that the heart may be set right and cleansed. Then, if you cannot have the gift of virginal chastity, at least choose that of a widow or a spouse; for in both sexes, male and female, there is flesh. Consequently, they also have seed and the passion that arouses to procreation. What advice should one give here? I answer: If you have chastity, continue in it; but if not, take a wife, lest you be polluted with the promiscuous lust characteristic of cardinals and perish.

The Hebrew verb צָחַק is just as broad in meaning as the verb "to laugh" is in German and in Latin. At times this verb is employed in its proper meaning. At times it is used by antiphrasis of sardonic laughter, which is bitterer than any weeping. At times it denotes joy or a joyful attitude or appearance, even in the case of lifeless objects, just as when we say: "The field laughs. The meadow laughs. The forest laughs," this is identical with being delightful or attractive. Thus we say in German: *Er lacht, das er schuttert, das ist, er ist frölich.* "He laughs so that he shakes, that is, he is merry." By antiphrasis: *Er lacht mein darzu in die faust. Wie hönisch lacht er mein!* "He laughs at me up his sleeve." "How scornfully he laughs at me!" Here a very sarcastic and bitter laugh is meant. The Hebrew verb has the same meaning in Ps. 2:4: "The Lord will hold them in derision. He will laugh at them." Likewise (2 Sam. 2:14): "And Abner said to Joab:[27] 'Let the young men arise and play before us.'" *Lass sie ein guten mut haben.* "Let them be

---

[26] The Franciscans were said to have been in Wittenberg ever since 1238.

[27] The Weimar text reads *Iob*, but we have followed the Erlangen text, which reads *Ioab*.

of good cheer." By antiphrasis: *Das heist auch gescherzt, wenn dir das schwert durch den bauch geht.* "This, too, is jesting if the sword goes through your belly." This is cruel fun or laughter. Consequently, in this passage "to laugh" does not denote "to lie together"; but the meaning is identical with what is stated above (Gen. 18:12) about Sarah's laughter. Ishmael laughed at Isaac, that is, derided him (cf. Gen 21:9). Similarly, in Ex. 32:6: "The people . . . rose up to play" does not mean "to worship idols," as the Jews dream,[28] but "to laugh and to be merry." Moreover, in the Hebrew there is a neat allusion which cannot be reproduced in any other language: "Isaac was Isaac—ing," Isaac, that is, the laughing, friendly, and lovable man, was being friendly with his wife; or the lovable man was loving his wife. He was conducting himself like a real Isaac, and he was doing this with the unconcern and confidence of a married man.

Accordingly, this example presents outstanding doctrine and comfort for Christian spouses. Then it confutes the completely pestilential papists and heretics, who have made mortal sins of all the words and doings of spouses. And I myself, when I was still a monk, used to feel the same way, namely, that marriage was a condemned kind of life. We used to debate whether it was permitted to love or court an honorable virgin. Likewise whether it was a sin to have fun with one's wife. And I was greatly amazed at the statement of Bonaventure, who was the most saintly among the monks, when he says: "It is not a sin if someone woos a girl with the intention of making her his wife. Indeed, this is really permitted. Consequently, one should not argue about this or have any doubt about it." [29] He also says that a husband may jest with his wife. I was looking for a far different statement and one that was more becoming to his vocation, for I was wont to explain these things in a way that did not differ from the interpretation given by the Jews.

Therefore you, young men, who are now growing up to marry in the future and to take part in public affairs, should be grateful

[28] Cf. Lyra *ad* Ex. 32:6.

[29] Luther consistently preferred the judgments of Bonaventure to those of Thomas Aquinas, even declaring: "I have the strongest doubts as to whether Thomas Aquinas is among the damned or the blessed, and would sooner believe that Bonaventure is blessed" (*Luther's Works*, 32, p. 258).

for the divine light and[30] blessing that we know that marriage is a sacred matter and that we are permitted to laugh and have fun with, and to embrace, our wives, whether they are naked or clothed. But we should abstain from the wives of others. This brings us extraordinary comfort. In addition, there is also the testimony of St. Paul. Even though he would want us to refrain from marriage entirely in order that the flesh might be clean, yet he permits it because God permits it (cf. 1 Cor. 7:1-2).

But from this one can take an admonition concerning the modesty and continence of married people. For some are such swine that they think that in marriage they are permitted to do anything they please with their wives. But they are decidedly in error. And they should know that they may indulge only in that wretched pleasure and embracing—not as though it were clean in the flesh, for both spouses are infected with original sin and the disease and frenzy of lust. But because God said: "I shall not charge this impurity against you, provided that you remain with the helpmate you have." Therefore we must live in the reverence and fear of God. Although God permits me to have a wife, yet there is sin in the flesh of both of us. That shameful lust is not good. For although, in conformity with nature, a husband is united with his wife with a better conscience than if his semen were to be wasted to no purpose or if he were to devote himself to acts of fornication and adultery, yet that, too, is not done without uncleanness. Consequently, those who practice shameful and execrable things with their wives in their bedrooms must be rebuked; for God has granted them some freedom from care, but only in accordance with His forbearance.

And this is the way one must understand Augustine's statement that he who loves his wife awaits the Last Day free from care.[31] How? In accordance with His forbearance. For if that were lacking, there would be adultery and defilement. But because this union was ordained by God, God does not charge them with anything shameful and unclean that takes place there. But that evil in marriage and copulation should not be defended as something good. The heathen said that it is in accordance with nature and not dis-

---

[30] From the Erlangen edition we have supplied *et*, which is missing in the Weimar text.

[31] See, among other such passages, Augustine, *De continentia*, chs. 22—23.

honorable for a young man to love, as the old man says in the comedy.[32] But God requires discernment from us in marriage and that we be sensible and know that although we are not condemned or considered guilty at the Last Judgment, yet we should not excuse the lust and shamefulness one finds in marriage. We should not say: "I have done a good deed by sleeping with my wife." But we should acknowledge the uncleanness and yet maintain that everything is clean because of the divine union, in order that we may possess our vessels in fear and reverence (cf. 1 Thess. 4:4) and that if any evil has been committed, it may remain within the bounds of marriage.

In this way we shall correctly understand and regard the kingdom of Christ. For it is one thing to be justified by the Law and another thing to be justified by grace. I have the use of the law and institution of marriage, but not because I am worthy. Indeed, I am unworthy of the bread I eat, of money, and of all my goods; "for the creation was subjected to futility," as Rom. 8:20 says. My wife serves me, a completely unworthy person in all the categories of substance, quantity, and quality; but in the category of relation I am worthy.[33] I am not worthy of having a wife or children in accordance with the substance or the truth of the matter, for I am a sinner. Then, however, I become worthy when God says: "I want to overlook and condone, because this is the way I have ordained it. But know yourself, and live in fear and reverence."

Thus we are all unworthy of marriage or of managing the affairs of state or the affairs of the church. I am not worthy to deliver one lecture or sermon. But we have a gracious, indulgent, and forgiving God, who has transferred us from the kingdom of wrath into the kingdom of grace and has bidden us, covered as we are with that veil of grace, to draw near to Him and enjoy His divine favors, even though we are unworthy.

9. *So Abimelech called Isaac, and said: Behold, she is your wife; how, then, could you say: She is my sister? Isaac said to him: Because I thought: Lest I die because of her.*

All these things are simply matters of the household and of the

[32] Cf. Terence, *Adelphi*, I, 2, 22.

[33] The Latin term is *praedicamenta;* cf. *Luther's Works*, 4, p. 259, note 35; also 3, p. 122.

government, and nothing is taught about the grand and truly spiritual things concerning which the Gospel preaches: about faith in Christ; about the Trinity; about the resurrection of the dead; about the victory over sin, death, and the devil. For this reason they are despised by these hypocrites, who pretend to have a great spirit [34] and sanctity. They say: "Of what concern are carnal matters to us?" It is as though they themselves were actually living without the flesh, as though they did not drink, did not eat, did not sleep, and did not have male and female sex, and finally as though they had no need at all of carnal things or were not at all concerned about them. But they have no understanding or knowledge of what the spirit or what the flesh is.

Accordingly, it is because of these fanatical notions that the Holy Spirit records such childish things and matters that pertain to the management of a household. And He points out that He also directs the physical activities without which this life cannot be guided or preserved. For even the enthusiasts themselves, much as they seem to shun carnal things, also have need of food, drink, and clothing. Why, then, would we not discuss how one should eat and live in godliness and with a good conscience? For in the church one must teach not only about the future life—as the Gospel teaches, without taking into account the present life, although it by no means despises this life—but we should regulate our life according to the Law and teach men how to lead a godly and honorable life until the last day. For we are born and die every day.

Consequently, one must teach how a wife should conduct herself toward her husband and how a servant should conduct himself toward his master. One should not steal, commit adultery, etc. "But these are carnal matters," the enthusiasts will say. Right indeed! But if it does not please you to make use of these, also give up food, drink, clothes, and the like. All these things are institutions and creatures of God given for this life, which should be spent in an honorable and godly manner until death. This must be said on account of that disgusting class of people who dream of another and, as it were, superheavenly life above the clouds, although they are utterly unable to do without this present life.

Let us see, then, what ensued after Isaac's deception. Abime-

---

[34] The Weimar text has *magnis spiritus,* but we have followed the Erlangen text, which reads *magni spiritus.*

lech summons him and says: "I saw you having fun with Rebecca, and from this I can conclude that she is not your sister, but that she is your wife; for a brother is not in the habit of jesting with his sister in this manner. Why, then, did you lie and say that she is your sister?" Isaac answers: "I thought I might die." At this point, as above, in chapter 12, one must speak about lying, concerning which Augustine argues sharply against Jerome on account of Paul's statement in the Epistle to the Galatians (1:20): "Before God, I do not lie!" [35] Augustine says that here Paul did not rebuke Peter in earnest but pretended to do so. Moreover, he says that there are three kinds of lies. It is a harmful lie when a falsehood is spoken out of a desire to deceive one's neighbor for the purpose of injuring him, his property, his reputation, or his very life. And this is worst when lies and false doctrine are spread under the name of God. God forbids this in the Eighth Commandment when He says: "You shall not bear false witness" (Ex. 20:16).

The second kind is the obliging lie, that is, a lie of love or compassion, as when the government happened to be searching for a thief to punish him and I knew where he was yet said that I did not know. In that case I am lying, not to harm but to help my neighbor. Or if I saw that someone had designs on the chastity of a virgin or matron, and I pretended not to know her, then I would be lying to help, and out of respect for, the girl. Thus Michal is lying to her father when she says that David went away, but she is doing this to help David (1 Sam. 19:11 ff.). Accordingly, where it can be done without harm to the government or to parents, one may protect and defend those whom they are seeking or are asking about. Rahab's lie in Joshua 2:5 is similar. Accordingly, it is an obliging lie by which one has regard for the welfare and the good name of the body or the soul. On the other hand, a harmful lie attacks all these, just as an obliging lie defends them and is not properly called a lie. Then this term is used ambiguously and is misapplied, because it is a very fine defense against danger to the soul, the body, and property. Therefore it is a respectable and pious lie and should rather be called a service of love, although Augustine calls it a lie and nevertheless tones it down by means of the epithet "obliging"; for the persecutor is deceived in order that the devil and the wickedness of the persecutor may be hampered

[35] A reference to the earlier discussion, *Luther's Works*, 2, p. 291.

and the innocent person may be defended. This is keeping the commandments of God, not transgressing them. Someone will object: "But the truth should not be concealed." My answer is that in such instances it should not be told unless you are driven to do so.

The third kind is the playful lie, when one jests with a person and yet preserves propriety, godliness, and faith. This is like the fun Isaac and Rebecca had, or when a husband plays with or fools his wife or little son. When this trick is discovered, it makes them laugh and be gay. Then the lie ends, and there is nothing but laughter or fun. This is also a useful lie, especially among those who are closely acquainted and are friends.

Accordingly, one asks whether what Isaac does is a sin. I answer that it is not a sin. No, it is an obliging lie by which he guarded against being killed by those among whom he was staying if he said that Rebecca was his wife. Yet it is a weakness of faith, because he did not make an open and firm confession and did not despise death. For that would have been a splendid and truly heroic virtue and firmness. But God wanted him to be weak, in order that there might be an example which teaches the church that God is not offended, whether you confess firmly, which is heroic, or are weak; for He overlooks this and leaves it unnoticed. And from this we see that we have a gracious God who can forgive and wink at our weaknesses and forgive our sins, provided that we do not lie harmfully.

Moreover, Isaac had no merely trivial reasons for his fear. Although he found the king in this kingdom just, saintly, and pious enough, yet he thought as follows: "Behold, because I have been compelled by the famine, I shall sojourn among nations which do not have the promise I have, namely, that the Lord wants to be my God, and that I must believe and continue in faith in Him. These people have neither the Word nor faith. Therefore one must take for granted, or at least fear, that they are godless and addicted to murder, adultery, and fornication. If they are not actually adulterers and murderers, nevertheless, when some slight occasion presents itself, they can fall into shameful acts of this kind. But now my wife is beautiful and could attract some ungodly man to fall in love with her because of her beauty. For this reason I am in great danger."

This is a well-founded fear and the kind of fear that is becoming to a steadfast man, as the jurists say.[36] But if it is becoming to a fearful man, it is useless. But the fear that is becoming to a heroic and courageous man is well founded and reasonable. Consequently, it is praised by the jurists and the theologians. For it is not heroic or characteristic of a brave man to be afraid of no danger at all and, because of some rash daring, to expose himself to unnecessary dangers. Such people are rash, not brave. He, however, who is truly brave properly combines daring and fear. In unavoidable dangers he is not afraid, where necessity, honor, and expediency demand an undaunted spirit. But where there is no necessity, he does not hurl himself rashly into danger. Thus well-founded fear can be becoming to him and can befit a steadfast man. This is the way Isaac fears and is weak. Yet he is excused, for he is fearful as a steadfast man.

But it pleases me to take from this passage the opportunity to discuss doubt, God, and the will of God; for I hear that here and there among the nobles and persons of importance vicious statements are being spread abroad concerning predestination or God's foreknowledge. For this is what they say: "If I am predestined, I shall be saved, whether I do good or evil. If I am not predestined, I shall be condemned regardless of my works." [37] I would be glad to debate in detail against these wicked statements if the uncertain state of my health made it possible for me to do so. For if the statements are true, as they, of course, think, then the incarnation of the Son of God, His suffering and resurrection, and all that He did for the salvation of the world are done away with completely. What will the prophets and all Holy Scripture help? What will the sacraments help? Therefore let us reject all this and tread it underfoot.

These are devilish and poisoned darts and original sin itself, with which the devil led our first parents astray when he said (Gen. 3:5): "You will be like God." They were not satisfied with the divinity that had been revealed and in the knowledge of which they were blessed, but they wanted to penetrate to the depth of the divinity. For they inferred that there was some secret reason why God had forbidden them to eat of the fruit of the tree which was in the middle of Paradise, and they wanted to know what this

[36] The usual phrase in legal documents, *in constantem virum*.
[37] See the fuller discussion of this below.

reason was, just as these people of our time say: "What God has determined beforehand must happen. Consequently, every concern about religion and about the salvation of souls is uncertain and useless." Yet it has not been given to you to render a verdict that is inscrutable. Why do you doubt or thrust aside the faith that God has enjoined on you? For what end did it serve to send His Son to suffer and to be crucified for us? Of what use was it to institute the sacraments if they are uncertain or completely useless for our salvation? For otherwise, if someone had been predestined, he would have been saved without the Son and without the sacraments or Holy Scripture. Consequently, God, according to the blasphemy of these people, was horriby foolish when He sent His Son, promulgated the Law and the Gospel, and sent the apostles if the only thing He wanted was that we should be uncertain and in doubt whether we are to be saved or really to be damned.

But these are delusions of the devil with which he tries to cause us to doubt and disbelieve, although Christ came into this world to make us completely certain. For eventually either despair must follow or contempt for God, for the Holy Bible, for Baptism, and for all the blessings of God through which He wanted us to be strengthened over against uncertainty and doubt. For they will say with the Epicureans: "Let us live, eat, and drink; tomorrow we shall die" (cf. 1 Cor. 15:32). After the manner of the Turks they will rush rashly into the sword [38] and fire, since the hour in which you either die or escape has been predetermined.

But to these thoughts one must oppose the true and firm knowledge of Christ, just as I often remind you that it is profitable and necessary above all that the knowledge of God be completely certain in us and that we cling to it with firm assent of the heart. Otherwise our faith is useless. For if God does not stand by His promises, then our salvation is lost, while, on the other hand, this is our comfort, that, although we change, we nevertheless flee for refuge to Him who is unchangeable. For in Mal. 3:6 He makes this assertion about Himself: "I the Lord do not change." And Rom. 11:29 states: "The gifts and the call of God are irrevocable." Accordingly, this is how I have taught in my book *On the Bondage of the Will* and elsewhere, namely, that a distinction must be made

---

[38] The reading *ferrum* in the Erlangen edition is clearly the correct one rather than the reading *ferrem* in the Weimar edition.

when one deals with the knowledge, or rather with the subject, of the divinity.[39] For one must debate either about the hidden God or about the revealed God. With regard to God, insofar as He has not been revealed, there is no faith, no knowledge, and no understanding. And here one must hold to the statement that what is above us is none of our concern.[40] For thoughts of this kind, which investigate something more sublime above or outside the revelation of God, are altogether devilish. With them nothing more is achieved than that we plunge ourselves into destruction; for they present an object that is inscrutable, namely, the unrevealed God. Why not rather let God keep His decisions and mysteries in secret? We have no reason to exert ourselves so much that these decisions and mysteries be revealed to us.

Moses, too, asked God to show him His face; but the Lord replies: "You shall see My back, but you will not be able to see My face" (cf. Ex. 33:23).[41] For this inquisitiveness is original sin itself, by which we are impelled to strive for a way to God through natural speculation. But this is a great sin and a useless and futile attempt; for this is what Christ says in John 6:65 (cf. John 14:6): "No one comes to the Father but by Me." Therefore when we approach the unrevealed God, then there is no faith, no Word, and no knowledge; for He is an invisible God, and you will not make Him visible.

Furthermore, God has most sternly forbidden this investigation of the divinity. Thus when the apostles ask in Acts 1:6, "Has it not been predestined that at this time the kingdom should be restored?" Christ says to them: "It is not for you to know the times" (Acts 1:7). "Let Me be hidden where I have not revealed Myself to you," says God, "or you will be the cause of your own destruction, just as Adam fell in a horrible manner; for he who investigates My majesty will be overwhelmed by My glory."

And it is true that God wanted to counteract this curiosity at the very beginning; for this is how He set forth His will and counsel: "I will reveal My foreknowledge and predestination to you in an extraordinary manner, but not by this way of reason and

---

[39] A reference to *On the Bondage of the Will* (*W*, XVIII, 689—690).

[40] Minucius Felix, *Octavian*, XIII, 1.

[41] Luther's familiar use of the scene in Ex. 33; cf. *Luther's Works*, 22, p. 157, note 125.

carnal wisdom, as you imagine. This is how I will do so: From an unrevealed God I will become a revealed God. Nevertheless, I will remain the same God. I will be made flesh, or send My Son. He shall die for your sins and shall rise again from the dead. And in this way I will fulfill your desire, in order that you may be able to know whether you are predestined or not. Behold, this is My Son; listen to Him (cf. Matt. 17:5). Look at Him as He lies in the manger and on the lap of His mother, as He hangs on the cross. Observe what He does and what He says. There you will surely take hold of Me." For "He who sees Me," says Christ, "also sees the Father Himself" (cf. John 14:9). If you listen to Him, are baptized in His name, and love His Word, then you are surely predestined and are certain of your salvation. But if you revile or despise the Word, then you are damned; for he who does not believe is condemned (Mark 16:16).

You must kill the other thoughts and the ways of reason or of the flesh, for God detests them. The only thing you have to do is to receive the Son, so that Christ is welcome in your heart in His birth, miracles, and cross. For here is the book of life in which you have been written. And this is the only and the most efficacious remedy for that horrible disease because of which human beings in their investigation of God want to proceed in a speculative manner and eventually rush into despair or contempt. If you want to escape despair, hatred, and blasphemy of God, give up your speculation about the hidden God, and cease to strive in vain to see the face of God. Otherwise you will have to remain perpetually in unbelief and damnation, and you will have to perish; for he who doubts does not believe, and he who does not believe is condemned (Mark 16:16).

Therefore we should detest and shun these vicious words which the Epicureans bandy about: "If this is how it must happen, let it happen." For God did not come down from heaven to make you uncertain about predestination, to teach you to despise the sacraments, absolution, and the rest of the divine ordinances. Indeed, He instituted them to make you completely certain and to remove the disease of doubt from your heart, in order that you might not only believe with the heart but also see with your physical eyes and touch with your hands. Why, then, do you reject these and complain that you do not know whether you have been predestined? You have the Gospel; you have been baptized; you have absolution; you are a Christian. Nevertheless, you doubt and say that you do not know whether you believe or not, whether you regard as true what is preached about Christ in the Word and the sacraments.

But you will say: "I cannot believe." Thus many are troubled by this trial, and I recall that at Torgau a little woman came to me and complained with tears in her eyes that she could not believe. [42] Then, when I recited the articles of the Creed in order and asked about each one whether she was convinced that these things were true and had happened in this manner or not, she answered: "I certainly think that they are true, but I cannot believe." This was a satanic illusion. Consequently, I kept saying: "If you think that all these things are true, there is no reason why you should complain about your unbelief; for if you do not doubt that the Son of God died for you, you surely believe, because to believe is nothing else than to regard these facts as the sure and unquestionable truth."

God says to you: "Behold, you have My Son. Listen to Him, and receive Him. If you do this, you are already sure about your faith and salvation." "But I do not know," you will say, "whether I am remaining in faith." At all events, accept the present promise and the predestination, and do not inquire too curiously about the secret counsels of God. If you believe in the revealed God and accept His Word, He will gradually also reveal the hidden God; for "He who sees Me also sees the Father," as John 14:9 says. He who rejects the Son also loses the unrevealed God along with the revealed God. But if you cling to the revealed God with a firm faith, so that your heart is so minded that you will not lose Christ even if you are deprived of everything, then you are most assuredly predestined, and you will understand the hidden God. Indeed, you understand Him even now if you acknowledge the Son and His will, namely, that He wants to reveal Himself to you, that He wants to be your Lord and your Savior. Therefore you are sure that God is also your Lord and Father.

Observe how pleasantly and kindly God delivers you from this horrible trial with which Satan besets people today in strange

---

[42] It is not clear which of his visits to Torgau Luther has in mind here; the best known of these was probably that of Easter, 1533, when he preached on the Second Article of the Apostles' Creed (W, XXXVII, 35—72).

ways in order to make them doubtful and uncertain, and eventually even to alienate them from the Word. "For why should you hear the Gospel," they say, "since everything depends on predestination?" In this way he robs us of the predestination guaranteed through the Son of God and the sacraments. He makes us uncertain where we are completely certain. And if he attacks timid consciences with this trial, they die in despair, as would almost have happened to me if Staupitz had not delivered me from the same trial when I was troubled. [43] But if they are despisers, they become the worst Epicureans. Therefore we should rather impress these statements on our hearts, such as John 6:44: "No one can come to Me unless the Father draws him." Through whom? Through Me. "He who sees Me also sees the Father" (cf. John 14:9). And God says to Moses: "You cannot see My face, for man shall not see Me and live" (Ex. 33:20). And we read (Acts 1:7): "It is not for you to know times or seasons which the Father has fixed by His own authority. But go, and carry out what I command." Likewise (Ecclus. 3:22): "Seek not the things that are too high for you, and search not into things above your ability; but the things that God has commanded you, think on them always, and in many of His works be not curious." Listen to the incarnate Son, and predestination will present itself of its own accord.

Staupitz used to comfort me with these words: "Why do you torture yourself with these speculations? Look at the wounds of Christ and at the blood that was shed for you. From these predestination will shine. Consequently, one must listen to the Son of God, who was sent into the flesh and appeared to destroy the work of the devil (1 John 3:8) and to make you sure about predestination. And for this reason He says to you: 'You are My sheep because you hear My voice' (cf. John 10:27). 'No one shall snatch you out of My hands'" (cf. v. 28).

Many who did not resist this trial in such a manner were hurled headlong into destruction. Consequently, the hearts of the godly should be kept carefully fortified. Thus a certain hermit in *The Lives of the Fathers* advises his hearers against speculations of this kind. He says: "If you see that someone has put his foot in heaven, pull him back. For this is how saintly neophytes are wont

[43] This is one in a series of recollections of Staupitz throughout the *Lectures on Genesis;* cf., for example, *Luther's Works,* 7, p. 192, note 44.

to think about God apart from Christ. They are the ones who try to ascend into heaven and to place both feet there. But suddenly they are plunged into hell." [44] Therefore the godly should beware and be intent only on learning to cling to the Child and Son Jesus, who is your God and was made flesh for your sake. Acknowledge and hear Him; take pleasure in Him, and give thanks. If you have Him, then you also have the hidden God together with Him who has been revealed. And that is the only way, the truth, and the life (cf. John 14:6). Apart from it you will find nothing but destruction and death.

But He manifested himself in the flesh to snatch us from death, from the power of the devil. From this knowledge must come great joy and delight that God is unchangeable, that He works in accordance with unchangeable necessity, and that He cannot deny Himself (2 Tim. 2:13) but keeps His promises. Accordingly, one is not free to have such thoughts or doubts about predestination; but they are ungodly, vicious, and devilish. Therefore when the devil assails you with them, you should only say: "I believe in our Lord Jesus Christ, about whom I have no doubt that He was made flesh, suffered, and died for me. Into His death I have been baptized." This answer will make the trial disappear, and Satan will turn his back.

Thus on other occasions I have often mentioned the noteworthy example of a nun who underwent the same trial. [45] For under the papacy there were also many godly persons who experienced these spiritual trials, which are truly hellish and thoughts of the damned. For there is no difference at all between one who doubts and one who is damned. Therefore whenever the nun felt that she was being assailed with the fiery darts of Satan (cf. Eph. 6:16), she would say nothing else than this: "I am a Christian."

We must do the same thing. One must refrain from debates and say: "I am a Christian; that is, the Son of God was made flesh and was born; He has redeemed me and is sitting at the right hand of the Father, and He is my Savior." Thus you must drive Satan away from you with as few words as possible and say: "Begone,

---

[44] This story is told earlier in these lectures also (*Luther's Works*, 3, p. 139, note 275).

[45] Luther recounted this anecdote in his sermons on the Gospel of John (*Luther's Works*, 22, p. 108, note 82).

Satan! (Matt. 4:10.) Do not put doubt in me. The Son of God came into this world to destroy your work (1 John 3:8) and to destroy doubt." Then the trial ceases, and the heart returns to peace, quiet, and the love of God.

Otherwise doubt about some person's intention is no sin. Thus Isaac doubts that he will live or have a pious host. About a man I *can* be in doubt. Indeed, I *should* be in doubt. For he is not my Savior, and it is written (Ps. 146:3): "Put not your trust in princes." For man is a liar (Ps. 116:11) and deceitful. But one cannot deal doubtfully with God. For He neither wants nor is able to be changeable or a liar. But the highest form of worship He requires is your conviction that He is truthful. For this is why He has given you the strongest proofs of His trustworthiness and truth. He has given His Son into the flesh and into death, and He has instituted the sacraments, in order that you may know that He does not want to be deceitful, but that He wants to be truthful. Nor does He confirm this with spiritual proofs; He confirms it with tangible proofs. For I see the water, I see the bread and the wine, and I see the minister. All this is physical, and in these material forms He reveals Himself. If you must deal with men, you may be in doubt as to the extent to which you may believe a person and as to how others may be disposed toward you; but concerning God you must maintain with assurance and without any doubt that He is well disposed toward you on account of Christ and that you have been redeemed and sanctified through the precious blood of the Son of God. And in this way you will be sure of your predestination, since all the prying and dangerous questions about GOD'S secret counsels have been removed — the questions to which Satan tries to drive us, just as he drove our first parents.

But how great would our first parent's happiness have been if he had kept the Word of God carefully in sight and had eaten of all the other trees except the one from which he had been forbidden to eat! But he wanted to search out why God had forbidden him to enjoy the fruits from that one tree. In addition, there was Satan, the malicious teacher who increased and abetted this curiosity. Thus he was hurled headlong into sin and death.

Thus God reveals His will to us through Christ and the Gospel. But we loathe it and, in accordance with Adam's example, take delight in the forbidden tree above all the others. This fault has been implanted in us by nature. When Paradise and heaven have been closed and the angel has been placed on guard there (cf. Gen. 3:24), we try in vain to enter. For Christ has truthfully said: "No one has ever seen God" (John 1:18). Nevertheless, God, in His boundless goodness, has revealed Himself to us in order to satisfy our desire. He has shown us a visible image. "Behold, you have My Son; he who hears Him and is baptized is written in the book of life. This I reveal through My Son, whom you can touch with your hands and look at with your eyes."

I have wanted to teach and transmit this in such a painstaking and accurate way because after my death many will publish my books and will prove from them errors of every kind and their own delusions.[46] Among other things, however, I have written that everything is absolute and unavoidable;[47] but at the same time I have added that one must look at the revealed God, as we sing in the hymn: *Er heist Jesu Christ, der HERR Zebaoth, und ist kein ander Gott,* "Jesus Christ is the Lord of hosts, and there is no other God" [48] – and also in very many other places. But they will pass over all these places and take only those that deal with the hidden God. Accordingly, you who are listening to me now should remember that I have taught that one should not inquire into the predestination of the hidden God but should be satisfied with what is revealed through the calling and through the ministry of the Word. For then you can be sure about your faith and salvation and say: "I believe in the Son of God, who said (John 3:36): 'He who believes in the Son has eternal life.'" Hence no condemnation or wrath rests on him, but he enjoys the good pleasure of God the Father. But I have publicly stated these same things elsewhere in my books, and now I am also teaching them by word of mouth. Therefore I am excused.

10. *Abimelech said: What is this you have done to us? One of the people might easily have lain with your wife, and you would have brought guilt upon us.*

---

[46] These prophecies of Luther were to be referred to in the Formula of Concord, Solid Declaration, Art. II, par. 44; see also our introduction, pp. xi—xii.

[47] Luther speaks this way, for example, in *On the Bondage of the Will* (*W*, XVIII, 614—618).

[48] Here, as elsewhere in these lectures (cf. *Luther's Works*, 7, p. 132), there are echoes of Luther's hymn *Ein' feste Burg.*

11. *So Abimelech warned all the people, saying: Whoever touches this man or his wife shall be put to death.*

The king shows remarkable goodness, justice, and godliness. Therefore Peter says in Acts 10:34-35: "God shows no partiality, but in every nation anyone who fears Him and does what is right is acceptable to Him." Although the king is not a son of Abraham, yet he is a saintly man and hopes for the righteousness of God, just as Cornelius did. Therefore Isaac came to him just as Abraham came to the earlier Abimelech, and from Isaac he receives instruction concerning true godliness and the knowledge of God. For Isaac undoubtedly preached the Word of God at that place. But Abimelech seems to have been a title given to royalty and not the name of a person, just as the name Pharoah was common to all the kings of Egypt.

Observe, however, how intensely the king detests adultery. Therefore this passage is outstanding. "Why," he says, "have you done this evil?" It is as though he were saying: "You would not deceive me and my entire kingdom in this manner, would you, so that we would offend God with such a grave crime without being aware of it? For not only I but my entire kingdom, was in danger if anyone of my subjects had lain with her." He surely was wrought up when he said this, and I believe that he was speaking of the honorable coition or cohabitation of a man and a woman, not of promiscuity, of which Isaac was chiefly afraid. But I think that the king meant to say: "Someone could have carried off your wife as if she had been unattached and could have taken her home and slept with her as married couples do. Yet in that case there would be a hidden sin of adultery. Even though he cohabited with her in a most honorable manner, as a husband does, yet he would be found out and justly be regarded as an adulterer."

These are words spoken by a man who fears God and is pious — words worthy of a prince and king who abhors even hidden adultery; and one can believe that he meted out far greater punishments for open cases of adultery and promiscuity. And even if Rebecca had been joined to someone else without the king's knowledge, yet he himself would not have been without fault. Among our kings and princes you will find nothing like this today. They would say: "Whether she is his sister or his wife, whether she is treated honorably or dishonorably, what is it to me?" But in Abimelech there was the fear of God. Therefore he was afraid that even hidden adultery would be committed in his kingdom. Undoubtedly the other princes and nobles of the kingdom were men like him.

Consequently, it was a great kindness that at that time God gave the church such saintly and godly hosts. Thus above (Gen. 14:13) Abraham had Eshcol, Aner, and Abimelech. For the church and the apostles must have a nook where they may live. Such a man was this Abimelech, who befriended Isaac, the saintly apostle and prophet of God. Therefore I think that he was one of the saintly kings. Even though he was not a son of the promise, yet he became a sharer in it, just as at that time many Gentiles were also saved.

Jerome has translated אָשָׁם with *peccatum grande*, "a great sin." But it is pointed out that at that time adultery was not regarded as a joke or a laughing matter, as today among Christians marriage is regarded as pastime, especially among the notables. And the papists consider adultery and fornication a pastime or a joke. Consequently, whether one understands this of adultery or of fornication, one can surely observe that the king's heart was filled with godliness and with reverence for God, who could not let either of these go unpunished. For the king is greatly disturbed. He does not regard this as a joke; he considers it אָשָׁם, that is, as guilt, *Für ein schuld, da unser Herrgott ein zuspruch zu hat*, "as guilt which our Lord God has the right to punish," as we pray in the Lord's Prayer: "Forgive us our debts or our guilts." And Ps. 34:21 states: "Those who hate the righteous will be condemned"; that is, they will be guilty. This is why the Latin word *hostia* means *Schuldopfer*, an "expiatory sacrifice." And in Ps. 5:10 we read: "Make them bear their guilt, O God." Here Jerome translates with "Condemn them, do not acquit them"; but consider them as condemned, guilty, and lost. It means about the same thing as what Paul calls κάθαρμα in 1 Cor. 4:13.

Accordingly, the king says: "You would easily have brought guilt and condemnation upon us." He not only stands in awe of and fears God, but he also shudders at that peril which would have arisen for himself and for his entire kingdom if someone else had carried her off and had taken her as his lawful wife. Furthermore, he is not satisfied with that sharp reprimand or reproof, but he also gives evidence by means of an edict that he is displeased and will severely punish those who lay violent hands on these guests. For the sake of these strangers he enacts a law and fixes the death penalty for those who transgress it. He even strengthens his decree by saying: "If anyone touches not only the woman but also the man and harms his body, domestics, goods, and reputation, he shall surely die; for I want him to be free and safe from every danger in my kingdom."

Moreover, you see how kind the Lord is to His saints. To be sure, He tests them, sends them into exile, lets them be exposed to danger of their reputation and their life, and permits them to be afflicted with famine and misfortunes of every kind; yet He provides excellent, quiet, and safe hospitality and grants peace in the midst of their enemies. These things are recorded to strengthen our faith—even if perils and misfortunes rush in, just as Isaac is living in the utmost danger—that God nevertheless leads and preserves us. For the church must have a place and nest on this earth. If one or another prince does not want to protect us, God will give someone else to provide hospitality in a kindly manner. And for the most part He is wont to choose a host without our advice or judgment, yes, even beyond and contrary to our hope and expectation. In this way Isaac obtained safety and quiet in that land, and later on he became exceedingly rich, with the result that the inhabitants begrudged him such great good fortune and he was compelled to move to another place. All this is related in order that we may believe in God, who leads and preserves us; for when we have the Word, we are indeed exercised by sundry perils, but in such a way that we do not perish or despair in the trial but rejoice in peace and give thanks to God.

12. *And Isaac sowed in that land, and reaped in the same year a hundredfold. The Lord blessed him,*

13. *and the man became rich and gained more and more until he became very wealthy.*

14. *He had possessions of flocks and herds, and a great household.*

All this that Moses relates about Isaac seems to be exaggerated; for it is said about a very wretched man, an exile, and a stranger who owned not even a footbreadth in that land, no farm, no barn, and no sodded roof of his hut.[49] But we have stated repeatedly that

---

[49] Vergil, *Eclogues,* I, 69.

these very saintly fathers are described for us as an example of a Christian and godly life, how it should be led in a "sober, upright, and godly" (Titus 2:12) manner on account of the future life. Thus we see that very saintly patriarch being plagued in various ways, yet living candidly in the Word of God which had been given to him richly in the promises: "I shall be with you. I shall give you all these lands. And in your Seed all nations will be blessed." He meditated diligently on these words and had them imprinted on his heart. We hear them listlessly and with deaf ears; we do not value the Word as highly as the fathers did. Therefore God wanted to point out how the very saintly men lived — not by bread alone but by every Word that proceeds from the mouth of God (Matt. 4:4); for it was impossible for flesh and blood to bear such great hardships of this life that is described here.

To him who is not on the very spot and reads or judges these things according to the flesh they seem to be insignificant and temporal matters about food, about a wife, about the household, pastures, and cattle. What about this? Here nothing is extraordinary or splendid. But to him who sets the proper value on the magnitude of these matters they will truly seem very serious and most important. For after that most generous promise the trial followed, and the danger in regard to the chastity of his wife and in regard to his own life. Meanwhile, however, he sustains himself with the word of the promise given above and sojourns in the land, which was promised to him by God and was his own, as an exile or foreigner; and he calmly lets strangers have dominion there. Now consider the circumstances, and put yourself on the very spot. What would you do if you had to put up with a strange master in your own house and were driven out of all your land and property? You surely would never put up with this.

Nevertheless, Isaac lives as an exile in the land given him by God, and in such a way that he is compelled to be afraid of the danger to his wife's chastity, that is, of a disturbance of his entire household, yes, of his own destruction. For if he himself had been killed, his whole household would have been in danger. We are pampered martyrs; we sit in ease and quiet, enjoy our possessions, and eat and drink in peace. But it is a great trial to dwell with one's wife and two sons and also with such a great household and so large a number of cattle and beasts of burden in a strange land, where food and all the necessities of life have to be purchased with money. There is no greater wretchedness than to wander about in the entire world without a fixed abode and one's own house, as the sayings of all nations bear witness, and also the well-known Saxon proverb which states: *Eigen wat, gut ist dat* ("One's own garment, that is good"). But to live because of the uncertain goodwill of friends and enemies is a most serious trial.

But such was the life of the saintly fathers. It was full of trials, even external trials in physical matters, in order that their faith in the promise might be exercised. For Isaac clings to heavenly things and depends on them, although he is still dwelling on earth. But without faith he would have been unable to live such a hard life. I wonder from what place he procured his household and servants unless perhaps from Arabia, which had a large supply of servants. Moreover, without a doubt many quarrels, many other annoyances in the household, and also thefts and plots had their origin among the shepherds and the domestics. But Isaac is patient and waits; for he has a God who gives him a promise, even though He is invisible and for a time deserts him. Yet He gives help at the right time.

Moreover, comfort follows this trial, lest Isaac seem to have believed and to have waited for the Lord in vain. Later on he will be tried again, and once more he will receive comfort. For these alternate successions of trials and comforts go on and on, just as night follows day. For in this way the word of promise and faith are put to use. Accordingly, Isaac sows in a foreign land, which nevertheless is his own, and in that year he reaps a hundredfold. Moreover, King Abimelech is conspicuous for his extraordinary piety; for he not only takes Isaac under his care and protection and forbids on penalty of death anyone to do harm to him or his wife, but he also grants him a part of the land, a field, and meadows for his cattle and his household. And although he lent it to him for a fixed sum of money, yet this, too, is honorable and deserving of thanks, because it is likely that it would not have been granted to him anywhere else.

Consequently, Moses praises this godly and pious king; and I have no doubt that Abimelech was saved, just as his father was, unless he is the very Abimelech who lived at the time of Abraham. Yet I do not believe that this is the case, for Isaac is now almost 100 years old. Moreover, these things lead to a recognition of the kindness of God, who comforts those who are His. After He has afflicted them and has tested their faith and steadfastness, He again lets the light and sun of His mercy and grace rise upon them and gives them a very fine dwelling place, with the result that he can not only live in peace but can also amass abundant wealth.

The Jews say that in that year there was great sterility in the entire land and that there was such an abundant yield only in Isaac's field, which he had rented.[50] But there is no need whatever for this Jewish amplification; in itself it is important enough that one measure yielded 100 measures. And it was undoubtedly a miracle and an unusual yield of the fields of that land. But 100 measures yield 1,000, and so on without end. I am saying nothing about the rest of the rural riches: butter, milk, eggs, and the like. In our regions there is an unbelievable and incomprehensible situation. It is an abundant and lucky yield if one measure produces five or six measures. Nevertheless, this is not yet a thirtyfold or sixtyfold return, about which we read in the parable in the Gospel (cf. Matt. 13:8; Mark 4:8).

Therefore let us learn from this passage to persevere in faith, lest we doubt or waver if some trial comes upon us. For note how generously God recompenses Isaac for the earlier trial, in order that we may know that He is not angry forever. And since we have the promise, let us hold out in trials and conclude: "The Lord, who said to me: 'Believe,' will surely keep His promise. Meanwhile I shall wait in accordance with the words 'Wait for the Lord, be strong, etc.' (Ps. 27:14), 'Be strong, and let your heart take courage, all you who wait for the Lord'" (Ps. 31:24). The godly should wait and persevere even in greatest dangers and adversities; for He has promised that He wants to take care of us. 1 Peter 5:7 states: 'Cast all your anxieties on Him, for He cares about you.'"

The exercises of faith are necessary for the godly; for without them their faith would grow weak and lukewarm, yes, would eventually be extinguished. But from this source they assuredly learn what faith is; and when they have been tried, they grow in the knowledge of the Son of God and become so strong and firm that they can rejoice and glory in misfortunes no less than in days of prosperity and can regard any trial at all as nothing more than a little cloud or a fog which vanishes forthwith.

Moses does not mention how many measures Isaac sowed; he

---

[50] Cf. Lyra *ad* Gen. 26:12-14, recounting various theories.

states only that one measure produced 100. If he sowed a 100 measures, he reaped 10,000. In accordance with the promise made above (v. 3), this is an extraordinary blessing. And now Moses continues to amplify this miracle and says that Isaac was greatly increased in wealth. And if this yield had lasted for two or three years, he would have prospered immensely. Although he would have been satisfied if one measure had produced 10 or less, God not only satisfies him but overwhelms him with His blessing and gives far more than is needed for his house and his domestics, no matter how numerous they are; for he needed barely a twentieth. Accordingly, God can easily enrich those who are His if instead of 1,000 measures, which previously were abundantly sufficient for a farmer, he gives 10,000 measures. Yet Isaac still has no property of his own in this land. He lives in his own land as though it were not his own.

Consequently, this is a great comfort, provided that we have a correct understanding of it; for God gives these things bountifully in order that we may learn to believe and to wait for the help of the Lord in affliction, and to thank Him for His kindnesses when we are prosperous. For the life of the saints consists in this. "The mountains rise, the valleys sink down" (Ps. 104:8). Now it is day; now it is night. Today there is honor; tomorrow there is dishonor, as 2 Cor. 6:8 says. But our eyes and heart should always be directed toward and fastened on the promise; "it will surely come, will not delay" (Hab. 2:3). Now another trial follows. By it Isaac's faith is exercised anew.

So that the Philistines envied him.

15. *(Now the Philistines had stopped and filled with earth all the wells which his father's servants had dug in the days of Abraham his father.)*

16. *And Abimelech said to Isaac: Go away from us, for you are much mightier than we.*

After God has comforted him, the very saintly patriarch is again hurled into varied and difficult trials; for the life of the godly must be arranged in such a manner that although they make use of this world, of marriage, food, drink, and all the necessities of life, yet the heart is set on heavenly things. Those who do not do this become gluttons and slaves of mammon. But the devil allows us no rest in this life. It is impossible for us to have peace with him, since he is God's enemy and enmity has been put between the children of the serpent and the Seed of the woman (cf. Gen. 3:15).

The first trial is this, that the Philistines, because of their hatred and envy, stop up all wells and fill them with earth. In this way they want to induce him to flee of his own accord. But Isaac bears all this patiently, and meanwhile he uses water purchased from others with money. Therefore since they are unable to drive him out in this way, they persuade the king to command him with a special order to leave the country. Then he is compelled to flee and to leave a land which is not rightfully under the jurisdiction of others but belongs to him. Therefore this trial is harder and sadder than it would appear to be at first sight and to one who looks at it only casually. At this point Origen brings forward some wisdom or other about the stopped-up wells — some wisdom that Erasmus greatly admires.[51] Meanwhile however, one loses the instruction in Christian living and the discussion of the account, which teaches us in a godly manner.

Isaac is rich and has an abundance of grain. He instructs his household in patience and godliness. But what happens to this saintly man and priest of God? Now, when he seems to have got possession of everything, the Philistines, stirred up by hatred and envy, deprive him of water in such a way that not even they themselves can have the benefit of it. If they had merely forbidden the use of the water, he would have been able to steal it secretly; but they stop up the wells completely by throwing earth into them, so that the use of the water is denied to all alike. Yet without water this life cannot be sustained, especially not among the cattle. To deprive of water is to deprive both human beings and beasts of burden of life itself. Therefore this was an exceedingly burdensome trial in the case of so large a number of domestics and cattle, and to withhold water in such great need is extraordinary wickedness. What else could Isaac think than that he, together with his beasts of burden and his household, would have to perish from thirst? He had this one comfort that he was able to send his servants to Gerar and to fetch water from that place in jugs and flagons — water

[51] Origen, *In Genesin Homilia*, XIII, *Die griechischen christlichen Schriftsteller, Origenes Werke*, VI, 113—121.

bought with money, just as we buy wine. Nevertheless, the very fact that he is forced to buy his own water adds to his pain; for he was actually lord over the water, the wells, and the entire land. Besides, his father Abraham had dug the wells.

Therefore let us learn from this that our trials are far lighter than the trials of the saintly patriarchs were. We are delicate martyrs, we who live amid an abundance of all things. Consequently, such accounts are completely without a precedent. Nor is there anyone today, even among the saintliest persons, who would be able to bear these things. They are compelled to wander through villages to Hebron, perhaps even into the desert as far as the Well of the Living and the Seeing (cf. Gen. 16:14) — for Moses does not record from what source they got the water — and to fetch drinking water from that place for themselves and for the cattle. Who would not be disturbed by such a great indignity? In all likelihood Rebecca sometimes said out of impatience: "In spite of all, we are lords over the land. Where is God's promise? Is it being fulfilled in such a way that foreigners enjoy our property after we have been driven out or surely have been deprived of everything that is necessary for enjoying it?"

Accordingly, these things that are mentioned about the water and the wells are not laughable, as they seem to be according to the judgment of the flesh; but they all served the purpose of putting faith into practice. For Isaac had the promise of God, who said: "I shall be with you." But now he is confronted with the opposite, as though he had been abandoned by God, who gave him the promise. Therefore we, too, should learn to wait for the Lord if we have His promise no matter what else happens, whether persecution instead of the presence of God befalls us or we feel His wrath instead of His grace. In spite of all, we should say: "I believe. I have been baptized. I have been absolved. I have God's promise of grace and mercy. I have enough. Whether night, day, tribulation, or joy befalls me, I shall nevertheless not forfeit His mercy or lose courage."

There is a second trial. After they have deprived Isaac of the water, the monsters come and corrupt the heart of King Abimelech, so that he cancels the lease of the meadows and the fields; and they claim all those farmlands for themselves. They do not understand that there is a miracle and an extraordinary blessing, but they suppose that the field is naturally so fertile and productive. Therefore they want to make use of it themselves rather than grant it to a stranger, who a little later on, after becoming wealthy, would be able to bring under his control, either by force or for a price, the fields and farmlands of the inhabitants and gradually the entire country. But in this way they bring a curse upon themselves. For it is not reasonable that the same fertility that Isaac had previously because of God's blessing was granted to them.

Moreover, perhaps the Philistines learned from the talk of some member of the household that this stranger boasted that ownership of this land had been promised to him. This indeed seemed completely unfair and deserving of hatred and exile. Therefore he is first driven out by a wrong done by individuals. Now this takes place by royal authority and by a public edict. For they had stopped up the wells for the purpose of causing him to leave on account of the lack of water without anyone compelling him to do so. But the trial is far more serious, because he is being driven out by order of the king, who, as he supposed, had up to this time been favorably disposed and friendly toward him and because of whose help and protection he could be safe from any wrongs whatever. From him he is now compelled to hear: "Depart from us; for you are much stronger, more prosperous, and richer than we are. You have more servants and cattle than we have." Thus Isaac is driven out because they begrudge him this blessing and cannot bear to see him becoming rich there. First they forbid the use of the water, then the use of the land.

This is the second trial that conflicts with the promise. Yet Isaac clings to this promise and holds out firmly. These are his thoughts: "God has delivered me from death, has preserved the chastity of my wife and has given fruit a hundredfold. Therefore I shall not regard it as a burden to leave this dwelling place, and I shall remain in the neighborhood in spite of all; for God has commanded me to sojourn in this land."

17. *So Isaac departed from there and encamped in the valley of Gerar and dwelt there.*

18. *And Isaac dug again the wells of water which had been dug in the days of Abraham his father, for the Philistines had stopped them after the death of Abraham; and he gave them the names which his father had given them.*

Isaac withdraws to another place, one that was not far from where he had been. Undoubtedly he did not do so without grieving his flesh and subjecting it to a trial. But what sort of land he had Scripture does not indicate; it only states: "He encamped in the valley of Gerar," in that corner. Moreover, three patriarchs — Abraham, Isaac, and Jacob — dwelt in these three places, namely, in Hebron, Beer-sheba, and Gerar. From this it is evident that God was particularly fond of those places. And these places are situated in the territory of the tribe of Judah toward the south and are four or five miles wide. There the saintly fathers wandered about. Sometimes they lived in Gerar, sometimes in Beer-sheba. And Moses calls it a valley, because there was no tilled place or fertile field in this valley of Gerar; for in the region of valleys the land is usually dry.

Accordingly, it was an extraordinary trial, in which Isaac learned not to live by bread alone but by every word that proceeds from the mouth of God (Matt. 4:4). This place the Philistines surely did not begrudge him, since he did not have good land where he could sow and reap; for torrents usually devastate the fields with their overflows. From what source, then, did he support himself and his household? If he had money, he bought the neccessary provisions. Then they dig other wells, which the Philistines will again stop up with earth, just as they did previously. Nevertheless, he will overcome these hateful acts and will continue to be invincible, even though various trials constantly follow these evidences of comfort. Thus Moses describes his strong and steadfast courage during that migration with the meaningful and emphatic words "Isaac departed." Isaac was driven and cast out of his own country. Nevertheless, he encamps. This is a military term. It is used in Ps. 34:7, where we read: "The angel of the Lord encamps, etc." אֹהֶל means "tent"; חָנָה means "to encamp." Later it is also employed for a dwelling place, but especially for a hut used in warfare.

Therefore Moses wanted to point out that the patriarch Isaac was undismayed in such great tribulations and very sure about this, that wherever he dwelt, there was some citadel or fortress in which he would be protected by God. So great is the power of the promises that Isaac seems to laugh at the devil and his members, who drove him from his very beautiful possession. For this is what he concluded: "If I cannot have a hundredfold here but am forced to give up what I had with perfect right, I shall nevertheless have a living. Indeed, I shall live protected and shall dwell in a camp. If I cannot dwell in the fertile fields of Gerar, I shall dwell in a valley near a torrent, which shall be for me a fortress fortified and walled not with wood and stones but with angelic hosts."

Thus Moses presents Isaac as a man who is bewildered and in the greatest tribulations and distress. Nevertheless, he describes his heroic courage and points out that he despised the world and clung firmly to his hope in God, which disposed him to say: "I shall have not only what I need but also protection and safety."

These things are presented to us as an example and a comfort; for if we have a promise, then it follows without fail that angels are round about us. This is why Ps. 34:7 states: "The angel of the Lord encamps around those who fear Him." Likewise Ps. 91:11: "He will give His angels charge of you." This they believed firmly[52] and without any doubt. Therefore we, too, if we are godly, should believe in the promise of Him who cannot lie. Then we are surely under His protection, and it is also certain that angels are with us. But if any evil befalls us beyond, or contrary to, this trust and protection, this happens because of a special purpose that is hidden from us and especially from our adversaries. But the godly should comfort themselves in this manner: "I know that I have guardian angels; but that I have to bear some misfortune, this I leave to the will of God. For I am in the camp of the angels. God is not a liar. Therefore He will not forsake me."

With this example Moses wants to remind us that we should be proud of the divine promise which we, too, have in rich manner in the Gospel. For since I know that I have been absolved from sins through the ministry of the Word and have been baptized, I should be elated and undismayed in all dangers, whether the body or the soul suffers to the utmost. "But I cannot believe this," you will say, "and be so stouthearted." I certainly grant this; for the flesh contends against the promise, as Paul says about himself in Rom. 7:23: "I see in my members another law at war with the law of my mind." Here he is speaking of sin in general and of the corruption of our entire nature, because of which it happens that we do not resist the law of our members so steadfastly and adhere to the law of the mind. And all the godly have the same complaint

---

[52] The Weimar text reads *infirmiter;* but the context makes the Erlangen reading, *firmiter,* evidently the correct one.

while they live in this flesh. To be sure, we have this wisdom, that we take hold of the promises of God in some way and superficially, and sigh every day that the flesh, which hinders faith, may be reduced to ashes; but we must try to grow in that heroic knowledge until we become perfect.

But without a trial we learn nothing and make no progress. For this is the warfare and the exercise of Christians through which we learn that we are under the protection of the angels, and that although we are plagued by severe and difficult trials, yet they do us no harm. This is our theology. It is not learned easily or suddenly; but we must meditate constantly on the Law and stand in battle array against the devil, who tries to draw us away from the study of the Word and to make our faith weak.

In this manner Isaac was harassed by the wrongs done by the Philistines. Nevertheless, he buoys himself up again and concludes as follows: "I shall dwell in this land contrary to the will of all who want me cast out, because the land is mine according to the promise. This will be my royal abode near that torrent." But I think that it was a valley like the one in Saxony between Düben and Eilenburg near the Mulde River.[53] Although he is not about to have a firm abode even here, yet he makes this statement in reliance on the promise; and he believed that he was living in a camp of angels. "For God does not lie. Therefore we shall not perish, since He has promised me this land. Consequently, even if we must perish we shall not perish." But Isaac learned this from his father Abraham, to whom similar things happened and who overcame them all with similar strength of faith.

Furthermore, mention is made here of the wells which the servants of Isaac's father had dug and which the Philistines stopped up after his father's death. These words must be brought into relation with chapter 21:25-26; for they explain what is said there about only one well, which the king's servants took away by force, where Abimelech excuses himself to Abraham by saying that he had no knowledge of it and where it is stated that later on he enters into a covenant with him. Perhaps it occurred to Isaac here that he is being vexed by the inhabitants of this land in the same way Abraham had been treated previously. Yet the fact that he is com-

---

[53] The valley of which Luther speaks was evidently almost due north of Wittenberg.

manded by the king to leave the country is harder to bear. He is being wronged not only by the servants; but the king himself, who was misled by the false accusations of the courtiers, expels him. For even though we think that Abimelech was a good man, yet he is compelled to follow the counsels of the princes in his kingdom.

19. *But when Isaac's servants dug in the valley and found there a well of springing water,*

20. *the herdsmen of Gerar quarreled with Isaac's herdsmen, saying: The water is ours. So he called the name of the well Esek, because they contended with him.*

21. *Then they dug another well, and they quarreled over that also; so he called its name Sitnah.*

This is a new blessing which God, out of special kindness, heaps on Isaac after the previous trial. For He gives him not only the wells that had been cleared again but also a new well of living waters — a well which had not been seen in this valley before. Moreover, Isaac is exceedingly fond of this well. He praises it highly and calls it a well of living waters. For it is a most beautiful comfort to have a well that flows constantly. Perhaps it flowed from the mountains. Augustine makes a distinction between a *puteus* and a *fons*.[54] He calls a *puteus* a well from which we are wont to draw water in vessels and in which the water, as though it were dead, does not flow. But *fontes* are wells that flow and by their flowing show life. They are similar to animals that are alive.

Thus God gave this living water to Isaac to comfort him. But the same thing happens to him that is stated in the proverb: "Some labor, others enjoy; some sow, others reap." When the Philistines see that Isaac has found a well of living waters and this most delightful spring water, they realize what a great advantage results from it; for it not only supplies water for the citizens and remains in the well, but it flows out and irrigates the entire land. For this reason the Philistines are pleased, although they themselves did not find or dig it. Indeed, they did not even see it in their territory. Nevertheless, they lay claim to it for themselves.

[54] Thus *puteum* (or *puteus*) was used also of a cistern, while *fons* referred to "living" or flowing water, or to an artesian well.

Moses is modestly silent about the king and the princes. He speaks only about the shepherds in the village, as though they had stirred up the quarrel over this spring water. But it was a serious quarrel because they say that it is rightfully theirs and adduce the words "The land is ours. Therefore what the land has produced and contains belongs to us." What should Isaac do? He is a saintly and upright man and is not quarrelsome. Consequently, he bears this injustice calmly, although it is a troublesome affliction that the wickedness of these people is so great that they even begrudge him a drink of the water God has granted him and take the water from him by force. For it had not been given to them or discovered by them but had been bestowed upon this saintly man by a special blessing. Here the jurists would have had a subject for at least 100 years of litigation. But Isaac yields to the time, the persons, and the pretexts; and he relinquishes the well. I would have prayed so much that God would have stopped the spring water and the well that had been discovered without any effort on their part.

But Isaac avenges the wrong in no other way than by giving the name Esek to the well as a perpetual reminder of such great wickedness, in order that he may bear witness that the wrong was caused by them, but that on his side there was the most blameless patience, which is a very holy virtue and sustains itself with the consciousness of what is right, just, and harmless. It does not offend the neighbor, much less God in His saints. This is the reason why Isaac does not inveigh against the Philistines; it is enough that he leaves behind the shameful name Esek as evidence of the wickedness of this people.

For such unjust acts of robbery lead automatically to vengeance and punishments, as Augustine's statement bears out. "Gain in the coffer," he says, "harm in the conscience." [55] No unjust gain is without most unjust harm. For he who has seized property has lost the faith. One acquires the devil with the property, and one loses God together with faith and justice. If you take away my property and leave me faith and a good conscience, then you have the chaff, but I have the kernels. No matter what you seize by any right and any wrong, you have already lost your faith and have God as your adversary, and together with the chaff itself you will be hurled

---

[55] This is actually not Augustine's own saying but apparently an older Roman proverb.

headlong into eternal destruction. Those facts are stated and impressed many times, but they are not listened to or believed. "Evil gains come to an evil end"[56] is a sentiment common to all nations. "Light come, light go." "The third heir gets no joy from ill-gotten gains." [57] The Germans say: *Ubel gewonnen, bosslich zerronnen. Unrecht gut wudelt nicht.* Nevertheless, we do not cease to rob and steal by means of false measures, false weights, and frauds of every kind.

I myself, after I had passed my twentieth year—for before that time a man neither sees nor understands anything in ordinary transactions—then indeed during 40 years I saw many rapacious, greedy, and usurious people who, when they had scraped together enormous wealth, nevertheless were barely able to keep it for 30 years.

In the same way I believe that little profit or pleasure came to this king and his princes from this unjust gain. Consequently, the statement of Ps. 37:16 should be kept in mind: "Better is the little that the righteous has than the abundance of many wicked." For injustice does not bestow happiness or peace of conscience. He who accumulates gets no pleasure from it, and the heir is impoverished. For in the house of the godless man it is wiped out.[58] Although riches are scraped together there, yet they are wiped out; for God blows, and he who accumulates does so into a pouch with a hole in it, as the poets relate about the sieve of the Danaides.[59]

Therefore he who is godly should be satisfied with a little, in accordance with the statement of Ps. 37:16. He should enjoy this, be glad with his wife and children, and abstain from unjust gain. The histories and books of all nations teach the same thing, namely, that it is far better for you to live on one or two guldens acquired in an honorable manner than on many thousands obtained in a shameful manner with harm to others. And I have heard a very noteworthy account about an honorable and pious citizen who, when he was about to give a dowry at the betrothal of his daughter, said to his son-in-law: "Behold, you have 30 guldens which I have obtained in a godly and an honorable manner without harming or

---

[56] Cf. Cicero, *Orationes Philippicae*, II, 27, 65.

[57] A favorite proverb of Luther's; see, for example, *Luther's Works*, 21, p. 208.

[58] The Weimar text has *erosio* here, but we have read *erasio* instead.

[59] Cf. Horace, *Carmina*, I, 11, 22.

cheating anyone." I would have taken this dowry in preference to 30,000 guldens; for God blesses what has been justly acquired, so that one penny is of greater profit than a gulden of a robber or a usurer.

Therefore this is a serious crime of the people of Gerar. Because of it they bring the curse of God upon themselves by doing violence and wrong to so saintly a guest. Of course, he himself does not avenge the wrong. Nor does he curse. Indeed, he would prefer to bless. In fact, there is almost an obligation to thank them for the well which they took away from him. But this giving of thanks is inauspicious and ominous. It is an inauspicious farewell when people filled with the Holy Spirit depart and say to a land: "Esek and Sitnah." Then a curse follows in short order. For this is what Isaac wants to say: "Here there is nothing but Esek and Sitnah." He would gladly say something else, but he cannot justify the wrong done by the people of Gerar. Consequently, he bids them farewell and at the same time upbraids them for their sin and for the wrong he suffered. He calls down no evil upon them; he only prophesies evil, namely, that at this place are the wells called Esek and Sitnah.

The Holy Spirit wanted to record this for our instruction (cf. Rom. 15:4) in order that we might know that one should not avenge a wrong. One may complain about it, but one may not take vengeance. Therefore Isaac does not take vengeance; he only points out his sorrow and, as evidence of the wrong, leaves behind the words, namely, that they are men of Esek and Sitnah, that is, that they are men who have inflicted wrong and are unjust. In the Hebrew עֵשֶׂק this does not sound good. It means "quarrel," "quarrelsome people," who do not seek peace, are not children of love but are children of strife and contention coupled with harm and damage to their neighbor. It means to inflict harm and violence, but with a show of right. "The land is ours," they say. This is the show of right. "Consequently, the well is ours." That is the wrong. It is a common and very wicked practice in the world that he who cannot do harm by force does so by means of plots, fraud, and wicked cunning. The Germans say: *Gewalt und unrecht thun, das ist Essig* ("Doing violence and wrong, that is vinegar"). It is a bad farewell, and it brings the people of Gerar no luck. May God protect me from hearing its like from a pious and godly person!

שִׂטְנָה. From this we have the word "Satan." This is what Isaac wants to say: "They are not only driving me out and taking the well away from me with a show of right, but they are also persecuting me in a hostile manner and are my enemies. They not only want to have the well and that new spring water which I found before and already gave them, but they are also taking away this well. What is the reason? They have a grudge against me; they hate me. Yet they do not need this well; they can be satisfied with that very fine stream from the new spring water. Why, then, are they taking it away? They cannot grant me what they do not need and from which they have no pleasure. They cannot let me have that from which they themselves get neither an advantage nor enjoyment. I have given them no reason for their enmity. They themselves derive no benefit from this well, but it is only violence; and it is stubborn petulance and the utmost wickedness. Farewell, therefore, and be Esek and Sitnah. Under that fine pretense take away the well which you neither need nor take pleasure in nor use."

People of this sort are the worst. They are not prompted to rob and sin for the sake of pleasure or some advantage. For they would not have desired or ever have bothered about the well if someone had offered it to them even for nothing; but because someone else, and especially Isaac, is enjoying it, they are inflamed with hatred and envy. But Isaac bears this calmly and says: "Keep the Esek, for you have such a grudge against me." This is an example for us, in order that we, too, may learn to bear with restraint wrongs done by others. He only bids them farewell and says: "Let Esek and Sitnah remain among you; I cannot stay in this valley." And he departs with a peaceful heart. This is matchless patience and unconquerable faith. Neither jurisprudence nor the arts nor medicine teach this. Holy Scripture alone presents these examples and this teaching.

22. *And he moved from there and dug another well, and over that they did not quarrel; so he called its name Rehoboth, saying: For now the Lord has made room for us, and we shall be fruitful in the land.*

23. *From there he went up to Beer-sheba.*

Isaac now goes to another place and digs another well. No quarrels at all arise over it. There the Lord comforts him again when He gives him a new well, which he calls Rehoboth; and he says: "The Lord has made room for us." These words proceeded from faith in the promise, for this is what he thought: "I have been forced to give up the very good wells, Esek and Sitnah; yet I shall not on that account give up my faith, but I must persevere and hold fast to the promise of God, who does not lie. Now at last we shall become rich, since we have a well of our own."

Observe, however, how God exercises his saints. Now things are sweet; now they are sour. Now He lets harsh things happen, now things that are pleasant. He who is truly a Christian will experience the same changes, as they are described in Ps. 4: distress, enlargement, tribulation, and comfort. But he names this well for the comfort: "It shall be called a well of comfort, a well of pleasure, just as the others were wells of tribulation, hatred, and spite. Thus in this well we have found not only physical but also spiritual comfort, in order that we may praise God, who is not forsaking us. Now we shall increase, be enlarged, and become rich in this land."

But not even this is lasting joy; for another migration follows, namely, to Beer-sheba. Yet Moses makes no statement at all to the effect that he changed his abode because the Philistines were persecuting him. Perhaps, however, he went away of his own accord and looked for a better place either because he was invited by others or for some other reason. There his household undoubtedly complained about the wickedness of the people of Gerar, who drove away this very good and saintly man. But God commends Isaac's patience and has presented it to all as an example; for He provides other hosts, who receive him in a kindly manner and gladly.

So much concerning the three wells and the outward trials with which the Lord exercised the very saintly patriarch. But a fervent and unconquerable faith shines in him. Because of it he persevered and overcame most difficult trials as an example for us, lest we despair in any perils. For as long as the Lord, who has given the promise, lives, we shall not be forsaken. But if He dies, the promise and everything will also go to ruin. While He lives, we need not despair, and we must take pains that our faith does not grow weak and that our hope does not cease. This pleases Him well and is salutary for us. Nor can any evil or trial, no matter how grave, last so long that it kills God. Because of this confidence all the saints had hope and were steadfast. Thus today, whether the Turk comes or some other evil, we should think as follows: "He who has set us apart into His church in order that we might believe and hope will fulfill what He has promised and will preserve us until that Day." This is what Isaac and all the patriarchs believed, and they were saved by this faith. Now, therefore, the outward trial is at an end, and Isaac appears to have vanquished the world through his patience and to have overcome his external enemies. But a little later he will be troubled by a domestic trial caused by his son Esau when he brings his two wives home. But once more a glorious promise precedes this trial.

24. *And the Lord appeared to him the same night and said: I am the God of Abraham your father; fear not, for I am with you and will bless you and multiply your descendants for My servant Abraham's sake.*

25. *So he built an altar there and called upon the name of the Lord, and pitched his tent there. And there Isaac's servants dug a well.*

Above I have often warned that in the historical accounts and legends of the patriarchs [60] one should direct special attention to the Word and should distinguish carefully between the works of the patriarchs and the Word of God as the chief part of the life of the fathers, namely, that we should note and observe primarily what and how often God speaks with them. For the Word of God is greater than the works of all men, even of the saintliest, yes, even of the angels.

In the accounts of the fathers this is the only and most desirable jewel, namely, that God speaks with them and with us. The world does not see this. Nor does it have an understanding of the value and exellence of this treasure. Nor do we ourselves pay sufficient attention to the fact that in our whole life the Word is the measure, the standard, and the most precious thing that guides our life, so that you can say: "I am doing this in the Word of God. The Lord has commanded this. This pleases God." Thus from the highest station in life down to the lowest we can be sure that God has commanded, that God has spoken. But if the Word is lacking, then he who can should flee, even if his life gives the appearance of being

---

[60] See, for example, *Luther's Works*, 4, p. 103.

angelic. Even if what one undertakes seems pleasing to God, especially religious, and pure, thrust aside that "it seems" if you are not sure about the Word. For why do you afflict yourself in vain and waste your time miserably, as the monks do in the papacy? The Turks do likewise, and the Jews proceed in accordance with the human opinion that they please God if they kill themselves with fasts and tortures of the flesh. Thus it is related about Bernard that he tortured his body to such an extent by not eating that because of the stench of his breath he was unbearable to the rest when the choir was assembled.[61] It is evident that in this way he wanted to curb and suppress lust. And this is the nature of all the works of human life that are undertaken without the Word.

Consequently, I give this warning diligently and frequently — and it must always be impressed — lest we be carried away by our own opinions or thoughts, however godly, angelic, and heavenly they may be. Thus Paul also warns in Col. 2:18: "Let no one disqualify you, insisting on self-abasement and worship of angels, taking his stand on visions." For they are without the Word. For God speaks with us and deals with us through the ministers of the Word, through parents, and through the government, in order that we may not be carried about with any wind of doctrine (Eph. 4:14). Children should listen to their parents, citizens to the government, a Christian to the pastor and the ministers of the Word, a pupil to his teacher. Apart from this Word all life is condemned, and all sects are lost. But if the Word is there, then I have sure comfort, whether I am a father or a mother or a child. Then I hear the Word, and I know what I should believe and what I should do; for God speaks with me, too, in the very station of life in which I live.

On the other hand, corruptions and distortions of the Word are a horrible wrath of God and severe retribution and punishment against those who have despised the Word; for if you do not want to listen to God in His sure truth, then indeed you may listen to falsehood under the guise of truth, as Paul, too, in 2 Thess. 2:10-11, declares concerning this punishment for contempt of the Word and very sad examples demonstrate the same thing. Today Greece listens to Mohammed. The West listens to the pope.

To be sure, there are admirable and commendable works and

---

[61] Luther refers frequently to this hagiographical anecdote, as, for instance, in *Luther's Works*, 4, p. 273, note 46.

examples in the accounts of the patriarchs, for these men walk in the Word of God; but more attention should be given to the Word, which guides the life of the patriarchs. It is the rule and standard according to which I can reach the conclusion that I am a preacher, a husband, a wife, a servant, a maid, a child, that God has committed this to me, and that for this reason it pleases Him, not on account of the works in themselves—for we are flesh—but on account of our guide and leader, namely, the Word of God, under which I walk. If I die, I do not die in the rule of Francis but in the rule and Word of the Holy Spirit.

Now let us look at the words themselves: "I AM THE GODS OF ABRAHAM." For in the Hebrew it is אֱלֹהִים, which in the plural number denotes Gods, just as above in chapter 1:1: "In the beginning God created, etc." We Christians must have no doubt about the oneness of God. But the nature of that oneness is inscrutable to reason and human wisdom, for it is a revelation of the Holy Spirit and of faith. The Jews and the Turks laugh at us and attribute a most impudent lie to us, namely, that we set up a plurality of gods and believe that there are three gods. Therefore they boast that they are the people of God and that they are honored with many brilliant victories and with the wealth of the entire world because they believe in one God, but that we have been afflicted with so many defeats because we invent more gods. For this reason they call us idolaters and horribly blaspheme the Son of God, as all their histories bear witness. Therefore our hearts must be fortified against these blasphemous utterances and this boast, which, as it appears to reason, is altogether too true and plausible. For it is completely certain that we believe in a God who is completely one and completely simple.[62] But the fact that the Turk does not understand our faith or doctrine properly and does not hear who that one and completely uncompounded God is—this is his own fault, not ours. For we teach and believe not only that there is one God, but that He is completely simple and completely one in His state of being one. We do not separate these three: the Father, the Son, and the Holy Spirit. We do not make separate gods. No, we believe in God who is completely one and completely simple.

Is someone going to say: "But I do not understand these

---

[62] The standard medieval discussion of the simplicity of God was that of Thomas Aquinas, *Summa Theologica*, I-I, Q. 3.

things"? Very well. Nor do you have to understand them. We believe in one God, who nevertheless is wont to speak about Himself and to count Himself in the plural. Just as above, as often as it has been stated, "in your Seed," that Seed, because He is without sin and also has the power to destroy sin, is God of necessity and in truth. In the same way God is called "the Gods of Abraham" in this passage. And we care nothing about those oxen and asses, the Turks and the Jews, who declare that they cannot comprehend this with human reason; for they do not have to either, since such important matters are established on the basis of divine revelation.

Furthermore, if we look at these words more carefully, we shall see that the resurrection of the dead can also be deduced from them. For just as it is stated in a common proverb that the letters of princes must be read three times,[63] so there is a much greater obligation to reread Divine Scripture a thousand times. We know that Abraham died and was buried by his sons Isaac and Ishmael. But now God says: "I am the Gods of Abraham." And Christ says (Matt. 22:32) that God is not God of the dead. Here, therefore, He restores Abraham to life and raises him from the dead. This is the well-known syllogism contained in Matt. 22:32, where we read: "I am the God of Abraham, and the God of Isaac, and the God of Jacob. He is not God of the dead, but of the living." God is not the God of that which is nothing. No One and Nobody do not worship God, and God does not rule over them. Abraham died, and God is the God of Abraham. Consequently, Abraham is living. "To be sure, he died and was buried; but for Me, God, Abraham lives and knows the Trinity of the Persons and Christ, his Seed; for God is not the God of nothing."

This reasoning the prophets, enlightened as they were by the Holy Spirit, saw and understood very clearly. The Turk does not see this, and the pope and his teachers have never understood it; for they go into Scripture with the understanding of a mule and an ass, as we read in Ps. 32:9. If they ever read Matt. 1:2, where it is stated that Abraham was the father of Isaac, etc., they thought that Abraham and Isaac were pious and plain men who were husbands and that in them there is nothing worthy of wonder. But if the Holy

---

[63] An axiom quoted earlier in these lectures (*Luther's Works*, 3, p. 114). The entire discussion of immortality in the paragraphs preceding this one suggests the hand of an editor schooled under Melanchthon.

Spirit comes as the Enlightener, then this light concerning immortality and eternal life shines forth; for if Abraham has God, and vice versa, it is necessary for God and Abraham to be living at the same time. For those statements mutually sustain and eliminate themselves, since God does not deal with the dead.

Isaac understood this doctrine concerning the plurality of Persons in the Godhead and concerning the resurrection of the dead, and he undoubtedly taught it; for it is the voice of the church and the preaching of the Gospel. First he prayed. Afterward he preached as follows: "To me it has been revealed by God that my father is living in the grace and mercy of God. Consequently, we shall not die either. For although we die to the world, yet we shall be separated from the godless, who seem to live and to have God in this world. But they have an angry God. We, however, will have a compassionate God both here and there."

What He adds, namely, "for My servant's sake," also belongs here. For how is Abraham a servant of God after his death? Will God not be able eventually to forget Abraham? Today he certainly still serves God, just as Adam, Abel, and Noah serve God. And this must be carefully noted; for it is divine truth that Abraham is living, serving God, and ruling with Him. But what the nature of that life is, whether he is asleep or awake, is another question. We do not have to know how the soul rests. It is certain that it is alive. Look at people who are in a trance or are sleeping; about them nobody can say what they are, even when they are sleeping physically. For they are without sensation and just as if they were dead. Nevertheless, one cannot say: "This person is dead." But according to the testimony of the entire world, he is alive while sleeping or dreaming. Yet when I am sleeping, I am not aware of being alive; for my senses and even reason itself do not perform their functions. Then nobody knows where he is. If we were alive while sleeping, we would be able to think in our sleep: "I am in this house, in this bedroom." Nevertheless, while dreaming I often think that I am in hell, in heaven, in Venice, or somewhere else. Accordingly, this is an important sign that I am alive and yet am not alive.

What, then, shall we suppose is the way in which the soul rests or lives? It undoubtedly has some way of its own in which it sleeps. I have no knowledge of this, just as I cannot understand physical sleep either; for I have often wanted to observe carefully the moment in which I fall asleep and the moment in which I would again become awake, but I was awake before I had noticed it. Such examples of our sleeping, which is a kind of death, prove that the souls of the saints are resting, as is stated in Is. 26:20 and 57:2, and far more peacefully at that than people who are sleeping. Indeed, these, too, are resting, and because of that rest people are never more alive than when they are sleeping; for the life of those who are awake is full of cares, troubles, hardships, and sicknesses. But physical sleep changes and overcomes illnesses. Thus the disciples say in John 11:12: "Lord, if he has fallen asleep, he will recover." Consequently, we shall be right when we say that we are most alive when we sleep and die; for then the spirit of life is most powerful. In the same way the souls, too, are sleeping. But how this takes place we do not understand.

Nor is this strange, since we do not understand other things that should be better known to us — things in which we were born and brought up. Look at your infancy, and give thought to whether you remember that you were in your mother's womb, that you lay in a cradle, that you sucked your mother's breasts, cried, ate pap, grew, etc. Yet we are certainly alive even during the first year, when the fetus is carried in the mother's womb. But how we lived we do not know at all. Thus also after its birth a year-old child knows nothing about life; it does not know that it is living. It does not reflect on life. In them we see life without life. Thus I have lived for 60 years.[64] I also lived in my mother's womb. But about that life I never knew a thing later on. Nevertheless, frequent movements show that there is certain and vigorous life of the fetus in the womb. So does the crying of the infant when it emerges. Now, however, since we cannot grasp this with our thoughts, we understand far less what the nature of that life after death is. Nevertheless, it is sure that we are living. Therefore this investigation must be given up and must be left to God, like the previous article, namely, how God is one and three at the same time in three Persons. But do this: Listen to the Word; let it guide you. But follow with your eyes closed. Then you will find how He is one and three.

In this way I hear in this passage that there is life in death and after death, and that there is a resurrection of the dead. Do not be concerned about how this will be, since when you are asleep, you

---

[64] Luther was born in 1483; but since he seems to be speaking approximately here, this is probably no key to the date of these lectures (see Introduction, p. ix).

do not know that you are living, even though you are living. Thus you lived in the womb and when you were an infant, even though you did not know it. Would God not have more ways of living than these two, so that there is a life without life and understanding? Thus the soul can have some way of its own of living — a way which is beyond our comprehension.

Meanwhile we should sustain ourselves with this comfort, and we should look for it with firm confidence. The voice from heaven sets it before us: "I am your God; I am the Gods of Abraham; you are My servants." As Is. 26:19 says: "Arise, O dwellers in the dust; because My dead bodies shall arise. Thy dew is like the dew of the meadows." There God speaks with the dead just as if they were living; and this very Word is the most powerful proof that we are not mortal, but that we are immortal even in death. For God speaks with us even in our own speech and in human language. God knows that this life is short. But why would He speak with us, and indeed in such a manner that He employs our own language, if we did not live forever? For otherwise He would be uttering His Word in vain for the sake of only a moment of time. But He does not speak in vain. Nor does He assume the voice of oxen or asses. He does not bellow with them. He speaks with man alone. Accordingly, where and with whomever God speaks, whether in anger or in grace, that person is surely immortal. The Person of God, who speaks, and the Word point out that we are the kind of creatures with whom God would want to speak eternally and in an immortal manner. Such a God or Gods, as He is called here, Abraham has; and he who clings to Abraham's promise has the same God and is a servant of God. Eventually he will live while he sleeps, even though he is dead.

But God repeats the blessing because the very saintly man, who has been vexed and tried in various ways, undoubtedly thought: "Wretched man that I am, what shall I do? Whither shall I turn? For the past trials are making us uneasy and anxious, so that we think: 'How long am I going to have this peace? Perhaps it will be for a month or two at most.'" For he was also forced to leave Rehoboth. And perhaps Rebecca began to complain and be indignant because of her rather unfair fortune and the frequent and varied changes. "Who will be able to bear and suffer this so long, to wander about so long and roam without fixed abodes?" For although these are carnal matters, yet they very greatly trouble faith.

Therefore I believe that Isaac was almost exhausted by such great misfortunes and that Rebecca grumbled. Thus Tobit's wife reproaches her husband with his alms. "It is evident," she says, "that your hope has come to nothing, and your alms have not appeared" (cf. Tobit 2:22). Such exhaustion, I suppose, existed here too. Furthermore, the complaints and shouts of the household increased it. Therefore the Lord comforts him and his whole household. "Fear not," He says. Accordingly, Isaac was afraid and terrified. His faith was in danger. For the devil exhausts the godly not only with the greatness of the trials but with his assiduity and his insistence. Therefore God says: "Be strong, My dear Isaac; fear not." And in this way He buoys up and puts new life into the man who is weary in his spirit. He does so with most beautiful comfort, namely, with the revelation of immortality. "You will live," He says, "and you will live eternally; for I am the God of your father, who is living. Therefore you, too, shall live."

One should take careful note of these words, because God does not speak in vain. In the first place, He says: "I am with you, but in a hidden manner." Isaac says: "I am not aware of it; Thou art standing far away." Thus Jeremiah complains (12:2): "Thou art near in their mouth and far from their heart." It is as if he were saying: "The others rejoice, dance, and exult; to them Thou art very near." Thus today the Turk boasts that God is on his side and that he has been honored by God with so many victories and such great wealth. For he has God's blessing in abundance. Meanwhile the devil seems to be very close to the Christians who are being captured or massacred by the Turks, but that God seems to be very far away. For the godless the devil is dead. In their opinion, God alone rules among them. But He is very far away from them, and they are, as is stated in Jer. 46:20-21, fatted calves for the day of slaughter and beasts for sacrifice. The same thing will happen to the Turks and to the pope, even though they interpret their successes as signs of grace, not of wrath.

But as for you, if God tries and scourges you, believe, and be satisfied with the Word you have in Ps. 91:15: "I am with you in trouble. I will deliver you, not only from trouble but from death, sickness, and shame. I will care for you." To be sure, the eyes do not see this, nor do the hands touch it; but to the believer all things are possible. And what has been said in this passage to the patriarch Isaac, the same thing is said to us: "I am with you, and I will keep what I have promised. From Me you must look not only for physical blessings but also for eternal blessings." "But assuredly the opposite is apparent," says Isaac. "It seems that Thou art cursing me. I must perish of thirst together with my wife, my children, and my whole household. This is not a divine blessing, is it?" God's answer is: "Fear not. You will not perish of thirst." And He adds: "I will multiply your seed for My servant Abraham's sake. I will multiply you not only now but also your seed and descendants in the future."

This is a repetition of the blessing together with an amplification by which He reassures him about eternal life and immortality. But why does He say "for Abraham's sake" and not "for Isaac's sake"? My answer is that He wants to praise the example of his father Abraham and to present it to be imitated. It is as though He were saying: "Even though you have not deserved that I should speak with you, yet I want to speak with you for your father's sake; so much do I love him." This is very sweet comfort, and it is much more gratifying than if He had failed to mention the example of Abraham and had said: "For your sake, Isaac." This is the last promise, and with it Isaac sustained himself [65] till the end of his life. Therefore he builds an altar there, and he remained in Beer-sheba till his death and was buried in the cave of which we read above in chapter 23. But he built an altar there not on account of the sacrifice but on account of the preaching of the Word. For wherever mention is made of the erection of an altar and the building of a tabernacle, there the establishment of a little church is pointed out—a church in which people came together to teach and hear the Word of God, to pray, to praise God, and to sacrifice. Thus our churches are places in which people assemble to worship and praise God. For an altar is not a place in the household; it is in the church, and the duties of the church are teaching, praising, the giving of thanks, etc.

Accordingly, Isaac delivered many very beautiful sermons there for approximately 70 or 80 years. He preached the mystery of the Trinity, of the incarnation of Christ, and of immortality, and all things that are read in the Gospel today and are being taught. Truly this was a beautiful chapel built under a tree under which he met with his household and his neighbors. I surely would have

---

[65] The Weimar text has *de,* but we have read *se* instead.

liked to see it. For it was not adorned with gold, silver, or jewels; but God spoke there by word of mouth. Nor was the tabernacle magnificent; it was constructed of trees. But it is impressive and outstanding because a highly distinguished prophet and the prophetess Rebecca dwell there, likewise many saintly people from their household who came together to Isaac when he taught. They heard him with great reverence, and they gave thanks to God for this teacher.

Thus after Moses has told about the physical and external matters that have to do with the care of the body — yet among them there are many outstanding examples of faith, love, hope, humility, and patience — he also inserts the religious activities and duties, the promises, the sermons, the words of praise, and the hymns with which the saints fostered their faith and comforted themselves in tribulation. For all sermons and the entire heavenly doctrine must be directed to the end that faith may increase, that the promise concerning the grace of God may be praised and take root in the hearts of men, and that patience and other fruits of faith may be increased.

Here, however, we retain the usual difference between these two expressions: invoking the name of the Lord and invoking *in* the name of the Lord. For the former means "calling upon," as in Ps. 50:15: "Call upon Me in the day of trouble." To invoke in the name of the Lord is to preach in the name of the Lord. Gen. 4:26: "At the time of Enosh men began to call upon the name of the Lord"; that is, at that time sermons began to be delivered, and preaching began. Strictly speaking, קָרָא means *ruffen, nennen,* "to call," "to name," "to read from a book," "to preach." Sometimes it also means "to meet." Moreover, I believe that this is why Mohammed titled his book the Alcoran;[66] for it is a compilation, or a textbook or his Bible, as the pope calls his decretals. Here, therefore, we take this word to mean "to teach," or "to read in a public assembly," provided that they had books.

At the same time the nature of the preaching is described. It was done in the name of the Lord; that is, they preached about our Lord God. It was the doctrine concerning God. It was not a useless preaching of human traditions, as the doctrine of the pope

---

[66] In 1542 Luther translated a *Refutation of the Alcoran* by a 14th-century Dominican, "Brother Richard" (*W,* LIII, 272—396); in 1543 he wrote a foreword to an edition of the Koran by Theodore Bibliander (*W,* LIII, 569—572).

is; but it was true and sound doctrine which gave pure instruction about the Lord and His name on the basis of the promise, in order that the faith which is a work of the First Table might be exercised. Then, in the Second Table, there was the doctrine about good works. For we have two kinds of doctrine. The one deals with the promises, which belong to the First Table. There God speaks with us and promises that He will be our God, in order that we may gain faith, love, and hope toward God. And this is by far the most extensive doctrine; it pervades works of every kind. The second kind of doctrine deals with works and the fruits of faith. Thus the chief parts of the Christian doctrine are the promise and the Law.

In the third place, the ceremonies are added, such as circumcision, which Isaac had from God. It, too, he transmitted to his hearers. And without a doubt he was a teacher completely free from error, one who trained and instructed the church diligently in the Word of faith and truth. And this he could do properly and well in a time of peace. For where there is no tranquillity, there is no time or place for constructing tabernacles or erecting altars, the people cannot be taught, and neither the government nor the household can be administered. A quiet place and a tranquil time are needed. But in a time of trial we should make use of what we have learned in peacetime, just as Isaac did. When he sees that he has peace because of God's kindness, he does not snore, is not spoiled by leisure, and does not strive to accumulate wealth; but he employs his time in such a way that he works most when he has leisure, since he understands that leisure has been granted to him for the purpose of establishing a church for the sake of his descendants.

We should do the same thing, while the monks and the clergy, who enjoy tranquillity, leisure, Rehoboth, and an abundance of everything, snore and gorge. But they misuse all these things most shamefully for gorging, pleasures, and every satanic villainy, although the treasures of emperors and kings have not been contributed to churches and religious establishments for these uses but have been gathered for the purpose of setting up and preserving practices of godliness. Thus when you have found leisure, as Isaac did, you should make use of these opportunities for the purpose of cleansing and spreading the worship of God. Thus the clergy should read and learn the Holy Scriptures in order that they themselves may also teach others concerning religion, pray, devote themselves to the altar, and preach in the name of the Lord.

26. *Then Abimelech went to him from Gerar with Ahuzzath, his adviser, and Phicol, the commander of his army.*

This account corresponds to an earlier one which is recorded in chapter 21:22 ff., so that it almost seems to be one and the same account. For there, too, Abimelech and Abraham quarrel about a well, and Abimelech excuses his lack of information by saying that the well was seized without his knowledge. But this account is clearer and explains the earlier one, for the gloss that there were many wells is added. Moreover, this, too, serves to comfort Isaac; for God has already buoyed him up with a promise and has given him leisure. As a result, he could be safe and could construct an altar and a tabernacle. And he uses this leisure in such a manner that he is by no means at leisure but does what is becoming to a prophet and priest of God. He labors in the Word and doctrine and is apt at teaching and ready to do so. In consequence, his comfort is increased, and Abimelech himself, who had driven him out, makes peace and a covenant with him of his own accord. I surely believe, however, that this Abimelech is the son of the Abimelech mentioned above (Gen. 20). But he is shrewder than his father, for he drives Isaac out and pretends not to know that his servants deprived Isaac of the wells.

Accordingly, one should recognize in the first place the kindness of God through which Isaac is reconciled to the king; for Solomon says in Prov. 16:7: "When a man's ways please the Lord, he makes even his enemies to be at peace with him." In the second place, this example shows what great power patience has to soften the heart of men. For it is an all-powerful virtue which makes an enemy one's best friend. Abimelech, who formerly hated Isaac to the utmost and could not bear him in his kingdom, returns of his own accord, without being asked, together with his princes and notables, not with the dregs of the common people but with Ahuzzath and Phicol. They offer peace, desire Isaac's friendship, and promise him security and favors of every kind. This is a great favor and honor with which God distinguishes Isaac. As a result, he has room or comfort, peace, protection, and defense in abundance not only from the king, who now no longer gives ear to the detractors and the wicked shepherds; but he also has the leading men of the kingdom as his friends, with the result that this shelter is strong enough and is without any fear and danger.

All this springs from the fact that Isaac persisted in his patience, did not leave off showing kindness to ungrateful people, and did not become less good because of the ingratitude and the wickedness of others. Just as a vine or a fig tree, even if it is torn to pieces and treated in the worst way, still does not degenerate into a bramblebush but remains a good tree, so Isaac is like a tree planted by streams of water which yields fruit abundantly and prosperously (cf. Ps. 1:3). But since he is so patient and forbearing, he opens the eyes of his neighbors and softens their hearts, so that they acknowledge and confess their sins and consider how greatly they have wronged him and how much and how undeservedly he has suffered up to this time without any fault of his or of his completely honorable wife and his whole household. Among these they always observed extraordinary kindheartedness, generosity, and hospitality. In addition, they saw that the manservants and the maidservants were well-mannered and properly instructed. For this reason they acknowledge the presence and the blessing of God in a household so honorable and pious. Thus Isaac's forbearance and kindheartedness lead his enemies to repentance and to knowledge of themselves. Consequently, they reproach and blame themselves for having driven out this godly and saintly man together with his household.

Therefore this example is in beautiful agreement with the statement of Paul in Rom. 12:20, which he took from Proverbs (25:21-22): "If your enemy is hungry, feed him; if he is thirsty, give him drink; for by so doing you will heap burning coals upon his head." For the human heart, no matter how much it has been irritated, can be softened and appeased if it is not filled with stubborn malice, such as Pharaoh's heart was. But if it has been provoked to anger by human weakness or some lack of knowledge and the calumnies of others, or even for just reasons, it can be so softened by kindness and forbearance that it glows and burns within itself as it acknowledges the kindness of him whom it regards as an enemy, and that it rebukes itself as it thinks: "Why did you hurt this pious man? Why did you persecute an innocent person?" These are the coals that catch fire because of patience, gentleness, and kindness. In this way Isaac's perseverance in his faith, hope, love, and hospitality moves and overcomes the king, so that the king has not only been reconciled with him but is also converted to the true worship and knowledge of God. For he undoubtedly heard the sermons and entered the tabernacle of Isaac to learn the Word of God from him. Thus God won the king himself and many others through the word of Isaac. For He has given His Word not only for our sakes but also for the sake of others, in order that we might share it with others.

In this way the very fine fragrance of Isaac's sound doctrine as well as of his blameless life was spread abroad among the king and [67] the princes. Consequently, they said: "Why did we drive out the saintly man who is an outstanding teacher and leads a saintly life, whose wife is a very virtuous matron, kindly, generous, and adorned with virtues of every kind?" Thus the hearts of the people in the entire kingdom and in the neighborhood were changed. Therefore whoever you are who have been exposed to wrongs inflicted by others, be patient, and wait. All these things are managed by God while Isaac sits still and undertakes nothing at all against the king and also has no understanding with him; for he only bears modestly and quietly what has been ordered, preaches, constructs a tabernacle, and devotes himself to the Word.

Thus we, too, are quiet and do not fight. But many have come to us even from among our enemies and have been converted, although I neither compelled them nor thought of it. Therefore this is a most pleasing comfort in agreement with the statement in Eccl. 7:8: "The patient in spirit is better than the proud in spirit." Therefore we, too, should accustom our hearts to be patient and to persevere in doing our duty, denouncing vices, and devoting ourselves to the Word. Then our neighbors and enemies will hear of it, and the fragrance of Christ will come to them, will captivate and take hold of them, just as here Abimelech comes of his own accord and becomes a saintly king like his father, even though he was not circumcised. For circumcision does not pertain to the heathen; it pertains only to this house of Abraham, to his descendants, and to his household. It was commanded to those alone who are in the people of Abraham. But the Jews did wrong when they circumcised proselytes, because they had no command in regard to this matter. For even at the time of circumcision many heathen were saved solely through the house of Abraham, in which there were the Word, the worship, and the altar of God, where the Word was heard in the name of God, and where the words of the promise

---

[67] The Weimar text has *ad,* but we have read *et* instead.

"in your Seed, etc.," were proclaimed. But God gave circumcision to the house of Abraham in order that there might be definite descendants and a definite place where the Word of God and Christ would be found even by the heathen. Besides, He did not say (Gen. 22:18): "In your name all nations will be circumcised" but "In your name all nations will be blessed." Therefore they could receive the blessing without circumcision.

Consequently, this entire account is a confirmation of the compass the church must have; for it must have defense and lodging in this life. Therefore Abimelech is led back through the Word to the chief and most important duty of a king, which is to uphold the law, to maintain peace, and to preserve justice and judgments. Above all, however, the king must guard the worship of God, protect the prophets, and support Isaac, in order that the knowledge of God may remain in his kingdom. That is the highest and the most splendid of all human works. It fills the hearts with true joy and with favor before God and men. Thus David congratulates himself exceedingly on this when he says in Ps. 60:6: "With exaltation I will divide up Shechem and portion out the Vale of Succoth." Why? "Because God has spoken in His sanctuary"; that is, "we hear the Word in my kingdom. The church has its tabernacle, worship, and priests in my kingdom." Therefore it is the chief and truly kingly duty of a king to defend the Word and to see to it that it is transmitted to posterity.

But the number of such kings is small; for the majority of the princes and kings in the world always hate and persecute the Word, destroy the churches, and harass the godly. Therefore this is presented to us as an example and for our comfort, in order that we may know that out of such a great number of princes who are enemies of the Word God selects the one or the other who cares for the church, loves and learns the Word of God. Thus Abimelech is baptized in the Holy Spirit, is circumcised with a spiritual circumcision, and believes in God, who is preached and worshiped in the house of Isaac. He becomes Isaac's pupil, friend, and patron. For this is the blessing of the godly which God promised in 1 Sam. 2:30: "Those who honor Me I will honor."

The Hebrews debate about the name אֲחֻזַּת , whether it is a proper name of a man or rather a common noun. Jerome thinks that it is a collective common noun and that it denotes not so much a person as a gathering or crowd of friends by whom the king was surrounded. [68] אָחַז means "to grasp," as friends are wont to grasp one another by the hands and to render services to one another. Therefore the meaning is that Abimelech and the grasping of his friends came, a joining together and multitude, as it were; that is, Abimelech came to Isaac with a whole crowd of his friends, whether they were in his kingdom or outside it. For undoubtedly many of the neighbors who were not under Abimelech's jurisdiction but were their relatives or friends gathered at Isaac's house. To all of them that pleasant fragrance of Christ came, so that they exhorted one another and said: "Come, let us go to the saintly man; let us listen to his sermons, etc."

But one can see how useful a person one prophet is in the world, as the words of Christ point out in John 15:16: "That your fruit should abide." For here the dignitaries and the nobles of the kingdom come to Isaac with their relatives by blood and marriage and with their friends, so great is his influence among them. And in this way the patience of the very saintly man is honored; for he overcomes evil with good, in accordance with what Paul teaches in Rom. 12:21.

27. *Isaac said to them: Why have you come to me, seeing that you hate me and have sent me away from you?*

28. *They said: We see plainly that the Lord is with you. So we say: Let there be an oath between you and us, and let us make a covenant with you,*

29. *that you will do us no harm, just as we have not touched you and have done to you nothing but good and have sent you away in peace. You are now the blessed of the Lord.*

30. *So he made them a feast, and they ate and drank.*

31. *In the morning they rose early and took oath with one another; and Isaac set them on their way, and they departed from him in peace.*

Isaac rebukes them and confronts them with the sin with which they have gravely offended him and his household. From this

---

[68] A reference to the institution of "friend of the king," referred to also in 1 Kings 4:5 and 1 Chron. 27:33; see also 1 Macc. 2:18.

reproof one can take the teaching and moral that one should live in faith, godliness, and patience, lest we flatter the dignitaries and cover and hide their sins. For if this happens, we burden ourselves with the sins of others. Although older people should not be rebuked too harshly lest the youth be insolent to the elder, as is stated in Is. 3:5, yet they should be admonished. And today the same corruption of morals is gradually spreading everywhere. But there should be a difference between one who is higher and one who is lower, between parents and children; for a father is more powerful and greater both because of his authority and out of necessity. Therefore a son should by no means conduct himself toward his father as a father toward his son, and God's Word says (Lev. 19:32): "You shall rise up before the hoary head." Thus Isaac does not conceal the sin of the king and his friends. Nor does he fawn on them. But he rebukes them with some respect and says: "Why do you come to me, since you are hostile to me? Do you not know that you have sinned? For why did you drive me out? Of course, I do refuse to converse with you; but I know that you are full of hatred and envy."

Thus sin should not be justified. Nor should a sinner be praised. But if it is an older person who has committed a sin, he should be admonished in a kindly manner. As if a son were taking his parents to task for some sin, he must say: "My father, my mother, these things do not seem to befit honorable people. Fornication, adultery, and other misdeeds are unbecoming to an aged person." But severer reproofs are sometimes proper for a prophet, as one can see in this passage in Isaac's example. Moreover, since the king, together with his friends, sees that this reprimand is just, they confess their sin and call him one who is blessed by the Lord, as though they were saying: "We acknowledge that we did evil when we persecuted you with unjust hatred, for we did not know that you are one who is blessed by the Lord. To be sure, we saw that you were growing and increasing in wealth; but we did not think that credit for this had to be given to God's blessing. But now our eyes, ears, and hearts have been opened, and we gladly acknowledge that you have been wronged by us without cause."

They do not excuse their sin, but they mitigate it. Nevertheless, they confess their fault sufficiently when they say: "We see that the Lord is with you." Thus they combine the confession of their sin with the acknowledgment of God's kindness and favor toward

Isaac. For he was still of the opinion that they had not yet been reconciled with him but were still his enemies. Therefore Abimelech says: "We are not ill-disposed toward you, since we see plainly that God is with you; and we also want to be associated with you in the same church and faith. We want to know and worship your God. Therefore let there be an oath between you and us. Even though we have not been circumcised, yet we want to learn the true faith from you and to share in the temporal peace and association, provided that you are our friend and do us no harm. We will never hurt you, just as so far we have done nothing but good to you."

Thus Abimelech excuses himself as much as he can. Although he did not take Isaac's possessions away from him and did not rob him of anything—so that the extenuation seems reasonable—yet his heart was embittered to such an extent by his servants that he ordered Isaac to leave the country. "Otherwise," says Abimelech, "since you were a sojourner in our land, we sent you away in a kindly way and in peace, without any displeasure. Even though the shepherds deprived you of your wells, yet for this wrong you were richly compensated by God's blessing. Therefore we ask you to forgive us."

This is the humbling and the conversion of King Abimelech. Isaac, on the other hand, does not quarrel, does not remonstrate, and has no dispute about anything. No, he rejoices in this goodwill shown by the king and his friends; and he prepares a feast, in order that the oath, the peace, and the protection may be approved and be firm. And after Isaac has been tested, he is exalted in this way above those who formerly hated and persecuted him.

32. *That same day Isaac's servants came and told him about the well which they had dug, and said to him: We have found water.*

33. *He called it Shibah; therefore the name of the city is Beersheba to this day.*

Another blessing is added. After peace has been made with Abimelech, God gives a new well. By this example we are reminded that one should look for comfort after tribulation, for this alternation is continuous in the life of the saints. Comfort follows tribulation. On the other hand, affliction follows comfort. But as long as God lives, it is certain that we, too, shall live; for (Rom. 14:7-8) "none of us lives to himself, and none of us dies to himself. If we live, we live to the Lord, and if we die, we die to the Lord." Whether it is day or night, whether cross or joy, everything belongs to God. Nobody is sick to himself, but everyone is sick to the Lord. He who sleeps, sleeps to the Lord. He who eats, eats to the Lord. All things are good if you hear the Word of God.

Concerning the Hebrew word שִׁבְעָה it has been stated above, in chapter 21, that it has a twofold meaning, namely, from the number seven and from the oath; and the Latin word *septem* seems to have been derived from the Hebrew, just as we Germans also say *sieben*. Jerome wants it to be explained in this passage as "abundance," because שָׂבָע also has this meaning, so that it is a well of abundance. But the rabbis of the Hebrews maintain that according to its true etymology it should be translated with "well of the oath." And this pleases me more, so that it is called the well of the oath, not of abundance, just as above it was called *Ein schwerborn*, a name also given to a certain well in Erfurt.[69]

Finally one should look for allegories in this passage. But I do not share the delight that Origen or Jerome take in allegories. I am not concerned with them except insofar as they embellish the historical meaning one gathers from the simple historical account. Here they are like interspersed flowers, but they prove nothing. This is what Augustine said about figures.[70] Yet if anyone wants an allegorical meaning, let him apply the three wells to the three principal parts of the Holy Scriptures: to the Law, the Prophets, and the Gospel. For the Law is עֵשֶׂק ; that is, as expressed in German, *es ist Essig;* it is vinegar in the soul,[71] because the Law works wrath. The prophets are שִׂטְנָה ; for when they stress the Law, hatred for God arises, not through the fault of the Law but because of the Philistines, Out of good comes evil. But the Gospel is רְחֹבוֹת , which, when it has been published in the entire world, brings about latitude of consciences. This can be the allegorical meaning of this passage. He who wants to do so may make use of it.

---

[69] See the earlier reference, *Luther's Works,* 4, pp. 86—87.

[70] The explanation of "figures" is the subject of Book III of Augustine's *On Christian Doctrine.*

[71] Cf. Plautus, *Pseudolus,* line 739.

34. *When Esau was forty years old, he took to wife Judith, the daughter of Be-eri the Hittite, and Basemath, the daughter of Elon the Hittite;*

35. *and they made life bitter for Isaac and Rebecca.*

These are examples of the very saintly patriarchs in which we observe not only outstanding faith but also instances of the most excellent practice of love, patience, and all virtues. So far we have seen how much Isaac suffered while he was troubled by outward trials, how he traveled about among the heathen, who, if they were not openly hostile, nevertheless, because of their jealousy, hatred, and plots, were most troublesome to him. And these were outward trials. Here, however, the beginning of far more horrible misfortunes follows after he has overcome all the trials by which he, together with his wife, his children, and his household, was plagued severely enough. From this he has already learned perfect patience. The heathen, among whom he had lived, have now been reconciled with him, and the church, which is peaceful and quiet, is growing and is increased by the large number of hearers who come together from everywhere. In addition, he has the physical blessing in abundance; for God bountifully bestows the fruits of the field, most delightful wells, and everything that he needs. In short, he has peace, quiet, and abundance.

Accordingly, now the trials in his household begin. They are far more burdensome than the earlier trials. Nothing but ginger, pepper, daphne, misery, and heartache now, when he is an old man and hopes for some end of his trials. He is tired and worn out by the misfortunes he has had to bear. For he is almost a centenarian, which one can gather from the fact that Esau and Jacob were born when Isaac was 60 years old. Esau takes a wife when he is 40 years of age. Therefore Isaac is a centenarian. Now, therefore, he is plagued and instructed anew by trials in his household. When everything seems to have been achieved and overcome, then a new cross and new distress begin.

But since the same thing happens to us, we should remember that this was written for us as an example in order that we may see how God plagues His saints, to whom He has given the Word and has promised eternal life, in so many ways and so harshly in this wretched life that St. Paul's statement (Acts 14:23) is completely true: "Through many tribulations we must enter the kingdom of God."

For in this manner Isaac endures misfortunes in his household, and the bitterest misfortunes of all, from the 100th year of his life up to his 180th year. All this he is compelled to bear and to swallow until his grandson Joseph is cast out into Egypt, for in that year or thereabouts he died. And he saw and bore every misfortune that will happen later on to his son Jacob, to his grandson Joseph, to Esau, who was a renegade, to Dinah, who was raped, and to Reuben, who went up to Jacob's bed. That vast sea of trials on which he is tossed about during these 80 years eventually engulfs him.

Consequently, these patriarchs are saints in the true sense of the word. In comparison with them we are altogether nothing. Indeed, all the bishops, martyrs, and apostles regarded them with admiration and thought: "To be sure, we are in the forefront and suffer much; but all this is nothing compared with the trials of the patriarchs." Therefore they regarded them so highly that in comparison with them they were ashamed of themselves; for the cross and torture of a martyr is a matter of an hour or a half-hour. *Es ist einem Martiri umb ein böse stund zuthun.* But here there is no end of trials, vexations, and daily misfortune. For what great misery it is to look upon and bear the misfortunes in his household with the utmost grief for 80 whole years! And these are no ordinary misfortunes. Nor does he share them with others. No, they are extraordinary and excessive. But Isaac's patience goes beyond all eloquence, just as the patience of Abraham and of Jacob is praised. From this it is sufficiently apparent that these three men were especially dear to God, and for this reason they are altogether worthy of being called patriarchs and very saintly martyrs. Furthermore, among all others we would justly call them a trinity, as it were, of saints if it were permitted to speak this way. For they were not overcome by the greatness, the large number, or the continuous recurrence of their trials; but with great courage they valiantly triumphed over all of them, and on the Last Day we shall finally see and wonder at the glory of their victories. Now, however, we may reflect and look upon them in one way or another. But before the eyes of the papists they are altogether hidden because of that one offense that they were married men, that they had wives, children, etc., and that they were not celibates. For in the papacy the only saintliness consisted in leading a celibate life. For this reason they cannot see those lights, which are in fact suns and moons of the most beautiful virtues.

Consequently, we are not only being trained to pattern after and imitate them but also to be ashamed and modest, so that we are ashamed of ourselves that compared with them we are altogether nothing. For here we must blush and say: "Augustine is nothing. Ambrose is nothing. Although they had gifts, they should not even be compared with these men who obeyed God in all respects with such great patience and humility." Therefore God does not say in vain that He is the God of Abraham, the God of Isaac, and the God of Jacob (Ex. 3:6). Accordingly we shall enumerate the trials in the household. *"When Esau was 40 years old, he married two wives, both of whom made life bitter for Isaac and Rebecca."* [72] Moses touches on this very burdensome cross with few words. He mentions Isaac's age because at that time people contracted marriages somewhat earlier than they did before the Flood. After the Flood it was customary and lawful for men to take wives when they were about 40 years of age. Afterwards Moses writes that Esau took two foreign wives. From this we can conclude that he did not want [73] to go to Syria and marry one of his kinswomen, which his father Isaac had done before him and Jacob will do later on.

Consequently, Moses seems to point out that Esau made a covenant with the Hittite men and youths, and that in order that this covenant might be firmer he contracted marriage with their daughters or sisters, even though the nations had long since been condemned by God, just as He enumerated these seven nations above and condemned them when He says (Gen. 15:16): "The iniquity of the Amorites is not yet complete." Esau undoubtedly knew this. Not that God rejected them completely; for Judah, one of the 12 patriarchs, is a father of Christ. From his seed came Christ, and he married Shua, a Canaanite woman. And Tamar bore Perez and Zerah as a result of fornication and incest. Accordingly, God condemned those nations. Nevertheless, He chose mothers from the race and blood of condemned peoples. And it is possible that Isaac was not displeased at first when Esau married Hittite

---

[72] These words appear in italics in the original.

[73] Although all the editions read *voluisse*, we have adopted the conjectural emendation suggested by the Weimar editors and have read *noluisse* instead.

women, and two at that. Perhaps he saw that this was customary among those nations. Thus Abimelech had many wives, and the same custom prevailed throughout the Orient. Therefore I think that neither of these two reasons offended and saddened the heart of Isaac and Rebecca. But the crosses and tribulations of the very saintly parents stemmed from the fact that they were forced to bring into their home those two daughters-in-law who were the cause of all the disturbances and of annoyances of every kind.

The celibate monks have no knowledge of the crosses and annoyances in a household. Yet it was surely a painful and burdensome cross for both parents, but especially for the mother, who had managed the entire household with great troubles up to her 90th year but now, exhausted by old age and household cares, is forced to receive these two young women into her own home and to support them from her own means, with the result that they torment and harass their mother-in-law and disturb and confuse everything as they please. For this is what Moses says: "They irritated and saddened the heart of Isaac and Rebecca." But Scripture does not describe the nature of the trials, and I do not believe that the parents were greatly disturbed because of some slight fault like the many insignificant annoyances that usually happen in a household; for both Isaac and Rebecca were very well trained to bear misfortunes and had the victory of the Spirit. Such people are not easily disturbed.

Consequently, there must have been some serious and special reason. But in one way or another we shall be able to discover and observe it if we consider the Decalog, which will point out what the causes of these trials were. Then let us make a comparison here with the example of Hagar, which was related above (Gen. 16:4). For since she ventured to rebel against her mistress and sadden her, what shall we believe that these two did not venture to do? For they undoubtedly boasted and said: "We are the wives of the first-born son; the primogeniture belongs to us." Isaac, you see, was spurned and despised; but Esau conducted himself as befits a priest, a prince, and a legitimate heir of the church and the house. Therefore the foreign women, as the wives of the first-born, also did not want to have the position of maidservants but wanted to be regarded and honored as ladies of the house. This prestige gave rise to great arrogance and haughtiness. As a result, Isaac and Rebecca had to suffer some exceedingly shameful treatment. And how would they behave otherwise, since, as has been stated above, Esau had a boastful disposition and savage manners? With what great arrogance shall we suppose that he boasted before his wives? "I am the first-born. To me belongs the succession of the inheritance. I have the divine promises which were made to my father. All these belong to me by divine right. I shall be the father of the future Seed. I shall have possession of the land." And as often as Isaac preached about the spiritual and physical promises among his household, so often did Esau arrogate them to himself. "I am the first-born and that heir of these promises, and you are the wives of the first-born. You have rule over the entire land. Our descendants will inherit and possess it. Jacob is far inferior to me. He has been cast aside and rejected."

This was the one sin and the one sorrow, namely, the arrogance of the two wives, Judith and Basemath, which the two saintly spouses were forced to endure; for in this manner it is correctly compared with the earlier example of Ishmael in the house of Abraham, where Ishmael boasted that he was the first-born, as even his father bore witness. On that occasion Sarah was indignant because he wanted to be the heir and to drive out her son Isaac. She said: "This is not what God said. No, in Isaac your descendants shall be named. Consequently, although Ishmael is the first-born according to the flesh, yet he is not the first-born according to the spirit."

The same thing happened in this household. Esau and his wives boasted of the priesthood and the sovereignty, and that Jacob should neither hope for nor expect anything else than one share or an insignificant little gift. With this he should be content, and he should be compelled to leave his father's house and go into exile. But Esau would remain and be the factotum and the prince, the priest, and the father of the Christ. Just as Sarah, however, resented Ishmael's boasting, so Rebecca was greatly disturbed and gave thought to how Jacob might keep the primogeniture. And this she eventually achieved. But it is still put off for 30 years, and only then does Jacob succeed his father, become the heir of his physical and spiritual possessions, and remain in his father's house. But Esau, together with his wives and children, leaves it. This is the judgment and special direction of God, who puts down the mighty from their thrones and exalts those of low degree (cf. Luke 1:52). For He neither wants to nor can endure haughtiness. Indeed, He rather casts down and overthrows the same ones whom He had shortly before placed on the throne. For He does both: He elevates those of low degree and places them on the throne, and He casts the same ones down from the throne.

But why does God do this, and why does He oppose Himself? I answer: The same ones whom He exalts because of their humility He puts down because of their pride. No emperor is so powerful that He cannot humble him. And it is easier for Him to overthrow some monarch than it is for me to kill a fly. For this is what He says to Saul (1 Sam. 15:17): "Though you are little in your own eyes, are you not the head of the tribes of Israel?" "But now," says God, "you are proud, and you do not obey My voice. Therefore I am deposing you." Consequently it is God's work to exalt the lowly and to put down the proud. The historical accounts of all nations prove the same thing. "He removes kings," says Daniel, "and sets up kings" (2:21). While kings are humble, He protects them and preserves their kingdom. When they become proud and persecute His saints, He removes them.

The example of Ishmael is horrible indeed. Because of his pride he is rejected and deprived of his primogeniture, especially so far as the spiritual promise is concerned (Gen. 21:9 ff.). Thus Esau, too, is proud. Therefore he is cast aside and is unworthy to be the heir of the land of Canaan and the father of the Messiah, who would rule in this land. Consequently, these bitter experiences had their origin from the First and the Second Table: from the First because of the priesthood, from the Second because of the rule. For the two wives of Esau boasted and said: "Our husband will have the worship and the church of God, and the Christ will be born from our husband. In the First Table he should teach; in the Second he should rule for a time." This is the right of the first-born of which he boasted with pride.

Above, however, the opposite was determined in the promise, where it is stated: "The elder shall serve the younger" (Gen. 25:23). For God expresses His promises in such a manner that when He promises grace and blessing He remains God. If His promise should be and remain firm, it is also necessary for God to remain and be acknowledged as the One who bestows and promises. But if I am proud, then I lose the promise; for the promise excludes pride and includes humility and the knowledge of God, who gives the promise.

But Rebecca and Isaac had to bear this bitterness for 30 years, for this is the length of time Jacob lived without a wife and in comparison with Esau was spurned and thrust aside even by the household. This situation caused his mother great and well-founded grief; for, what is commonly said, namely, that all mothers-in-law hate their daughters-in-law,[74] should not be said about this saintly woman. This situation is far different because she is troubled about the primogeniture of Jacob, just as Sarah was troubled. Here nothing should be concealed, no wrong should be tolerated, and one should not depart from what is right; for there is a divine promise. Moreover, to surrender or give up the Word and to deny the promises of God is not patience; it is laziness, yes, contempt for God. For I could bear anything at all, provided that Christ is not taken away from me.

"But," someone will interpose, "should a Christian not keep silence, show patience with humility, and also forgive the wrongs of those who hurt us?" I answer: Patience, humility, and all other obligations of love cease when I have to lose Him for whose sake I am suffering. When one has to lose God and deny His Word and the worship that is owed to God, one must have no patience. Here we must be steadfast and sure concerning the promise of God which pertains to us, lest we permit it to be taken away from us in any way. Thus when Rebecca sees that Esau and his wives are giving themselves grand airs as if he were a king and they were queens, and to the extent that they consider themselves the heirs in physical as well as spiritual things, her patience comes to an end, and she thinks: "I shall have to sweat, in order that the blessing may not be snatched away from my son, but that he may be the heir according to the promise." And the Holy Spirit gives Rebecca the advice about which we shall hear later—the advice which leads Isaac, the father, who is blind and does not know what he is doing, to transfer the primogeniture from Esau to Jacob. And just as Abraham was compelled to listen to the voice of Sarah, so Isaac is compelled to obey Rebecca even against his will; and this she brings about by means of a sinless and pious deception,

---

[74] Cf. Terence, *Hecyra*, II, 1, 4.

in order that the inheritance may be taken away from the false first-born and may be restored to Jacob, the true first-born.

This one cause of their bitterness was surely greater than we, who read this carelessly and have no understanding of such struggles, can imagine. To this misfortune the second one was added, namely, idolatry. For the two daughters-in-law, who had not been properly instructed in the heavenly doctrine, opposed the true worship and religion of God. Perhaps they brought the ancestral traditions of the Hittites into the house of their father-in-law and infected the church of Isaac with this leaven. It certainly grieved the hearts of the very saintly spouses when heresies and sects arose because the women held fast to and defended their ancestral superstitions. For when the church has been set up in the best way and there is agreement among those who teach and those who believe—one mouth, one heart, one pen—when we all teach and write the same thing, and then someone arises who throws all this into confusion, who wants to be the doctor and the teacher and to attract the whole church to his side, this is by far the worst and saddest state of affairs. Thus Arius arose and destroyed the church at Alexandria. For these two, namely, quarrels about the primogeniture and heresies, are sisters and twins, so to speak. The heretics see that they cannot become famous if they remain in the common fellowship and harmony of the church. "What shall I do?" they say. "My name is being completely obscured; it is not being honored in other kingdoms and lands. Consequently, I must try a way by which I could raise myself from the ground in order that people may see what I am able to accomplish." Then a quarrel about the primogeniture and the title of the church arises. But the true church is trodden underfoot by ambitious spirits of this kind. Thus here Isaac and Jacob are not regarded as the true church by Esau and his wives. They said: "They are foolish, and they have a picayune spirit. One must aim at higher things, *man muss höher faren.*" [75] In our time Münzer spread abroad words like this: "To be sure, Luther and others started the Gospel; but they did not promote it." [76] In the same

---

[75] Here Luther uses the German expression, "man muss höher faren," which we have elsewhere translated: "who thought that they had to interpret this far more boldly than St. Paul does in his simple message about Christ" (*Luther's Works*, 24, p. 32).

[76] See also *Luther's Works*, 30, p. 254.

way those two ladies urged Esau to reform the church. They said: "You are the master. You may manage everything as you see fit. You will not be able to err. Come, let us also introduce the religion of our Hittite fathers. What about father Isaac? He is an ignorant man, remains in his simplicity, and teaches us only how to pray. Those simple things are without any show and ostentation; they do not move or arouse the hearts of men. Things that shine and glitter in the eyes of men should be brought into the church. Our Hittite fathers worship the moon and the sun. Consequently, let us at the same time respect the religion and ceremonies of the Hittites."

This was the bane of that church, for human traditions and ceremonies are very showy and strike the eyes of the people. They move the common people, so that they marvel at that outward splendor. In this way these two foreign women attracted many of the household, and even the neighbors, to themselves; and they said: "Isaac is a silly old man; he cannot be responsible for anything. Rebecca milks the goats and the cows. Therefore let us establish a different and far more sublime worship of God." Thus the false church began to prevail because of its outward splendor, but the promise and sound doctrine concerning God was despised. What misery Isaac and Rebecca were compelled to see and bear! Esau, together with his wives, was preferred, and he despised his parents. And so they neither worshiped God nor honored their parents, but along with their followers they vexed and grieved the very pious parents.

But the same thing is also happening today to us, who see that so many dissensions and sects are arising. For this reason the church is distressed and grieves exceedingly, but one cannot guard against this evil. Moreover, when the primogeniture has been taken away, then idolatry is altogether sure to follow. Consequently, the church of Isaac was in great danger. This arose on account of the first-born and his wives, both of whom grieved and, if I may speak this way, embittered the heart and soul of Isaac and Rebecca. Nor could Isaac keep silence about or conceal his grief, for there was strong and constant vexation. They not only vexed, as the Vulgate has it,[77] but they kept on vexing by per-

---

[77] Luther is suggesting the imperfect form, *offendebant*, instead of the perfect form, *offenderunt*.

sisting without interruption and habitually in causing the irritation. They did not cease to irritate those two, Isaac and Rebecca. This happened not only once, twice, or three times; but the vexing lasted for a long time — until that violent outburst which now follows.

CHAPTER TWENTY-SEVEN

1. *When Isaac was old and his eyes were dim so that he could not see, he called Esau his older son, and said to him: My son; and he answered: Here I am.*

2. *He said: Behold, I am old; I do not know the day of my death.*

3. *Now then, take your weapons, your quiver and your bow, and go out to the field, and hunt game for me,*

4. *and prepare for me savory food, such as I love, and bring it to me that I may eat; that I may bless you before I die.*

THIS chapter deals with the amazing transfer of the blessing of the primogeniture from Esau to Jacob and describes the divine judgment which has so far been concealed but is finally disclosed. Above all, however, one must note the computation of the time, in order that we may know in what year this event took place.[1] For at this time Esau and Jacob were 77 years old, because Jacob goes to Mesopotamia at the age of 77. About this there is no doubt; the computation demonstrates it clearly. Thus if the previous 60 years of Isaac's age before the birth of his sons are added to the 77 years, the total is 137 years. Esau took two wives when Isaac was 100 years old. Beyond these 100 years he then lived 36 or 37 years. Therefore what follows took place when Isaac was 137 years old.

But after Jacob has served in Mesopotamia for seven years, he does not become a bridegroom until he is 84 years old. Esau took his wives 44 years before this time and was already the father of many children, and from these he undoubtedly also had grand-

---

[1] As we have noted in previous volumes of these *Lectures on Genesis* (e. g., *Luther's Works*, 1, p. 334, note 1), Luther had compiled a choronology, which he — and apparently the editors who compiled the *Lectures* — employed in the exposition of Genesis.

children. For he has been a husband for 37 years, during which numerous children are begotten, especially from two wives. Consequently, he has a large household and a tent of his own together with his wives and children, as will become clear below. He is the prince and lord in Isaac's house and has two ladies of the house and many children and grandchildren. And he hopes that nothing will prevent him from succeeding his father. Jacob is wretched and disheartened. He has no hope at all but is looking only for a gift, and after receiving it he expects to be sent away from his father's house and to leave everything else to his brother Esau. This expectation of both lasts 37 years.

But eventually Isaac thought: "Look, you are more than 137 years old, and now you must think about departing from this life and about making arrangements for your descendants." For after the Flood the fathers no longer reached the age of 200. And by that time, of course, nearly all had died except Eber alone. All the majesty of the patriarchs had been buried. Only Isaac and Eber are left, and Eber dies two years later. Consequently, Isaac alone, together with his sons, is the patriarch and pope in the world. Therefore he thought: "The rest of the fathers, with the exception of one or two, did not live 200 years, and I will not hope for a longer life." "When Isaac[2] was old," says Moses — namely, when he was 137 — "and his eyes were dim" — perhaps not so much because of his age as because of some other mishap. Otherwise in old age, however, not only the eyes but the taste, the touch, and all the senses and members become weak; for old age is the prelude to death. Just as infants, too, are dead, so to speak, and see without seeing and taste without tasting, so old people turn out to be children again and become childish. Their eyes grow dim, and it becomes more and more difficult for them to hear. Consequently, the failing of the senses begins immediately at birth, and as death approaches, all the powers and senses become weak again. Accordingly, when, either on account of his age or because of the occurrence of sickness, his eyes grew dim, so that he was no longer able to see, he called his older son Esau to himself in order to bless him before he died.

Here, however, a difficult and troublesome question arises.

---

[2] The Weimar text has "Jacob" here, but we have followed the text of the Erlangen edition (and the sense of the paragraph) and read "Isaac."

Why, after the prophecy given to Rebecca above (Gen. 25:23), does Isaac go ahead with his determination to bless the older son? For it is certain that he heard what was said to Rebecca through the divine prophecy, namely, that "the elder shall serve the younger," and also that "two peoples, born of you, shall be divided, of which the elder shall serve the younger." And for this reason Rebecca supports Jacob, the younger son; but Isaac, on the other hand, favors the older son, Esau.

Here the Jews make the silly assertion that Isaac had no knowledge of the answer contained in the prophecy; for, as they say, Rebecca had concealed it from him.[3] But this is absurd and contrary to the nature and custom of spouses, who are wont to share such matters with each other. Nor was Rebecca able to conceal the pain she felt as a result of the struggling of the infants in her womb. She undoubtedly complained that she was in danger of her life, and at her husband's bidding she goes to Eber or to Shem to seek his advice and opinion. Then he answered: "You will not die, but two peoples are in your womb, and you will be the mother of twins, yes, of two peoples. Nor will your sons die in infancy; but they will grow and have the promise of life, so that they know that they will be patriarchs of very great peoples." When she heard this, she returned to her husband and joyfully related the prophecy: "Shem said that I would give birth to twins who will live and beget two peoples."

What, then, does Isaac think now, after the divine prophecy has been given that the older must become the younger? This is certainly a difficult question, and this entire chapter is quite amazing. Moreover, the commentaries of others who have expounded Genesis are altogether dull and worthless. I incline toward the pious thought that there was a friendly and kindly disagreement about the meaning of the prophecy. Rebecca could say to the father: "It surely seems that Jacob will be the first-born." Isaac, on the other hand, said: "You do not understand it correctly. To me it seems that this prophecy has already been fulfilled in such a way that Esau overcame Jacob, the older son, in your womb when he wanted to overpower the younger son. But Esau came out as the older and must remain the older." Rebecca thought the opposite and held fast to her opinion until later, when that amazing

---

[3] These opinions are recounted in Lyra *ad* Gen. 27:1.

transfer took place. Meanwhile, however, there was a friendly disagreement between the spouses. Isaac tried to get Rebecca to change her mind and said: "You are mistaken, my dear Rebecca; you do not understand the oracle correctly." Rebecca answered: "Esau will not be the first-born." And she had very weighty arguments. For Esau was a hunter, has made covenants with the Hittites, and brings two very wicked wives into his father's house. He has not taught his children to be obedient to their parents. From this she concluded that Esau should be cast aside. And she did this at the prompting of the Holy Spirit, who reminded her that Esau, who was born first, is the older and that the other son is the younger.

Thus each parent calls him whom he or she loves the older and the younger son. Friendly mistakes of this kind occur every day between spouses. The same thing happened here with regard to a matter that was not unimportant, and this controversy lasted up to the time of that turning point and reversal. Rebecca concludes that Esau is the older and that for this reason he cannot become the first-born according to the prophecy. Furthermore, he had despised and sold the right of primogeniture. All this she considered carefully, just as women have their own thoughts too. But Isaac holds fast to the opposite opinion and has the rule or law on his side. Esau is the first-born. Consequently, the right of primogeniture is his due. Just as when you say in grammar: "Nouns, ending in *a* are feminine in gender, but certain ones are excepted," [4] so Rebecca makes an exception and a transfer. The father adheres to the rule without an exception. In addition, Esau is in possession, rules the house, and is the lord; but Jacob remains in the position of a servant, is unmarried, and, since his place is that of a servant, gives no directions whatever during these 37 years.

That comparative description of the persons helps; it sheds light on the account. Esau manages everything, not only in the home and in governmental affairs but also in the church. When his father is away, he preaches, prays, sacrifices, and kills the animals. He is king and pope in that church. His wives are proud ladies and queens. They undoubtedly boasted that they were in possession, that their husband Esau had the priesthood and

[4] See also p. 308, note 42.

the rule. Jacob, on the other hand, is cast aside, dead, and buried, like a decaying tree trunk and "a root out of dry ground," as Isaiah (53:2) says about Christ. But this is a work of God, who can make a green tree out of a dry trunk.

Meanwhile, however, since this is how matters and opinions stand, Esau is regarded as the chosen one; but Jacob is regarded as the rejected one, in accordance with the rule and judgment of all in the house and with the authority of Isaac, the father. Only Rebecca, the mother, resists. She has had patience during these 37 years and has put up with many exceedingly shameful and rude deeds of her son and his wives. She was compelled to see Esau in possession, ruling, preaching, and administering the priestly office, and Jacob in the position of a servant who brought water and fire to the sacrifices and assumed other domestic and menial tasks.

These thoughts and words do not seem incongruous at this place. For disputes of this kind about doubtful matters occur often in life. Thus there was a similar disagreement between Augustine and his mother Monica.[5] His mother used to pray night and day for her son that he might be delivered from the sect of the Manichaeans, to which he was devoted for nine years. He was engrossed to such an extent that nobody was able to deliver him or to oppose him in debates. His mother had called upon many to confer with him and to remove this error. But he could neither be overcome nor turned back by anybody. Consequently, his mother was pitiably troubled and had no comfort. Then one night she had a dream in which there appeared to her a young man who insisted on a certain rule and said to her in a friendly way: "Woman, why are you weeping?" She said: "I am grieving over the complete loss of my son." The youth answers: "Where you, there he." When the mother awakes from sleep, she joyfully relates the dream to her son. "I have finally found comfort," she said, "and the promise that you are to be converted to my rule." And she recounts the words of the youth. Then Augustine turns this statement around and says to his mother: "You did not hear correctly, but this is what he said: 'Where I [undoubtedly referring the little word "I" to himself and his doctrine], there you.'" But his mother was not at all impressed; she

[5] Augustine, *Confessions,* Book III, ch. 11.

persisted with the greatest firmness in her understanding. And Augustine confesses that he was deeply moved by that steadfastness of his mother, with the result that he went over to her opinion all the more easily.

Such quarrels are common not only between spouses but also between friends, as for example between Pomponius and Cicero,[6] and here between Isaac and Rebecca. And they not only argued about the meaning of the oracle, but they also made a careful comparison of the dispositions and the morals of each of the two sons. "My dear Rebecca," said Isaac, "you see that Jacob is unassuming and dejected in spirit, and that he cares neither about the rule nor about the priesthood. Esau carries a bow, arrows, and a sword; he will be more eager and ready to rule." We are wont to expect much from those who, as we see, do things a little more eagerly and vigorously. Furthermore, he clings to the literal sense of the prophecy, just as the Jews cling to the carnal understanding of Scripture; for Isaac, who is blind and an old man, does exactly what they do. On the other hand, the very saintly matron, vexed by the bitterness of Esau's wives and by her son's pride, is enlightened by the Holy Spirit to support Jacob and to say to her husband: "Esau will by no means be the lord. His conduct displeases me, no matter how well he seems to be suited to rule. Jacob humbles himself, is obedient, and is trodden underfoot by his brother. Therefore the promise has not yet been fulfilled; for the humble are exalted, and the proud are humbled." For this is an infallible rule of Holy Scripture, as Peter says: "God opposes the proud but gives grace to the humble" (1 Peter 5:5).

Consequently, since God's government is in agreement, Rebecca lays stress on this rule. Because Esau realizes that he is honored and highly esteemed by his father and on this account is proud and puffed up because of his popularity, he will be humbled. And later on God decrees the opposite, so that the other son, namely, Jacob, who is cast aside and sits in the dust, is elevated. These are the judgments of God. And I am saying this in order that one may be able to understand more easily why Isaac is deceived in such an astonishing way, so that the thing seems

---

[6] Titus Pomponius Atticus (109—32 B. C.) was Cicero's correspondent over a period of many years.

almost incredible. For one has to conclude that he was well acquainted with the prophecy and adhered stubbornly to the opinion that Esau was the older—Esau, who had first been trampled on by Jacob in the womb and who now, in turn, will trample on one who is older than he is, namely, on Jacob; for otherwise it will not be possible to bring the text into agreement.

The father, like Abraham, who regarded Ishmael as the firstborn, adhered to the letter.[7] But Rebecca had stronger arguments. Therefore although she puts up with Esau's pride and insults, yet she directs her mind to all opportunities, in order that she may be able to transfer the primogeniture from Esau to Jacob. She does not begin to consider that plan this year or this day. No, she turned it over in her mind for a long time in various ways and thought: "I shall see how I can regain the blessing for my son." And it is credible that she did not form it spontaneously or because of her own ingenuity, but that she was reminded by the Holy Spirit through the patriarch Eber of that exception from the rule. He informed her that by divine authority the blessing belonged to Jacob and not to Esau, by way of an exception from the rule, although the latter defended himself with the inflexibility of the law and the rule. But, as Paul says, the children of the exception, not the children of the Law, are the heirs (cf. Gal. 3:18). Therefore Rebecca does not depart from her opinion, and she has the utmost confidence that Jacob will be the heir and lord. Isaac, on the other hand, clings to the rule and law until that moment when the mother and the son begin to deceive the father with their lies.

Accordingly, Isaac summons his older son Esau and asks him for the food which, as Esau knows, he enjoys. From this one gathers clearly that he was firmly convinced in his heart that Esau was the older, for he is full of confidence when he makes this statement, as saintly people are wont to do. They are not double-tongued or deceitful in their hearts; but to what they are inclined, they are inclined wholeheartedly. They are either "all or nothing at all."[8] On the other hand, deceitful people are undecided, fickle, and double-tongued. But here the heart of ISAAC, the father, is undivided. With full confidence and con-

[7] Cf. *Luther's Works,* 3, p. 75.

[8] The Latin is *aut nihil, aut totum.*

viction he inclines toward his son Esau and says that he is the first-born. Later on, therefore, when he realizes that he has been deceived in this artlessness and undivided confidence, he is most severely disturbed. This results from that artlessness, which does not split the heart into conflicting opinions, just as he who believes in one God cannot have two gods; for here God demands the whole heart when He says (Deut. 6:5): "You shall love the Lord your God with all your heart." Consequently, his excessive confidence is the cause of the deception.

Moreover, Esau is described as very obedient and good. Therefore Isaac puts all confidence of the succession in him and speaks with him just as if he were his successor. "My son," he says, "it is time for the promise to be fulfilled. You are the older and the first-born. Therefore we shall see to it that you succeed me in the rule and the priesthood. For I am afraid that between you and your brother there will be a quarrel the seeds and beginnings of which I have now seen for more than 30 years. Therefore in order that dissensions between brothers may be guarded against, I have decided to appoint a definite successor and prince for the state and the church." But he chooses Esau because Esau is completely submissive and believes Rebecca his mother, who loved Jacob and hoped that he would be the first-born, is in error. Therefore Isaac's words come from a heart that was fully convinced and certain that Esau must be declared his successor. "Go," he says, "take your quiver and bow, etc., and bring me something, that I may eat and that my soul may bless you before I die." Here there is no suspicion that it can happen differently. Nevertheless, he will be deceived.

Furthermore, it is clear from these words spoken by Isaac that Esau was able to ingratiate himself with his father. Scripture does not state that he honored his father; it states that he flattered him and was extraordinarily complaisant. "Jabbering is part of the trade." He was able to accommodate and adjust himself to any nod of his parent. Then he feigned extraordinary solicitude and concern toward his father. This was more than his brother did. Therefore Isaac despairs of Jacob, who stays close to his mother and is modest and quiet, as though born for a menial position. But Esau is the lord in the house. He is accustomed to hunt and to bring his father choice foods from the hunt, not everyday foods, such as a hen, milk, or cheese—the kind of food Rebecca and

Jacob were in the habit of supplying—but game. And in this way he shows devotion and kindness toward his father that are far superior to the devotion and kindness shown by Jacob and his mother. And by means of such complaisance and zeal Esau increases the goodwill felt toward him by his father, who favored him very much in other matters. Of course those whom we want to deceive have to be treated in this manner.

But he was also diligently aided by his wives, who cajoled the old man with their flattering remarks and meanwhile greatly disturbed the mother; for they knew that Esau's honor and the contempt in which Jacob was held displeased her. But Rebecca thought: "O Esau, you are honoring your father, to be sure; but as the saying goes, 'it is not you, but yours,' that one is after.[9] You are not thinking of your father; you are thinking of yourself." For it is not his purpose to honor his father with his whole heart, but he is seeking the rule and the priesthood for himself and for his wives and children. Rebecca realized this. For this is the way all hypocrites are minded. They are wolves in sheep's clothing (cf. Matt. 7:15), with which they make an impression on parents, masters, brothers, etc. Isaac does not notice this, but Rebecca sees it clearly and will thwart this trick by means of an amazing plan. Accordingly, Esau was an obedient son, but God had no knowledge of it. Jacob, on the other hand, does not seem to bestow any honor or reverence on his father, but in God's judgment he alone honors him; for God "looks at the heart" (1 Sam. 16:7). Esau brings rabbits and game, and he flatters his aged parent. For this reason he is loved more. But it is pure hypocrisy. Therefore the artlessness of Isaac, who lets himself be duped by this hypocrisy, becomes greater.

But it is a bad example, and godly people should learn to hate this kind of hypocrisy and to fear the Lord. For God is not concerned about whether one does many great things. Esau, for example, apparently fulfills the Fourth Commandment to the highest degree, but he does anything but this; for his heart is not upright and sincere. Nevertheless God demands this above all. Furthermore, Esau is not concerned about his father; he is con-

---

[9] The Latin phrase, *non propter te, sed propter tuum te*, seems to be a proverbial expression describing the exploitation of a personal relation for the sake of gaining something; the nearest equivalent in English is the saying, "I do not want you, but yours."

cerned about his primogeniture. This will be more apparent after he has lost the blessing. For if he had loved his father truly and from the heart, then he would have borne that curse calmly and would have said: "Father, although something else seemed best to me and to you, yet I shall also obey my mother and calmly bear this transfer of the blessing." But his purpose is far different; for he says: "The days of mourning will come, and I will kill my brother." But is this how parents are to be honored? Therefore God, who searches the hearts (cf. Rom. 8:27), saw this satanic and murderous heart. To be sure, Esau conceals this for a time, lest his father notice it; but later on it bursts forth.

But honor to parents demands that you remain obedient even if they arrange something contrary to your wish. Therefore Moses describes Esau as an outstanding hypocrite who deserved well of his father because of special services and yet deceived him with this hypocrisy. Hence even if Isaac, who is blind and old, is made sport of by his seemingly very obedient son, God nevertheless judges justly (cf. 1 Peter 2:23) and transfers the blessing from the wicked hypocrite Esau to the pious and guileless Jacob. And this is presented to us as an instructive example, in order that we may learn to fear God, who is not deceived by our hypocrisy but looks at the heart. Therefore it is best to act guilelessly and to live with an upright heart. Nor should one jest with God in religion or in the management of the state or the household, for such jesting and hypocrisy never goes unpunished. Accordingly, after the hypocrite has conspired with his two wives and his children to deceive his father and to have Esau appointed as the heir, now Rebecca's counterplan follows. She acts with extraordinary daring and frustrates and thwarts all the plans of her husband Isaac and their son.

5. *Now Rebecca was listening when Isaac spoke to his son Esau. So when Esau went to the field to hunt for game and bring it,*

6. *Rebecca said to her son Jacob: I heard your father speak to your brother Esau:*

7. *Bring me game, and prepare for me savory food, that I may eat it, and bless you before the Lord before I die.*

8. *Now therefore, my son, obey my word as I command you.*

9. *Go to the flock, and fetch me two good kids, that I may prepare from them savory food for your father, such as he loves;*

10. *and you shall bring it to your father to eat, so that he may bless you before he dies.*

Here belongs a description of the rites which the fathers used both when bestowing and when receiving a blessing. But Moses relates merely as a matter of history what the first-born had to do and how he had to be dressed in order to receive those fiefs of the blessing. Beyond this he adds nothing, although they made use of definite and special rites. Thus when the princes receive fiefs from the emperor today, they are not dressed in the ordinary or customary manner but put on royal garments with distinctive helmets and arms.[10] These are ceremonials which the world uses to make public and adorn what is being done. Thus Moses laid his hands on Joshua (Deut. 34:9), and Scripture says: "You shall invest him with your dignity" (cf. Num. 27:20, 23); that is, you shall honor him with a short address before the people, in order that they may know that he has been praised by you and deserves to be heard and followed by them. This is what we do when convocations are held at schools and when degrees are announced.[11] The same thing is done at weddings. The couple goes into the church and is arrayed in new attire, the neighbors are invited to the festivities and the rites, and a feast is prepared in honor of the groom and the bride.[12]

In the same way they made use of some rites when receiving the blessing of the primogeniture. First it was necessary to prepare some food for the father. This was not done without a sacrifice. Both offered a sacrifice to God, and thus the beginning was made with a sacrifice, just as in our public assemblies we commence with a prayer or thanksgiving, and just as we pray when we lay hands on those who are being ordained for functioning in the

---

[10] This is a reference to the customary rituals followed in the investiture of noble vassals with their feudal privileges.

[11] From contemporary accounts and woodcuts it is evident that the Reformation had not eliminated the academic ceremonies surrounding the *Promovierung* of doctoral candidates, despite the objections of Carlstadt.

[12] Luther himself had prepared a brief manual proposing the form of the wedding ceremony (*W*, X-I-2, 720—725).

church. Thus Esau began with a sacrifice. Later he gave his father something to eat.

The second ceremony was this: He had to put on pontifical vestments appropriate to the priestly pomp and that blessing of the primogeniture. And here Moses points out that Rebecca had possession of the priestly vestments. Jacob does not concern himself about them and despairs of the primogeniture, but she guards them carefully. At that time, however, both Esau and Jacob were 77 years old. Nevertheless, these vestments were in the custody of their father and mother, from whom they had to be requested whenever it was necessary to use them. And I think that Rebecca did this for the special purpose of having in her power the vestments, the crown, the scepter, the robe of state, and other things that pertained to the dignity of the primogeniture. Approximately this is what we are able to gather from Moses in regard to the ceremonies.

But now a very weighty question and an almost unsolvable problem presents itself. Did Rebecca and her son Jacob have the right to lie, to deceive the very saintly patriarch who was a blind old man, in such an important matter, and to deprive brother Esau of the blessing and the primogeniture? For, in the first place, they sin against the Law and the rule. In the second place, they sin against the prophecy, which Isaac did not understand in the way she interpreted it. In the third place, they sin against the wish and the authority of the father. Besides, Rebecca appropriates to herself the regal and priestly vestments and brings Jacob, who has been adorned with these, to his father, who had never thought of appointing him as his heir. This is great rashness and boldness coupled with extraordinary deception and very great harm, for this lie is not playful or obliging but is decidedly harmful.[13] The primogeniture, you see, is a matter which people quarrel about in the church and which brings with it eternal as well as temporal life. Consequently, it is a great crime of which you would never consider anyone, even the most worthless person, capable, much less such saintly people as Rebecca and Jacob. It seems that nothing more vicious can be mentioned or thought of, even according to the world. It is a very wicked deception in exceedingly important matters; it is contrary to the prophecy and contrary to divine Law. Furthermore, Esau has the possession and the manage-

---

[13] See the earlier discussion of various kinds of lies (p. 40).

ment of the household, the government, and the church; yet, contrary to all this and contrary to his father's wish, he is dispossessed by his brother Jacob.

But I have nothing from the fathers, Augustine, or others to help me in explaining this question; for they all ignore this passage.[14] Consequently, we shall have to guess. And it is surely an amazing thing for this woman to have the courage to do something so important, to expose her son to such great danger in his brother's absence and against the will of his father, who comes close to being aware of the deception and is stunned when he hears the voice and feels the hands of Jacob. For this is what he says: "The voice is Jacob's voice, but the hands are the hands of Esau." Likewise: "How is it that you could find it so quickly?" And Jacob himself shudders at his mother's plan, trembles, and says to his mother: "I am afraid that I shall bring a curse upon myself instead of a blessing." But Rebecca follows the spirit that seizes her, and with great courage she removes those dangers and all obstacles from her eyes.

And it seems that she did not carry this out on her own initiative, but that she conceived it as a result of the advice of others. But she was unable to persuade her husband to transfer the blessing to Jacob contrary to the rule. For this reason she often came to Eber and complained that Isaac was unwilling to depart from the rule and to bless Jacob. Then she heard Eber say: "Do whatever you can to deceive him and to seize the right of primogeniture. Leave nothing untried, for faith is not without the Word." [15] Therefore she undoubtedly listened to the spoken Word and pondered it in her heart. Otherwise she would not have had the courage to attempt this. For the Holy Spirit does not come without the Word, but He comes through His lyre; that is, He wants to come through meditation on the Word or through the spoken words of the father, the mother, or others. Otherwise the devil comes. But, as David, Isaiah, and all Scripture bear witness, the Holy Spirit comes with the Word and through the Word, according to the statement: "Blessed is he who meditates on the Law of God day and night" (cf. Ps. 1:1-2).

---

[14] As the discussions by Jerome, Augustine, and Lyra illustrate, this is an exaggeration.

[15] On the theological principle underlying such speculations cf. *Luther the Expositor*, pp. 103—107.

Furthermore, God is wont to transgress the rule now and then on account of the fact that those who are children according to the rule and the law are wont to misuse their rule. And to that extent the law is of no benefit to them; for if you begin to misuse it, God repeals it. Esau was proud in opposition to the prophecy and thought to himself: "Jacob is rejected, dead, and buried." And he oppressed his wretched brother and also tolerated the impudence and the harshness of his wives toward his parents. Therefore when pride comes, then the rule is at an end. For God does not establish kingdoms and empires, and does not bestow other gifts on men in order that they may become haughty and rage against the poor and the afflicted; but whatever He gives, whether wealth, power, or beauty, He gives for His own glory and for the benefit of the neighbor.

Hence the purpose of God's gifts is not the pleasure or the tyranny of those who have the gifts, but the lawful use should be directed toward the glory of God and the welfare and benefit of the neighbor. But although people receive God's blessing, sovereignty, priesthood, power, strength, and intelligence, and have the efficient, formal, and material cause, they are not concerned about the final cause.[16] But why are you a king? Why are you a prince, a priest, a father, or a mother? "In order that I may be blessed in this life," you will say, "in order that I may indulge in pleasures, in order that I may gratify my lusts. I am learned and rich in order that I may get a great name and glory among men." But then the rule of which you boast is completely done away with, because God does not want His blessings poured out for any other purpose than for His own glory, for the praise of Him who bestows them, and for the welfare of the church. The government is held in honor in order that it may benefit the state. Husband and wife are joined together in order that they may bring children into the world and rear them for the benefit of the home and the state. But the world cuts off the final cause in all the gifts of God.

Rebecca noticed this and looked at and considered the prophecy more carefully than her husband did. He clung only to the rule, namely, in this way: "Esau was born first. Jacob was born later. Therefore Esau is the first-born." Rebecca, on the other

---

[16] Here again, as earlier in the *Lectures on Genesis* (for example, *Luther's Works*, 2, pp. 125—126), Aristotle's distinction of causes is being employed.

hand, relied on the promise. She has the formal cause in her favor, not the material cause; for Esau's life and conduct are not in agreement with the prophecy. Hence she thought: "My son behaves in such a way that I see that he will not be the first-born. Furthermore, he sold his birthright, despised the final cause of the primogeniture, and said: 'For the present I shall take away only the red pottage.' That is to say: 'Provided that I am the master, the prince, and the priest, I care nothing about the final cause pertaining to the benefit of the church. I am interested in my own desires and my own glory.'" Thus Isaac upholds the rule, but Rebecca upholds the exception. For Esau behaves in such a manner that he neither is nor can be the first-born. Furthermore, the prophecy is in agreement with what God inspired contrary to the rule.

This is the epitasis and the catastrophe of the matter.[17] Rebecca and Jacob continue to cling to the exception and to the spirit on account of the fact that Esau had sold his birthright and, because of the misuse of his birthright, is judged unworthy of it. Consequently, the question can be answered in favor of Rebecca and Jacob. That which has been given to me by God and concerning which I know that it belongs to me I can claim by using any deception and scheme; for at the risk of committing a mortal sin I am bound to plan, invent, pretend, and conceal in order that what has been committed to me by God may come to pass.

Lyra says that Jacob and Rebecca should not be excused.[18] Nor do we absolve them entirely from sin. They were human beings who had the passions of the flesh just as we have. But it is not necessary to charge them with lying or to reproach them with any deceit; for when God said: "I want Jacob to be the first-born," then the law was abrogated. "But where there is no law, there is no transgression," as Rom. 4:15 says.

Accordingly, since Jacob and Rebecca, as a result of the prophecy and of Esau's evil fruits and morals, were sure that the primogeniture belonged to Jacob, they were in duty bound to disregard the law and rule and to follow the exception by which God transferred the primogeniture from Esau to Jacob. Therefore Rebecca gave thought to how she might be able to deceive her husband

---

[17] The technical terms are *epitasis* and *paroxismus*.

[18] In his discussion of Gen. 27 Lyra cites the opinions both of the rabbis and of the church fathers on whether this deception should be excused.

Isaac, her son Esau, and all who were in the house; for now she is not obeying the rule or the law. No, she is obeying God who transfers and dispenses contrary to the rule. Therefore she did not sin.

And I believe that this is the simple and true answer to the question concerning the deception, the lie, and also the harm done to Esau and all who were on his side, that is, to the entire church in the house of Isaac. For they all obeyed Esau and regarded him as the first-born, since he had held that right and lordship for more than 37 years. Therefore they had no doubt at all that he would remain the first-born. But now, when the blessing of the primogeniture was to be ratified, a sudden and unlooked-for change of events occurs contrary to the plan and agreement of the entire church and of the patriarch Isaac. For because of Esau's rejection Rebecca seeks to accomplish God's transfer in accordance with the prophecy, with Esau's contempt for the primogeniture, and with his fruits and life, which were unworthy of this honor. And in this matter cause and effect are in agreement, and the confirmation of the Holy Spirit is added. But Isaac is deceived. To be sure, this in itself is a serious and horrible sin against the husband, against the father and the neighbor, yes, against the brother and against the rule; but as it pleased the Lord, so it happened. For the First Table embraces obedience to parents, brotherhood, and love. The Second Table yields and is nothing when it impinges on the First. To combine love for one's brother or father with an insult to God is to hate God. "If anyone comes to Me," says Christ (Luke 14:26), "and does not hate his own father and mother and wife and children and brothers and sisters, yes, and even his own life, he cannot be My disciple." Here God abrogates the law. Consequently, I am not held to obey in the Second Table. But in the event that there is no conflict between the First and Second Table, then the law and obedience remain.

If the government tolerates me when I teach the Word, I hold it in honor and regard it with all respect as my superior. But if it says: "Deny God; cast the Word aside," then I no longer acknowledge it as the government. In the same way one must render obedience to one's parents. But if they say: "I want you to become a monk or a priest devoted to papal idolatry," then one should by no means obey it. For this is what Moses says in Deut. 33:9: "Who said of his father and mother: 'I regard them not'; he disowned his brothers and ignored his children. For they observed Thy Word." God wants us to deny ourselves and our life in the Second Table if it is contrary to the First. But if they are in agreement, then reverence for parents is reverence for God. If, on the other hand, they conflict with each other, then an exception is necessary.

"But is it proper and necessary to state that the government, parents, and every authority must be obeyed?" It is proper. I acquiesce in the rule. "Then why do you not observe the rule if either the government or your parents demand that you follow their religion?" I answer: This is an exception. The First Table must be given precedence over the Second Table. If parents prescribe or command something contrary to God, then the Fourth Commandment, which previously was valid and unalterable, is abrogated. For in the First Commandment it is stated that one must love and honor God above all things, and Acts 5:29 says: "We must obey God rather than men."

This is the way we, in carrying on the work of the Gospel, decide against the authority of the emperor and the pope and against all the ungodliness of the pope without any preceding legal hubbub.[19] We made no charges against the pope. Nor could we do so, for there was no judge. We have honored the pope, our parents, and the emperor; but because Christ says: "My sheep hear My voice; a stranger they will not follow, but they will flee from him" (John 10:27, 5), we should not have waited until a decision was reached in human fashion whether we did right or wrong by separating ourselves from the pope; because when one has learned what God's will is, there must be no debating about rights, rules, or the like, but God's command must be obeyed without any deliberation; for neither the pope nor the parents nor the emperor have this title: "I am the Lord your God" (Ex. 20:2).

In this way one can easily answer this rather difficult question about what Rebecca and Jacob did. The law and the rule ordained that Esau was the first-born; but God, with His First Table, made the transfer. Indeed, He changed that law and decreed as follows:

---

[19] At the Diet of Augsburg in 1530 and at earlier confrontations, it had been claimed that the Reformation stood in violation of the Code of Justinian; the princes and free cities who supported the Reformation claimed the legal rite, under the feudal law of the Holy Roman Empire, to reform the churches within their own principalities.

"Esau I did not want; Jacob I did want." Hence Rebecca and Jacob did not sin. No, they acted in a godly and saintly manner. They had every right to despoil Esau and to deprive him of that fief of the primogeniture. They were unable to obtain it by force, for this could not be done without a quarrel. For so far as the promise and the legal authority were concerned, the church as well as the government and the entire house of Isaac would have opposed Jacob. Esau, you see, was superior in power and right. Jacob was far inferior; he was despised and oppressed. Therefore Rebecca attacked the matter with skill, ingenuity, and a very beautiful stratagem; and she did this in accordance with the will of God, who grants a successful outcome in a matter so difficult and so full of great dangers.

The word מַטְעַמִּים means "a tasting" and corresponds to the expression which Luke employs about Peter in Acts 10:10: "And when he became hungry, he wanted to taste food," that is, to eat. Moderation in food and drink is pointed out, so that there is more a tasting than excessive eating and drinking, in order that the body may be nourished and supported, not burdened.

Moreover, there was a very beautiful rite for receiving the fief and blessing of the primogeniture. According to this rite, he who was to be blessed had to bring rather choice foods to the parent who was about to bestow the blessing. The mother exercises her authority when she gives this command: "Obey my word." She does so in order to comfort her son and to inspire him with courage to carry out such an arduous and difficult thing. She has the prophecy on her side. Therefore she proceeds simply and wholly in faith. And Moses used this word "command" particularly to indicate that the mother exerted herself to persuade her son; for he is reluctant, and he argues with his mother about the command.

11. *But Jacob said to Rebecca his mother: Behold, my brother Esau is a hairy man, and I am a smooth man.*

12. *Perhaps my father will feel me, and I shall seem to be mocking him, and bring a curse upon myself and not a blessing.*

13. *His mother said to him: Upon me be your curse, my son; only obey my word, and go, fetch them to me.*

14. *So he went and took them and brought them to his mother; and his mother prepared savory food, such as his father loved.*

חָלָק means "soft" or "smooth," *glat*, "without hairs." This is a weighty excuse with which he tries to nullify his mother's command. He reminds her of the great difficulty of the thing she was attempting. It is as though he were saying: "Take care that you do not happen to hurl me into the danger of taking away a curse instead of a blessing." He is a good dialectician, and he brings up a sufficiently strong argument with which he tries to divert his mother's heart from the undertaking. "What if my father will say: 'You have caused me to make a mistake when I pronounced the blessing. I revoke the blessing.' In that case I shall bring a curse upon myself. You and my father will easily find an excuse, but because of this compliance and my obedience I will be brought into the utmost peril."

Here, therefore, a second question concerning this very saintly woman arises. Although she is driven by the Holy Spirit and proceeds in her faith, yet she does many rash things and involves herself and her son in very many dangers. It is a very fine plan for her to get ahead of the older son so shrewdly, to cook the kids, to deceive the father with an extraordinary trick almost beyond a woman's capacity, to wrap up Jacob's hands, and to cover their smoothness with the skins of the kids. But this is a foolish thought, for she does not realize that the father can examine his son in another way than with his eyes, which are blind. She does not see that large window, namely, the voice, which betrays a person most, even if the other senses are unable to judge. Nor can it be disguised or changed in any way. Indeed, a conclusion based on the voice is more certain than if you look at the face itself. Therefore Rebecca would have brought her son into the greatest danger if God had not controlled everything in a wonderful manner. For listen to the father's reply. After Jacob says: "I am your son Esau," he immediately recognizes the voice of Jacob and says: "The voice is Jacob's, but the hands are Esau's." Then Jacob was undoubtedly stunned and thought that he had not considered everything properly. I certainly would have run away immediately when the father answered: "The voice is Jacob's, the voice is Jacob's," etc.; for this catastrophe is full of danger.

But all this serves to comfort the saints, whose counsels and undertakings must be successful because they are undertaken in faith; for "everything works for good for him who believes" (Rom. 8:28). Faith does not rest, and it can do everything; it can even deceive a saintly man and, in a measure, the Holy Spirit. Thus

Rebecca goes ahead and does not consider how she is exposing herself and her son Jacob to great danger. For Isaac could have said: "Why do you want to deceive your father and rob your brother? Do you suppose that I do not hear and recognize your voice?" (There the matter really hung in the balance.) Stricken with consternation by these words, Jacob would have thought: "O mother, what have you done? My father is taking notice of my voice. This did not occur to us. Otherwise we would have taken precautions against this giveaway." Thus he was in the greatest distress. But he goes ahead in obedience to his mother, who said to him: "Your curse be upon me!" Therefore it was outstanding faith that opposes itself to Jacob's hesitancy. "Do not argue," she says. "I order. I command. If any evil results from this, I want it to redound to me, whether it is a curse or a blessing. Just proceed in my name, at my command and order. If you are cursed, I shall bear it." Nobody can speak this way [20] unless he is filled with faith and the Holy Spirit. For to let a son go in this manner and to expose him to completely certain danger of a curse and yet to believe in this way that if the affair turns out badly, you would be willing to bear all misfortunes and the curse itself—not everybody can do this, but it is a work of most fervent faith.

Then she prayed: "O heavenly Father, grant that my son may carry out everything properly and successfully." It did not occur to her that the father would recognize the voice. Therefore he who wants to lie must be cautious, must be endowed with a very good memory and with great intelligence and cunning.[21] I would surely not be able to excel at all in this respect; I would soon ruin everything. Nor was Rebecca cautious enough; what she should have guarded against most she foresaw least, so that she might as well have hanged herself, as the saying goes.[22] But faith is victorious and overcomes all mistakes and dangers. Just as Rebecca believed and prayed, just as Jacob obeyed, and just as the prophecy, too, finally agreed, so the outcome also agrees. For faith makes those who hear deaf, those who see blind, and vice versa. In short, it does not fail and it destroys nothing. Or if it stumbles now and

---

[20] The Weimar text has *Si* here, but we have followed the Erlangen text and read *Sic*.

[21] An allusion to Quintilian, *Institutes*, Book IV, ch. 2, sec. 91.

[22] Cf. Terence, *Phormio*, V, 4, 4.

then because of folly or rashness, yet God usually foresees and corrects this, so that the mistakes are covered and finally turn out to be fortunate.

I know that I have often done many things foolishly and very rashly, so much so that I thought: "Why has God called me to preach when I do not have as much knowledge, discretion, and judgment as the importance of the office demands?" Although I performed everything with a pious and sincere heart, with pious devotion and zeal, yet a great deal of nonsense and many failures arose, with the result that heaven and the whole world seemed about to go to ruin. Then I was compelled to fall on my knees and to ask for help and counsel from God, who is powerful and turns a denouement in a tragedy into a catastrophe in a comedy while we are sleeping. Thus He creates Eve while Adam is sleeping. He takes a rib from him while he is sleeping, closes the place with flesh, and builds the rib which he took from Adam [23] into flesh. Here someone may say that God had silken fingers, because He performs such a great work so nimbly and so easily.

In the same manner He also governs His saints. Even if they have erred seriously in their thinking and have been guilty of great folly and rashness, from which countless evils can arise, yet He brings about a happy outcome, like the denouement in a comedy.

So great is the power of faith and prayer. Indeed, prayer is truly all-powerful. Therefore Isaac is deceived knowingly, purposely, and visibly, so to speak; for he says: "The voice is Jacob's, the hands are Esau's," and yet allows himself to be deceived, just as we see in the books of the heathen that masters are deceived by slaves, as the well-known character in the comedy says: "If I were not a stone, I could have seen clearly." [24] God deals with His saints in such a way that they are not aware that anything foolish and rash has happened.

Accordingly, we should be careful to remember this example. It reminds us that the power of faith is so great that it makes those who have very keen sight or hearing blind and deaf, with the result that they are deceived even though they hear and see. And

---

[23] All the editions of the *Lectures on Genesis* read *de muliere*, "from the woman," here; clearly "from the man" or "from Adam" is the sense of the passage.

[24] Terence, *Heautontimorumenos*, V, 1, 43.

the question can be answered in this way, that although Rebecca acted rashly, yet on account of her outstanding faith she had divine providence as her guide, so that although father Isaac heard Jacob's voice, he, filled as he was with confidence and unconcern, was deceived in spite of this.

An incredulous person is not easily deceived; but he who trusts anyone rashly is easily deceived, in accordance with the well-known statement in Prov. 14:15: "The simple believes everything but the prudent looks where he is going." Consequently, those whom we desire to deceive should not be approached at a time when we know that they are wary and alert; but first all distrust must be removed, and they must be made to trust us. Their hearts must be allured by means of some persuasion, just as Davus and Syrus [25] in the comedies lure their masters into deceit, so that they close their eyes, sleep, and trust you. For thus Isaac has no doubt at all about the trustworthiness of his wife Rebecca and of his son Jacob; he thinks that they are so pious and faithful that they cannot act craftily or deceitfully against him. Therefore even though he was warned by Jacob's voice, yet he could not suspect any evil but supposed that Esau had changed his voice in a joking manner, not in order to deceive his father.

And this is the common way of all life, not only in the case of the saints but in common life among all men, as the examples in the comedies prove. He who believes rashly is deceived. On the other hand, you will try in vain to deceive him who does not readily believe. But many such things happen in the life of the saints in order that we may see how God governs His saints, turns their foolishness and rashness into the greatest wisdom, and grants to their plans, which at first seemed very stupid, very beautiful results. Saintly people act unwisely often enough, just as here Rebecca errs shamefully in her thinking. Yet she forces her way through because she believes.

Therefore at the beginning of this chapter the following facts should be carefully noted: in the first place, that the First Table must be given precedence over the Second; in the second place, that God pardons the foolishness and rashness of His saints, yes, even causes it to turn out successfully. Consequently, if you do

---

[25] Davus is the slave whose speech introduces the *Phormio* of Terence; Syrus is the slave of Micio in the same author's *Adelphi*.

anything wrong in any walk of life, you should not despair; but you should acknowledge your mistake with humility and think as follows: "God, who was able to lead Rebecca and Jacob out of such great danger, is all-powerful. Therefore I, too, shall not despair but shall be confident that He will bring me out of this misfortune." Although Rebecca's plan was rash, it had a fortunate outcome, because God brings the plans of the ungodly to nothing but honors and helps His saints.

Accordingly, you must beware both of being haughty because of your wisdom and plans and of despairing if your deliberations turn out badly, for GOD controls and blesses the mistakes of the godly. I have often been guilty of very great indiscretions and foolish acts; but I did this with a good intention, not because of a desire to harm and not knowingly, but unwisely and foolishly, when I desired to counsel faithfully. Then I surely had to pray that God might cover and correct my mistake. Nor can it happen otherwise in affairs that are disturbed. For in this way the greatest and best men in the state often do the most harm with foolish and rash plans; and if God did not have compassion on them, everything would be in a topsy-turvy condition.

Such is our life; it is very wretched indeed. When we try to be very wise and to give the best advice, we often cause the greatest havoc, to such an extent that if our errors were not corrected because of God's compassion and providence, everything would be utterly overturned. For the same thing happens to us that happened to a certain peasant who was driving his wagon with difficulty because the wheels, as they seemed to him, were too blunt. In order that the horses might pull the wagon with less difficulty, he sharpened the rims of the wheels. But with this plan he accomplished so little that the wagon, with the wheels, sank deeper into the mud and could not be moved from the spot at all. This is the kind of wisdom we arrogate to ourselves. According to it, nothing seems easier than the management of affairs, just as the well-known character in the comedy says: "I should have been king," and as the poets have beautifully portrayed such arrogance in the story of Phaethon.[26] For today, too, you could hear many who cry out: "If I were in Dr. Martin's or Philip's place, I would give them

---

[26] Terence, *Phormio*, I, 2, 20; Phaethon, son of Helios, had tried to drive the chariot of the sun but was struck down by a thunderbolt of Zeus.

better advice!" Of course! We see that great princes stumble and that the best bishops often show themselves as the most foolish.

Then what? Should nothing at all be done, and should all managing be shunned entirely? Not at all. Rather let everyone diligently and faithfully do his duty which has been committed to him by God. But let him beware of relying on his own strength or his own wisdom and of considering himself such a great man that everything should be directed in accordance with what he counsels. For it is incurable and damnable rashness and arrogance on my part when I claim to be such a person and such an extraordinary man that I can manage the state, the home, and the church wisely and properly. But if you are a judge, a bishop, or a prince, you should not feel ashamed to fall on your knees and say: "Lord God, Thou hast appointed me as prince, judge, head of the household, and pastor of the church. Therefore guide and teach me, give me counsel, wisdom, and strength to attend successfully to the office committed to me."

This is what Solomon did. After he had heard in a dream (1 Kings 3:5): "Ask what I shall give you," he prayed (cf. 1 Kings 3:7-8): "Lord God, Thou hast given me a great people; give me wisdom, that Thy servant may be able to judge and discern between good and evil." And Scripture declares that this prayer pleased God very much; for it is a very beautiful confession. The king was very wise and pious. Nevertheless, he called himself a little child (1 Kings 3:7). Moreover, he says (1 Kings 3:7): "I am but a little child; I do not know how to go out or come in." Therefore the author adds (1 Kings 3:10-12): "It pleased the Lord that Solomon had asked this. And God said to him: 'Because you have asked, and have not asked for yourself long life or riches or the life of your enemies, but have asked for yourself understanding to discern what is right, behold, I now do according to your word. Behold, I give you a wise and discerning mind, so that none like you has been before you and none like you shall arise after you.'"

Hence everyone should learn to acknowledge his weakness humbly and to ask GOD for wisdom and counsel. For men are not summoned to govern because they should arrogate to themselves perfect knowledge of everything, but because they should be taught and learn what God is and what He does through the government and the rulers, who are the instruments of God's works through which God rules the people. Then they become truly wise and successful in governing. But if they follow their own counsels and their own thoughts, they do nothing properly. No, then they disturb and confuse everything. Therefore one must take refuge in prayer, set forth the difficulty of the office to God, and say: "Our Father who art in heaven, etc., give me the wisdom that sits by Thy throne" (Wisd. of Sol. 9:4).

But above all a ruler in the church should pray in this manner: "Lord God, Thou hast appointed me in the church as bishop and pastor. Thou seest how unfit I am to attend to such a great and difficult office, and if it had not been for Thy help, I would long since have ruined everything. Therefore I call upon Thee. Of course, I want to put my mouth and heart to use. I shall teach the people, and I myself shall learn and shall meditate diligently on Thy Word. Use me as Thy instrument. Only do not forsake me; for if I am alone, I shall easily destroy everything." The sects and the sectarians do the opposite, for they ascribe to themselves the wisdom and the ability to rule and to teach. Therefore they burst rashly into the church, do not pray, and do not believe that the administration either of the church or of the state is a gift of God; but they force themselves in as teachers and leaders. Therefore it eventually happens that they confuse and hinder what has been profitably built by others.

The same thing[27] happens in the state to those who rely on their own counsels and wisdom when they assume an administrative office. Consequently, if you are in the government, beware of depending on your own wisdom; beware of yourself, and pray privately with folded hands: "Heavenly Father, be Thou with me; help, guide, and direct me." Thus Moses turns back to God the entire matter of leading the people out and declines to do what God commanded unless God Himself is the leader and manager. He says (Ex. 33:15): "If Thy presence will not go with me, do not carry us up from here." But when you have prayed in this manner, proceed with a stout and dauntless heart, and have no doubt about a happy and successful outcome. Thus I, too, often cast the keys at the feet of the Lord, as the German proverb puts it; that is, I turned back to Him the administrative office that had been committed to me. For this reason the matter had an outcome

---

[27] The Weimar text has *item*, but we have followed the Erlangen text and read *idem* instead.

far different from what I had foreseen or thought. And if I had made some mistake, He Himself corrected it in accordance with His goodness and wisdom.

Moreover, in the management of the household father and mother are the instruments through which the house and household affairs are governed. But they themselves should also acknowledge that by their own power, diligence, or effort they can never bring up their children properly and successfully. Therefore they should cry out: "Lord God, heavenly Father, help us that our children may turn out well! Grant that the wife may live in chastity and honor, and that she may remain steadfast in the knowledge and fear of God!"

But you could find many who do not acknowledge this higher power and wisdom in governing. If any obstacles are put in their way, they suppose that they will set things right more properly if they employ greater severity in their punishments, so that their subjects are held in check by the fear of the punishments and are driven to obey even against their will. Surely there is need of discipline—and rather stern discipline at that—especially in the matter of these morals of ours; but it is completely certain that you will never achieve anything without prayer. For governing is a divine power, and for this reason God calls all magistrates gods (cf. Ps. 82:6), not because of the creation but because of the administration which belongs to God alone. Consequently, he who is in authority is an incarnate god, so to speak. But if they force their way into the government of the church, the state, or the household rashly and without due preparation, exclude God, do not pray, and do not seek advice from God but want to rule everything with their own counsels and strength, then it will eventually happen in the management of household affairs that an honorable and chaste wife will become a harlot of the worst kind and that the children will degenerate and come into the power of the executioner. In the civil government the state will be thrown into confusion by insurrections, wars, and countless other perils. In the church heresies, Epicurean contempt for the Word, desecration of the sacraments, etc., will arise. Why? Because such a head of a household, prince, or pastor does not recognize GOD as the Author of all counsel and government but by his presumption and arrogance destroys himself and others over whom he rules.

I thought that on the basis of this passage these things had to be said as an example and as doctrine—in the first place, in order that we may know that the First Table has supremacy over the Second in accordance with the statement of the First Commandment which says: "I am the Lord your God" (Ex. 20:2); in the second place, in order that we may acknowledge the mercy of God, who guides His saints in a wonderful manner even in their rashness and foolishness, in order that we may trust God with all our hearts and learn that faith devours not only the sins but also the rashness, foolishness, and thoughtlessness of the saints.

This is the subject matter and the main point of this chapter. Now we shall read the text in succession and be spectators as this amazing story is told.

15. *Then Rebecca took the best garments of Esau her older son, which were with her in the house, and put them on Jacob, her younger son.*

The second ceremony is added by Moses. It involved fine and precious apparel; for this is the meaning of the Hebrew word חֲמֻדֹת, "desirable and precious apparel." It is frequently employed in Holy Scripture. To Daniel the angel says (Dan. 9:23): "You are greatly beloved," a dear and esteemed man; and of the centurion it is stated in the Gospel account (Luke 7:4) that he had a slave who was worthy, that is, a dear and precious slave. So Rebecca brought out those fine and magnificent garments—*die lieben, schönen, herrlichen kleider*—the priestly garments, which undoubtedly were very beautiful, as they are described in Moses (Ex. 28:2 ff.). For they used special attire at their religious rites, just as we do in our churches. We call it *Ornat*, vestments. These Rebecca has with her in the house, and from this it is evident that Esau had not yet been established in his position, even though he was in possession of it and governed the church. He was a licentiate to the papacy [28] and performed the functions of a priest, but he was not yet established in this position and had not received the fiefs. Therefore he does not have the vestments in his control. Rebecca, who took possession of the vestments and kept them, undoubtedly guarded against this by a special design, although the vestments belonged to father Isaac. For she waited

---

[28] A *licentiatus* was one who had the right to lecture but had not yet received the doctor's degree.

for the opportunity to turn them over to him who would receive the fiefs from his father and would be established in the succession.

16. *And the skins of the kids she put upon his hands and upon the smooth part of his neck;*

17. *and she gave the savory food and the bread, which she had prepared, into the hand of her son Jacob.*

18. *So he went in to his father and said: My father; and he said: Here I am; who are you, my son?*

It is strange that his mother puts the skins only around his neck and does not also cover his face. The only thing that occurred to her was that he would have to hold out his hands to his father and that if he had to give his father a kiss, the latter, in turn, would put his arms around his son's neck. For this reason she wanted these two parts especially to be covered. But she thinks that the smooth face cannot easily be noticed, since Isaac had a beard and would be kissed on his beard.

Moreover, while decking him out she perhaps also reminded him to imitate Esau's voice as carefully as he could, lest his father distinguish between the voice of Esau and the voice of Jacob, since he immediately asks: "Who are you, my son? Are you Esau whom I have sent to hunt? It seems to me that I am hearing the voice of Jacob."

19. *Jacob said to his father: I am Esau your first-born. I have done as you told me; now sit up and eat of my game, that you may bless me.*

20. *But Isaac said to his son: How is it that you have found it so quickly, my son? He answered: Because the Lord your God granted me success.*

Jacob answers his father in a long speech, and his father listens intently to it and finally reaches the following conclusion: "The voice is Jacob's, the hands are Esau's." But when Jacob says that he is the first-born, this is a plain lie. Furthermore, he hurried— rather unwisely. For his mother did not foresee that this speed would arouse his father's suspicion. Therefore Isaac says: "How is it that you have found it so quickly?" This one blow is very hard, and Isaac is reminded of deception and a trick. "How is it that you are returning so quickly from the hunt? Have you been able to hunt and catch game so soon? If you had returned in the evening or tomorrow, you would have come quickly enough." But Jacob answers: "The Lord God granted me success." It is true. God must take the responsibility. Jacob lies magnificently. He says that he had hunted game, although he had taken two kids in the stable. But Isaac is silent and feigns ignorance, because he is unconcerned and fully confident that it is impossible for him to be deceived by the son or by the mother.

21. *Then Isaac said to Jacob: Come near, that I may feel you, my son, to know whether you are really my son Esau or not.*

22. *So Jacob went near to Isaac his father, who felt him and said: The voice is Jacob's voice, but the hands are the hands of Esau.*

This is another blow, and one that is far more serious. Now things look bad. He is commanded to draw near in order that his father may touch him. Then he sweat profusely and silently found fault with his mother's plan. "O dear mother," he asked, "what have you done? To what have you driven me?" After he has come near, he hears his father say: "The voice is Jacob's, the voice, the voice." At that point I would have let the dish fall and would have run as though my head were on fire. Then I would have got rid of the dish and would have taken to my heels at once. For Isaac is on the right track that will lead to a discovery of the deception when he notes the difference between the voice and the voice, and that blow should have awakened him. But he sinks back into sleep and thinks that there is shamming of some kind because of which Esau is imitating his brother's voice. Jacob approaches confidently and hears these words. Here, then, the plan of Rebecca and Jacob ends. Indeed, it makes a false step. But GOD brings it about that Isaac is intent on his duty of blessing and removes this blow from his mind.

But now all this must be applied to our instruction, in order that we may learn how great the power of faith is and that to him who believes all things are possible. For faith causes that which does not exist to exist and makes possible everything that is impossible. You have seen Rebecca's foolishness and rashness, how she decked out her son Jacob to deceive his father and put skins of kids around his hands and neck in order that his father might think that Jacob actually was hairy.

The situation is full of danger, inasmuch as Jacob trembles and turns away from his mother's plan. "Lest perchance my father touch me," he says, "and be aware, and I bring upon myself a curse instead of a blessing." But the faith of this very pious woman is so great that it forces its way through all this. Jacob went in pretending to be Isaac's son Esau. He has hairy hands, which have been made so with cunning and deceit. But he does not deceive his father in every respect, for Isaac knows Jacob's voice in spite of this. You see, therefore, that God compensates for this rashness in a very beautiful manner through the woman's faith, for the sake of which the exceedingly foolish plan must become very good and very successful.

Thus Holy Scripture presents the accounts of the saints in such a way that it gives praise to the power of faith. Consequently, he who has the Word of God should consider himself blessed and should turn his eyes away from present things to those that lie in the future and are invisible. For the Word of God, especially the promise, does not speak of present things; it speaks of things that lie in the future and have been experienced by no one. Faith attaches itself to a thing that is still an utter nothing and waits until everything comes about. It is a knowledge and wisdom of darkness and nothingness,[29] that is, of things which it has not experienced and are unseen and almost impossible. He who wants to be a Christian must meditate well on and fix this in his heart. For all other branches of knowledge are taught on the basis of syllogisms, inductions, and experiments. They do not have their basis or beginnings in what is nothing, and especially not on what is unseen, impossible, absurd, and foolish; but faith, which takes hold of the promise, fixes the heart on what is altogether absurd, impossible, and contained in the Word and God's promise.

For this is what Jacob does: His mother tells him to receive the blessing from his father. Here utter nothingness stands in the way; for the blessing belonged to Esau, not to Jacob. Impossibility was standing in the way. He thought: "How indeed could I be

---

[29] In the persistence of such language even in Luther's late years scholars have noted the continuing influence of the German mystics.

blessed? The blessing is owed to my brother. Besides, he is hairy. I am smooth. There is danger that I shall get a curse from my father. Therefore so far as the thing is concerned, it is impossible; for the blessing is not mine. For my father intends to bless Esau. About me he is not at all concerned. Furthermore, it is possible that a curse will cling to me, who have a smooth and hairless skin, if my father notices the deception. Therefore we shall surely run into trouble, dear mother." But against all this his mother says: "Let that curse harm me, if any curse comes." She is a woman who is not a woman; she is a human being with a woman's spirit. But she has such great ardor that she overcomes the most stouthearted men, for she thinks that she can force her way through, so that the blessing is bestowed on him to whom it was not owed according to the law and the rule. She believes what is utterly impossible, absurd, foolish, and dangerous. She has no doubt that Jacob must be blessed, no matter to what degree everything resists and opposes this.

Thus faith and its power is a thought of the heart, or, if I may say so, an opinion which attaches itself to what is nothing, what is impossible and absurd.[30] She has only the Word of God, which says (Gen. 25:23): "The older will serve the younger." But as their mother she decided who of the two was the older. In addition, there was the enlightenment of the Holy Spirit. Consequently, she had a correct understanding of this word. Isaac, on the other hand, remains inflexible, like an immovable rock, and clings only to the law and the rule that Esau is the first-born; but the mother is not influenced at all by this law and rule.

We should adjust ourselves in the same way. When we have the Word, then we should cast aside discussions contrary to the Word and care about nothing, whether we are confronted with things that are foolish, impossible, or finally contrary to the law of nature and of Moses. No, we must follow directly what God has said. But if reason approaches and argues about the Word, then all is lost. This is the cause of that conflict of the flesh against the spirit about which we read in Gal. 5:17, where Paul is speaking about those lofty sentiments, such as believing what you do not understand and what is impossible according to reason.

---

[30] The slogan *Credo quia absurdum* had been attributed to Tertullian, but it does not appear as such in the corpus of his writings.

One must do the same thing in one's calling and eventually even in death. When GOD appoints me leader against the gates of hell (Matt. 16:18), against the raging of the whole world, and against the weakness of my flesh, in what frame of mind must we be in these circumstances? For who am I to fight first against so many hosts of all demons and men, and then against the weakness of my flesh? I answer: "One must be mindful of God's command." The Lord says: "Go, and you will prevail; I will be with you." Thus He tells Moses to go to the Egyptian king and to lead the people out of tyranny and the iron furnace. Does that not seem foolish and impossible, to lead out such a great people, and to lead them out in such a manner that they do not leave a hoof behind, as Moses says to Pharaoh (Ex. 10:26)? But according to my reason I would have said: "You will not lead out even a hoof, much less such a great people; for the king is powerful and a cruel tyrant." But Moses speaks in no other way with Pharaoh than as if he had already led that huge multitude out, even though it seems to be a fictitious story, a foolish and completely impossible thought, if you take reason into account. For whatever faith dictates and the Word promises must be done, because God is the Word and the Word is God (cf. John 1:1). He who has the Word has the power of God, as Rom. 1:16 says.

Outwardly, to be sure, it appears to be no different from a human voice and foolishness on the part of the man who is speaking, just as Peter says to Cornelius in Acts 10:26: "I, too, am a man." Peter has the Word, and in Cornelius' ears it has the sound of a human voice. Nevertheless, it does wonders of all kinds. Thus we should be encouraged against all dangers which threaten from the Turks and other enemies. Indeed, we should be encouraged against death itself. For if we have been absolved through the mouth of a brother or a minister, we must not look at the human being who is speaking. Nor should our eyes be directed toward danger or death. And one should not consider the grave, the corruption, the worms, and the decay to which I am exposed. For reason without faith thinks: "It is not possible for a dead body, which is buried, consumed by worms, or burned and reduced to ashes to live, is it?" Indeed, reason flatly denies this and says: "It is not true." The spirit, on the other hand, contradicts and says: "It is true. Even though I am now destined for death, I seem to myself to be living; and I shall arise from the grave with glory and with a transfigured body."

Therefore faith is an all-powerful battle which, in opposition to the battle of the flesh, clings to the Word and the promise with one and the same prospect. For here we are not speaking of historical faith,[31] which is nothing more than knowledge, as when I know that David overcame Goliath and the Philistines. Although this is an example of faith, yet for me it is only a historical account; and if I had to lay Goliath low or tear a lion to pieces, then the historical account would serve no other purpose than that of a kind of admonition to spur me on to similar courage. But if this were my thought: "David and Samson won very glorious victories, therefore I, too, shall have to do the same," this would be impossible for me. For even David did not perform such glorious deeds without a great struggle. For he was in the flesh, just as we are; he had flesh that contradicted, waged war, yes, held him captive. The same thing is true of us. He felt much more unbelief than faith; for faith seems and is weak, because the flesh not only wages war but even takes captive, as Paul says in Rom. 7:14.

Formerly I had no other conviction than that Paul gave no thought at all to exerting himself and battling against the flesh. But he says (2 Cor. 12:7): "A thorn was given me in the flesh, a messenger of Satan, to harass me." He teaches me what faith is. I see the glorious victories of the saints and the martyrs. But my faith cannot accomplish this. And they also exerted themselves and overcame death. They did not do this without a great conflict. Thus we, too, have the same Baptism, the same God to give consolation, and the Holy Spirit, the Comforter who offers us rich comfort in the Word. And although I gladly hear the account of the conflicts and the victories of the saints, I cannot do the same things. Therefore one must take hold of the Word (Ps. 27:14): "Wait for the Lord; be strong, and let your heart take courage." God does not abandon even him who is weak in faith. Indeed, the apostles themselves and the prophets were not strong in faith, especially when they were about to do great things through faith. Moses trembles at the Red Sea and cries out (cf. Ex. 14:15), for the the flesh not only waged war against him but took him captive. "For you see," the flesh suggested to him, "that there are mountains on both sides. Egypt is behind us, and before us is the sea, through which we shall not be able to pass with the

---

[31] On Luther's polemic against *fides historica* cf. *Luther's Works*, 22, p. 153, note 120.

children, the women, and the cattle." Thus he was being forced to despair, as it were; for the law of his flesh and of his members (cf. Rom. 7:23) kept telling him: "Behold, we are bereft of all aid! What have I done by leading the people out? We shall all have to perish." Here begin the sighs that are too deep for words, as Paul calls them (Rom. 8:26). This cry cannot be written down. Nor can it be described in anyone's words, for this expression "THE SIGHS OF THE HEART" is powerful beyond measure. It fills heaven, penetrates the clouds, and reaches the ears of the Divine Majesty, so that God answers: "Why do you cry?" (Ex. 14:15.) Yet he did not cry; but he was aghast, his hair stood on end, and his voice stuck in his throat.[32] But He who searches the hearts understands what the spirit wants when it sighs (cf. Rom. 8:27).

I am repeating this and impressing it rather carefully because in the eyes of reason faith is a trivial matter and a worthless notion as it were, which anyone can grasp with his mind. People think that it is a historical matter and that it is easy. But when one encounters the Red Sea, death, and victory over sin, death, and hell through us, then God's power is coupled and joined with human weakness; omnipotence is combined with nothingness and the utmost foolishness and finally brings a weak person to the point that he does things that are impossible and unbelievable. Thus Christ says in John 14:12: "Greater works than these will he do." For in this way the church does all things, even though it is weak. It prays, and it bears and devours all the violence and rage of the devil and of men; it also consumes and removes weakness, sins, death, etc.

Rebecca proves this power and might of faith with her exceedingly dangerous deed, where it was a matter of an eternal curse or an eternal blessing. For the blessing is eternal life; the curse is death. There is a debate about whether or not Jacob, and his mother with him, would be eternally cursed. In a conflict so great and arduous Rebecca sets the kingdom of heaven before her eyes as open and appoints herself the mother of the blessing. On what basis? On the basis of the Word. For nobody does anything successfully or believes without the Word. This text, "The elder shall serve the younger," gave her courage. From it she concluded that the blessing belonged to the younger, not

---

[32] Vergil, *Aeneid*, III, 48.

to the older. To be sure, Isaac did not understand it; but the mother pondered it carefully, and the Holy Spirit collaborated. He gives no one faith through mere speculations. No, He gives it through the Word; for the flesh wars against the spirit, and nothing results from the thoughts or speculations of the flesh. For since the things that are of the Holy Spirit are not apparent, everything seems hostile and dead. But when the heart takes hold of the Word, then the enlightenment of the Holy Spirit follows, and the power and might to do amazing things.

23. *And he did not recognize him, because his hands were hairy like his brother Esau's hands.*

It could also have happened naturally and in a normal way that although he heard the voice, excessive eagerness and determination to give the blessing prevented him from recognizing his son. For a person who is intent on one thing does not concern himself about other matters, even though he sees them and grasps them with all his senses. This is wont to happen not only spiritually but also physically, as can be seen in the case of people who have melancholia. While others are talking, drinking, entering, or leaving, they neither hear nor see anything; for the thoughts of the heart have been diverted from their senses. Therefore when a melancholy heart is occupied with thoughts of other matters, it pays no attention to what is clearly presented to the senses. Such a person is present when others converse and tell stories and tales. Yet he hears nothing of this. Indeed, the heart wanders, as it were. When eating and drinking, a person who has melancholia does not know what he is eating or what he is drinking, whether it is beer or wine. They relate about Bernard that he drank oil instead of wine when he was engaged in earnest meditation.[33] And this happens far more frequently when spiritual confusion is added and a spiritual heart is wholly intent on spiritual matters.

We must imagine that the same thing happened to Isaac, who hears and recognizes Jacob's voice and does not conceal this; for he says: "The voice is Jacob's; the voice is Jacob's." Nevertheless, he is torn in another direction, because that one

[33] *Sancti Bernardi vita prima,* III, 1, *Patrologia, Series Latina,* CLXXXV-1, 304.

thought occupies his mind, how he wants to bless his first-born son. At the same time he considers how important a matter this blessing is and puts together all the promises that were made to Abraham. Therefore Isaac is occupied not only with natural thoughts, as lovers and people with melancholia usually are, but also with thoughts that are spiritual. Moreover, even before this Rebecca detected in him melancholia of this kind. It often happened that her husband was unaware of what was going on when she placed food before him. Finally Isaac was fully convinced that the mother, together with her son, neither could nor wanted to deceive him. Therefore he says: "The voice indeed is the voice of Jacob." Yet he abandons the thought and becomes engrossed in spiritual thoughts. The Jews are wrong when they imagine that although Isaac was aware of and detected the fraud, he pretended not to know; [34] for they have no knowledge of the powers of the Spirit, which are stronger than melancholy thoughts. When a person's heart is occupied with these, they render him altogether senseless and ecstatic.

So he blessed him.

The blessing does not begin as yet, for the text goes on to state that Isaac asked: "Are you really my son Esau?" But Moses means that when Isaac had touched and felt Jacob's hands, he was taken completely by surprise, dumbfounded, and out of his mind, and that with regard to this blessing he concluded and affirmed in his heart that it should be unalterable and permanent. It is as though he were saying: "The blessing has now been given and is definite." Thus later (v. 33) he will say to Esau: "And he shall be blessed." For it is the Holy Spirit who blesses through Isaac. Therefore one may not revoke or change anything. This was an extraordinary impulse and operation in the Holy Spirit. On this account he concluded within himself, after he had felt the hands and the neck, that he wanted to bless his son. Nor did he change his decision, even though many arguments were advanced against it.

This is what Moses means by this preface: "So he blessed him." It is as though he were saying: "The blessing predetermined for Jacob is now unalterable and confirmed. After this, whoever

[34] Cf. Lyra *ad* Gen. 27:23 and the *Additio*.

desires it will be disappointed in his hope; for the Holy Spirit does not revoke His operations and, as Malachi says, is not one who changes." "For I the Lord do not change" (Mal. 3:6). And in Num. 23:19 we read: "God is not man, that He should lie, or a son of man, that He should repent." When God has rendered a verdict, He does not change or retract it, as men are wont to do. Thus here the Holy Spirit touched Isaac's heart and said in his heart: "I am now blessing." Rom. 11:29 states: "The gifts and the call of God are irrevocable." Therefore Moses says: "So he blessed him"; that is, it had happened.

24. *He said: Are you really my son Esau? He answered: I am.*

25. *Then he said: Bring it to me, that I may eat of my son's game and bless you. So he brought it to him, and he ate; and he brought him wine, and he drank.*

26. *Then his father Isaac said to him: Come near and kiss me, my son.*

27. *So he came near and kissed him; and he smelled the smell of his garments, and blessed him, and said: See, the smell of my son is as the smell of the field which the Lord has blessed!*

The soul is the spirit or the life of man in the external senses. The soul sees, hears, speaks, weeps, and laughs. This is what Isaac wants to say: "Inside, in my heart, it had been decided that I want to bless you. Now my soul will bless you; that is, I will bless you with the external senses. You have been blessed according to the spirit. Now I will bless you with my soul." For this reason ceremonies are added. For even spiritual things that are external cannot be administered without external ceremonies. The five senses and the entire body have their own gestures and rites under which the body must live as if under certain masks. Therefore Isaac blessed not only in his heart but also with the external senses and ceremonies. Sons who were to be blessed had to bring their father some rather delicious food and wine. After this they approached and kissed their father. These are really civil ceremonies, and today they are retained among kings and princes when fiefs are bestowed. We also observe them in the schools when we create doctors of theology.[35]

After the ceremony had been observed, Moses says again: "And he blessed him," namely, externally, when he had smelled the fragrance of his garments. For a sense which moves the Holy Spirit is always present, and the Holy Spirit moves hearts through external things, as for example through the Word, through ceremonies and objects which move the heart through an external sense. But after these operations of the Holy Spirit Isaac takes courage, and he now, as if in a trance, is entirely convinced that this is his first-born son; for he is made confident by the fragrance of the garments. But these were the priestly robes of Abraham and Isaac, which they preserved with the utmost care by applying cassia and other fragrant substances, lest they be nibbled at by moths. Thus today we make use of nard or the like. Consequently, Isaac thought: "This is Esau, my first-born son; for he is clothed in the priestly robes." Thus he was deceived in the spirit, and now he is deceived by a sense.

But he employs a fine comparison: "The smell of my son is as the smell of the field which the Lord has blessed." For farmers know very well what the smell of a field is like when the harvest approaches, and how delightful that smell is. In like manner, the smell of vineyards is very pleasing and completely invigorating when the vintage season approaches. Accordingly, Isaac congratulates himself and gladdens his heart because of the blessing to be pronounced on his son. He thinks: "Now I have an heir and successor with whom I am pleased and delighted just as if I were walking in a field or in some fragrant vineyard the smell and fragrance of which would refresh my whole body and soul. Now I shall die gladly and in peace; for I leave behind me a lord and teacher of my house, a father of the future generation, and a priest." Thus Moses describes Isaac as intoxicated with joy [36] and drunk, as it were, with the best and happiest thoughts about his son and successor. He drinks wine and is of good cheer; but he is intoxicated, if I may say so, more with the Holy Spirit and spiritual thoughts. For his one and chief comfort is the knowledge that he has an heir of that blessing which was to be looked

[35] Cf. p. 109, note 11.
[36] Cf. Terence, *Phormio*, V, 6, 16.

for through Christ. And he undoubtedly added the fact that the promise given to Abraham was now in effect and was being extended to the third heir.

This blessing is far different from and much more sublime than the consecrated water concerning which the papists make many false assertions.[37] They were blessings concerning eternal life over against eternal death. They were priestly and regal blessings that reached into the life to come. Nevertheless, they cannot be administered apart from this life, and it is necessary for us to have physical blessings as well, for we cannot enjoy the eternal blessing without the temporal blessings. God must bless the field, supply bread, meat, and all the other necessities of life. But "man does not live by bread alone" (Matt. 4:4), and the physical blessings are given because of that eternal blessing. Therefore the spiritual promises always include the temporal promises.

Thus when Christ sends His disciples to teach the Gospel, He says to them (Luke 10:7): "Remain in the same house, eating and drinking what they provide." Likewise: "Eat what is set before you" (v. 8). For the Lord gives the physical blessing, bread and wine, since this life cannot do without these physical blessings. The Gospel is the chief blessing, but the other things are added for those who seek the kingdom of heaven (Matt. 6:33). The first blessing deals with eternal life; the second is physical, and concerning it Christ says in Matt. 6:31: "Therefore do not be anxious, saying: 'What shall we eat?' or 'What shall we drink?' or 'What shall we wear?' For your heavenly Father knows that you need them all." Thus here, too, we shall see Isaac add this external blessing to the blessing of eternal life, which one cannot have without the physical blessing.

28. *May God give you of the dew of heaven, and of the fatness of the earth, and plenty of grain and wine.*

29. *Let peoples serve you, and nations bow down to you. Be lord over your brothers, and may your mother's sons bow down to you. Cursed be everyone who curses you, and blessed be everyone who blesses you!*

---

[37] Pope Leo IV, who died in 855, commanded the priests: "Every Sunday, before Mass, bless the water with which the people and the places of the faithful are to be sprinkled." *Decreta, Patrologia, Series Latina,* CXV, 679.

This is the form of the blessing, and its first part pertains to the sustenance of the body; for without this we cannot live even in the kingdom of God so far as this life is concerned. For the body must be nourished if we must teach and govern the church. Accordingly, the first part pertains to the management of the household and to household supplies, in order that wife, children, and domestics may have the necessities of daily life. In the Lord's Prayer this is called "daily bread," that is, everything that is needed in the house for the sustenance of the body. "May God give you," says Isaac, "of the dew of heaven, and of the fatness of the earth, and plenty of grain and wine." These are temporal things. On earth we have need of the dew of heaven, that is, rain from heaven, and of the fatness of the earth, that is, fertility of the soil. For one sows in vain on rock, in water, or in a forest. One must sow in fertile and productive land. Then there is also need of rain. And he makes this part of the blessing rich and delightful enough; for he says that he would have plenty of grain and wine to live on, that he would live not only on water frugally and austerely, but would live in abundance and sumptuously. "You will have the wherewithal to take excellent care of your body," says Jacob. "Consequently, it will be nourished plentifully enough and amid an abundance of all things, not just barely." Thus Moses says in Deut. 32:15: "The loved one grew fat and frisky, became fat and gross and gorged."

Accordingly, Jacob is sure of sustenance in the household for himself and his descendants. And that sustenance will not be meager. No, it will be sumptuous and luxurious. And one can surely see in the Books of the Kings how this promise was fulfilled. Therefore the godly should acknowledge that they have their earthly things because God gives and blesses. Nor should they dream, as the heathen and the unbelievers do, that either the good or the evil things in this life come about by chance. On the contrary, they should acknowledge that these great gifts come from God. Therefore they should be grateful to God for these benefits, as the apostles declare in Acts 14:17: "He did good and gave us from heaven rains and fruitful seasons, satisfying our hearts with food and gladness."

The monks and other unlearned people before these times taught contempt for temporal goods, vineyards, and fields. Yet they themselves regarded these with the greatest longing. They ate and drank what was finest and best. Contrary to these dreams of the monks, we should learn that physical benefits are also blessings of God.

The second part of the blessing has to do with the state and pertains to authority; for Jacob is appointed lord over peoples and nations. His descendants will be princes and kings, not only heads of households. For peoples will serve him when they will be subjected, not to heads of households but to princes and kings. Not only one people but many peoples and many tribes will be subject. This was also fulfilled at the time of the judges and the kings, when the Children of Israel occupied the land of Canaan, when they not only subjected the Idumaeans but also exterminated all the peoples and kings of that land.

The third part of the blessing is spiritual and pertains to the priesthood. "The brothers born of the same father and the same mother will bow down to you. Perhaps they can enjoy the same authority in the state and in the household, but you alone will get the priestly authority." And this is the chief part of the blessing. Earlier he said: "Peoples will serve you, and the tribes of the earth will bow down to you." This bowing down is a civil matter. But this is something else and has reference to the brothers and sons of the same mother. Although it could be referred to the state, it is more properly understood of the third part of the blessing, since he had mentioned the state previously.

These, then, are the three hierarchies we often inculcate, namely, the household, the government, and the priesthood, or the home, the state, and the church.[38] The home has the daily bread and is a daily realm, as it were. The government has things that are temporal and is more than a daily realm, because it endures throughout all time, excluding eternity. But the priesthood is above the household and the state; it pertains to the church and is heavenly and eternal. In this manner excellent provision has been made for Isaac's son; for he has been appointed the heir, so that he, together with his descendants, has his own household, realm, and church. And it is a rich and magnificent blessing by which he has been established with regard to the future inheritance,

---

[38] This definition of the three hierarchies, which includes the "secular" realms, is directed against the notion of celestial and ecclesiastical hierarchies in Pseudo-Dionysius; cf. *Luther's Works*, 1, p. 235.

which he could hope and wait for with certainty and without any dispute.

But this blessing is more than an empty sound of words or some verbal wish in which one person tells and wishes another person good things, as when I say: "May God grant you pious and obedient children." These words are nothing more than wishes with which I give nothing to the other person but only desire something eagerly for him, and it is a blessing that depends entirely on events and is uncertain. But this blessing of the patriarch Isaac states facts and is sure to be fulfilled. It is not a wish; it is the bestowal of a good thing — the bestowal with which he says: "Take these gifts which I am promising you verbally." For it is one thing when I say: "I would wish you to have a strong and healthy body, and to be gifted with fine talents," where the Word by which you get these things does not follow. It is another thing when I offer you a bag of money and say: "Take the thousand guldens I am presenting to you," or when Christ says to the paralytic (Matt. 9:6): "Take up your bed and go home." According to an ordinary blessing, He would say: "Would that you were well and in full possession of your strength!" But the sickness would not be removed. Nor would a restoration of his strength ensue. Therefore it is only a verbal blessing.

In Holy Scripture, however, there are real blessings. They are more than mere wishes. They state facts and are effective. They actually bestow and bring what the words say. We also have blessings of this kind in the New Testament through Christ's priesthood, which is our blessing when I say: "Receive the absolution of your sins." [39] If I said: "Would that your sins were forgiven you; would that you were pious and in God's grace!" or "I wish you grace, mercy, the eternal kingdom, and deliverance from your sins," this could be called a blessing of love. But the blessing of a promise, of faith, and of a gift that is at hand is this: "I absolve you from your sins in the name of the Father and of the Son and of the Holy Spirit; that is, I reconcile your soul to God, remove from you God's wrath and displeasure, put you in His grace, and give you the inheritance of eternal life and the kingdom of heaven." All these things have the power to grant you forgiveness immediately and truly if you believe, for they are not

---

[39] See Luther's formula of 1531, *Luther's Works*, 53, p. 121.

our works; they are God's works through our ministry. Accordingly, they are not blessings that express wishes; they are blessings that have the power to bestow. When I baptize you in the name of the Father and of the Son and of the Holy Spirit, it is just as if I were saying: "I am snatching you from the hands of the devil and bringing you to God, and I am doing this truly and in fact."

In the same way the patriarchs had in their hands the power to bless, that is, to teach on the strength of a definite promise that their descendants would have sustenance, dominion, and the priesthood. This is no different from what it would be if Isaac were saying: "I am giving you grain; I am handing over to you dominion and the priesthood." The Jews treat these blessings too coldly; for they understand them only in a human way and as being expressed in the optative mood, not in a definite statement. But a blessing is the kind of statement that determines and settles something, a clinching statement or verdict. Such power is surely something great, for it really brings and grants physical goods for the household, temporal goods for the government, and spiritual goods for the priesthood. For this power they praised God, who had granted it to the men through whom He pronounced blessings and bestowed benefits of every kind.

But the fact that we see the very saintly patriarchs hand down and receive these goods with such sure faith, while we have such a cold and indifferent attitude toward our own blessing in the New Testament—this is great and deplorable wretchedness. I certainly am greatly ashamed of myself and chagrined whenever I compare myself with them. For look at this woman Rebecca, who lives in flesh and blood just as we do; and look at Isaac and Jacob. But with what a sure, living, and firm faith they are carried along to those future goods, so that they do not concern themselves about the presence of the flesh! Indeed, they seem to be sleeping and snoring in this physical life in view of the things that are promised to them for the future.

We have a richer gift, or surely one that is no smaller in measure and abundance. But we do not have the same faith; we snore, we are half-dead, our eyes are dimsighted, our ears are hard of hearing, our hearts falter and waver; they have, and they do not bother about what they have. For to pronounce absolution, to administer the sacraments of Baptism and the Lord's Supper, and to proclaim the forgiveness of sins from the Gospel is something far greater than if Isaac blesses Jacob. For it is just as if I were saying: "I give you the kingdom of heaven, power over the devil, and no matter how much you die, I keep you from perishing." Of course, we do not do this with our own strength; but we do it by virtue of the authority and command of God, who has given men the power to lead one another to eternal life through the priesthood of Christ.

Thus we indeed have far richer promises than they, but we also snore more and disregard this treasure of God's riches and goodness. For we are not grateful to God; we do not rejoice and exult wholeheartedly at this good fortune. We have it in great abundance; but we disregard and despise it, although everything is just as sure as those blessings of the patriarchs. Indeed, what is most horrible of all, the more abundantly we have, the more the world rages and persecutes.

Therefore the vigilance of the fathers, who accepted the promises and blessings with greater spirit and faith, should stir up our hearts and drive out this lethargy. Then we should make much of our gifts, which are equal to or greater than their gifts, even though they, too, are exceedingly great and excellent. We do not have the fathers speaking with us; but we have the Son of God Himself, as the author [40] of the Epistle to the Hebrews says (1:2). We hear Him saying: "I absolve you, I give you the keys of the kingdom of heaven, the power to baptize, to save, to tread demons and hell underfoot. I give you this divine power in order that you may do the same works that I do, and greater works than these" (cf. John 14:12).

But we, who are listless and sleepy, have thoughts like these: "Christ is true God and man. Consequently, it is not surprising that He bestows these gifts on men. But that men should give the gifts of this life and of the life to come to one another—this seems absurd, impossible, and unbelievable." But this was not the way the saintly fathers felt; they esteemed God's blessing very highly and gave thanks to God with rejoicing. Therefore we should blush when we compare ourselves with them, and we should censure and correct our sluggishness.

Now in the last part, the holy cross follows. Yet at the same

[40] On Luther's views about the authorship of Hebrews cf. *Luther's Works*, 35, p. 394, notes 43—44.

time it is victory through and in the cross. For this is what Isaac says: "Cursed be everyone who curses you." This passage is taken from chapters 12 and 22, where the Lord says to Abraham: "You will be cursed, but I will turn the curse into a blessing." But the fact that Isaac pronounces this verdict shows that he has great power—power at which hell, together with its demons, and the whole world, with all its might, are compelled to tremble. For this is what he wants to say: "I know that these blessings will be odious to the devil, the world, and the flesh. I know that this is bound to happen, O Jacob. To be sure, I am heaping great gifts on you; I am exalting and glorifying you. For you will be a father without poverty, a king without hindrance, a priest and a saver of souls against the will of the gates of hell (cf. Matt. 16:18). But remember that all these things are a matter of promise, that they have not come to fulfillment in the complete victory which is still hoped for and in prospect. Therefore you will have these things in such a way that it will seem to you that you have nothing at all. For you will be assailed in the household, in the state, and in the church. The ungodly will envy you all these things, and you will be cursed by them in such a way that the curse has been made ready alongside the blessing. Although I am blessing you, the devil and the world will come, your brothers will come, and will curse you; they will persecute you and attempt to defeat and destroy your blessings."

And eventually the outcome was in accord with the prophecy. For how much Jacob suffered immediately after the beginning of the blessing! His brother Esau threatens him with death. Here the household cross is laid upon him. He is the father of descendants to come; but day and night he is in danger of his life, is exposed to murder at the hands of his brother, and with much concern and great difficulty he is spirited away by his parents in order that he may avoid this danger. He is compelled to be in exile in Syria for about 20 years. A fine blessing indeed! He surely could have thought: "Father, how does what you said about the dew of heaven and the fatness of the earth agree with such great troubles?" For he does not have even a crumb of bread when he goes to Syria. Poor and destitute, he serves for 14 years, and in that servitude he suffers many indignities. For this reason his father warns him that he will feel the curse instead of the blessing.

But later, when the famine arises in the land of Canaan, he, together with his whole household, will be most seriously imperiled. In fact, he will be in extreme danger of his life. How cruelly and shamefully the Children of Israel are eventually treated in Egypt! Where, then, is the blessing? I answer: "Man does not live by bread alone, but by every word that proceeds from the mouth of God" (Matt. 4:4). Man is buoyed up by the Word; he is sustained by the Word. Therefore even though for the present there is no bread in his household, yet he does not die. Nor is he forsaken. But faith in the Word of God feeds both his body and his soul in the midst of poverty and eventually also changes hunger into plenty and abundance. For "those who seek the Lord shall lack no good thing" (Ps. 34:9-10). On the other hand, it is stated about the rich: "The rich suffer want and hunger." And again (Ps. 37:2): "They will soon fade like the grass."

But this must be accepted and waited for with faith. Thus Jacob concluded in faith that nothing would ever be lacking in his household. And eventually the outcome was in very beautiful accord with this; when the blessing followed, he became richer than his father-in-law, Laban, but through trials. He was tried but not forsaken. For the blessing is assailed but not overcome. It is battered and jostled but not felled. Thus the psalm states (Ps. 118:13-14): "I was pushed hard, so that I was falling, but the Lord helped me. The Lord is my strength and my song; He has become my salvation." The Lord bestows a blessing mixed with patience and adorned with reminders of the holy cross, in order that we may be instructed in our trials and learn that our life depends not on bread alone but on every word of God. In the end, however, God surely and without fail supplies us with bread after we have been disturbed in faith about whether we are willing to believe God in His promises. For He makes a promise; but He tests us and withdraws His blessing, as though no blessing should be expected. But He really reflects on and is aware of the blessing when we feel the curse. Consequently, the blessing can be assailed and repressed; but, as is said about truth, it cannot be overwhelmed and subdued.[41]

And this was the curse or cross in the household that disturbed the patriarch harshly enough. But look also at the state among his descendants. Look at David, who was the first king according to

[41] This appears to be an allusion to 1 Esdras 4:38-41.

the blessing, at how often, I ask you, his kingdom is shaken and in danger, as though it would collapse every moment, first at the time of Saul, then through his son Absalom and his wicked counselor Ahitophel. And at the time of Absalom his evil conscience was an additional factor. But in spite of this he buoyed himself up and sustained himself with God's promise, as is stated in Ps. 21:1: "In Thy strength the king rejoices, O Lord." Likewise (Ps. 63:11): "But the king shall rejoice in God; all who swear by Him shall glory." And in 2 Sam. 15:25-26 we read: "If I find favor in the eyes of the Lord, He will bring me back . . . but if He says: 'I have no pleasure in you,' behold, here I am, let Him do to me what seems good to Him." For the kingdom was promised to him and was established for him, but not without very great vexation and without trials on his part.

In the same way more of the curse than of the blessing is seen in the church. For this we, too, learn from experience—we who are in the same profession and to whom Baptism, the power of the Keys, and the Sacrament of the Altar have been given. But how many even very pious people there are whom Satan assails and infatuates to such an extent when he removes from their sight these heavenly blessings that they seem to retain nothing at all of these blessings! Indeed, they feel the curses and anguish of hell more than they feel the divine and heavenly blessings. Others rush into manifest acts of wickedness and manifest contempt, and cast the blessings aside. But those who retain these blessings and love them are so weak that they have need of many and frequent admonitions and repetitions to arouse them and to sharpen the Word of God in them, as Moses says (Deut. 6:7).

Meanwhile, however, nothing departs from the blessing. No, the blessing remains unalterable, firm, exceedingly rich, and greater than we understand. Paul has the same complaint when he says (2 Cor. 12:7) that a thorn was given him in the flesh and also (Acts 14:22) that we must enter the kingdom of heaven through many tribulations. Accordingly, curses will not be lacking. But go forth to face them more boldly, be strong, and cling steadfastly to the blessing, no matter how much everything seems to be full of a curse. For this is what we should conclude: It is sure that I have been baptized. I have heard the Word from the mouth of the minister. I have made use of the Sacrament of the Altar. This is the divine and unchangeable truth. Even though I am weak, it is sure and unalterable. They are exceedingly powerful and rich possessions, but the heart is slippery and vacillating when taking hold of them. But we should not deny them. This is the only thing against which we should be on our guard. And if we are unable to confess with a loud shout, let us at least make ourselves heard in a low murmur as best we can. If we cannot sing when we praise God, let us at least open our mouths, in order that we may continue steadfastly in the blessings into which the Son of God has placed us—the blessings which cannot be kept without a great struggle and trials of various kinds. For in this manner the fathers had sure and firm blessings, but not without a trial. And for this reason Christ so assiduously exhorts us to persevere. "By your endurance you will gain your lives" (Luke 21:19). You are children of the kingdom, your sins are forgiven, the devil has been overcome and laid low under your feet, sin and death will do you no harm; but you are blameless. Therefore bear the hostile curses with equanimity.

But after Isaac has mentioned the curses, that is, the cross and the trials which accompany those outstanding and rich blessings, he goes on to add: "BLESSED BE EVERYONE WHO BLESSES YOU!" It is as though he were saying: "They will not all curse or assail you, but many will come who will bless you and share in your blessings. This will be the fruit of your trials if you continue steadfastly in the faith." Thus Christ says (John 12:24): "Truly, truly, I say to you, unless a grain of wheat falls into the earth and dies, it remains alone; but if it dies, it bears much fruit." One Christian who has been tried does more good than a hundred who have not been tried. For in trials the blessing grows, so that with its counsels it can teach, comfort, and help many in physical and spiritual matters. Thus in the world you are cursed, but at the same time you are filled with a heavenly blessing.

Now let us also look at the grammatical explanation of some words. To bow down means to bend, incline the body, and show respect for the other person. The use of this word is extensive. Above (Gen. 23:7) Abraham bows down to the Hittites. Then it is used figuratively of spiritual bowing, which means to bend down before the Creator; for one bows down in one way to the Creator and in another way to the creature. But does he say: "Be lord over your brothers," although he has only the one brother, namely, Esau? This is a unique expression of Holy Scripture by which all grandsons are called sons and the sons of brothers are called brothers. Those who were born to Rebecca and her daughters were called sons. Thus Esau is the father of his sons and his grandsons. But in Holy Scripture not only brothers by the same mother but also the descendants and grandsons are called brothers.

30. *As soon as Isaac had finished blessing Jacob, when Jacob had scarcely gone out from the presence of Isaac his father, Esau his brother came in from his hunting.*

31. *He also prepared savory food, and brought it to his father. And he said to his father: Let my father arise, and eat of his son's game, that you may bless me.*

Now, when the blessing has been finished, a lamentation and the altogether different blessing of Esau follow. And this in the second part of this account. But the words of Esau's speech should be carefully considered; for Jacob had not said in the third person: "Let my father arise" but "Sit up, I ask you." But that hypocrite employs unusual rhetoric, just as saints of this kind are wont to employ words that are suitable for adornment, refinement, and show. Jacob presented his request in a simple and plain conversational manner. This man makes use of rhetorical amplifications that would never have entered Jacob's mind. "Let my father arise," he says, "and eat of his son's game." This is how proudly he rhetorizes. It is as though he were the sole and only-begotten son, but Jacob were not a son. For such is the way of hypocrites; they call themselves the church and [42] have a greater mask and more splendid dress than those who are truly godly. But in the godly there is neither so much boldness nor splendor. Thus Jacob does not have the courage to accost his father so arrogantly. Here Moses makes no mention of the robes. Nevertheless, Esau undoubtedly wore them. Perhaps Rebecca secretly put them back in their place, since she was no longer concerned about keeping or watching over them. She thought: "Let him go, for all I care; let him clothe and adorn himself as rhetorically as he wants; my son has already obtained the blessing."

32. *His father Isaac said to him: Who are you? He answered: I am your son, your first-born, Esau.*

[42] The Weimar text has *ut*, but we have followed other editions and read *et*.

33. *Then Isaac trembled violently, and said: Who was it, then, that hunted game and brought it to me, and I ate it all before you came, and I have blessed him?—yes, and he shall be blessed.*

Here he begins to lie deliberately, and he uses words that are truly impressive and high-sounding. "I," he says, "am your firstborn son." He makes his speech uncommonly expansive, as befits such an orator. Jacob is a simple dialectician. In the eyes of Esau he is completely contemptible, despised, and accursed; he does not deserve to be called Isaac's son, much less the firstborn son. But the Holy Spirit has decided that the opposite is true: "For Jacob already has the blessing; but you, Esau, are by no means the first-born. You have not forgotten, have you, what you did when you said: 'I am about to die; of what use is a birthright to me? Give me the pottage.' (And he sold his birthright and went away after he had eaten, and he despised it, considered it worthless.) The Holy Spirit has not yet forgotten this, as you dream. If you sold it to your brother, you have been justly condemned. Therefore you are lying when you say that you are the first-born son, for you squandered the birthright when you ate the pottage and cast it aside with extraordinary contempt." God wants to be glorified for His favors, and the person who honors Him He glorifies in turn; but those who despise Him shall be lightly esteemed as 1 Sam. 2:30 states. This is a horrible example of that statement.

But Isaac shudders and is stricken with great and violent dread at Esau's words, since he is afraid that perhaps by God's design some stranger had seized the blessing and that his descendants would be deprived of it. This was no inconsequential dread, for he was afraid that that glory of the blessing, the kingdom, and the priesthood would be transferred from his house in accordance with some plan of God. Thus the same danger confronts him when Esau threatens his brother Jacob with death,—the danger that if Jacob should perish, the blessing would be given to strangers. Nevertheless, Isaac is not induced to change the blessing once it has been bestowed. But he says that whoever it is who seized the blessing is blessed and will be blessed since God's gifts cannot be revoked. Later, however, he recalled the matter more carefully and thought: "Behold, I heard Jacob's voice; he deceived me by covering his neck and his hands with skins. Surely he is the one I blessed."

34. *When Esau heard the words of his father, he cried out with an exceedingly great and bitter cry, and said to his father: Bless me, even me also, O my father!*

35. *But he said: Your brother came with guile, and he has taken away your blessing.*

At this point the question is raised why Isaac did not revoke the blessing, since Jacob took it away with guile.[43] Lyra relates the opinion of the Jews that when Isaac heard Esau's complaint, he wanted to revoke the blessing; but then, by God's will, he saw hell open and ready for him if he revoked it. For this reason he was terrified and did not revoke it but rather confirmed it. This is what Lyra says about the opinion of the Jews. These people, however, do not explain the words of Scripture but rather obscure them. Consequently, one should not imagine that Isaac, even though he was violently terrified, gave thought to a revocation; for he knew that the blessing was an utterly permanent and unchangeable work and gift of God. Thus when I give Baptism to someone, then my heart and will are completely certain that I really want to baptize. But if he who is being baptized acts deceitfully, I have still administered a true Baptism which is not my own but is truly a divine work.

In this way Isaac also said: "I have blessed him, and he shall be blessed." And this he previously decided earnestly in his own mind, and it was not without special deliberation that he put it off to the end of his life. Therefore he was certain that when he blessed, he was uttering a definitive statement pronounced and confirmed by divine authority. And it was the same blessing that he had received by hereditary right from the fathers: from Adam, Noah, Abraham, and the others. Such statements cannot and must not be changed, for God does not change His gifts. He does not revoke Baptism, absolution, and the other gifts He bestows through His Word. If He forgives me my sins, then they have truly been forgiven.

People also debate about the guile, whether the saintly fathers acted with guile and whether they sinned by acting with guile.[44]

---

[43] The Weimar text has *nam,* but we have followed other editions and read *eam.* The source of this information about rabbinic exegesis is Lyra *ad* Gen. 27: 34-35.

[44] According to Lyra *ad* Gen. 27:32, Rabbi Solomon attempted to cover up the guile by pointing the words of Jacob to read: "I am the one who is bringing you food."

For we have often heard that they lied inordinately, not only obligingly but also actually. But in this deed there is no sin. Although in the fact and in the sight of men there is fraud and deceit — for Jacob deluded his father with his hairy hands and by covering his neck with skins — yet before God it is not a fraud, because the primogeniture and the blessing which he had bought from his brother and previously already had by divine authority was owed to him, since it was destined for him in accordance with the prophecy, which declared (Gen. 25:23): "The older shall serve the younger." Consequently, to contrive a plot and to take away from another by deceit what God has given to you is not a sin. Thus although the despoiling of the Egyptians is truly a despoiling according to human judgment, the Israelites did not sin by despoiling the Egyptians, since God had commanded them to say to the Egyptians (Ex. 11:2): "Lend me a silver vessel and clothing with which to adorn the feast of the Lord" when they were intending to flee. They had God's clear command, which said: "I want you to defraud, to despoil the Egyptians"; for the Egyptians owed the Israelites pay for their servitude and for the exceedingly harsh tyranny. Yet this was surely insignificant and poor compensation for such a long oppression of the people and for its slain children.

This is how one should also regard this fraud on the part of Jacob; for when the saints perpetrate a fraud and have a command of God in regard to it, then, although it is a fraud in the sight of men, yet it is a saintly, legitimate, and pious fraud. Therefore there is no need to ask and debate in what way and whether Jacob sinned, but one must consider that what he took away from his brother by fraud had previously been granted to him by divine authority. Thus in their wars the saints frequently deceived their enemies, but those are lies one is permitted to use in the service of God against the devil and the enemies of God.

Thus a fisherman deceives a fish by enticing it with bait, and it was not unreasonable on the part of the fathers to apply this to Christ.[45] For He came into the world clothed in flesh and was cast into the water like a hook. After biting Him, the devil was suddenly pulled back out of the water by God, thrown on dry

---

[45] Cf. *Luther's Works*, 26, p. 267, note 69, on this metaphor in the church fathers.

land, and crushed. This means that Christ presented to the devil His weak humanity, which covered that eternal and unconquerable majesty. Then the devil struck at the hook of His divinity, and by it all his power as well as the power of death and hell was overcome, as is stated in Col. 2:15: "He disarmed the principalities and powers and made a public example of them, triumphing over them in Him." But Satan could rightly have complained that he had been shamefully deluded and deceived, since he had thought that he would kill a man and was himself being killed after being decoyed by Him into a trick. But by God's wonderful counsel the same thing happened to him that is commonly said:"That cunning might deceive cunning."

36. *Esau said: Is he not rightly named Jacob? For he has supplanted me these two times. He took away my birthright; and behold, now he has taken away my blessing. Then he said: Have you not reserved a blessing for me?*

Here begins the hatred against his brother. "Is he not rightly named Jacob?" he says. "For he has supplanted me these two times." But both are false. You, Esau, are lying. Do you not know what you did earlier? You sold the birthright of your own free will when you said: "I am about to die; of what use is a birthright to me?" You despised the blessing which is efficacious even after death. Furthermore, you disregarded the authority of God, by which it was said (Gen. 25:23): "The older shall serve the younger." Therefore you are no longer the first-born; but that purchaser is the first-born, and he has the blessing with full right. Nor may one demand it back from him, for it is a gift of God that is not changed. But you are lying, and you are falsely accusing your brother of having taken away both the birthright and the blessing.

And from this it is clear how the passage in Heb. 12:16-17 is to be understood. There we read: "That no one be immoral or irreligious like Esau, who sold his birthright for a single meal. For you know that afterward, when he desired to inherit the blessing, he was rejected; for he found no chance to repent, though he sought it with tears." For the reason why he accomplished nothing with his repentance and tears is that it was not a true repentance. This is indeed true and firm, that God, who does not deceive or lie, has offered His mercy to all men who truly repent; and repentance for sin always finds room before God. This must be firmly maintained and defended, just as God has borne witness to it with many examples and books of Holy Scripture.

But there is another repentance that is not genuine but is false. The Germans call it "a gallows repentance," [46] namely, when I repent in such a way that I am not ashamed of having offended God but am ashamed because I have done harm to myself. Such a repentance is very common, and I myself have often repented in this manner; and I felt sorry that I had done something foolishly, unwisely, and with harm. I was more ashamed of the foolishness and harm than of the sin, than of the guilt or offense. But to feel sorry only for the harm that has been done is a repentance of which God has no knowledge. Indeed, even our own hearts have no knowledge of it, as is evident in the case of Esau; for he does not say: "Now I realize that I have sinned. Why did I offend God by selling my birthright? Now I shall gladly do without the blessing, provided that God forgives me this sin." This would have been a true repentance, with which he would have been concerned about appeasing God on account of the sin that had been committed. For true repentance looks at God's wrath on account of sin. It earnestly desires that He be appeased; it shuns the wrath of God. It not only produces grief on account of the harm and no anger and hatred against the brother, but this is what it says: "Provided that God were willing to be gracious to me, I would gladly bear any harm and evil whatever."

You hear nothing of this from Esau; he has a repentance because of punishment, not because of sin. Therefore he does not find a repentance for the punishment, for he does not seek a repentance for sin but is stubborn in his sin, just as Saul, too, did after he had transgressed the command by which he had been ordered to kill Amalek together with the men and women and with all the flocks and cattle (1 Sam. 15:3). But he spared the king and the cattle. And when he was reproved by Samuel, he answered: "The people spared the best of the sheep and of the oxen, to sacrifice to the Lord your God" (1 Sam. 15:15). This was

---

[46] The German is *Ein galgen rew;* the more common English term is "deathbed repentance."

[W, XLIII, 533, 534]

not an acknowledgment of the sin; it was an excuse and a defense under the pretext of saintliness. Therefore the prophet is deeply disturbed and announces to him the very sad verdict: "Because you have rejected the Word of the Lord, He has also rejected you from being king" (1 Sam. 15:23).

Thus Adam, too, tried to excuse his sin and flung back the blame not only on the woman but also on God (Gen. 3:12): "The woman," he said, "whom Thou gavest to be with me, she gave me fruit of the tree, and I ate." In the same way Eve also excused herself and accused the serpent, who had deceived her. This should by no means be called repentance, for the feeling of true penitence is like this: "Alas, why have I offended God? Why have I stirred up His wrath and judgment against myself? Let Him make of me whatever example He wants provided that He forgives and pardons my sin." Thus in the Book of Judges (10:15) the children of Israel pray: "We have sinned; do to us whatever seems good to Thee; only deliver us." Such a prayer is proper for those who are truly and sincerely repentant. "By all means, let the Lord do with me what He wants, provided that He is propitious to me!" And then God is completely ready to grant pardon and to forgive, and He offers forgiveness of sins immediately.

But Esau's words prove how far he is from this true humility and from the acknowledgment of his sin. With these words he lies most shamefully by saying that he is the first-born when he is not and by saying that the birthright which he previously had given up voluntarily belongs to him. Finally—and this is far more serious—he accuses and condemns his innocent brother. Himself, the guilty one, he excuses and praises. "He is rightly named Jacob" he says, "for he has supplanted me." Not even with a word does he mention his sin. He does not say: "I have sinned. Until now I did not realize and did not understand that I sinned. Now I am being taught by the punishment itself and by God's judgment. Now it is time to acknowledge my sin; for I realize that God has been horribly offended by my sale, by my contempt. But I do not begrudge my brother this blessing. No, I am sincerely fond of him, and I am glad that he got this blessing. I have sinned, and I am heartily sorry, not so much because the blessing has been lost as because God's wrath has been stirred up against me." He does not say or think this at all. Indeed, he glories in his wickedness. "I am righteous; my brother is wicked. He has fraudulently taken away what belongs to me, and he has possession of what does not belong to him. May this turn out badly for him!" In this manner he condemns the righteousness of another and defends his own sin. Finally he conceives horrible hatred for his brother, begrudges him the grace which God has bestowed on him and which he himself has lost in a lawful way and by his own fault. Over and above this, he threatens him with death. Truly a fine repentance!

Hence it is nothing else than grief over the loss of his possession and the harm that has been suffered. In this way even thieves and criminals grieve over their wicked deeds, not because they come to their senses in earnest or detest their misdeeds, but because they are tormented by the fear and thought of punishment. Under the papacy we did penance in this manner for our sins, since we were driven to confession every year; [47] for even then people would rather have indulged in sins if it had been permitted. And soon after Easter they would return to their natural inclination and be glad to have been delivered from that torture of confession. Accordingly, to repent is to feel seriously God's wrath because of sin, so that the sinner is troubled in his heart and plagued by a desire for salvation and for the mercy of God. But he who can should buoy up and comfort this person, lest he despair and perish, as Judas despaired. For such a heart does not feel otherwise than that it would gladly throw everything overboard, provided that it found comfort and had help even from a very little child who proclaims the promise of salvation. It thinks: "Provided that I am freed from God's wrath, by which I am wretchedly tortured, I shall care nothing about recovering what I have lost. If I have acted foolishly, I shall surely pay the price or penalty for my folly, provided that God is gracious to me." But this is how Esau felt: "If I had my birthright, I would not care about whether God is gracious or not."

Accordingly, this is how one should understand that statement in Hebrews (12:17): "He found no chance to repent," for there was no true repentance.[48] But he grieved over the harm he had

---

[47] This was required by the canon *Omnis utriusque;* cf. *Decretalia Gregorii IX, Liber V, Titulus 38, De poenitentia et remissionibus, c. 12, Corpus iuris canonici,* edd. Aemilius Ludovicus Richter and Aemilius Friedberg (Leipzig, 1879—81), II, 887.

[48] In his preface to the Epistle to the Hebrews of 1522 Luther had said of this

suffered and over his folly through which he lost the birthright and his glory. Therefore he rushed horribly into hatred for his brother and for God, who blessed Jacob through his father Isaac.

This is an outstanding pattern and example of one who repents falsely. Therefore it should be noted, in order that we may learn to distinguish true repentance from that which is false and feigned, which we call "a gallows repentance." For when a thief sees that punishment on the gallows is imminent for him, he also grieves and would gladly live longer. But if God gives him this grace and light that he truly acknowledges his sin and God's wrath, he is no longer concerned about his life, provided that he gets help, lest his soul's salvation be in doubt. And then he should be instructed and buoyed up with the mercy and grace of God revealed in Christ, not with confession or papistic satisfaction. Otherwise he would be done for.

37. *Isaac answered Esau: Behold, I have made him your lord, and all his brothers I have given to him for servants, and with grain and wine I have sustained him. What, then, can I do for you, my son?*

Jacob's blessing includes the three hierarchies: the domestic, the royal, and the priestly. For the purpose of administering these three he also gives him the goods of the world. In the state he has the rule and government among the people; in the church he has the stewardship of the forgiveness of sins and of eternal life. Consequently, Jacob is a bishop, has the prophecy, has the Word, forgiveness of sins, and the worship [49] of God. Next he adds: "I have made his brothers subject to him in the state, and he will make peoples subject to himself." This happened under David, who was the first to fulfill the blessing when he subjected the Syrians, the Philistines, the Arabians, and the Edomites. "What, then, shall I now do?" says Isaac. "What shall I give to you beyond these three blessings? He has taken everything, and this has undoubtedly happened in accordance with the special plan and

passage: "This is contrary to all the Gospels and to St. Paul's epistles; and although one might venture an interpretation of it, the words are so clear that I do not know whether that would be sufficient." In later editions the word "is" was changed to "seems, as it stands, to be." *Luther's Works*, 35, p. 394.

[49] The Weimar text has *cultuum*, but we have followed other editions and read *cultum*.

will of God, whose blessing this was. Therefore I cannot change it." But Esau does not give up. Indeed, he urges his father with prayers and entreaties [50] to bless him too.

38. *Esau said to his father: Have you but one blessing, my father? Bless me, even me also, O my father. And Esau lifted up his voice and wept.*

This is why it is stated in the Epistle to the Hebrews (12:17): "Though he sought it with tears." For this is that anxious and fervent entreaty with tears with which he seeks often and anxiously but too late and in vain. For once God has withdrawn, and once the Word and the grace of God have been taken away, it is not easily found again. Formerly there was a very beautiful church at Rome, and it had a larger number of confessors and martyrs than there were anywhere else in the entire world; but what horrible darkness and abominations followed when it was taken away! Now even if they were pining away with crying and wailing or were really dying with Esau, yet they are achieving nothing toward recovering that former light and grace of God.

Before these times, in the papacy, we cried out for eternal salvation, for the kingdom of God; and we afflicted our bodies violently, yes, killed them. We did not do this with the sword or with weapons; we did it with fastings and by castigating the body. We sought, we knocked night and day (cf. Matt. 7:7). If I myself had not been delivered by the comfort of Christ through the Gospel, I would not have lived two years. In this way I tortured myself and fled from the wrath of God. Nor were tears, sobs, and sighs lacking. But we accomplished nothing. Therefore it is not without a purpose that Paul is so careful to warn (2 Cor. 6:1-2) "not to accept the grace of God in vain." "Behold," he says, "now is the acceptable time; behold, now is the day of salvation." Therefore let us make use of the grace that has been offered while we may; let us open our mouths and hearts and permit the blessing to be poured into us. For when it has been taken away, we are done for.

The Germans use a proverbial imprecation that is not evil: "May God afflict lazy hands with boils." That is, "May evil betide

---

[50] The Weimar text has *obscurando,* but we have followed other editions and read *obsecrando.*

remiss and lazy hands." They urge us to avail ourselves of the opportunity at hand without delay. Thus when the Gospel is taught, let us hear and learn it with grateful hearts, as Christ says (John 12:35-36): "Walk while you have the light, lest the darkness overtake you. The light is with you for a little longer. While you have the light, believe in the light, that you may become sons of light."

And surely the example of the Jews proves adequately what horrible darkness laid hold of them when they no longer believed in Him who did such great signs before their eyes. For they fulfill this figure of Esau uncommonly well. They cry out day and night. They have been castigating the body with fasts and prayers for 1,500 years. They pray most fervently: "Lord God, send the Messiah for Thy name's sake, for Thy Word's sake, and for Thy kingdom's sake." Even stones and rocks could be moved by these prayers and lamentations. But they find no place for repentance. Not that there is no place for repentance; but they are going to heaven by a wrong road and want to acquire the blessing by their own merits, which is impossible. They do not acknowledge their sin; but they justify themselves, just as Esau does. They say: "We are Israel." Thus Esau said: "I am your first-born son." "O God," they say, "the heathen have taken away the birthright and the blessing." Although they feel God's wrath, they do not want to acknowledge their sin. But to feel sin and the wrath of God because of sin is very great grace, and salvation is close to such sinners. As a result, they are easily brought to repentance. But to defend and excuse sin is "to pass judgment on God," that is, to condemn in His words, as Ps. 51:4 says. Therefore Esau is an example of all the Jews.

Therefore we, too, when we were monks, were accomplishing nothing with our castigations; for we were unwilling to acknowledge our sin and ungodliness. Indeed, we had no knowledge of original sin. Nor did we realize that unbelief is a sin. We even concluded and taught that one had to be uncertain about God's mercy.[51] Therefore the more I ran, and the more I longed to come to Christ, the farther He withdrew from me. After confession and the celebration of Mass I was never able to find rest in my heart, for the conscience cannot have sure comfort on the basis of works. Therefore let us enjoy the blessing we now have and the grace

---

[51] Cf. the more extensive discussion of this in *Luther's Works*, 26, pp. 377 ff.

that is offered after the light of the Gospel has reappeared, and let us not be indifferent or ungrateful. For once the blessing has been taken away, it is not in our power to recover it; it can be recovered only by reason of a free gift of God, and in such a way that He is influenced by no one's tears, cries, and exertions.

First I saw this well, namely, that the free gift is absolutely necessary for obtaining the light and the heavenly life, and I worked anxiously and diligently to understand the well-known statement in Rom. 1:17: "The righteousness of God is revealed in the Gospel." [52] Then I sought and knocked for a long time (cf. Matt. 7:7), for that expression "the righteousness of God" stood in the way. It was commonly explained by saying that the righteousness of God is the power of God by which God Himself is formally righteous and condemns sinners. This is the way all teachers except Augustine had interpreted this passage: the righteousness of God, that is, the wrath of God. But every time I read this passage, I always wished that God had never revealed the Gospel — for who could love a God who is angry, judges, and condemns? — until finally, enlightened by the Holy Spirit, I weighed more carefully the passage in Habakkuk (2:4), where I read: "The righteous shall live by his faith." From this I concluded that life must come from faith. In this way I related the abstract to the concrete, and all Holy Scripture and heaven itself were opened to me. At this time, however we see that great light very clearly, and we may enjoy it richly. But we despise and disdain this jewel and heavenly treasure. Accordingly, if one day it should be taken away again, we shall cry and knock once more, as Christ says about the foolish virgins in the parable (cf. Matt. 25:11). But we shall cry and knock in vain. Therefore let us fear God and be grateful. Above all, however, my own example and the example of others should move you. We lived in death and hell and did not have the blessing so abundantly as you have it. Therefore occupy yourselves diligently with the doctrine of the blessing, and think about it, in order that you may be able to keep it yourselves and also to make it known to others. As for ourselves, we have done our duty.

39. *Then Isaac his father answered him: Behold, of the fatness*

---

[52] See Luther's description from the year 1545 of this struggle, *Luther's Works,* 34, pp. 336—337. We have conjectured the reading *laborabam* here, even though all the editions read *laborandam*.

of the earth shall your dwelling be, and of the dew of heaven on high.

40. *By your sword you shall live, and you shall serve your brother; but when you break loose, you shall break his yoke from your neck.*

He gives him a share of the domestic blessing, for the blessing pertaining to the state and the blessing pertaining to the church are in the possession of his brother Jacob. Yet this is not a blessing; for he only says: "You are destined to have a fruitful land," that is, food and clothing. Lest the carnal Jewish people have nothing at all, he gives it a carnal promise. Then he adds: "By your sword you shall live"; that is, "You shall defend yourself with the sword, but you shall not conquer or rule. Everything is to be understood without a blessing. God has not appointed you lord over other peoples, much less over your brother, whom He has previously excepted. And He has appointed Jacob lord over his brothers. You will have to be satisfied to dwell in a fertile land, to defend yourself with the sword, so that you may be safe from your enemies, but in such a way that you are subject to your brother and serve him." These two things should now be compared with each other. Jacob is the teacher in the church and the political magistrate above his brother Esau, and his blessing is called a blessing. But the blessing of this man Esau is not called a blessing. For the text does not read: "It will be your blessing." No, it states: "Of the fatness of the earth shall your dwelling be," and it is the same word that is used in Ps. 1:1: "In the seat of scoffers." Holy Scripture has carefully guarded against calling Esau blessed; for the blessing extends far and wide, to what is fat, and to all possessions. Nor does it say: "May the Lord God give to you"; for if "the Lord" is added, it becomes a blessing. Therefore this is what Isaac means: "God will not bless you by virtue of this blessing; but it will come about that you will have something that God will give you, just as He gives to the Arabians and the Egyptians, who had fortuitous nourishment and protection without acknowledging God's blessing." This should be carefully noted. Those two words "God" and "blessing" do not appear in the text. Therefore it is not a blessing.

Besides, he adds: "But when you break loose, etc." This is also an unusual little statement; for Isaac would gladly give him more and is careful to ask what else he could bestow on him. But these words pertain to Herod and his generation. The Jews explain them as dealing with the time of King Joram in the days of Elisha.[53] Because of the godlessness of the king the Idumaeans revolted against him (2 Kings 8:20). And this is not a bad conclusion, for then Edom broke the yoke and freed itself from Israel's domination. But I think that the words are understood more correctly of Herod, who was the son of Antipater, the Idumaean who had great authority and honor at the time of Julius Caesar and harshly plagued the kingdom of Israel. Accordingly, it came about that he shook the yoke from his neck and also had dominion.[54]

But this leads to the question how the prophecy or promise was fulfilled, namely, that Jacob is blessed and that the older will serve the younger, but that the younger will rule (Gen. 25:23). And below it will follow that Jacob bows to Esau, both he himself and his domestics, children, and wives (Gen. 33:1-3). On that occasion he will draw up four lines, and they all prostrate themselves before Esau and bow down to him. Then the Idumaeans have dominion in Israel for a long time; and Herod, along with his descendants, rules powerfully almost up to the time of the destruction of Jerusalem. Nevertheless, Jacob received the blessing on the basis of what is stated in Gen. 49:10-11. How, then, are these two facts reconciled?

I answer: A rule that lasts one hour or one day is not properly called dominion. Thus when the people had been led away captive to Babylon, it could also have been said to have lost the rule. But it did not actually lose the rule, for it was only chastened. The rule was not lost; it was postponed. In the same way Jacob bows down to Esau. He wrestles with the angel in such a way that he almost despaired of the rule and the blessing. For he had no other feeling in that struggle than that he would be subjected to his brother and that his brother would slay him, his household, and his wife. But after the struggle he is called Israel by the angel, and he is appointed king in that struggle the moment he succumbs. "For you have wrestled with God," says the angel (Gen. 32:28). "You will wrestle more with men." One does not lose the blessing or the rule

---

[53] Lyra *ad* Gen. 27:39-40, referring to his previous comments on Gen. 25.

[54] Josephus, *Antiquities of the Jews*, Books XV—XVII; *The Jewish War*, Book I, chs. 18—33.

when one is tried in his faith in regard to the rule and the blessing. Thus Abraham is tried for an hour in regard to his son's life when God says to him (cf. Gen. 22:2): "Sacrifice your son to Me." But he did not lose his son on that account. No, he got him back richly and with profit, just as the angel gives additional confirmation of the blessing of Jacob at Jacob's request. "I will not let you go, unless you bless me" (Gen. 32:26). Consequently the blessing did not cease. Nor was it removed. But it was tested and assailed, in order that it might become firmer and surer.

But what about Herod, who certainly ruled over Jerusalem and Judah with great insolence and cruelty? I answer: Then the prophecy of Jacob, which said: "The scepter shall not depart, etc." (Gen. 49:10), was fulfilled. For Mary, the mother of Christ, had already been born, and the parents of John the Baptist were also living after Herod had ruled six or, at the most, 10 years, although this was not confirmed before Christ's birth. Thus Philo gives evidence that he ruled for six years with legitimate power and for 31 years with arbitrary power, which is by no means worthy of being called a rule.[55] But his father Antipater before him was only a prefect of Judea. Moreover, he did not have a tranquil rule; for the Jews were constantly in rebellion because of the promise, which they clung to pertinaciously. And since it had been said: "You must serve your brother Jacob," it seemed intolerable that the Jews should be compelled to be subject to their servant Herod. Therefore Herod ruled, but not with legitimate power.

Finally one can also give this answer, that he had obtained the rule, not by divine authority, by which kings had previously been appointed in Israel and Judah, but through the tyranny of the Romans as a result of God's wrath, in order to destroy that kingdom which was now coming to an end and was gradually being destroyed. Therefore his dominion is not contrary to the promise, for that very time was the end of the kingdom in which Christ was to be born.

And these are the two contrary promises of the two brothers. Jacob has obtained the blessing that concerned the household, the state, and the church. Esau has no blessing at all; he has only

---

[55] The only references to Herod in the genuine works of Philo appear to be *Ad Flaccum*, 25, and *Legatio ad Gaium*, 294—300, neither of which discusses these facts.

a promise such as the rest of the nations had, as, for instance, the Syrians, whose dominion the Jews occasionally endured. But they did not lose the rule except at the end, in order that the prophecy of Jacob might be fulfilled. He had foretold (Gen. 49:10) that when Shiloh came, the rule, together with the priesthood and the Law, would have to be terminated.

41. *Now Esau hated Jacob because of the blessing with which his father had blessed him, and Esau said to himself: The days of mourning for my father are approaching; then I will kill my brother Jacob.*

Concerning the repentance of that godless man Esau we have stated that he wept and, as Jerome translates,[56] roared with a mighty outcry because of the blessing that had been stolen from him, even though he himself had previously sold it of his own accord. Now words befitting such a penitent follow; for as the repentance is, so are also the fruit of the repentance and the satisfaction. For this is what he says: "The days of mourning for my father are approaching." Why? "Because I will kill my brother." Truly a beautiful repentance! He is angry not only with his brother but also with his parents and with God Himself, whose blessing, as he knows, it is and from whom alone it was also to be expected. This, of course, is the way one should repent! Before this he was weeping and crying out: "O father Isaac, bless me, too, your son!" Now he is enraged and is planning a triple murder, for first he wants to kill his brother. This, of course, is rendering satisfaction to God for the sin in penitence! Then, however, he wants to hurl both of his parents into exceedingly deep mourning, in order that in this way they, too, may be killed. He will kill his brother with a cudgel or a sword; he will kill his parents with mourning and grief. Godless Esau knows that this will happen. Therefore he says deliberately and wittingly that he will kill his parents with this sorrow.

This is certainly a case of being carried away by devilish rage and malice, while these are his thoughts: "If I am not to have the blessing, I will see to it that all the others are also deprived of it. Neither my brother nor my parents nor the entire church shall retain it." For there are only two brothers to whom the blessing,

[56] Cf. p. 149.

or the succession in the rule and the priesthood, pertains. And if Jacob had been killed, the inheritance of the blessing would nevertheless not have returned to Esau; for he would have been either executed or driven into exile, just as Cain was. Therefore the church and the blessing of God in the house of Isaac were in very grave danger. And here you see the nature of Esau's repentance. It is simply a devilish rage by which he casts out of his heart all respect for and fear of God and his parents. And he completely forgets about all godliness and honor, in such a way that if he were able, he would want the blessing destroyed together with his father, his mother, and the whole church. For if his raging had continued and Jacob had been killed, Isaac, a very tenderhearted old man, and his mother Rebecca would surely have died of wretched and bitter grief. Just as because of the murder of his son committed by Cain it would have been impossible for Adam to live unless God had preserved him in a miraculous manner,[57] so such piercing pains would have killed these parents.

Therefore you see how the devil rages in the home life and the household of even the saintliest people. It is not without cause that we warn so often and exhort and cry out so often that you should pray diligently and without ceasing. For the devil is not far away. No, he is in our midst. Observe what a disturbance he caused in the very holy church of the fathers, in the house of Isaac, where Esau is plotting the destruction of his brother, the murder of his parents, and the overthrow and devastation of the entire church. On the other hand, this grief is justifiable, and Esau has good reason to be so greatly disturbed. But it is his own fault; for he himself sinned, since he esteemed lightly and despised what he now desires so much. And now, when he feels God's wrath, he is driven to madness because of grief and impatience.

Let us recognize this great malice of the DEVIL. It is because of this malice that he has his own children in the homes of the saintliest people. They plot against the lives of their brothers and their own parents. Isaac is a very saintly patriarch, the father of the promise; Rebecca is a very saintly woman and the mother of the same promise. But Esau was born from their flesh and blood. He longs for their death, and he himself plans to bring it about. Of what will we not have to be afraid? But the grief of parents

[57] Cf. the discussion of this in *Luther's Works*, 1, pp. 283—284.

is far more piercing and far bitterer than that of children, than that of brothers or relatives. For there are very great and intense emotions that God has created in the whole nature of things and has implanted in parents toward their offspring. And if at any time their hearts are wounded by grief or sorrow on account of a misfortune suffered by their children, this is a very real plague and a poison for their lives. Therefore parents are easily killed, if not by the sword, then by sorrow and grief. I myself have seen that many very honorable parents were slain by godless children because of sadness of heart. Young people neither consider nor understand this. But children should be taught and warned, lest they become murderers of mothers and murderers of fathers; for an exceedingly horrible judgment and punishment of God awaits them, as Paul says (1 Tim. 1:9): "The Law is laid down for murderers of fathers and murderers of mothers." Children often fall smugly into various misdeeds without having any regard for respect toward parents. Daughters sully their chastity and disgrace their pious and honorable parents. But with these shameful acts they kill father and mother; for father and mother are endowed with that very tender affection and love toward their offspring which is not so intense and ardent in children. Indeed, they do not even understand it.

Therefore let the youth beware and learn to honor and respect their parents and to regard these words "father and mother" as most sacred objects of veneration. Indeed, let them hold that they should rather die than offend their parents. For in this life they have nothing by which they are influenced more than by the love and affection of their children. For this reason they are very easily hurt, even if you are not aware of it but are engulfed in sin and in the flesh and attach little importance to their concern and solicitude for you. But woe to you if your respect and reverence are not appropriate, for in this way you will suddenly become the murderer of your father or the murderer of your mother before you think of it. And then you will look in vain for their blessing. Indeed, you will be more likely to bring upon yourself the gallows or the sword and a horrible curse. For this is what the Word of God says (Deut. 27:16): "Cursed be he who dishonors his father or his mother." Likewise (Ex 21:17): "Whoever curses his father or his mother shall be put to death." And also (Lev. 20:9): "He who curses his father or his mother, his blood shall be upon him."

Here Esau actually curses his father, if not in words, nevertheless in fact; for this is what he means when he says: "The days of mourning for my father are approaching." The usual translation is "The days will come." But the Hebrew word means that they are near, that is, "It will not be long until I shall disturb the joy of my father, my mother, and also my brother Jacob, just as they have disturbed my own joys. I shall compound gall and wormwood for them, as the common saying is." These are certainly words of an exceedingly horrible curse which prove that he is being driven by the devil and the Furies.

Accordingly, this is one of the greatest misfortunes of the human race, namely, the foolishness and wickedness of children with which they kill their parents before they understand how great their sin is. For they do not know what great distress and what great grief their parents suffer on account of the wickedness of their children. But the parents feel it, waste away from heartache, and are consumed. Therefore it is not without a purpose that God used the word "honor" in the Fourth Commandment; for He does not say: "Obey, listen to your parents." No, He says: "Honor them." He wants this name to be regarded as sacrosanct; for God knows the wickedness of original sin, which is so powerful that it impels people to kill their parents and to rage against their own blood. David was severely plagued by this evil, and he learned what great grief and what great distress the wickedness of children causes. For he felt that his son Absalom was his enemy who was plotting against his physical and eternal welfare and life but eventually incurred a horrible curse when he met with destruction befitting his deeds.

Therefore I urge and earnestly beseech all young men to shun and detest this sin and to accustom their hearts to respect their parents and to that end to implore God's help with unceasing prayers. If this happened in the house of Adam, in the house of Abraham between Ishmael and Isaac, and in the house of Isaac between Jacob and Esau—I am now passing over very many examples of the heathen—what shall we parents not look for, and what will you children not be afraid of? For you see that the devil is in our midst; you also see exceedingly sad examples of punishments in all ages—examples which befall insolent children who disgrace their parents and torment them with their insolence. How wretched and sudden Esau's downfall is before he foresees or thinks of such a sad event! And how would he think of it, since in his father's house he alone is in control of civil affairs and rules the church, inasmuch as he is the lord and prince of the house?

For this is the picture of the house and the household of Isaac. The aged father is rid of all the duties of the head of the household and of the entire administration, whether in the household or in civil or church affairs. For he is blind, not, as I think, because of old age but because of some other mishap or trial, so that this, too, was added to the mass of his afflictions and his cross. For he was a saintly man, and God loved him. Therefore he was vexed by many trials. Consequently, deprived as he is of the use of his eyes, he is compelled to abstain from all governing, unless perhaps some verbal admonition or command has to be given. Rebecca is the mother of the household, but without authority. Similarly, Jacob, too, was scorned and despised. Esau alone, who has two wives and many children, is the lord. For Jacob is not blessed until 37 years have elapsed after Esau's marriage, which he celebrated when he was 40 years old. And now both are 77 years of age. In the meantime, however, Esau begot many children.

Consequently, even if Rebecca, as the mother of the household, assumed part of the management, yet she did this with the greatest difficulty and very great annoyances; for her two daughters-in-law were heathen and godless ladies of the house, who despised their mother-in-law as a silly old woman. Besides, it is usual that all daughters-in-law find it annoying to be ruled by their mothers-in-law. But these women were not foreigners; they were natives in this land, who had married Esau, a poor and abject foreigner. Therefore they opposed Rebecca proudly and with the height of contempt. This poor Rebecca lived in great anxiety and in the utmost contempt, as has been stated above in Gen. 26:35 that both were מָרָה, a bitterness, for the two parents. They continually harassed and tormented the very pious woman. For they were the queens in the house. Esau was a junker who was related by affinity to the nobles and important persons of the land. Jacob was an exile shortly to be cast out, for Esau was planning to appoint his own children as his heirs, and undoubtedly his relatives by marriage and his two wives urged him to do this. Hence he is completely sure of his rule and priesthood, for he governs the house in his father's place as his father's deputy. But Rebecca, his very saintly mother, walks in the mire of many waters and suffers many indignities from her daughters-in-law; for the father, who is an old man and has been deprived of his sight, has given up all management.

How much Rebecca suffered in the meantime! How many wrongs and affronts she had to bear without speaking about them! Hence it is not without a reason that she favors and protects Jacob, in order that he may obtain the blessing, while Esau gives orders so proudly in the house, and his relatives by marriage exult with such great arrogance and boast that through this prince Esau even the Hittites themselves wanted to rule. Then Rebecca undoubtedly poured out anxious and fervent prayers tearfully before God when she saw that the glory of the promise was to be transferred to the heathen, namely, to the Hittites. "O God," she cried, "prevent their attempt from succeeding!"

Accordingly, when the community and Esau, the very haughty prince, were flourishing in this way, while Jacob, together with his mother, was despised and thrust aside, Esau had no other persuasion than that he was a king by every divine and human right. To this are added the devotion, the favor, and the beneficence of his father Isaac, which is a confirmation and completely sure evidence. Relying on this, he is no longer at all concerned about having sold and repudiated his birthright. He is smug about everything, as though he had been placed in heaven itself and in Paradise.

Observe, however, how suddenly and unexpectedly the wrath and the judgment of God overwhelm him. His father commands him to go out hunting and to bring him choice food, since he was to be blessed. On that occasion Esau undoubtedly had relatives by marriage and other friends as companions. And so he goes out with dogs and the rest of the crowd of hunters, who congratulated him. And the household also boasted: "Tomorrow Isaac will bless Esau, our prince and priest." Everything was full of joy and exultation. But what happens? Esau returns home with pomp and grand expectation. He offers his father the food he had prepared. Then all things, all hope, and all joys suddenly collapse, and he himself is dashed to the ground as though struck by a thunderbolt from heaven. Therefore he had abundant reason to be angry. To think that such great joy and pomp are so suddenly changed! What fearful and great maledictions he then hurled at his brother! What weeping there was, what confusion, wailing, and dismay of the whole household, of the wives and the relatives by marriage! For he who had been a lord, a king, and a priest at six o'clock in the morning has become a servant by evening. Thus, contrary to all hope and expectation, they are all suddenly deprived of their great hope.

The flesh cannot be patient in a misfortune of this kind. Esau thought: "What shall I do now? The shame is too great for me to be able to bear and endure, to such an extent have I, a king and a priest, been affronted in my father's house. And my brother, who up to this time has been cast aside completely, will now be the lord over me." And he added curses and maledictions. "Ah, let the devil in hell lay on! Let hellfire lay on!" That unexpected downthrow from such great hope could not fail to disturb him most violently.

Accordingly, you see what a great and horrible evil it is to sin smugly and not to repent; for this caused this misfortune of Esau, who, because of God's wrath, was deprived of every heavenly blessing, just as Lucifer fell from heaven before he foresaw or thought of it. When he lost the blessing, as it then was, he at the same time also lost his father and mother and the entire inheritance, together with the kingship and the priesthood. Therefore he is insanely angry and enraged when he says: "The days of mourning for my father are approaching." For this is how he spoke to his relatives by marriage, with whom he took counsel, and to the household, which saw that he was burning with wrath and rage. In addition, his children wept and shed tears. They saw that they had been deprived of and disappointed in their proudest hope. They spurred him on to rage. They said: "You are not going to let so many good things be taken away from you so suddenly, are you?" "I will not permit it," he said, "but I will play havoc with that joy." Such words he undoubtedly bandied about among his relatives by marriage and his wives, those two cancers of Rebecca who inflamed him more when he was already insane as a result of his fury.

And this is the condition and picture of the house of Isaac, the very saintly patriarch. It is in an exceedingly disturbed state on account of the plan of the Holy Spirit, which Rebecca carried out in order that the blessing might be transferred from the older son to the younger. For a very great disturbance had to follow, since all those grand hopes and plans of Esau had been brought to nothing; for he was already in possession of the priesthood and the rule and could not fear his downfall or expulsion. But this is an outstanding example of the divine punishment because of which that exceedingly proud prince and lord suddenly falls, so that in almost one moment he who shortly before had promised himself an eternal rule is brought to the rope.[58] This we should carefully set before our eyes, for the perversity of human nature is such that while we are sinning, we are smug; but when we feel God's wrath and punishment, we are wretched and desperate, just as in the house of Esau there was very great lamentation and wailing. His wives, his children, and the whole household wept aloud. He himself is driven to despair and madness, because the wrath of God is something serious and horrible; for Esau is inflamed to such an extent that he wants to kill his parents and to destroy the church.

42. *But the words of Esau, her older son, were told to Rebecca; so she sent and called Jacob, her younger son, and said to him: Behold, your brother Esau comforts himself by planning to kill you.*

Esau did not conceal this threat; but while his children and wives wept and his relatives by marriage raged in anger and indignation, he said publicly: "Never mind! The joy of Jacob and of my parents will not last long; I shall bring it about that they, too, will grieve and lament with us." When someone of the servants, who was more upright and faithful than the rest, heard these words, he ran directly to Rebecca and reported them to her. And she herself could not have thought anything else than that he would be greatly disturbed and that he had a very just reason for being angry, since he had lived all his 77 years in the sure hope ot possessing the blessing, and his father had intended it for him with the greatest zeal and kindness. All this is now lost. Indeed, it also occurred to Rebecca that she was the source and cause of all these evils and of the horrible confusion, although actually she was not. But Esau's sin, and chiefly God's prophecy, in which it had been stated that "the elder shall serve the younger" (Gen. 25:23), was responsible. Therefore Esau brought this evil upon himself through his own fault; for he offended and despised God, regarded the glory

[58] See p. 118, note 22.

and honor of primogeniture of little value, and sold it at a very cheap price, namely, the red pottage.

Observe, then, how much evil originated from this one sin; for beside the divine prophecy Esau's sin is the cause of all this confusion. And with these two facts Rebecca comforted herself: in the first place, with the divine prophecy; in the second place, with the sin of Esau, who begins to rage and not to repent after he, too, has come to know and feel the wrath of God. Yet to sin and to feel the punishment and not to acknowledge that it is being inflicted by God's just judgment, but only to be indignant and angry about the good thing that was lost—this is not repentance; it is rage against God. In like manner, we today, when we are afflicted by the war with the Turks, by the plague, and by famine, or are harassed in other ways by the devil, all complain about the greatness of the misfortunes. But you would hear no one say: "We have sinned. We have done evil. Lord God, have mercy upon us; be mindful of Thy mercy, which is of old" (cf. Ps. 51:4; 25:6). We do not turn to God, who punishes us. Thus Is. 9:13 has the same complaint: "The people did not turn to Him who smote them, nor seek the Lord of hosts."

Accordingly, we all cry and complain pitiably about the punishment, the fierceness, and the cruelty of the barbarian enemy and about the evils by which we are overwhelmed; but we do not grieve about sin. Therefore our repentance is an Esauitic repentance. But eventually we shall hear what is written in Prov. 1:24-28: [59] "Because I have called and you refused to listen, have streched out My hand and no one has heeded, and you have ignored all My counsel and would have none of My reproof, I also will laugh at your calamity; I will mock when panic strikes you, when panic strikes you like a storm, and your calamity comes like a whirlwind, when distress and anguish come upon you. Then they will call upon Me, but I will not answer." For what is more shameful than that we demand from God safety, deliverence, and a blessing in physical and spiritual matters, and meanwhile practice idolatry in spite of this, kill a brother and parents, and also give free rein to lusts of every kind? This will not end without sure and exceedingly sad punishments. For the same threat occurs in Is. 65:12-13: "Because when I called, you did not answer, when I spoke, you did

---

[59] The original has "Prov. 4."

not listen; but you did what was evil in My eyes and chose what I did not delight in. Therefore thus says the Lord God: 'Behold, My servants shall eat, but you shall be hungry; behold, My servants shall drink, but you shall be thirsty.'"

But the godly and the innocent also have their misfortunes and afflictions, and they are very often involved in common evils; for among so many thousands or in such a great multitude some godly people must always remain. But when they pray, they are not cast aside or forsaken as the ungodly are. No, they experience what is stated in 1 Peter 4:17, namely, that judgment begins with the household of God. The godless, however, must drink the dregs. For when those who pray and worship God from the heart suffer, this is the surest evidence that destruction threatens those who are godless and smug. And the former, of course, taste only a little from the cup of wrath (cf. Rev. 16:19). But what will be the outcome for those who have not believed the Gospel? Thus today we are in the company of those who have deserved destruction and perdition, and we are now experiencing that judgment begins with the household of the Lord; for we are enduring the common tribulations, and they are severe enough, just as Daniel and the other godly people in the Babylonian exile bore the common misfortune. But far harsher things are announced for tyrants and enemies, as the voice of God bears witness in Jer. 49:12 against the Ammonites, the Idumeans, and others: "For thus says the Lord: 'If those who did not deserve to drink the cup must drink it, will you go unpunished? You shall not go unpunished, but you must drink.'"

Therefore in such tribulations the heart must be prepared to be patient, in order that we may take God's judgment in good part; for nothing will harm us, who are repentant, do not participate in the sins of the ungodly, and pray earnestly. But woe to those who will have to drink the dregs! For such people become worse as a result of the punishment ordained for them and do not acknowledge the sin they have committed. They cry out and rage because of the misfortune. They are not sorry for their sin. If you cried out because of sins, God would hear you; but since you hide, excuse, and defend sin, "I will not hear your cry about the punishment," says the Lord. This should be considered in regard to the reason for this very sad and sudden fall of Esau, in order that we may learn to understand and shun the reasons for punishments, and in order that in the common dangers we may retain hope and prayer, lest we be overcome by the misfortunes and desert to the godless.

Accordingly, after Rebecca has received the message that Esau is angry and is breathing out murder against his brother, she addresses her son Jacob and says: "Your brother is comforting himself by planning to kill you. He is seeking revenge by which he may comfort and avenge himself. This is surely very bad comfort. Therefore flee to my brother, lest we tempt the Lord. Yield for a time to Esau's rage, lest occasion be given for his anger." In this way she intervenes as mediator and does not yet despair of appeasing Esau, just as love believes and hopes all things (1 Cor. 13:7). Then she also prayed that his heart might be soothed, and by means of blandishments and gifts among his relatives by marriage and his wives she undoubtedly sought to cause them to conciliate the angry Esau. She also tested the heart of Esau himself with friendly words, in order that he might not rage so much. "Be satisfied with what your father has given you," she said. "You have enough. God will give you other and greater possessions." She made use of plans and blandishments of this kind in order to allay this turmoil, for she was a very shrewd and clever woman. But she did so in a pious and God-fearing manner.

43. *Now therefore, my son, obey my voice; arise, flee to Laban my brother in Haran,*

44. *and stay with him a while, until your brother's fury turns away;*

45. *until your brother's anger turns away, and he forgets what you have done to him; then I will send and fetch you from there. Why should I be bereft of you both in one day?*

The Hebrew word חֵמָה denotes a violent anger, which is a glowing heat, as it were. It is from יָחַם, "to heat," "to glow," as the poet describes anger: "Wrath becomes inflamed, and resentment flares up in his sturdy bones." [60] In this way Esau, too, burned with anger. Consequently, Rebecca thinks that her son should consider flight, lest it seem that she was rashly exposing him to danger if she kept him with her; for a heart inflamed with anger has the audacity to do anything. Thus it is commonly said that anger is a brief madness.[61] Hence one must get out of the way of madness,

[60] Vergil, *Aeneid*, IX, 66.
[61] Horace, *Epistles*, I, 2, 62.

lest an angry person vent his rage on you and inflict harm that can never be healed afterwards. It was wise on the part of Rebecca to consider and say: "We do not want to test God and say: 'He who has blessed you will also preserve you.' To be sure, God does what He has resolved; but He does so through means." Therefore she believes that the church and the blessing must be protected. Nevertheless, she makes use of the means God has granted for avoiding the danger.

This example should be carefully noted on account of those who refer everything to predestination and thus do away with all the activities and means God has ordained.[62] For this is what they say: "If these things must happen, they will happen of necessity, even without work on my part." Or if they should expose themselves to needless dangers, they promise themselves protection and defense, since God would do this of necessity in accordance with His promise. These thoughts are wicked and impious, because God wants you to make use of the means you have at your disposal. He wants you to embrace the opportunity presented to you and to use it, since it is through you that He wants to accomplish the things He has ordained. For thus He wanted your father to beget you and your mother to nourish you, although He would have been able to create and to nourish you without parents. Thus in common life the necessary works have to be performed. One has to sow, plant, seek provisions, etc. Afterwards God will do what He wants. But if you say: "I will not give milk to the child; for if it ought to live, it will live," you will deceive yourself and sin grievously. For God has given breasts to the mother in order that she may nurse her child. Although He could nourish the infant without milk, He does not want to do so. Consequently, one should make use of the means ordained by Him.

Thus Rebecca could have concluded with certainty: "My son Jacob will not be killed. Nor will the blessing be revoked." Nevertheless, she does not neglect her duty, but she says to Jacob: "Flee to my brother Laban until your brother's anger ceases and is allayed. Although God could protect you, every opportunity the devil might have must be forestalled. You see how your brother is now wandering about in the house in a towering rage, and if he were to take hold of you, he would undoubtedly kill you. Or if

---

[62] See p. 256.

Esau's heart were to be appeased by his father, yet there is no less danger from his relatives by marriage, his wives, and his children, who could not be so easily placated. Even though Esau has been placated, they will design evil against you, since they know that they are doing something that pleases their father Esau. Therefore since you are able to flee to my brother and to avoid this danger, make use of this opportunity and plan. Meanwhile we shall placate both the relatives by marriage and the daughters-in-law. We shall instruct them concerning the divine will, namely, that God foresaw and ordained this in this manner. Just go away for a time. I shall exert myself that their hearts may be appeased. I shall go to them, talk with them, and pray to God."

This is outstanding prudence on the part of the very saintly woman, who takes excellent care of herself and of her son in such a great disturbance, which she has stirred up, and in such great danger. For both the house and the church of Isaac were greatly disturbed and confused. Nor could hearts embittered by just resentment become gentle so suddenly. Rebecca sees this. Nevertheless, she does not tempt God. Nor does she despair. For both things must be done: God must not be tempted in dangers, and one must not despair of deliverance.

This serves to teach and comfort the church, whose image is presented here. For it is always in very great dangers and evils —dangers and evils which, according to human reason, one cannot escape; and "Save, Lord; we are perishing!" (Matt. 8:25) is its usual cry and label. Nevertheless, it does not perish. It is tossed about by unceasing waves and storms, so that nothing else than destruction is in sight. And we cry out: "We are perishing!" Nevertheless, there is safety in God. Thus in such great difficulties Rebecca and Jacob rely on God's promise and eventually surmount and overcome these difficulties.

Then one should also learn this from this example, in order that we may not despair immediately about people who sin but may consider that word which Christ speaks in reply to His disciples when they urged Him not to return to Judea because shortly before this the Jews had wanted to stone Him. He asks (John 11:9): "Are there not twelve hours in the day?" This means that in time hearts change, are mollified, and are placated, with the result that they amend their wickedness. In time that rage and heat of anger is allayed, and it is surely likely that Esau was pacified to a great extent during the twelve or more years Jacob remained in Mesopotamia. In addition, there was his temporal success, which was by no means diminished. Indeed, his godless presumption that he would keep the blessing in spite of all was increased, since the opposite of what was in Jacob's blessing was clearly taking place. For although he had been appointed heir of the royal authority and of the priesthood, he does not have very much success, because he is driven into exile, and his lot and his entire life seem more like a curse than a blessing. But Esau remains in possession, since Isaac, after being deprived of his sight, had given up the management of the household and the church. Therefore Esau remains lord of the house during Jacob's absence and engages in his usual works, just as he had done up to this time.

When the two daughters-in-law and the relatives by marriage saw this, they, too, were easily satisfied. They thought: "Well, let him who has been blessed go. We remain in the house. He is a fugitive." And this confidence was greatly increased, since Jacob was away for so many years. They said: "Perhaps old Isaac was out of his mind when he was deceived by the stupid Rebecca. This blessing did not please God; and the fact that he is forced to be an exile is an important sign that he was not blessed. We are the wives of the prince and priest; we are the daughters-in-law of Isaac, to whom the promise was made. Consequently, we shall not bother about that fugitive." Such undoubtedly were the thoughts of all who were in the household of Esau; for when there is prosperity and a false persuasion about the blessing is added, people say at once: "God is well disposed toward us." But prosperity and a godless opinion make people proud and smug. Thus it is possible that Esau, together with his wives and children, was also mollified when he thought, yes, was fully convinced, that Jacob's blessing was of no use, since the latter was not being protected by a divine miracle, but God was forsaking him and permitted him to be driven out of the house, even by his father and his mother. Therefore he could not conclude anything else than that God had made this blessing ineffectual.

But we should not think that this took place without a severe trial and the utmost grief of the parents. Surely Rebecca's faith again began to be in trouble, for it grieved her greatly that Esau remained in his former power during Jacob's absence. Yet the sentiments of such godly parents cannot be adequately explained or weighed. My own faith surely would not be able to bear that much. She has now been a mother for 77 years, for that many years have elapsed since the prophecy was spoken when she still had the twins in her womb. "The elder shall serve the younger," it stated (Gen. 25:23). During these years she waited anxiously for the blessing, and Jacob waited with her. For this reason he lived in a state of celibacy, without a wife and children, as one who was cast aside and scorned. Meanwhile Esau married two wives when he was 40 years old, and now he has children and children's children. He is the lord, prince, and priest in the house. Rebecca has been compelled to bear and look at this every day for such a long time. Nevertheless, she holds out even while her two daughters-in-law are in control. They were two sources of bitterness for her, because they tormented the aged Isaac and the true lady of the house; for Rebecca had to turn over to them the keys and all the management. Therefore consider whether this faith and hope of Rebecca, who waits so patiently for the blessing, is not outstanding.

What about Isaac? In addition to various trials and vexations, he had the misfortune and the almost unbearable cross that in his old age he was deprived of his sight. In his venerable old age he does not see the sun and other things that were necessary and pleasing for him to look at. Occasionally he hears complaints from his wife Rebecca, from his son Jacob, or from the rest of the household about the arrogant rule and the outrages of the Esauites. This he can deplore and complain about, but he cannot correct it. And from the antecedent one deduces the consequent, namely, that his son Esau has degenerated completely, since he was captivated more by the religion and the customs of the heathen than by the godliness and the teaching of his father; and because his daughters-in-law were heathen, they were also hostile to the true doctrine and were quite insolent on account of their husband's authority.

Therefore the faith of these most saintly parents is tried and exercised to such an extent that our hearts are unable either to grasp or understand it by reflecting on it; and this continued, not for 10 or 20 but for more than 100 years. But what a great misfortune it is for such a great man, whom God loved to such an extent that He blessed him and promised him the inheritance of the kingdom of heaven and of eternal life, to sit in darkness, in sorrow, and in vexations of every kind for so many years! God lets him be deprived of his eyesight and be tortured by so many great troubles. Why, then, shall we murmur? Why shall we be angry with God if some adversity or some misfortunes befall us? Although those afflictions of the patriarchs are nothing when compared with Christ's suffering, yet they affect our hearts more; for Christ's suffering is not perfectly understood by us, and we do not believe that He was such a wretched and abject man as He actually was. Furthermore, everybody thinks that since He was God, He could easily bear and overcome everything. And surely there is nobody who could compare himself to Isaac and could show the same endurance and steadfastness in misfortunes. The faith of these parents was surely put to a test and found purer than gold, and in this faith and hope they finally obtained what they longed for.

The Hebrew text has יָמִים אֲחָדִים, *diebus unis*. Our translation into Latin has *paucis diebus*, "a few days." In German it would be *ein oder zwen tage*, "one or two days." At the end she tells why she orders him to go away: "Why should I be bereft of you both in one day?" For the very sagacious woman sees that if Esau were to kill his brother, he, too, as a murderer, would have to be punished with death in accordance with the law universally approved from the beginning. Or he, like Cain, would be driven into exile or would be killed by a man, that is, by the government. But at this point Rebecca seems to be in doubt about the truth of the divine promise and blessing, since she sends her son away because she is afraid of his angry brother. For why does she not keep him with her, since she knows that he should expect with certainty that God will keep him safe?

I answer as above: Of course, Rebecca could have said: "Stay with me; have no fear at all of your angry brother, because the Lord will be concerned about you. He will protect you in accordance with the blessing." But she does not do this; for by her example she wants to teach that one should believe everything God says and put all hope in Him, but should not tempt God. Her faith is altogether sure and firm because of the word and promise he has, and she could have concluded: "My son has the blessing. Let that happen which must happen. He cannot perish. I will let him stay at home." This is what has been stated earlier about godless and irreligious people who refer everything to some fated governance of God.[63] But this godly and sensible woman makes use of the means that are at hand and have been provided by God. Thus one should not say: "I do not want to eat. I do not want to drink. If I am to live, I shall live. If I am not to live, food or drink will be of no benefit." Likewise: "I am a man. Therefore I shall be a father even if I do not marry." Who would not regard someone with such thoughts as mad? For you must make use of the gifts of God that have been put at your disposal. You must not leave it to predestination or to a promise. We should not speculate on the outcome of affairs without the Word; on the other hand, we should have no doubt about a promise. Where there is no promise, there nothing should be attempted; but one should follow the example of Rebecca, who could rely on this promise: "Jacob will live because he must become the father of descendants." But she does not despise the means that are offered. Indeed, she makes use of them to enable her son to escape the danger. This is surely what it means to believe and yet not to tempt God.

On the other hand, not to believe God when He promises and to tempt Him are one and the same thing, and a very serious sin is committed on both sides; because God wants us to make use of the creatures He has given, and He has given them for us to use. Consequently, one should not tempt God as the Jews tempted Him in the wilderness and were severely punished. This example is also adduced by St. Paul in 1 Cor. 10:9. And one must detest that exceedingly pernicious madness of the fanatics which, in spite of all, is becoming widespread today, as has been stated previously. For such people undermine all godliness by leaving everything to predestination even though they have no word on which to base what they do.

Furthermore, Rebecca sends Jacob [64] away not only that he may avoid his brother's fury, but also because she is thinking about providing a wife for her son, as will follow later. Nor does she think as the fanatics do. She does not say: "He has the blessing. It is all the same whether he remains in the land or not. Whether he marries or not, he will nevertheless be the father

---

[63] Cf. p. 42.

[64] The Weimar text reads "Joseph" here, but obviously "Jacob" is meant.

of the Seed and will have everlasting offspring. Or even if he marries a Canaanite woman—and I regard the Canaanite women as unworthy of this honor—yet the Lord will bring it about that she becomes a worthy mother of this Child." She has no such thought, but she shuns these Canaanite women, from whom she has always turned away; and for Isaac's sake she does as much as she can to induce Jacob to take a wife from her own people.

Hence in all our affairs and actions this example of Rebecca should admonish us to do what lies in our power, that is, to make use of the means in accordance with the promise and later to entrust the outcome and the predetermination to God. For you have the Word and the commands of God; and you should know that you must walk according to them, lest you stumble. But those who stray outside the promise and devise a special outcome for themselves on the basis of the divine promise lose both God's command and His promise. But this is contempt for the God who commands and promises. Rebecca, a woman with very much experience, wants to avoid this great sin. Although she was now sure about the promise, yet she was concerned about the outcome. Therefore she makes use of the means that had to be employed. She goes to her husband and tells him where their son should seek a wife. Isaac sends their son away in order that it may be possible for him to avoid the Canaanite women and to take some other woman as his wife—a woman born from his own stock. Besides, Moses makes no further mention later on of the fact that she promises to send someone to ask Jacob to come back. And it seems that she dies in the course of those 20 years during which Jacob served Laban. For this is the last mention of Rebecca in this entire account.

46. *Then Rebecca said to Isaac: I am weary of my life because of the Hittite women. If Jacob marries one of the Hittite women such as these, one of the women of the land, what good will my life be to me?*

Observe once more the prudence and shrewdness of the godly woman, who does not tell the father why she is sending their son away. She does not point out how great the misfortune and disturbance of the house is, namely, that brother wants to kill brother; but with godly shrewdness she conceals this tragedy from her husband. From this one should derive moral instruction — surely very fine and beautiful — in order that we may learn to be peaceable and to be frank, candid, and skillful in interpreting, extenuating, covering, and correcting even what has been wrongly said and done by others, to put the best construction on things, not to aggravate but to excuse and mitigate even the worst cause, as this one is, when a brother plots against the life of a brother. Rebecca alone takes it on herself, shoulders it, and remedies it in such a manner that both the plan and the wicked attempt are thwarted and Isaac, who is old, gray, and venerable, is not saddened. If Isaac had found out, he could have been consumed and killed by sadness of heart; for it is likely, as we have pointed out above on the basis of the account, that during so many years he endured numerous indignities from his son, who ruled with such arrogance. And if this final misfortune had been added, he would have wasted away because of the distress and grief of his heart.

Therefore Rebecca advances a different reason for this departure of Jacob, namely, marriage. She does not want him to contract marriage in that land with the daughters of Heth but wants him to wed some other woman, who is of her own lineage. For a godly and believing person must have a healing tongue, as is stated in Prov. 12:18: "There is one whose rash words are like sword thrusts, but the tongue of the wise brings healing." Therefore let us accustom ourselves to be pious mediators in evil causes, in accordance with Rebecca's example, and not to inflict too much harm on him who sins and him who is guilty, just as she wisely takes care of her son Esau. She does not want to accuse him before his father, and at the same time she spares her very pious husband, who is old and sightless, lest she perturb him. She prefers to suffer and swallow this misfortune herself.

If she had been a wicked woman, she would have blown on the fire and would have poured oil and pitch on the flame; for this is what perverse natures that are inclined beyond measure to calumniate and to revile are wont to do. But the tongue of a righteous man is a tongue of life; for he speaks well of God and uses his tongue to compose dissensions, to mitigate and allay offenses, and to buoy up and strengthen distressed hearts. Thus a beautiful example is related about Monica, the mother of Augustine.[65] If at

---

[65] Cf. Augustine, *Confessions,* Book IX, ch. 9, par. 21.

any time quarrels had arisen among the women who were her neighbors, and she heard many bitter and harsh statements made on both sides, she did not spread them abroad or carry them from one to the other; but she carefully concealed them, and meanwhile, when she came to one of those who hated one another, she pretended that the other woman had spoken of her in the best and most proper manner. In this way, although the other woman had no knowledge or information about the matter, she would be appeased, with the result that she rid her heart of all offense and grudge. Thus the tongues of godly people must also be healing—tongues that "can cure and likewise mitigate and show mercy," as is stated in Ecclus. 36:25.

But a harsh and abusive tongue often stirs up a huge sea from one little drop and a huge fire from one spark. Therefore let us shun that vice and follow the example of Rebecca and Monica, in order that when we hear the worst, we may say the best and explain in the best way, unless it happens that someone's welfare is endangered because of the other person's implacable hatred. Then he who is in danger should be warned, in order that he may be able to beware of the violence or the plot of his adversary. Thus he who reported Esau to his mother Rebecca in this murderous quarrel did what was best and by that very fact was a healing tongue, because he ordered him whom the danger was threatening to get out of the way. Consequently, plots and murders should not be kept secret but should be revealed. This messenger who reported Jacob's danger from his brother should not have said: "Esau is well satisfied. He has nothing evil in mind. He loves his brother." But the devil in the other court,[66] who urged and inflamed his prince to commit murder, had to be accused and revealed. For if he had not given the information, he would have aided the murderer; but because he brought the message, he prevented the murder.

This is moral instruction, which is transmitted here with profit; for we see in this example that both the plot and the murderer are thwarted. And everything is kept secret with amazing cleverness, lest the murderous threats of Esau be reported to his aged father. And Rebecca surely gives a very good reason; for Jacob had already been appointed heir, the blessing had been bestowed

[66] The term "court devil" was a favorite with Luther; cf. *Luther's Works*, 22, p. 246; 13, pp. 146—224.

on him, and the entire church had been entrusted to him. "Now a staff to lean on must still be put into his hand," she said to Isaac; "that is, he should have with him a wife as a companion and a help." This is a very proper statement, not only in regard to what is useful and proper but also in regard to what is necessary; for if he is destined to enjoy the blessing, he must have a wife. Up to this time he has lived without a wife, since he was cast aside and did not count. Now Esau has been cast aside. Consequently, a wife must be given to Jacob, who has obtained the blessing and later will assume the entire rule. With this rhetoric she persuades Isaac to send their son away, for it is an argument based on necessity — an argument which surpasses all arguments with regard to what is useful and honorable. Thus in Gellius we find the proper statement of Metellus that if we want to have citizens, we must also have wives, etc.; for marriages must be preserved for the sake of descendants.[67]

"But why do you not betroth one of the Canaanite maidens to him?" "They do not please me," she says. And the rhetoric she employs is different from that which is useful and proper. "I do not want him to marry a woman like those two daughters-in-law of ours. You have seen, my dear Isaac, how much we have suffered during these 30 years from the wives of Esau, how they have trodden me underfoot but have despised you and have behaved with the utmost arrogance, yes, in an exceedingly tyrannical manner. If you want me to be safe, do not let him marry a heathen woman from the daughters of this land or from other Canaanites; for they hate us, since they hear that we have the promise of this land. This they cannot bear. Therefore they want to drive us out by force and injustices of every kind."

Moreover, Scripture does not expressly mention her brother Laban, to whom she was about to send her son. Perhaps Isaac asked: "Whence, then, shall we choose a maiden for him?" Then she replied: "Let him go to my brother Laban." To this advice the aged Isaac gave his assent, and he entrusted everything to her judgment. For Rebecca now governs the house, but with great difficulty and danger, since matters are so confused and in such a bad state.

---

[67] Aulus Gellius, *Attic Nights*, I, 6. (At this point the translation by George V. Schick ends, and that of Paul D. Pahl begins.)

Accordingly, after this consultation Jacob is sent into exile. He who has been blessed and appointed as the heir is cast out of the house and flees from his enraged brother. A beautiful blessing indeed, and certainly an excellent beginning of the promises he holds! "For I have been appointed heir," he could have thought, "and I am being cast out. And he who has been cast out stays and gains possession of everything in the house. How does this agree with the promise and with such a rich blessing?"

This, then, is one of the wonderful examples of the divine government by which God shows that He requires confidence in His Word and promises, even if the opposite of what is contained in the promise happens. He does so in order that we may accustom ourselves to trust in God in things that are absent and are placed far out of our sight. For Jacob has the promised blessing, but he has it in accordance with faith, which is a matter of things that are hoped for, not of things that are visible (cf. Heb. 11:1). Thus I believe that God, who promises, loves me, has regard for me, cares for me, and will hear me; and this I regard as something present and at hand, although it is not visible. Therefore Jacob lives in faith alone. He is wretchedly cast out, is lonely and destitute, and has nothing in his hand but a staff and a morsel of bread in a little sack.

This is the beginning of the blessing, for what is begun through faith is not yet in one's possession but is hoped for. Thus God has promised us eternal life and has given absolution and Baptism. This grace I have at hand through Christ; but I await eternal life, which is promised in the Word. Those who live by this Word are saintly and blessed; but the godless live only by bread, not by the Word. Therefore they do not believe and do not wait for eternal life. Jacob waited 77 years for the blessing that was to come. Now, after he has obtained it, he is forced to go into exile and begins his rule and priesthood with a very great cross, with a very great calamity, and with extreme poverty. He is forced to be cut off from his very dear parents, and his parents are cut off from their dearly beloved son for such a long time.

If a person looks at and hears this only in passing, he considers it unimportant and easy. But one learns by experience how difficult and full of trials it is to leave parents, a blessing, and an inheritance, and to flee to a place of wretchedness and poverty. This is the wonderful government of God which the flesh can by no means bear, for it is a government that consists in faith. But this is written as an example for us in order that we may learn to depend on the invisible God and to be satisfied with the fact that at all events we have the comprehensible Word of this invisible and incomprehensible God. And let us order our lives in such a way that we have nothing from our invisible Creator but the Word and the sacraments, likewise parents and magistrates, through whom this life is governed in accordance with the Word. And let us wait for the promise itself in hope and long-suffering, for God will not lie. Nor will He deceive us. To be sure, the flesh believes with difficulty; for it is accustomed to things that are at hand and is moved by the things it feels and sees. But the flesh must be crucified and mortified; it must be withdrawn from the things perceived by the senses and must learn, in order that it may be able to live and act in accordance with the things that are invisible and are not perceived by the senses. This is the mortification of the perception of the flesh, which simply wants to sleep smugly on both ears [68] in matters that are at hand and visible. Therefore when it has felt the opposite, it is vexed and sorrowful.

Therefore this example should be set before men's eyes to show how Jacob is appointed king and priest, and how he is invested with his rule and priesthood. For such is the wretched pomp and ritual connected with anointing and investing this king. He is not clothed with a royal robe, is not adorned with a fillet or a royal crown. No scepter is put into his hands. But he is equipped with a bag and a staff and is driven into exile. The blessing, however, is left to his brother Esau, to whom it did not by any means pertain. But finally, after Jacob has been mortified through faith in the invisible God, the visible blessing follows, the seed of Jacob takes possession of the land, and Christ is born from that seed — Christ, the eternal King and Priest whose kingdom and priesthood is contained in this blessing.

Thus David was anointed as king over Israel after Saul had been condemned and rejected by God (1 Sam. 16:1, 13 ff.). But in spite of all this Saul remains in the rule as before and governs successfully at home and against his enemies. Indeed, he persecutes David himself in a cruel way as a deceitful man and one

[68] Cf. Terence, *Heautontimorumenos,* II, 3, 101.

who is plotting against the kingdom. In the meantime David, like a fugitive and an exile, wanders about in the land where he had been declared king by God. Thus history testifies that he wandered about in this manner for 10 whole years while Saul pursued him and plotted against him every day. Surely to be an exile for 10 years in one's own land does not seem to be ruling, does it? What could be stranger, what more shameful, than to be declared king without a kingdom, without a scepter, and without a fixed abode, yes, to be bereft not only of the land and the kingdom but also of one's own home, wife, and children?

But Christ's example goes beyond all this. Did He not, according to the prophet (Is. 53:3), become the most despised and rejected of men? When He wants to ascend into heaven and to enter into His glory, when He is about to overcome death, sin, and the devil, He is nailed to the cross, dies, and is buried as the most rejected of all men and demons. This is not an entrance into glory or a victory and triumph over death, is it? It surely is; for these are God's hidden ways, which must be understood not according to the flesh and human understanding but according to Scripture and Christ Himself, who says to His disciples (Luke 24:26): "Was it not necessary that the Christ should suffer these things and enter into His glory?"

In the same manner Jacob had to be an exile for 20 years and afterwards at last to become a king and priest. David had to be driven hither and thither for 10 years and seek out the most varied byways where he might hide in safety for one night, at times for one hour. He is not a king appointed and confirmed by God, is he? Yet you hear him praising his kingdom in a wonderful way, as he sings (Ps. 63:11): "But the king shall rejoice in God; all who swear by Him shall glory; for the mouths of liars will be stopped." That is, those who think that he is a king appointed and anointed by God will exult. But where were they? For the whole kingdom and all power were in Saul's hands. David himself did not have even a footbreadth in the land.

Thus we who believe the Word of God are the church. We have a most certain promise, into which we have been called and baptized, and by which we are nourished and sustained; we have the Sacrament of the Altar and the power of the Keys. But we are not Christians and have not been baptized in order that we may get possession of this land. Nor have we been baptized and born again into this life; we have been baptized and born again into eternal life. But what happens in regard to us too? Surely this, that when the church must be glorified and brought to those eternal joys which it awaits in the Word and in hope, then it is subjected to countless persecutions of tyrants and devils; it is harassed and torn by false brethren in many most pitiable ways. This is not what being led to eternal life means, is it? Indeed, it means being exposed to eternal misery. Yet hearts must be buoyed up and strengthened against this way of the cross. For we have the Word and the promise. Therefore the glory that has been promised is sure to follow. And meanwhile the church lives and is preserved by faith, which concludes firmly that GOD does not lie. And it learns this wonderful wisdom which is hidden from the flesh and reason, namely, that God is wonderful in His saints (Ps. 68:35) and that His counsels are wonderful. This is also why our Lord and Leader Jesus Christ has His name and is called WONDERFUL in Is. 9:6.

Accordingly, this points out that we should be instructed, in order that if we want to live in a godly manner, we may establish a way of life that is different from the way to which the world and the flesh are accustomed. For we must depend simply on the invisible God and give thanks to God with joy that we have the Word of God, which makes the promise. Concerning this Word Peter says (2 Peter 1:19): "And we have the prophetic Word made more sure. You will do well to pay attention to this as a lamp shining in a dark place, until the day dawns and the morning star rises in your hearts." For the Word is the light of our life. Otherwise we have nothing of the glory. I know that I have been baptized; I know that I have eaten the body and blood of Christ, that I have been absolved, called, and taught by the Word of the Gospel. I have nothing more of eternal life. I do not yet have a glorified body, which surpasses the splendor of the sun and the stars. No, I have a heart that is still weighed down by many great evils and terrors. I carry around a body that is exposed to many infirmities and to death. Nothing is less apparent in the body as well as in the soul than eternal life. But the promise will not deceive us. Therefore let us cling to and persist in faith and hope, and let us be content with the Word which promises. In addition, we have this external life and fellowship; we have parents, magistrates, the external ministry of the Word, and the external goods that are necessary for this life. All this is a preparation and an approach, as it were, to the life to come.

This is the proper and chief doctrine of the church. It has been handed down by the Holy Spirit. The world and the flesh do not know it. It teaches us that we are lords and heirs of eternal life in no other way than the way in which Jacob was an heir of the blessing. When he had obtained it, he was sent into exile from the land and the house of his father. For this is the way the Divine Majesty deals with His saints, and this is the faith of the saints concerning which we have spoken up to this point. Now matters pertaining to morals follow, likewise the fruits of faith.

CHAPTER TWENTY-EIGHT

1. *Isaac called Jacob and blessed him, and charged him: You shall not marry one of the Canaanite women.*

2. *Arise, go to Paddan-aram to the house of Bethuel, your mother's father; and take as wife from there one of the daughters of Laban, your mother's brother.*

THE first part of this chapter is not theological, for it does not relate examples or spiritual doctrine concerning faith and other spiritual acts of worship. Yet the things dealt with here require and include both faith and the fear of God. But it is a section pertaining to morals. It deals with marriage, a topic that should be retained in the church and should be diligently urged because of the necessity and the dignity of marriage. For after the doctrine of the Gospel and faith, which is the proper doctrine of the church, marriage should be honored and respected above all. And this should be done because the world and the flesh do not understand what marriage is and how highly it should be esteemed. To be sure, men usually define it in the following way: "Marriage is the union or companionship of man and woman; it maintains inseparable companionship for life." [1] But this is not the whole definition, for the final cause and the efficient cause are lacking. It is taken only from the material cause, for the union of man and woman is material. But the following definition is truer and is complete: "Marriage is the lawful and divine union of one man and one woman. It has been ordained for the purpose of calling upon God, for the preservation and education of offspring, and for the administration of the church and the state."

Therefore in the Christian doctrine, in which, after the doctrine of the Gospel and faith, we teach how we should conduct

[1] *Corpus juris canonici, Causa* 27, *Quaestio* 3, cap. 3, Richter-Friedberg (cf. p. 154, note 47), I, 1063.

ourselves in a godly and honorable manner in this life, marriage is the first and chief thing; for it is the beginning and origin of the whole life. And Satan rages no less against this way of life than against the church. This is apparent from the fact that a proper and salutary marriage and mutual love are very rare not only among married people themselves but also so far as the children and the neighbors are concerned. For it is hedged in by thorns and thistles. At the beginning, to be sure, this is not apparent to young people, when, impelled by love and blind lust, they rush rashly into marriage. But afterwards, when they feel and experience troubles and difficulties of every kind, they repent too late and in vain.

Therefore Christians should so prepare themselves and so arrange their life that they do not consider marriage a rash or fortuitous matter depending on our judgment and a fortuitous outcome but regard it as a lawful and divine union. Clear proof of this is the fact that God created man and woman, and that neither a man alone nor a woman alone is born, but that both man and woman are born. Therefore this union has its origin in the first birth, and for this reason it is truly lawful and divine. Furthermore, God did not institute marriage for the sake of lust and the pleasures of the flesh. This is not the final cause, but marriage serves a twofold purpose: in the first place, to be a remedy against lust; in the second place—and this is more important—to be a source and origin of the human race, in order that offspring may be born and the human race may be propagated, or, as the jurists say, to replenish the city.[2] But from the Holy Scriptures one should add the purpose of bringing up children in the discipline and fear of the Lord, in order that they may be equipped to govern the church and the state.

Therefore the godly should be careful to maintain and observe this chief point, that both sexes were created by GOD for lifelong, inseparable union and companionship; that is, it is GOD'S will, by which He wants us men and women to be lawfully united, in order that we may bring up offspring to serve the church and God. When we firmly retain this, we shall also more easily bear and overcome all the troubles and difficulties to which married people are exposed in this unhappy life. For ever since man was

---

[2] The Latin phrase is *ad replendam civitatem.*

subjected to death and Satan through original sin, Satan does not cease to vex and afflict married people horribly both in body and in soul. This is what mars this kind of life so much and makes it so troublesome, odious, and hateful that nature shrinks from marriage in no other way than it shrinks from the cross, as the examples and the exceedingly foul words of the heathen testify. And today you could hear many who studiously assemble all the disadvantages and all the difficulties by which they allow themselves to be alienated from the thought of marriage.

Nor do we think that men should be forced into marriage reluctantly and against their will. For if you have the gift of being able to abstain from it and to avoid it without sin, abstain from it by all means, if you can do so without sin. But if you cannot avoid being joined to a woman without sinning, use the remedy shown by God. And if you do not seek the function of bringing children into being, at least seek the remedy against sin, in order that fornication and adultery may be avoided as well as pollutions and promiscuous lusts. For there is more than enough misery in the fact that we are oppressed by misfortunes of every kind, by sin and death. Do not heap sin on sin and load yourself with an evil conscience by committing other misdeeds. Yet, they say, marriage is a way of life too wretched and too troublesome! I reply: It is a twofold way of life: a life of sin and a life of punishment. Now consider which is better, to live in punishment without sins or, on the other hand, in sins without punishment. Reason is so corrupt that it cannot bear those punishments for sin with equanimity. Therefore it seeks the things that are agreeable, joyful, and pleasant; but it flees the cross and troubles. Thus when Socrates was asked whether it was better to marry or not to marry, he replied: "Whatever you do, you will regret it. If you marry an ugly woman, you will have punishment; if you marry a woman who is beautiful, you will have her in common." [3] He looked only at the punishment and the misuse.

But a Christian should resolve as follows: The punishment must be despised, and every annoyance must be removed from one's eyes. Besides, one must venture in the name of the Lord. For one must think of a life without sins, without uncleanness,

---

[3] The wife of Socrates, Xanthippe, was known, perhaps unjustly, as a shrew; hence this comment.

without defilement and stains, in order that you may be able to have a good conscience before God. For one should not hope for the kingdom, blessedness, or eternal life in this life. Original sin, the weakness of the flesh, and the devil do not allow this. But if wretchedness must indeed be borne, we should bear it with God rather than with the devil. For although those who flee the burdens of marriage live a pleasant and agreeable life, have their harlots, whom they sometimes cast aside and sometimes receive as they please, what kind of conscience are we to think that such men have? Surely a very evil one. And, what is most serious by far, they also endure the same annoyances. Indeed, they endure more of them. They are plagued more cruelly by harlots than they would be by their wives. Therefore they bear a twofold punishment. They bear the one that is common, and to it they add the punishment that is eternal.

Therefore after the dogmas of the church have been taught, these matters concerning marriage should also be taught and carefully inculcated in the church in order that men may know how to live without sin in this life. Then the hearts of godly men should also be buoyed up and exhorted to [4] despise the annoyances of marriage. For a husband should behave as a man not only at night but also at other times in enduring the punishments and the will of God, in bearing and swallowing the impudence of the household, the wrongs of neighbors, and whatever other troubles occur. Therefore the best men and the best women should be chosen for marriage. Thus Abraham and the other saintly fathers excelled in strength both of body and of spirit. The others, who fear the burdens and annoyances of marriage and for this reason abstain from it, do exactly what is stated in the proverb. "They go from the smoke into the fire." [5] For they seek a kind of life different from that which has been born in sin. But there they find the devil and hell, because they are not able to escape lust, the disease of origin, sin, and death, which clings to the flesh and the heart.

Therefore take heart, and bear in mind that this life is nothing else than misery itself. You will overcome the troubles, toils, and difficulties of this misery if you look to God, your Creator and Father, to whose will and ordinance you should submit yourself

---

[4] We have supplied the word *ad,* which is missing from the Weimar text.

[5] Ammianus Marcellinus, *Res gestae,* XIV, 11—12.

in humility and patience by concluding as follows: "I believe in God, who has created me a man; and I shall thank Him that I have His Word and that it has pleased Him for me to be a husband, to be a wife, in order that I may bring up offspring and govern the household, and that through the Gospel I have the promise of eternal life and consolation in this present life." Thus Paul says in 1 Tim. 4:8: "Godliness is of value in every way, as it holds promise for the present life and also for the life to come." And in Rom. 15:4 he writes: "Whatever was written ... was written for our instruction, that by steadfastness and encouragement of the Scriptures we might have hope."

In this manner we should learn to think and judge more properly about marriage than the flesh and the world are accustomed to do. And we should exhort the youth to suffer and bear with equanimity whatever evils occur. They should accustom themselves to prayer and say: "Lord God, I am Thy creature, created a man by Thee and ordained to this kind of life in which I am now constantly entangled in many evils and difficulties. But grant that I may truly acknowledge that I am Thy creature and that Thou art my Father and Creator. And grant that I may await help and protection from Thee."

Such a prayer is necessary for all married people, because we all experience the cross and the troubles that have been imposed on us. And would that one day celibacy may be removed from the establishments of the priests and the bishops, and that they may be permitted or commanded to marry, just as the ministers of our churches live piously and honorably in matrimony. Then they would not gaze with longing at bishoprics and canonries. But this wish of ours is futile. They are beasts of the field and the dregs of the earth.

This had to be said about marriage at the beginning of this chapter because Moses narrates how Isaac summoned his son Jacob and spoke with him about setting up a household and taking a wife. And the marriage began with God's strength, ordinance, and call. But what kind of miseries and annoyances he will have in marriage we shall see in what follows. For in the whole marriage he has nothing of his own, nothing joyful and pleasant, except offspring. Otherwise he is exceedingly wretched; he lives in exile and serves his father-in-law Laban, who treats him shamefully.

But when God, through the mouth of the father, orders Jacob himself to take a wife, this is the ordinance of and the call to marriage. But the father adds another commandment, namely, that he should not choose a wife from the Canaanites but should rather take a wife for himself from the daughters of Laban. Accordingly, this passage pertains to the teaching about the authority of parents and the consent they must give to the contracting of marriages. For we have rejected and condemned clandestine betrothals and marriages, for since the rebirth of the completely clear light of the Gospel we know that marriage is sacred and permissible, and that it is a divine ordinance. It is not disgraceful or dishonorable to become a spouse, as we thought in former times because we had been led into error by the monks. No, it is honorable and sacred. We know, of course, that it has been horribly dishonored by lust, and for this reason many considered it disgraceful to court a girl and to contract a marriage, as though it were something foul and unclean. That work of procreating children was not distinguished from other sins, from fornication and adultery. But thanks to God's kindness we have now learned and are sure that marriage is honorable, as is stated in Heb. 13:4: "Let marriage be held in honor among all, and let the marriage bed be undefiled." And we are also sure that it is God's will and institution that everyone should have his own spouse, who has been lawfully joined to him. Therefore there is no reason why we should shrink from this kind of life or why, deterred by shame and modesty, we should enter into it secretly and stealthily, contrary to the honor and the will of our parents. A girl should not be afraid to approach her parents and to ask them to give her an honorable young man in marriage. And parents have now been properly trained and are prepared to counsel their children. There are also godly pastors and magistrates who, by reason of their authority, are able to persuade parents not to show themselves hard and difficult.

Therefore those secret betrothals should be avoided, and the very sacred covenant of marriage should be made with honor to God and with respect for parents. A clear example of this doctrine is set forth in this passage. For the authority and the command of father Isaac precedes. He orders his son not to marry a Canaanite woman, and Jacob obeys this order with the greatest willingness. Esau did the opposite. He took two Hittite wives against the will of his parents. By doing this he grievously offended them, with the result that both Isaac and Rebecca complained with sorrow that they were being wretchedly harassed by their daughters-in-law. This was a very grievous sin and crime. But in other respects we already endure more than enough annoyances in marriage. Why, in addition to this, do we cause ourselves other more serious evils and God's wrath by sinning and by despising our parents? Why do we not prefer to contract marriages in the name of the Lord, as Jacob did? Yet even then there will be no lack of difficulties and troubles of every kind. But you will bear them more easily if you bring to marriage the knowledge which enables you to say: "Thus it has pleased my parents, my friends, my guardians, and God." For you do not approach it in reliance on your own reason and wisdom. You did not disregard the authority and the consent of those whom God wanted you to respect. Therefore you are sure of God's protection and goodwill. But if you do not do this, an evil conscience, which will increase and aggravate all annoyances, is added to the common evils. What else is this than heaping evil on evil and increasing Satan's raging against you?

But I have also dealt with this point at greater length above and elsewhere.[6] It must be diligently inculcated that clandestine marriages are forbidden not only by the civil laws of the emperors but also by divine examples and testimonies. This must be done because of the pettifogging jurists [7] who prefer the decrees of papal law to the authority of Holy Scripture and civil laws. They are ashamed to confess and acknowledge that they once taught things that are absurd. Yet the theological profession is far more sublime. Nevertheless, we are compelled to acknowledge countless very gross errors on the part of the theology of the scholastics. But these jurists try knowingly and skillfully to retain and defend manifest error. This is decidedly shameful. For the civil laws openly contradict this and testify that the children of a household must have the consent of their parents when they contract

---

[6] For earlier references in these lectures cf. *Luther's Works*, 4, pp. 226—227; also the treatise of 1524 on the subject, *Luther's Works*, 45, pp. 385—393.

[7] The Latin word is *iurisperditi*, which may be Luther's own coinage; the passage is evidently a critique of the Lutheran jurists who continued to employ the canon law, as for example, the members of the faculty of law at Wittenberg.

marriage. The examples of Holy Scripture contradict this. Then of what concern to us is the stupid pope with his decrees?

Isaac forbids his son to marry a heathen woman and orders him to go to his mother's brother Laban and to take a wife there. Although Isaac does not force him to marry a woman pleasing to his father, yet he wants him to choose an honorable woman whom he himself will love and marry. The father's order must precede; the son must obey. Nor should he be forced to marry a woman whom he hates; but the love of one who is betrothed should be free, and a father should not stand in the way. He should promote it and give help. This is the true and orderly way to contract a marriage. It should not be overthrown, for the day's own trouble is sufficient (cf. Matt. 6:34), that is, the troubles of marriage which you will have in sufficient abundance when you have entered this kind of life. As much as you can, therefore, you must avoid offending your parents and God. Rather begin marriage with the good favor and the good will of God and your parents, so that you may be able to complete the course of your whole life, if not without punishments and annoyances, at least without blame, if not with unalloyed joy, at least with an innocent heart or a good conscience and God's good pleasure. The tribulation of the flesh is sufficient. And may God preserve us from the tribulation of the spirit!

On the other hand, however, those who shrink from marriage altogether, either under the pretext of sanctity or to be able to live with greater freedom, should be exhorted to take up this very saintly kind of life, lest they pollute themselves with the unmentionable lusts that are customary in the establishments of the clergy and the cardinals. If you do not have the gift of chastity, you should marry a wife in the name of the Lord. If you cannot become rich, you should be content with daily food. If you cannot be a king and lord, be a servant. Believe in God, and wait for eternal life in this wretched and unhappy life, which does not last forever but is very brief. Or even if you live to be a hundred, what is such a brief span of time compared with eternity? We Christians know that another, better life remains—a life which we wait for and for which we must always have regard. And because in the meantime this body of ours does not live chastely and continently, we should by all means endure the laws of thorns and thistles in marriage, and we should rejoice that God regards us with kindness and protects us in these miseries. For it is pleasing to God that you toil and sweat among the thorns of marriage. Let His grace be sufficient for you (cf. 2 Cor. 12:9), and do not let the difficulties deter you. Furthermore, consider the toils and troubles of the very saintly patriarchs, and you will see what great troubles Jacob alone endured in marriage.

3. *God Almighty bless you and make you fruitful and multiply you, that you may become a company of peoples.*

4. *May He give the blessing of Abraham to you and to your descendants with you, that you may take possession of the land of your sojournings which God gave to Abraham!*

5. *Thus Isaac sent Jacob away; and he went to Paddan-aram to Laban, the son of Bethuel the Aramean, the brother of Rebecca, Jacob's and Esau's mother.*

Above Isaac gave blessings to his son Jacob. These he repeats in this passage with a wish. But the blessing, as we have also pointed out above,[8] is the very thing that has been handed over and given forthwith. Thus Baptism is handed over to me now, and forgiveness of sins is handed over; for I do not hope for the remission of sins, but I have it forthwith in faith. I do not believe that Christ is going to suffer for me. No, through faith I am sure that He has suffered for my sins and risen for the sake of my righteousness (cf. Rom. 4:25). Therefore it is not a mere prayer or wish; it is that by which through the power of the Keys I hand over to you now the remission of sins, the grace and favor of God, in order that you may be able to conclude with certainty that you have God, who is well pleased with you. This I hand over to you as a sure possession. Thus the church has the favor and goodwill of the Divine Majesty, of the Father, the Son, and the Holy Spirit, forthwith, of Christ and the angels, who give their congratulations, and of all creatures, who applaud and wait for its redemption, as is stated in Rom. 8:19.

A blessing is a far different matter from a wish. Yet a wish is added in this passage. "May God bless you, that is, make you fruitful, etc.," says Isaac. Above, the blessing has been spoken;

[8] Cf. p. 140.

here the prayer is added. For it has often been stated that ever since the beginning of the world there are and always have been two priestly offices. The one is teaching, which takes place in the sermon or in absolution, in which I hand over the grace of God confirmed by the blood of Christ. The other is praying for oneself and others, which usually takes place after the sermon. For a prayer should follow every sermon. A good Our Father should follow a good sermon.[9] For one should pray for the increase of faith, in order that we may grow in the blessing, lest the devil take it from us. Therefore both should be done: teaching and praying. For these are the two priestly offices: to hear God speaking and to speak with God, who hears us, to descend and to ascend. Through the blessing, through preaching, and through the administration of the sacraments God descends and speaks with me. There I hear. On the other hand, I ascend and speak into the ears of God, who hears my prayer.

One should note the special name for God in this place, It is שַׁדַּי, from שַׁד, that is, "breasts," "teats." God considers it befitting His dignity to be called this name, and it agrees with the Greek term πολύμαστος, "many-breasted."[10] He wants to be praised for nourishing and cherishing, for He cherishes all creatures. He is not only the Creator, but He is also the Sustainer and Nourisher. Above (Gen. 17:1) He employed the same name when speaking to Abraham: "I am God Almighty," He said; that is, "I cause all things to grow, increase, live, and be nourished." Therefore Jacob implores God, who is not only the Creator but also the Nourisher and Sustainer, to give his son the land of his sojourning. "It is your land," he wants to say, "but you are a guest and a stranger in it. Someone else has possession of it, although you regard it as yours and it is owed to you by divine right." Accordingly, Jacob does not have possession of the land owed to him. This was surely burdensome and difficult. For us, however, it would be altogether intolerable if I had my own house and someone else lived in it. I, a guest, would be compelled to buy bread, wine, and all necessities with my own money in order to nourish and clothe that stranger. Therefore the faith of the very saintly patriarchs was great, and these words of Isaac, which are filled with faith, bear

[9] See *Luther's Works*, 53, pp. 78—80.
[10] Cf. *Luther's Works*, 3, p. 83, note 4.

witness to this. And they undoubtedly understood that the eternal and spiritual promises were included in these physical promises of the land of Canaan. Accordingly, they hoped for another fatherland (cf. Heb. 11:14), since the temporal blessings are promised and yet are given to others. So far enough has been said about faith and the promise of the blessing, likewise about marriage.

6. *Now Esau saw that Isaac had blessed Jacob and sent him away to Paddan-aram to take a wife from there, and that as he blessed him he charged him: You shall not marry one of the Canaanite women,*

7. *and that Jacob had obeyed his father and his mother and had gone to Paddan-aram.*

8. *So when Esau saw that the Canaanite women did not please Isaac, his father,*

9. *Esau went to Ishmael and took to wife, besides the wives he had, Mahalath, the daughter of Ishmael, Abraham's son, the sister of Nebaioth.*

It seems that Esau, who was furious, becomes a little milder after he sees that his brother Jacob has withdrawn from his father's house. For he thought: "I have enough, provided that I remain in the house and in possession. That brother of mine, who has been blessed, is gone and has left the blessing behind." He thinks that it was only an accidental blessing with which his father blessed him in order that he might have a small portion with which to sustain himself in his exile and sojourn. It was most pleasing to him that Jacob did not resist his parents but obeyed so readily and, content with little, withdrew into exile. "He could have urged his father," he thought, "to bestow a greater blessing on him, just as I, by urging and insisting, have wrested from him the permission to remain in the house now. But my father, my mother, and my brother Jacob are simple folk. My parents send their son into exile, and the son is completely willing to obey; for he trembles at my threats and my wrath. Therefore he wisely considers his own interests by fleeing. For I am the master and the ruler; up to this time Jacob is and always has been a servant."

This is certainly an excellent example of godless people,

who are wont to flatter and console themselves even with Holy Scripture in spite of the fact that it is completely opposed to them, just as godly and God-fearing people, on the other hand, turn statements and words spoken for them and for their life and comfort around and receive them as though they had been pronounced for their perdition. A godly man fears the wrath of God when he should hope for mercy. Godless people, on the other hand, distort the passages dealing with God's mercy and grace and refer them to themselves. Thus the papists and the Turks dream that they alone are the beloved and accepted children of God. They dream that they are sitting on the lap of God the Father. They want the examples of punishments and the threats to be far removed from them. But we fear these and think that they pertain to our perdition, although God does not want to terrify us but wants to console, strengthen, and gladden us.

Thus Esau saw — and saw with special pleasure — that his parents sent Jacob away out of fear of their angry son's wrath. Nothing more agreeable could have happened to him. Therefore he, in turn, wants to do his father a favor and to gratify him, lest he seem to be ungrateful and disobedient toward his parents. For when he hears that his Hittite wives displease his father, he thinks: "Behold, I will marry one woman who will please my father." And he goes to his paternal uncle Ishmael and marries Ishmael's daughter. But Scripture does not point out whether that hypocrisy and deceit pleased his father or not. I do not think so, for Isaac did not believe that the blessing was attached to Esau but knew that it was owed to Jacob. He also saw that whatever Esau was doing he was doing hypocritically and deceitfully. But this is a striking and excellent example of godless men and hypocrites, who flourish in this life and have everything in abundance. They get their kingdoms and the wealth of the world with glory and pomp, just as our bishops do. But in the end it will be seen who is calling the tune.

Up to this point Moses has related the history of Isaac and Rebecca in a few words. In it he has told about the very grievous trials and struggles which both endured with great courage at home and abroad, in the Word and in faith. For after Isaac had received the promise about the multiplication of his descendants, he had to live with a sterile wife for 20 whole years. But when her prayer is heard, she becomes pregnant and gives birth to twins, yet not without a trial and danger to her life. Later, after the birth of the children, new abodes must be sought because of the famine. It is necessary to sojourn with the children and the household among the Philistines. Here Rebecca's chastity is endangered. Then the quarrels and the enmity of the shepherds, yes, even of the king himself, must also be borne. But amid all this the saintly people are buoyed up and sustained by the Word and the promise, and the hearts of the king and the adversaries are also placated and reconciled again.

Finally, however, when they were now rid of the external trials, a domestic cross is added because of the wickedness and the obstinacy of their son Esau and the two daughters-in-law, who, as we have heard, plagued their aged parents very harshly. And Rebecca especially was affected more seriously by this, since, in addition, she was concerned lest the primogeniture and the blessing be transferred to Esau contrary to the meaning of the divine oracle. This is what the father himself was trying to bring about and Esau was proudly arrogating to himself. But here the wonderfully divine power of the Word shines forth in the promise — the Word which had to remain immovable and firm even though Isaac himself resisted on account of his mistaken notion. Therefore he is beautifully deceived by the counsel and cunning of Rebecca, who retained the true meaning of the promise. Contrary, therefore, to every expectation and unknowingly he confers the blessing on Jacob, to whom it was owed. But Esau lost the blessing and paid a fitting penalty for his godlessness and his contempt. The fact that these examples of the extraordinary struggles and of the troubles in which the whole life of this patriarch abounded occur in the church is profitable. They inflame the hearts of the godly to similar endurance, expectation, faith, and invocation in adversity.

Now the history of the patriarch Jacob follows. To it we shall not inappropriately assign the FIFTH BOOK of Genesis.[11] For after he had obtained the blessing from his father and heard his counsel and admonitions about taking a wife, no further mention will be made of Isaac and Rebecca until the 35th chapter, where Moses will relate how Isaac, old and full of days, died and was gathered

---

[11] The "fourth book" of Genesis had begun at 25:11; cf. *Luther's Works*, 4, p. 320.

to his people (Gen. 35:28). But although in the meantime Esau rules in the church and house of Isaac and persecutes his fugitive brother in a hostile manner, Jacob alone is the patriarch and, if I may say so, the light of the world because of the promise and the blessing. All the others are dead, and his father Isaac because of his age is no longer able to govern the church. Accordingly, we shall see, how God also leads this patriarch in a wonderful manner and exercises him by means of great dangers and difficulties, in which he will experience the presence and the protection of God just as Abraham and Isaac experienced them and triumphed bravely over all evils and troubles in faith in the promises of God.

10. *Jacob left Beer-sheba, and went toward Haran.*

11. *And he came to a certain place, and stayed there that night, because the sun had set. Taking one of the stones of the place, he put it under his head and lay down in that place to sleep.*

The first point is altogether striking and is worthy of careful treatment. For it contains manifold and rich doctrine almost too grand for us to attain with our explanation. For Jacob goes into exile. He has been compelled to flee the rage of his brother and to leave to the fratricide the blessing owed to him. The latter, however, has been placated by the very fact that the possessor of the blessing flees and leaves him in full possession of it for so many years. These matters in the divine administration are undoubtedly foolish and absurd to our eyes, namely, that the heir who is destined to be the stone at the head of the corner is rejected by the builders (cf. Ps. 118:22; Matt. 21:42). He had been destined to be the ruler in the house, and the government of the house and the church was entrusted to him by divine authority. But to flee from and desert all this is not to have possession of the house or to govern the household and the church. Therefore reason concludes that in the divine promise there are meaningless and empty words, because the realization does not follow but tends in the opposite and contrary direction.

But these matters pertain to our doctrine; for theology is not philosophy, which looks at the things that are at hand, is inflated by prosperity, and is crushed when the same prosperity has been removed. Reason and all the Epicureans argue that God seems to be a liar, because He promises in a kindly manner and puts forth good words but gives things that are evil. He gives Jacob a blessing and, on the other hand, allows it to be taken away. On the contrary, Esau, who has been cursed, remains in the house with his children, his wives, and his whole relationship, and governs everything just as previously he was head of the household and a priest of the church. Jacob goes into exile and abandons his blessing. This indeed is the administration of divine matters! The cornerstone must be rejected in order that we may learn to distinguish between divine and human government, and also that Jacob's blessing has not been lost, but that this is only a trial, to see whether he is willing to cling to it firmly in faith and to wait. For this way Abraham is also ordered to sacrifice his son, as though he were about to lose him (Gen. 22:2). Soon, however, he recovers him with greater glory and profit (Gen. 22:12). Thus David, after being anointed to be king (1 Sam. 16:13), lives in exile for 10 years, is a servant of servants, and is king only in name and in accordance with the empty words which he heard from Samuel. Yet he holds out, and he perseveres in faith and expectation, until the outcome corresponds in richest abundance to the promise.

This is the constant course of the church at all times, namely, that promises are made and that then those who believe the promises are treated in such a way that they are compelled to wait for things that are invisible, to believe what they do not see, and to hope for what does not appear. He who does not do this is not a Christian. For Christ Himself entered into His glory only by first descending into hell. When He is about to reign, He is crucified. When He is to be glorified, He is spit on. For He must suffer first and then at length be glorified.

Moreover, God does this in order to test our hearts, whether we are willing to do without the promised blessings for a time. We shall not do without them forever. This is certain. And if God did not test us and postpone His promises, we would not be able to love Him wholeheartedly. For if He immediately gave everything He promises, we would not believe but would immerse ourselves in the blessings that are at hand and forget God. Accordingly, He allows the church to be afflicted and to suffer want in order that it may learn that it must live not only by bread but also by the Word (cf. Matt. 4:4), and in order that faith, hope, and the expectation of God's help may be increased in the godly. For the Word is our life and salvation. If in this life the children of Adam can say and believe what is commonly stated, namely, that what is postponed is not taken away, why should we Christians not think and believe the same thing?

To be sure, it is difficult and troublesome to hold on to this help and consolation. Thus Solomon says in Prov. 13:12: "Hope deferred makes the heart sick." But the promised blessing consoles and sustains the heart. Accordingly, one must be carefully fortified and strengthened against the displeasure of the flesh, which fights against faith and the spirit during this waiting, as that murmuring of the flesh is described in the examples of two wives, the wife of Tobias and the wife of Job. The wife of Tobias says: "It is evident that your hope has come to nothing, and your alms have not appeared" (cf. Tob. 2:14). And Job's wife says: "Do you still hold fast your integrity? Curse God, and die" (Job 2:9). Job's friends kept reproaching him in the same way. "Where is your faith now?" they asked. "If you were pleasing to God, He would not allow you to be afflicted in this way." These are the flaming darts of the devil (cf. Eph. 6:16) with which he tries to overthrow us in order that we may despair and fall away from God. But the consolation so often repeated must be opposed to this. It is a postponement, not a loss. It is our mortification, not our destruction. It is an upbuilding. The blessing is being postponed. But wait, and persevere in faith. Nor should you sing what we read in the psalm (115:2): "Why should the nations say: 'Where is their God?'" No, you should think (Ps. 42:6): "Why are you cast down, O my soul, and why are you disquieted within me? Hope in God; for I shall yet praise Him." Things will still turn out well. For David is fighting against himself when he says: "My soul, you are disquieting me." For what you want is not at hand. At all events, wait, and be content; for God and His Word are present.

Therefore if carnal men can console and buoy themselves up with the conviction that what is postponed is not lost, why should we not do the same thing? The administration of human affairs is also full of such examples. For it often happens that some prince promises by letter and seals to give farms, a castle, or something similar. Here, too, the gift is not given immediately; but one must wait for the opportunity. One must wait for the place, the person, and the time. How much more we should wait for the blessings promised by God, who does not deceive and cannot lie but surely keeps and fulfills His promises! Thus Jacob firmly believes His promise. In the meantime, however, he endures this delay and postponement. He knows that he has become a ruler of the church and of the whole earth, for the blessing has been transferred from the house of Abraham to the house of Jacob. Yet he goes into exile and lives among those who are idolaters.

We are surrounded by such examples as by a cloud. For the whole church and every Christian, yes, Christ Himself, our Lord, endures this will and government of God, which means that He tries but does not condemn, that He postpones but does not take away. This, then, is the Christians' own doctrine. It depends on the Word and concludes with certainty that God will not fail to give what He has promised. But the devil and the flesh cannot endure this wonderful government. We can endure the postponement of something promised among men more easily than we can endure a promise made by God; for original sin stands in the way, lest in divine matters we bear what is not so troublesome to bear in human matters.

Therefore is it not shameful that although we have such sure and firm promises about eternal life and the blessing, we still have doubts about God's will or at least are weak in faith? I have been baptized and have the hope of eternal life. Yet I cannot believe as firmly as would be the case if a prince promised me some estate and confirmed his promises by letter and seals. That strength and firmness of faith in this patriarch of ours is all the more praiseworthy. For when he is about to take up the government of the house which he has in accordance with the institution and blessing of God, he flees and leaves his adversary and enemy Esau in possession of the rule. Esau performs and enjoys everything that belonged to Jacob. Yet Jacob's faith is by no means shaken. It does not waver or fall away, even though it appears that the blessing is altogether vain and worthless. Yet I do not doubt—indeed, I gladly think—that those very saintly patriarchs were human beings, that they had flesh and blood just as we have. For if Peter, Paul, and the other apostles had flesh and blood, they were also afflicted with something that was human. For flesh and blood wrestle against the spirit.

Therefore there is no doubt that Jacob sometimes felt doubt and was tried. Was the blessing vain, or was it established? For his flesh was true flesh, and the devil was his foe. Accordingly, he felt not only an external trial, when he was forced to go into exile and was driven from his house and his own possession; but in addition there was an internal trial far more serious and on a far higher plane, when he thought: "What if your mother has deceived you? For you see that your brother remains in possession and acquires the blessing. What if God has changed His purpose? For Esau has the thing itself. I have nothing but meaningless words." And because of this twofold trial God will console him later with a new word.

Accordingly, one should learn patience from the examples of the patriarchs, who were tried in every way, yet not without sin, from which Christ alone was free (cf. Heb. 4:15). Surely Jacob was not tried without sin. He was not Christ Himself. Nor did he have a flesh free from sin. And he was tried as an example for us, in order that we might learn what faith is and what a Christian life is. For it is a life that has a definite promise which is not only postponed but brings the opposite to pass. Jacob should be king and priest by divine dispensation. But something happens that is far different from what has been promised. Then he thought: "Nothing will ever come of it; the outcome will not correspond to the promise." But faith wrestled against the flesh and said: "Flesh and Satan, you are lying; for God has spoken and has made a promise. He will not lie, even if the opposite happens or I die in the meantime." Thus faith spoke and ordered the light to shine out of the darkness (cf. 2 Cor. 4:6). Therefore faith is not a laughable, cold quality that snores and is idle in the heart. No, it is agitated and harassed by horrible trials concerning the nothingness and the vanity of the divine promises. For I believe in Christ, whom I do not see. But I have His Baptism, the Sacrament of the Altar, and consolation through the Word and Absolution. Yet I see nothing of what He promises. Indeed, I feel the opposite in my flesh. Here, then, one must struggle and do battle against unbelief and doubt.

But formless faith [12] is powerless and cannot sustain and bear those assaults. True and living faith, however, which overcomes doubt, is in reality an exceedingly lively "quality," if indeed this

[12] Thomas Aquinas had discussed *fides informis* in the *Summa Theologica*, II—II, Q. 4, Art. 4.

is what it should be called;[13] and it is a restless blessing in our heart, which the devil assails and attacks every single moment. One learns and feels in the agony of death above all whether it is a formless faith or a true and living faith. For a Christian dies, is buried, and is consumed by worms. In short, he is reduced to nothing. This is certainly contrary to all the divine promises. What, then, should he do? Then he surely finds out that faith is not a meaningless quality, since it overcomes the terrors of death and says: "Even if you were to bear on your neck the burden not only of death but also of a thousand devils and of hell itself, yet I will not make God a liar." For in such agony the hearts of the godly are disposed to say: "Even though hell were to pour out all its flames and spew out every evil on me, yet I remain in that faith. I believe in Jesus Christ, His only Son. Lord God, preserve me through Christ, lest that blasphemy which says 'Thou art a liar' arise. To be sure, I feel the contrary; but I have Thy Word, which does not deceive. Indeed, it is all in all to me."

In this manner Holy Scripture commends the fathers and sets forth shining examples of their faith, and there is no other doctrine in the world beside Holy Scripture which teaches that faith alone conquers the world (cf. 1 John 5:4). This faith consists in having the Word in our hearts and having no doubt about the Word. Meanwhile it simply suffers the opposite, is not crushed, and is not wearied to the end, that is, until the promise comes. Job stoutly endured the reproach of his wife, for he replies (Job 2:10): "You speak as one of the foolish women would speak. Shall we receive good at the hand of God, and shall we not receive evil?" If we have had life and up to this time have eaten and drunk while God nourished and supported us, why should we not also bear some adversity? The wife of Tobias also fell (Tob. 2:14). But David remained firm and steadfast for 10 whole years, although he was a king without a crown, without a land, without a people, yes, had even been declared an enemy and a rebel by the Saulites. Later, when Absalom drove him from the realm, he merely said (2 Sam. 15:25-26): "If I find favor . . . He will bring me back; but if He says, 'I have no pleasure in you,' behold, here I am, let Him do to me what seems good to Him." This is what it means to hold firmly to the promise, which says (Deut. 8:3): "Man does not live by

---

[13] Cf. *Luther's Works*, 27, pp. 335—336.

bread alone, etc." This is stated about faith and the promises. It must be repeated and carefully inculcated both here and in many other places, for the flesh always resists.

Here an additional question arises. Why did the very saintly parents, Isaac and Rebecca, send their son to idolaters? For we shall hear below that Laban had gods of silver, etc. Therefore they hurl their son into evident danger and by so doing seem to be tempting God. For when I approach certain and manifest danger, then it is correct to conclude that I am tempting God.

How, then, can faith stand alongside that temptation by which they involve their son in the danger of idolatry and other examples of the worst kind? For Laban not only worshiped the silver gods; but he was greedy, niggardly, and full of vices, as will appear below. Therefore Jacob could have been corrupted as a result of his association with him and could have been contaminated by many vices contrary to faith and good conduct. I answer: Where was he to go? He had to take a wife, and preparation had to be made for the government of the church and the house. But the Canaanite women were altogether idolatrous and had no Word at all. But there, in Nahor's house, some knowledge of godliness remained; for the line or succession of the fathers from Noah up to Abraham, in which Nahor, Abraham's brother, is numbered, had the Word. For although the church was transferred to the house of Abraham, yet the Word and zeal for true godliness also remained in the family of Nahor. Scripture makes no further mention of the patriarch Lot. But Nahor had a family or posterity in which Job, who was from the land of UZ, was born (Job 1:1). Some contend that he was descended from Edom. But Jerome and others derive his origin from Nahor, Abraham's brother.[14] Therefore Job is a cousin of Isaac himself, because he springs from the family of Nahor. They say that Balaam, who at first was a saintly man and a godly priest, was also born from the same family. But later, after he had been corrupted and ruined by the gifts of the king of the Moabites, he lapsed. They also maintain that the man who is called Elihu in Job is Balaam. But we leave those matters in doubt. Nevertheless, it is reasonable to believe that this line of the patriarchs preserved the knowledge of God even outside the church

[14] Cf. *Luther's Works,* 4, p. 185.

of Abraham and that it remained in the purer and true religion. This can be the first answer to that question.

Secondly, even though the profession of sound doctrine is retained, yet hypocrites are always close by, and those who are truly godly are compelled to endure in their gatherings those who serve mammon or are given to other vices. Nevertheless, they are in agreement in regard to doctrine and the use of the sacraments. They are Christians in name because they do not fight against and persecute the doctrine. But they have their own carnal wisdom and live mostly for the belly. But if one had to beware of all those and live only with godly people, where there are no hypocrites, then we would have to go out of this world, as Paul says (1 Cor. 5:10). The church cannot prevent hypocrites, that is, false brethren, from being in their gathering, provided that they do not attack the doctrine and condemn us, as the Babylonians did in the days of Abraham, provided that they let us live with them and let us teach the truth. Indeed, let them be slaves of mammon and have their own opinions, provided that they remain quiet and keep faith and the public peace. If they are true enemies, they will burst forth, with the result that either they will no longer be willing to endure us or we will not be able to live with them. But we cannot guard against those hypocrites. And there is some hope that they can be improved. In regard to him who is greedy or given to other vices, feels his sin and does not defend it, we will have hope that he can be corrected. A kind of foolishness or weakness is characteristic of this life and of human nature, and we cannot be perfect in all respects; for according to the flesh we cannot do what the spirit wants. For this reason we pray: "Forgive us our debts." We do not defend sins. We do not sow errors and false opinions instead of true doctrine. But every Christian is harassed by the devil and the flesh, and he acknowledges the wickedness and corruption of his nature, as Paul complains about himself in Rom. 7:19: "The evil I do not want is what I do."

Thus Nahor retained the promises made to the fathers, although not so purely as Abraham, who had been separated from them in order that he might be the father of the church. Yet he had some light. Therefore Jacob could not have found a better place to which to betake himself. The common saying that one must plow with oxen if there are no horses must be observed. For we are human beings, and as human beings we are compelled to put up with those who, even if they sin, are nevertheless willing to be admonished and corrected. Therefore it is not tempting God to associate with men like Laban, with whom Jacob lived. Undoubtedly many from this house of Nahor were saved, and among the other nations they were a kind of light by teaching and propagating the true knowledge of God. Thus Job was an honorable man. So were the friends of Job. Balaam was a most honorable prophet, and in the beginning he was truly godly and had special gifts of the Spirit. In the beginning he blessed the people of Israel truly and properly. Later the devil corrupted him. For this is how it can happen that the pure and sound doctrine remains even when those who were sound at first have been corrupted.

As citizens, therefore, we cannot avoid association with those who are manifestly godless. The church could not avoid the tyranny of the Romans. Abraham could not keep away from Ur. But when I know that a person is greedy and openly inflicts a wrong on others, steps must be taken to prevent him from being admitted to the church and to Communion. From this he can and should be excluded. This, therefore, is the way one can reply to the question why Isaac and Rebecca sent their son to Haran. They did so because the people there still agreed with them partly in doctrine, even though they, too, had their faults. And there was continuous and constant friendship between Nahor and Abraham and their descendants. At that time they were lights, so to speak, of that age. They, not the Chaldeans, had the promise and the Word. But where the ministry of the Word is, there the church is. Conversely, where the true church is, there the Word is.

But let us look at the words and the grammar. For these words are spoken with much feeling and indicate great sadness, namely, that after Jacob has been appointed ruler and heir, he leaves Beer-sheba and sets out for distant Haran. But everyone can make his own guess with what great grief the good and saintly patriarch was smitten. He undoubtedly traversed that long journey with many tears and with frequent sighs and sobs, for he fled in secret that he might hide himself from the fury of his brother Esau, lest Esau pursue him, seize him on the journey, and do him some violence. Therefore he sets out alone, without a servant, without a guide or a companion. It certainly was great misery to go into exile and darkness in this way, to depart from father and mother, to leave that most pleasant association with his parents, and to allow his furious brother, together with his wives, to rule during his absence on that journey. Furthermore, Jacob was a human being subject to human feelings, just as we are. Indeed, the more spiritual he was, the more the wickedness of very evil men, likewise his own sins and troubles, affected and tormented his heart. For saintly men are very tender and are moved more deeply than those stocks and logs, the monks and the self-righteous. Therefore Jacob's departure was sad and troublesome enough without the danger which threatened from his brother. It was not a pleasant promenade; nor did he rest or proceed more slowly, as men do who feel secure and are safe from all snares. No, he hurried; he ran. Nor did his parents give him a companion in order that he might more easily conceal his departure from his brother Esau. For Esau could have blocked his way and killed Jacob, as he had decided. But Moses uses the figure which they call hysteron proteron. For Jacob fled before Esau discovered [15] that he had fled.

Finally the fiery darts of the devil (cf. Eph. 6:16) were added to this great perturbation of his heart. In this way the devil incited him to think: "Behold, what have I done? I have seized the blessing of my brother, have disturbed the house, and have enraged my brother and his whole household and relationship." Undoubtedly Jacob was not free from this trial; and although he overcame these trials, they nevertheless greatly tormented and distressed his heart. Accordingly, the saintly patriarch proceeded on his way in this great grief and unrest with worries and tears. For every circumstance was of such a nature that there was every reason for it to wring tears from him.

Haran is the city to which Terah, Abraham's father, fled from Ur of the Chaldeans and where he lived. From there Abraham was called to the land of Canaan. But Nahor, who was Abraham's brother, and his descendants remained there. Jerome says that it was called Charran.[16] It was situated in Mesopotamia between the Tigris and the Euphrates. Here the Roman people suffered a great defeat when Crassus led them against the Parthians, who

---

[15] We have followed the conjecture suggested by the Weimar editors and have read *resciceret* rather than *resisteret*.

[16] Jerome, *De situ et nominibus locorum Hebraicorum, Patrologia, Series Latina*, XXIII, 934.

seized the eagles and standards from the Romans and wretchedly slew Crassus himself.[17]

"HE CAME TO A CERTAIN PLACE, ETC." In the Hebrew Moses uses an extraordinary word, פָּגַע, which cannot be translated into German. For it has the same meaning as when we say *er traffe eben an*, or "a place met him," *Begegnet*. This word also means "to intercede," as above in chapter 23, verse 8, "with Ephron": "Intercede for me that he may sell me the field." Properly speaking, therefore, it does not mean "to come" but means "a place met him," "he happened upon a place." Hence it is applied to intercession, because he who intercedes meets the man who is to be placated. In German we say: *Er kam on gefer an den ort* ("He happened upon the place"). Therefore it is just as if Moses said: "Jacob, sad and disturbed, had not thought of resting in that place; it happened this way contrary to expectation." Much less did he think that he would see a vision that night, but being in flight he wanted either to proceed farther or to stop on the nearer side of that place. He had not intended to spend the night there. This is how it happened. Nothing was further from his mind than spending the night there or seeing that vision. But because the sunset takes him unawares, he is compelled to stay there.

Therefore Moses points out that Jacob was disturbed and concerned about his own peril and about the condition and safety of his parents, whom he had forsaken, and that in this state of grief he had hurried to arrive quickly at the desired place yet had stopped there because night was rushing on. Moreover, those who are exhausted by sorrow, flight, anxiety, and bodily fatigue are easily lulled and gently fall asleep. Thus Christ found the disciples in the garden "sleeping for sorrow" (Luke 22:45). Sometimes grief makes it impossible for others to sleep. But our patriarch falls asleep because he has been exhausted by his cares and as a result of his journey.

But what kind of couch, what bed, what covering did he have? He lies on the ground, and as a pillow he puts under his head a stone which he has found in that place. It seems that he did not dare entrust himself to any city or village, for he suspected every-

---

[17] This battle at Charran (Latin *Carrhae*) took place in 53 B. C.; cf. Plutarch, *Crassus*, XXVII—XXVIII.

body. So he spends the night in the fields, in a spot which was deserted and dark after sunset. He had no hay or straw to spread under him, just as the disciples in the garden had neither feathers nor pillows. But just as anyone had sunk down on the ground, so he rested while either lying or sitting, and he slept no less sweetly and pleasantly than if he had had feathers or hay spread under him. Thus the patriarch Jacob enjoys complete rest in that desert, even though he has been put in the greatest danger and grief because of his flight and because he has been torn away from his very dear parents. For the trials are exceedingly great and severe; and if the heart is afflicted and oppressed by their severity, it has need of rest in order that it may revive a little and that the grief may be assuaged.

מְרַאֲשֹׁתָיו points out what is placed under the head and is derived from the word for head. The Jews say, as Lyra recounts, that Jacob placed three stones under his head and that when he had awakened, they were joined into one.[18] For here he says "stones" in the plural number, but afterwards he says "stone" in the singular. Whether the Jews have this from the fathers or not, I do not know. It would be a fine thought if it had originated from the fathers. For it would seem that he wanted to leave behind indications of the future faith in Christ. But the Jews have no understanding whatever of Jacob's dream, which follows.

12. *And he dreamed that there was a ladder set up on the earth, and the top of it reached to heaven; and behold, the angels of God were ascending and descending on it!*

13. *And behold, the Lord stood above it and said: I am the Lord, the God of Abraham your father and the God of Isaac; the land on which you lie I will give to you and to your descendants;*

14. *and your descendants shall be like the dust of the earth.*

This is a very beautiful sermon and an extraordinary gem of this whole history, which should be accurately and carefully examined because, as we have often stated, in the legends and histories of the fathers and saints one should observe chiefly

---

[18] Lyra *ad* Gen. 28:11, adding that he preferred to expound this to refer to the Trinity.

that God speaks with them. It is for this reason that they are saints and are called saintly. For there are two kinds of saintliness. The first is that by which we are sanctified through the Word. The second is that by which we are saintly on the basis of what we do and how we live. But these two kinds of saintliness must be most accurately distinguished. For the first and purest kind of saintliness is the Word, in which there is no fault, no spot, no sin; but it is so saintly that it needs no remission of sins, because it is God's truth, as we read in John 17:17: "Sanctify them in the truth; Thy Word is truth." In that saintliness we, who have been called through the Word, glory. It is outside us; it is not our work. It is not formal righteousness; [19] but it is a heavenly saintliness communicated to us through the Word, and indeed through the spoken Word. Therefore we proclaim that righteousness and oppose it to all forms of righteousness and saintliness of the pope and all hypocrites, for it is unpolluted saintliness. I have the Word. I am saintly, righteous, and pure, without any fault and indictment, insofar as I have the Word. Thus Christ Himself says (John 15:3): "You are already made clean by the Word which I have spoken to you."

But the pope has no knowledge of this saintliness. All self-righteous people despise it and cling to the righteousness of the Law. They do not ascend to the heavenly saintliness by which we are acceptable before God because of His Word. Therefore the legends of the saintly patriarchs should be observed above all when God speaks with them. For from the Word you learn how great the saints are, even if they never performed a single miracle. Yet that is impossible. But before the flesh does anything, we are saintly through the Word. Therefore I conclude: "The Word is not my work. Consequently, when I glory in my work, I lose the Word. On the other hand, if I glory in the Word, my work perishes."

Of this no one can persuade the papists, who constantly bark out that old saying, "Reason strives for what is best, etc." [20] But let us remember that there are two kinds of saintliness. One is the Word, which is saintliness itself. But this saintliness is imputed to those who have the Word. And a person is simply accounted

---

[19] On "formal righteousness" cf. *Luther's Works,* 26, pp. 127—129.

[20] Cf. *Luther's Works,* 2, p. 42, note 54.

saintly, not because of us or because of our works but because of the Word. Thus the whole person becomes righteous. Therefore the church is called holy and we are called holy because we have irreprehensible holiness not from us but from heaven. And this saintliness should not be despised. Nor should we be ashamed to be called saintly. For if we do not glory in this saintliness, we do wrong to the true God, who sanctifies us with His Word. "But I am a sinner," you will say. "I know that you are a sinner, and if you were not, I would not want to sanctify you; you would have no need of the Word. But because you are a sinner, I sanctify you," says God.

The other saintliness is a saintliness of works. It is love, which does what is pleasing. Here not only God speaks, but I strive to follow God when He speaks. But because weakness clings to us, this righteousness is not pure. But the Lord's Prayer reigns, and it is necessary to pray: "Hallowed be Thy name" (Matt. 6:9). This pertains to our saintliness and the saintliness of works, which is formal and pertains to the saintliness of the Decalog and the Lord's Prayer. But the first saintliness must be referred to the Symbol, to the Creed; for I do not take hold of the promise of the Word through the Ten Commandments. Nor do I do so through the Lord's Prayer. But with them I grasp my love and my works. Through faith, however, I take hold of the Word, that is, purity itself.

These things cannot be adequately stated and inculcated. Yet there is an easy distinction between the commandment and the promise. The Word, which justifies the believer without my love and my righteousness, is one thing. It is something else when I take hold of the commandments of God, so that I do not steal, do not commit adultery, etc. But the papists are submerged in and overwhelmed by their own darkness to such an extent that when they hear this doctrine, they do not hear. Nor do we ourselves retain it firmly enough. Learn, therefore, from the reading of these histories what we have always been accustomed to do in our reading, namely, to linger at this passage, when God speaks with the patriarchs; for here the best and most precious things are to be read.

Now let us look at the sermon itself, and from it one surely sees in what great sadness and anguish of heart Jacob found himself. For he is in outer darkness, so to speak, driven from his home and fatherland, forsaken and solitary, uncertain where he can hide in safety. In addition, the devil has come—the devil, who is wont to torment afflicted hearts in a thousand strange ways, so that the truth of the common saying that no disaster is alone becomes apparent. For Satan "prowls around like a roaring lion" (1 Peter 5:8) and seeks where he can most easily climb over the fence and with what stratagems he can overturn the leaning wagon. He climbs across where the fence is lowest; and if the wagon is unsteady, he turns it over completely. Thus temptation is added and piled up for those who are afflicted and tried, so that it hurls them headlong into despair, into blasphemy or impatience.

These are the works of the devil; these are his customary and constant snares. Therefore besides the physical cross and the exile, Jacob was undoubtedly assailed by the fiery darts of the devil (cf. Eph. 6:16). Perhaps he thought about how he had stolen the primogeniture and about how he had deceived his father. For in this way the devil is wont to make a great and enormous sin out of an excellent work. The fact that God speaks with him is a sign of this very grievous trial. For He is not wont to pour forth His discussions and words in vain. He does not speak unless an important and necessary reason impels Him to speak. Nor is He wont to address or to console those who laugh at Him, who exult and rage against Him in the pleasures or wisdom of the flesh, who live smugly, without fear of and reverence for God. "Wisdom is not found in the land of those who live pleasantly," says Job (cf. 28:13); it is found under the cross of those who are oppressed and are in conflict with spiritual trials. Then there is both a reason and a place for consolation; then God is present and consoles the afflicted "lest the righteous put forth their hands to do wrong," as Ps. 125:3 says. And "He will speak peace to His servants" (cf. Ps. 122:8). For if He were absent too long, no one could endure and persevere in those trials and ragings. This, then, is a great consolation in his great and exceedingly sad perturbation, and it appears that this, rather than bodily exhaustion, lulled Jacob to sleep. For the devil came to terrify him within his heart while he was in flight and in exile.

But this is Jacob's dream: A ladder has been placed on the earth —a ladder which touches heaven with its top. On it the angels are ascending and descending. And the Lord Himself is reclining on the top of the ladder and is speaking that promise to this third patriarch. He is not speaking through a man. No, He Himself is speaking, a fact which, as we have stated, should be carefully observed in the histories of the fathers.

Moreover, the ladder is a picture or an image, as it were, that has to have a meaning. For the angels are spirits and fire, as we read in Ps. 104:4: "Who makest Thy angels spirits and Thy ministers a flaming fire." Therefore they have no need of a ladder on which to ascend or descend. Much less does God Himself have need of a ladder to recline on when He has to speak to Jacob, the heir of the promise. But the images and pictures suggested by this ladder have been explained in various ways, and it is not worthwhile to gather and recount them all.

Lyra says that the rungs refer to the patriarchs who are enumerated at the beginning of Matthew's Gospel in the genealogy of Christ.[21] For both sides indicate that Christ descends from sinners as well as from righteous men. The angels, he says, refer to the revelation of the incarnation of Christ — the revelation which took place through the fathers, the prophets, and the apostles. He interprets the ascent as the devotion of the saints when they pray. This thought is not irreverent. But it does not seem to be the principal explanation of allegory.

The *Glossa ordinaria* interprets the ascending angels as the blessed angels who minister to God in heaven.[22] Then it interprets the descending angels as those who do so to minister to men, as is written in Hebrews (1:14): "Are they not all ministering spirits sent forth to serve, for the sake of those who are to obtain salvation?" And in Dan. 7:10 we read: "A thousand thousands served Him; and ten thousand times ten thousand stood before Him."

Gregory calls the angels preachers who give thought to Christ when they ascend and later, when they descend to the church, serve the members of the church.[23] But who could enumerate all the speculations? Although they are godly, yet, like many things in the fathers, they have not been expressed at the right time

---

[21] Lyra *ad* Gen. 28:12-14.

[22] "The angels ascending and descending are evangelists and preachers," *Glossa ordinaria ad Gen.* 28:12-14.

[23] Gregory, *Liber regulae pastoralis*, Part II, ch. 5, *Patrologia, Series Latina,* LXXVII, 33.

or at the right place. It is true that a preacher must first ascend through prayer in order to receive the Word and doctrine from God. He should also study, learn, read, and meditate. Later he should descend and teach others. These are the twin duties of priests: to turn to God with prayer but to turn to the people with doctrine. But these matters should be left where they belong.

But because mention is made of this ladder in the first chapter of the Gospel of John, we should look rather at that text. For there the Lord Himself seems to interpret this picture. When Philip brings Nathanael to Christ, he says: "Behold, an Israelite indeed!" (John 1:47.) Here, as Augustine says, he reminds us of that ladder of Jacob, who is also called Israel.[24] This is what Christ says (John 1:50): "Because I said to you: 'I saw you under the fig tree,' do you believe? You shall see greater things than these." And He adds (v. 51): "Truly, truly, I say to you: 'You will see heaven opened, and the angels of God ascending and descending upon the Son of Man.'" We should believe and be content with this explanation of our Savior; for He has a better understanding than all other interpreters, even though they agree properly in this point, that this dream signified that infinite, inexpressible, and wondrous mystery of the incarnation of Christ, who was to descend from the patriarch Jacob, as God says: "In your seed, etc." Therefore He revealed to Jacob himself that he would be the father of Christ and that the Son of Man would be born from his seed. God did not speak this in vain. Indeed, He painted that picture of the ladder to comfort and console Jacob in faith in the future blessing, just as above (Gen. 22:18) He gave the same promise to Abraham and Isaac in order that they might teach and transmit it to their descendants as certain and infallible, and expect a Savior from their own flesh. In this way God strengthens Jacob, who, like the useless trunk of a tree, is wretched and afflicted in a foreign land; and by means of this new picture He transfers to him all the blessings, to assure him that he is this patriarch from whom the Seed promised to Adam will come.

Therefore we must understand the angels in their proper meaning, as Christ calls them in John 1:51, where He speaks of them as "the angels of God," that is, the blessed ones. They

---

[24] Augustine, *In Joannis Evangelium Tractatus*, ch. I, Tr. VII, 23, *Patrologia, Series Latina*, XXXV, 1449.

ascend and descend on Christ or upon Christ. The LADDER signifies the ascent and the descent that are made by means of the ladder and by means of the rungs. If you remove the ladder, it signifies nothing else than the ascent and the descent. The angels, however, do not use a physical ladder or an imaginary one. Nevertheless, there is an ascent and a descent, that is, an angelic ladder, so to speak. This is the principal meaning, just as Christ Himself explains the descent and the ascent of the angels upon the Son of Man without a ladder.

But what is this ascent and descent? I reply that it is this very mystery that in one and the same Person there is true GOD and man. Accordingly the unity of the Person fulfills this mystery. And we, who believe, fulfill the Word of Christ (John 1:51): "You will see . . . the angels . . . ascending and descending." For we believe in the one Lord, His only-begotten Son, born of the Virgin Mary, true God and man. This mystery is so great, so grand, so inexpressible, that the angels themselves cannot marvel at it enough, much less comprehend it. But, as is stated in 1 Peter 1:12, these are "things into which angels long to look." For angels cannot rejoice and marvel enough at that inexpressible union and unity of the most diverse natures which they do not reach either by ascending or by descending. If they lift up their eyes, they see the incomprehensible majesty of God above them. If they look down, they see God and the Divine Majesty subjected to demons and to every creature.

These are marvelous things: to see a man and the lowliest creature humbled below all, to see the same creature sitting at the right hand of the Father and raised above all the angels, and to see Him in the bosom of the Father and soon subjected to the devil, as is stated in Ps. 8:5: "Thou hast made Him a little lower than the angels." Likewise in Eph. 4:9: "He had descended into the lower parts of the earth." This is a wonderful ascent and descent of the angels, to see the highest and the lowest completely united in one and the same Person, the highest God lying in the manger. Therefore the angels adore Him there, rejoice, and sing: "Glory to God in the highest" (Luke 2:14). On the other hand, when they consider the lowliness of the human nature, they descend and sing: "And on earth peace."

When we see the same thing in the life to come, we, too, shall feel and speak far differently from the way we feel and speak now. For now these are things such as the angels do not comprehend. Nor can they be satisfied. Indeed, they always desire to look into this inexpressible goodness, wisdom, kindness, and mercy poured out upon us when that Person, who is the highest and is terrible in His majesty above all creatures, becomes the lowest and most despised. We shall see this wondrous spectacle in that life, and it will be the constant joy of the blessed, just as it is the one desire and joy of the angels to see the Lord of all, who is the same as nothing, that is, the lowest.

We carnal and ignorant human beings do not understand or value the magnitude of these things. We have barely tasted a drink of milk—not solid food—from that inexpressible union and association of the divine and the human nature, which is of such a kind that not only the humanity has been assumed, but that such humanity has been made liable and subject to death and hell yet in that humiliation has devoured the devil, hell, and all things in itself. This is the communion of properties.[25] GOD, who created all things and is above all things, is the highest and the lowest, so that we must say: "That man, who was scourged, who is the lowest under death, under the wrath of God, under sin and every kind of evil, and finally under hell, is the highest God." Why? Because it is the same Person. Although the nature is twofold, the Person is not divided. Therefore both things are true: the highest divinity is the lowest creature, made the servant of all men, yes, subject to the devil himself. On the other hand, the lowest creature, the humanity or the man, sits at the right hand of the Father and has been made the highest; and He subjects the angels to Himself, not because of His human[26] nature, but because of the wonderful conjunction and union established out of the two contrary and unjoinable natures in one Person.

This, therefore, is the article by which the whole world, reason, and Satan are offended. For in the same Person there are things that are to the highest degree contrary. He who is the highest, so that the angels do not grasp Him, is not only comprehended but has been comprehended in such a way, is so finite, that nothing is more finite and confined, and vice versa. But He

---

[25] Cf. *Luther's Works*, 22, p. 492, note 176.

[26] The Weimar text has *humanum,* but we have followed other editions and read *humanam.*

is not comprehended except in that Word as in breasts in which milk has been set forth and poured. Faith takes hold of this Word, namely, "I believe in the Son of God, our Lord Jesus Christ, who was conceived by the Holy Spirit, born of the Virgin Mary (these are the breasts), suffered under Pontius Pilate, was crucified, dead, and buried; He descended into hell; the third day He rose from the dead; He ascended into heaven and sits at the right hand of God the Father Almighty, after subjecting all the angels to Himself." Here there is God and man, the highest and the lowest, infinite and finite in one Person, emptying and filling all things.

This, then, is the ascent and descent of the angels of God and of the blessed, who look on this, pay attention to it, and proclaim it, as can be seen on the day of the nativity. They descend as though there were no God up in heaven. They come to Bethlehem and say: "Behold, I announce great joy to you, The Lord has been born for you" (cf. Luke 2:10-11). And in Heb. 1:6 we read: "When He brings the First-born into the world, He says: 'Let all God's angels worship Him.'" They adore Him as He now lies in the manger at His mother's breasts. Indeed, they adore Him on the cross, when He descends into hell, when He has been subjected to sin and hell, when He bears all the sins of the whole world. And they submit themselves forever to this lowest One. Thus, therefore, the angels ascend and see the Son of God, who is begotten from eternity. On the other hand, they descend when they see Him born in time of Mary. And whether ascending or descending, they adore Him.

This is how Christ explains this ladder. I regard this as the chief and proper explanation of this passage. And this is that great and indescribable dignity of mankind which no one can express, namely, that by this wonderful union God has joined the human nature to Himself. Ambrose and especially Bernard take great pleasure in this passage, which is exceedingly delightful, and in this work of the incarnation.[27] And it is right and godly for them to do so. For this pleasure will be a joy above all joy and will be eternal blessedness when we truly behold there our flesh, which is like us in all respects in the highest as well as the lowest

---

[27] See, for example, Ambrose, *De excessu fratris Satyri*, II, 100, *Patrologia, Series Latina*, XVI, 1402; Bernard of Clairvaux, *Sermones de tempore*, Sermon I, *Patrologia, Series Latina*, CLXXXIII, 36 (cf. *Luther's Works*, 22, 103).

place. For He did all this for us. He descended into hell and ascended into heaven. This sight the angels enjoy forever in heaven, and this is what Christ means when He says (Matt. 18:10): "Their angels always behold the face of My Father who is in heaven." They look constantly at the divinity. And now they descend from heaven after He has been made man. Now they look upon Christ and wonder at the work of the incarnation. They see that He has been made man, humiliated, and placed on His mother's lap. They adore the man who was crucified and rejected, and they acknowledge Him as the Son of God.

Bernard loved the incarnation of Christ very much. So did Bonaventure.[28] I praise these men very highly for the sake of that article on which they reflect so gladly and brilliantly, and which they practice in themselves with great joy and godliness. Bernard thinks and imagines piously enough that the devil fell because of that envy on account of which he begrudged men such great dignity, namely, that God would become man. For he thinks that when Satan was a good angel in the sight of God, he saw that one day the divinity would descend and take upon itself this wretched and mortal flesh and would not take upon itself the nature of angels. Moved by that indignity and envy, thinks Bernard, the devil raged against God, with the result that he was thrown out of heaven. These thoughts of Bernard are not unprofitable, for they flow from admiration for the boundless love and mercy of God. The devil was a very handsome angel and a decidedly outstanding creature. But when he saw that it had been predetermined that God would assume human nature and not the nature of the angels, he was inflamed with envy, anger, and indignation against God for not being willing to take him, who was a most handsome spirit, and for not being able to become a participant in the divinity and in such great majesty. It pained him that that wretched mass of human flesh had to be preferred to himself; for he thought that all this became him better than it did this sinful flesh, which is liable to death and all evils. And, what is most surprising, this opinion crept into the Alcoran, no matter who the author or what the occasion, was. It certainly seems that the devil himself suggested to the author of the Alcoran that

---

[28] Bonaventura, *De incarnatione verbi, Breviloquium,* IV, *Opera omnia,* VII (Paris, 1866), 282—295.

good angels became demons because they refused to adore Adam.[29] Satan could not conceal this sin of his. Therefore he imposed it on this instrument of his to stir up hatred against God. He distorted the true cause of the Fall, as though the angels were compelled to adore Adam, that is, a creature, and that when they refused, they were hurled headlong from heaven and became angels.

This is almost in agreement with what Bernard imagined, and by what he himself points out the devil betrays in what respect he sinned. He wanted to be like God. When he saw that it would come to pass that GOD would lower Himself in such a way that He would assume man, he thought that this honor most properly suited him. This is how the ancients understand the well-known passage in Is. 14:13. They refer it to this fall and sin of the devil. The passage reads as follows: "You said in your heart: 'I will ascend to heaven; above the stars of God I will set my throne on high.'" For then he would truly have become like God if God had assumed him into the unity of His Person as He assumed man. The fact that the humanity has now been assumed makes this man the Son of God, because He is one Person. This man born of the Virgin Mary is God Himself, who created heaven and earth. The angel would have been adorned with the same glory if the Son of God had become inangelate,[30] so to speak, and had taken up that most beautiful spirit. For then it would have been said: "That Lucifer is true God, the Creator of heaven and earth."

This, says Bernard, is what the devil seems to have sought to achieve. But when he had been repulsed, he was inflamed with great hatred, wrath, and envy against God for honoring the human nature in this way with the divine nature and because he himself was compelled to adore the human nature in the divinity. This is the origin of that hatred and rage of the devil and the world by which he plots and sets in motion the destruction of our nature with whatever darts and devices he can, for it is the height of his monstrous hatred against the Seed of the woman, the Son of God. It is He who is involved. It is an ancient and inveterate

---

[29] On this conception of the fall of Satan cf. Koran, II, 36; VII, 12; XVII, 60.

[30] The Latin word used here is *inangelatus*, which may be Luther's own coinage; Tertullian, however, had spoken of a *caro . . . angelificata, De resurrectione,* 26, *Corpus Christianorum, Series Latina.*

hatred, conceived and rooted in heaven, so that it can never be eradicated. Accordingly, the ladder is the wonderful union of the divinity with our flesh. On it the angels ascend and descend, and they can never wonder at this enough. This is the historical, simple, and literal sense.[31]

Later there is another union — a union between us and Christ, as John expresses it in a very beautiful manner. "I am in the Father, and the Father is in Me," says Christ (John 14:10). This comes first. Later He says: "You in Me, and I in you" (John 14:20). This is the allegorical meaning of the ladder. But the allegory should nourish faith and not teach about our affairs or our works. Therefore we are carried along by faith and become one flesh with Him, as Christ says in John 17:21: "That they may all be one; even as Thou, Father, art in Me, and I in Thee, that they also may be one in Us." In this way we ascend into Him and are carried along through the Word and the Holy Spirit. And through faith we cling to Him, since we become one body with Him and He with us. He is the Head; we are the members. On the other hand, He descends to us through the Word and the sacraments by teaching and by exercising us in the knowledge of Him. The first union, then, is that of the Father and the Son in the divinity. The second is that of the divinity and the humanity in Christ. The third is that of the church and Christ.

This is the true meaning. The devil hates it, and perhaps he foresaw it in heaven. Therefore he does not cease fighting against the ladder and this ascent and descent to draw us away from it. This he sets in motion through all sects and heresies in order that he may divert men from the knowledge of Christ, from His divinity and His humanity, and in order that he may draw the whole church and the members away from Christ. Therefore God wanted to give a veiled indication of this great sacrament of the incarnation of the Son of God to this very saintly man, not only for his own consolation in order that his faith might have respite in such great troubles and in his great tribulation, but also that for the future it might be a prophecy for all his descendants. For what Moses wrote concerning the patriarchs he did not write primarily

---

[31] It should be noted that according to this statement, the literal sense of Jacob's ladder refers to Christ, while the allegorical sense, given in the next paragraph, refers to the union between Christ and the believer.

for their sakes. They had no need at all of these writings; they were already dead and gathered to their fathers. No, Moses wrote in order that the churches might be instructed and strengthened up to the end of the world. For we cannot treat of and teach diligently enough that great compassion and the honor the Heavenly Father paid us by deigning to send His Son into the flesh. Nor can we understand this by meditating on it. Indeed, as has been stated, not even the angels can be satisfied by ascending and seeing God's Son in heaven and, on the other hand, by descending to where they see Him lying in the manger, crucified, dead, and descending to the depths of hell but lifted up in turn out of hell and sitting at the right hand of the Father.

In short, one must learn that God and man are one Person. He who believes this article knows now that all things are comprehended and hidden in that Person. Thus Paul says in Col. 2:3, 9: "In whom are hid all the treasures of wisdom and knowledge. . . . In Him the whole fullness of deity dwells bodily." No wonder Satan begrudged this knowledge and honor of ours and is still angry. For he is an exceedingly proud spirit who cannot look upon that humility as the good angels do but continually looks up to heaven and wants to be like the Highest. This is why he fell so horribly.

The additional content of this sermon has often been dealt with above and is repeatedly confirmed in what follows.[32] In the first place, God is named in the plural number; for He is called אֱלֹהִים. In the second place, God is God of the living, not of the dead (cf. Matt. 22:32). These three patriarchs, Abraham, Isaac, and Jacob, live even though they are dead. Therefore we, too, shall live when we are dead, since we have the same God. These points are always repeated and confirmed.

Lastly, the land of Canaan is promised to the third patriarch in spite of the fact that they did not hold even a foot's length in it as Acts 7:5 says. But because of the promise they received, and hoped for, another land. And they understood that when God spoke to Abraham and the other fathers in these physical promises, He also made a promise to the dead, who in faith would have not only this land but also the future fatherland. Concerning the

---

[32] See, for example, *Luther's Works*, 1, pp. 59, 285.

seed He says: "It will be as the dust [33] of the earth." Above (Gen. 26:4), when speaking to Isaac, He compared it to the stars of heaven. Likewise to the sand of the sea. Here He mentions the dust of the earth. This has been discussed above.[34]

> *And you shall spread abroad to the west and to the east and to the north and to the south; and by you and your descendants all the families of the earth shall be blessed.*

15. *Behold, I am with you and will keep you wherever you go, and will bring you back to this land; for I will not leave you until I have done that of which I have spoken to you.*

Here a new word, פָּרַץ, is used — a word which was not employed before in this promise. Below, in Gen. 38:29, Moses also employs it when Perez, the son of Judah, is born, and the midwife says: "What a breach you have made for yourself!" And in 2 Sam. 5:20, when David had overthrown the Philistines, he said: "The Lord has broken through my enemies before me," and he called the name of the place בַּעַל פְּרָצִים. From this word comes פָּרִיץ, "a robber," "a footpad," as in Ps. 17:4. And from this has also come *parix,* the name of a small bird, a tomtit, because it is a cruel bird.[35] Therefore this word has a wonderful meaning: "You will be divided. You will break out. You will spread out to all four parts of the earth." This is different from, and more complete than, what He stated above (cf. v. 13): "I will give you this land." "Nor will you spread out alone, but you and your descendants will spread out and rush or break out of this corner into all four parts of the world." But He enumerates these directions in the opposite way. First He names the west, for this is what the sea means; then the east, and finally the south. Here not only the possession of the land of Canaan and of the future blessing according to the promise is pointed out but also the fact that Jacob will reign in the four parts of the world. And He will explain this later.

But He makes a remarkable insertion: "All the families of the

---

[33] The Weimar text has *populus,* but we have followed other editions and read *pulvis.*

[34] Cf. *Luther's Works,* 4, pp. 151 ff.

[35] Thus, according to Luther, the name *parix* in Latin has a Hebrew origin.

earth shall be blessed in you." He means to say: "Not only will you possess the land in which you are sleeping, but you will break out in such a way that the Blessed Seed will proceed without any resistance and will be spread out with might into the whole world." God really speaks in a very friendly way with Jacob, as though He were saying: "The serpent will try to oppose himself to this blessing and resist it. He will attack not only one part in the land of Canaan—the part which will take possession of the rule and the physical blessing—but he will also resist the part which will be spread out through the world in all four directions. There he will assail the spiritual blessing with all his might. He will not cease; for there is no end of his enmity, of which mention has been made above in the first promise (Gen. 3:15). But the exceedingly wretched throng that has the spiritual blessing is weak and afflicted. It is a poor little flock, as Christ says in Luke 12:32, rejected, despised, and not worthy of being regarded as the church. Indeed, it is not worthy of being regarded as a people at all, much less as the people of God. "What is that poor throng?" the devil will think. "I will devour them in the twinkling of an eye." "But let him ravage without measure, tear, persecute, resist, and hinder," says the Lord. (And again He holds up before him the word meaning to proceed against.) "I will proceed against him. I will be a פָּרִיץ against a פָּרִיץ."

This is how God consoles Jacob, and in him the whole church, in order that he may be certain about his descendants. For although Esau exercises dominion after Jacob has been cast off and driven into exile, and even though he is really king and priest in the meantime, so that everything is full of despair and nothing is less likely than that Jacob will be the future heir and ruler in the house or the church, yet this is of little importance. "Be stouthearted, and endure. For not only will you be the heir in the house, and not only will the blessing of Abraham and the possession of this land be bestowed on you; but I also assure you that you will be a patriarch over the whole earth and the father of the Blessed Seed, through whom all the nations will be blessed. And I will accomplish this when I rage against him who rages."

Therefore God points out that through the might of God and the Holy Spirit He wants to force His way through against all the wisdom and power of the prince of the world. We know that this has been fulfilled, and we are finding out that it is being fulfilled even now. The devil has always raged with horrible fury against the people of God from the time of the judges, the kings, and the apostles up to the end of the world, so that one can think of nothing fiercer and crueller than the ruler of this world (John 16:11) and god of this world (2 Cor. 4:4). "But I, in turn, will be a פָּרִיץ. I, in turn, will force My way through and rage," says God, "in order that he may feel the insuperable might and power in this פָּרִיץ." God accomplishes this with His might, with no wisdom and no power of ours. For everything in us is weak and worthless; but in that nothingness and worthlessness, so to speak, God shows His strength, according to the saying (2 Cor. 12:9): "My power is made perfect in weakness." "When you think that you have been devoured and destroyed, I will force My way through and bring it to pass that you rise and reign." Thus Christ was strongest when He was dead and weakest. For in that weakness He condemned the world and the ruler of this world together with all their power and wisdom.

Accordingly this word should be carefully noted. Moses undoubtedly understood it well and took very great delight in it. The patriarchs, too, paid close attention to these emphatic, brilliant, and significant words. He could have used greater simplicity, just as previously He simply said: "You shall spread abroad." But He preferred to use a stronger word, a military word pertaining to the camp. St. Paul considered this when he said in 2 Cor. 10:4: "The weapons of our warfare are not worldly but have divine power to destroy strongholds." All ministers of the Word are called soldiers and generals. God Himself is called in Scripture the God of armies, soldiers, and warriors, פָּרִיצִים, yet without the might of the flesh, without human strength and wisdom, but with the strength of the Holy Spirit, in the greatest weakness, humility, and modesty.

But what will be the outcome of this battle? "And all the families of the earth will be blessed by you and by your descendants. There will be no carnal tyranny. I will not rage in such a way that I harm and destroy men. This the mighty men in the world do. With their tyranny they rage with the sword and fury only in order that some may exercise dominion over others and may practice their cruelty on those who are under them. But My raging, My strength, and My victory must be salutary, blessed, quickening, kind, and merciful, which does not harm or injure men but blesses all, saves all, and liberates them from sin, death, and the devil. And through that raging I will destroy the tyranny and raging of the devil, and this victory will benefit the whole world through your descendants." In this way God explains this bursting forth by means of these words: "In you shall be blessed."

Above (Gen. 26:4), however, He spoke of "all the nations." Here He speaks of "families," a word which extends less widely than the word "nation"; for every nation has many families. This blessing, then, will be extended not only to the nations in general but also in particular to the families among the nations, not that all from every family will receive the blessing, but some from all families will embrace it. Accordingly, in this place the blessing is clearer and more explicit; it is expressed in stronger and more meaningful words. Here the word is not reflexive,[36] meaning "they will bless themselves." No, it is simply passive, meaning "they will be blessed." The word used above is stronger, yet when He says here: "They will be blessed," He has adequately expressed the fact that He will break out into the four parts of the earth. For "they will be blessed" signifies the same thing as the statement that they will hear the preaching. But to hear the preaching and to believe and receive it when it has been heard differ, just as the word above designates not only the preaching when it has been heard but also those who receive it when it has been heard. Thus Ps. 34:2 says: "My soul makes its boast in the Lord"; that is, "I am not only praised in the Lord," but, transitively, "I—the soul which has been praised—am encouraged," or "My soul glories when it hears the preaching of the blessing; it admits and receives that blessing."

Therefore He points out that this blessing, which comes from Jacob himself, must be published abroad. For the Gospel concerning Christ the Savior cannot be preached without adding that He was born from Abraham, from Jacob. For we must have sure proof that He was in all truth the Son of Man, a natural man, and not a specter, not an apparition, as Manichaeus raved.[37] Therefore we have His ancestors, who were true men. Nor can He be

---

[36] The verb is in what the Hebrew grammars call the Niphal, which may have either reflexive or (sometimes) passive meaning.

[37] Cf. *Luther's Works*, 13, p. 96, note 34.

named without these fathers, without Abraham, Isaac, Jacob, and Adam, in order that He may have a definite lineage, a true father, a true mother, and that it may be certain that He is from a human seed and that He took upon Himself human nature, not the angels, not any other creature. Accordingly, a definite place was assigned to the nativity of Christ for the fathers and the prophets, and definite persons from whom He had to descend were named. Consequently, we cannot doubt that He is in very truth our flesh and blood, bone of our bones. Accordingly, when He is preached and praised, His parents, from whom He assumed flesh, are named at the same time. And at the same time we, too, are included—we for whose sakes He became the Seed of Abraham, Isaac, and Jacob, not the seed of angels. Therefore He so carefully inculcates and so often repeats the words "in your seed, etc." It is as though He were saying: "Know for sure that you will have descendants. Now you are alone, without a wife, without children. You are exiled. But later you shall have children's children and that Son who will make children of God."

Therefore this is a glorious promise not only for the present life—although it embraces this too—but also for the life to come. For if he must fill the four parts of the world, he must by no means have died; or if he dies, it will be necessary for him to be brought back to life. Accordingly, it is a great and sublime promise. Indeed, it is greater than Jacob was able to comprehend, just as we cannot embrace its greatness either with our hearts; for the human heart is too narrow to be able to comprehend and take hold of it. I think that after the patriarch Jacob had been awakened from his sleep, he was drenched to such an extent with joy and gladness when he thought about this promise that he was altogether beside himself, thunderstruck, and ecstatic.

But this should be applied to our use, in order that we may acknowledge the magnitude of God's grace, which has been revealed and given to us through the Gospel. For we are absolved through the Word, and on the authority of Christ we are told: "I baptize you; I extend to you the body and blood of Christ; I tear your soul by force from the power of the devil; I set you free from eternal death and damnation; and I make you a child of God and an heir of eternal life." These words which God speaks to us are so grand, eternal, and infinite that we cannot grasp them; for my nature is too weak to be able to endure them. This weakness draws us back and hinders us, so that we do not feel such great joy and gladness as those words and divine promises really bring. For if I could take hold of them as I desire and wish, it would be not at all strange if I suddenly expired for joy. For think what a great thing it is that by the word of a man and the laying on of hands the kingdom of God is announced and bestowed, likewise victory against the devil, sin, and death, and that one is put into the company of the angels and into possession of heavenly and eternal blessings. But how few there are who believe these things as they should! Much less do we comprehend them, but we only take hold of them in one way or another. Yet they are completely true. And surely we must die in this faith. Otherwise we shall fall from our salvation and not remain safe and sound against the devil for even one moment. For he rages horribly when he hears that this is taught in this way, and he persecutes those who preach it or who listen to this doctrine and embrace it.

But [38] we should listen with grateful hearts and with joy, and we should believe at least weakly. Only let us not fight against it, blaspheme, persecute, reject, and deny. The reason why we do not comprehend it firmly and perfectly lies in the wretchedness of our flesh and in the narrowness of our heart, which cannot grasp that incomprehensible glory. Thus Paul says in 2 Cor. 9:15: "Thanks be to God for His inexpressible gift!" Nevertheless, we toil and exert ourselves that we may finally comprehend it as we have been comprehended (cf. Phil. 3:12). Of course, we hold it in our grasp as much as we can with a weak faith, and we must rest content with the consolation that God commands that he who is weak in faith should be welcomed (Rom. 14:1). For the law of my members (cf. Rom. 7:23) resists in us; it makes war and takes me captive, and does not permit me to take hold of so many great blessings more firmly. For GOD promises and gives an inexpressible treasure, the forgiveness of sins, eternal life, the grace of GOD, the inheritance of heavenly blessings, victory, and the power to trample the devil underfoot. Therefore must I, wretched little man and worm that I am, fight against so many angels, against principalities and powers, against the rulers of darkness (Eph. 6:12), and indeed without the sword of the flesh, without strength, without wisdom, without power? But how?

---

[38] The Weimar text has *verbo* (perhaps because of the *audiamus*), but we have followed other editions and read *vero*.

Believe in the Seed of Abraham, the Son of God. This faith is our victory which overcomes the world (1 John 5:4), vanquishes the devil, and destroys the gates of hell (cf. Matt. 16:18). But it is still a slender grasping and a tiny spark of faith. Therefore in that slender grasping it does not yet appear how great the thing we believe is. May the Lord grant that we endure in faith to the end!

Accordingly, this is a twofold promise concerning the Seed of Jacob, in whom all the nations of the earth are to be blessed, that is, a promise concerning Christ which he includes in the temporal promise as in the one that is less significant, just as a child is wrapped in rags, a gem is inserted in gold, or a precious treasure is kept in an earthen container. The temporal blessing is great and rich enough, but the one about raging into the world is greater. But He repeats the temporal blessing and binds it up into a little bundle with this temporal promise concerning the descendants. For He says: "And behold, I am with you, etc. You have the eternal promise and the temporal one concerning your descendants. Now I shall add this third point: I will be with you on this journey and during this exile so far as your person is concerned, and I will even protect you yourself; for in order that the things I have promised may be fulfilled, you must live and be protected. Your brother Esau is plotting against you. The devil hates you when you sleep and when you are awake; but I want to walk with you, and I will be your companion." O what a desirable and stout companion! "I will not only go with you to escort you; but I will be your wall, your protector. I will fight for you — I, who am to be your Son from your seed, through whom all the families of the earth will be blessed. I will be with you, I will shield you and protect you."

This is certainly a great consolation which Jacob clings to and believes. But he does so with a faith that is weak enough, as we shall hear below, when he will be plagued with very grievous trials and with an outward appearance completely contrary to the other things God has promised. For he will be compelled to suffer and bear wrongs and annoyances from Laban for 20 years. This is not keeping watch day and night, is it? Nevertheless, God kept His promise, and eventually [39] the outcome was in accord,

---

[39] The Weimar text has *tamen* (perhaps because of another *tamen* earlier in the sentence), but we have followed other editions and read *tandem*.

although according to the flesh the opposite seemed to happen.

Therefore it is an extraordinary promise, and, as I have stated before, it should be carefully considered; for in the legends of the fathers special attention must be paid to the part in which they hear God speaking. For our life consists in the internal sanctity which is the Word or the blessing applied to us. It does not consist, as even the best among our adversaries contend, in our works. Yet we do not deny that good works must be done, that the body must be castigated, and that the lusts of the flesh must be resisted. The world, of course, is taken in by this hypocrisy and by the outward appearances of the works in order that they may remove the Word of God from sight. For human folly cannot distinguish between the Word of God and our work. Yet this distinction is easy and decidedly necessary. But for hypocrites it is difficult and impossible — not to understand but to take hold of.

Our adversaries cry out that a formal righteousness of works is needed.[40] This the world admires. But is this enough, even if you praise a man to me as altogether saintly? To be sure, the works of the saints are great and praiseworthy, and we admit that love is necessary, that one must abstain from evil lusts, that the flesh must be mortified, etc. "But you do not do this," they say. Yet even if we were to do all this, we would not be righteous on this account, would we? And why do you extol and admire this so much? Surely in order that you may suppress that other divine sanctity. To be sure, we concede that there is a righteousness of works, but in such a way that it is not preferred to the former righteousness and that a distinction is made between precious and cheap, between greater and lesser. This distinction is necessary both in the whole life and especially in this doctrine. Indeed the dumb animals understand that there is a difference among foods. A dog understands that meat is better than bread. Therefore let the sanctity of works be something, and let it be necessary! But we want[41] the sanctity of the Word to be exalted above it and to be preferred to it, that is, the sanctity of the promise, namely, that we live before God not by a formal and intrinsic sanctity but by the sanctity of the Word and of faith.

Therefore one should make a proper distinction, namely, that

---

[40] See also the discussion on p. 213.

[41] We have adopted the conjectural emendation suggested by the Weimar editors and have read *volumus* rather than *nolumus*.

the sanctity of works is one thing and that the sanctity of the Word and of faith is something else. The latter sanctity conquers the devil and makes me a child of God. This does not take place because of the sanctity of the flesh or works, not even of the Decalog, in which we do not even comprehend that sanctity. For we have only some beginnings of it. This, then, should be the first and chief proclamation, and it should not be underestimated. Thus our adversaries insidiously urge the sanctity of works in order to obscure the sanctity of the Word or of faith. We praise the virtues of the patriarchs, their modesty, patience, humility, chastity, and love, and the pilgrimages undertaken with obedience to God; and we teach and imitate other services of godliness. Nevertheless, we should have far greater preference for this, when God speaks with them. To listen to God's Word when He promises and blesses is different from hearing a commandment by which you are ordered to do or to suffer something.

It is clear and manifest enough that there is a difference between the Word, which promises, and the commandment, which orders to do something. Therefore the legends of the saints and all life should be divided into these two parts: the Word of God and our work. The former belongs to God alone; the latter is ours, namely, love, patience, and the castigating and crucifying of the flesh. This is a life; but it is a life of works, and it does not take hold of the sanctity of the Word, which is the soul of life. Therefore the Word has to precede; for it is the Word and promise of God, who blesses, promises, receives us into grace, and forgives sins. This surely must precede: "Your sins are forgiven you; I am your God; do not fear the devil; I am with you; I will protect you; I will not forsake you." But after the forgiveness of sins this follows: "Take up your bed and go home" (Matt. 9:6). This precedes: "Take heart, My son"; that is, "First acknowledge Me as propitious, as placated, as being favorable, and as absolving you. First receive My blessing, in order that you may be freed from sin and death. Afterwards, when you have been healed, take up your bed and walk; teach, and do works." Thus after Jacob has first been strengthened in faith because of grace and the blessing, he walks, works, and suffers, as is stated in what follows: "He awoke from his sleep, etc."

So far, then, we have heard this glorious promise given to the patriarch Jacob not only concerning the blessing of his descendants and concerning Christ but also concerning the present guidance and protection in exile, in order that he may be sure of life, of food, of his return, and of victory over all future sufferings and tribulations. For below we shall see that he was afflicted with great evils before these things were fulfilled. Yet through all those kinds of death and countless misfortunes he must be brought back and remain blessed and the heir of the descendants and the future inheritance. Therefore these examples are especially memorable [42] because they not only show that God spoke with the fathers but also testify that when God speaks, He does not lie, even though everything seems to proceed and happen in the opposite way, that the world is furious, and that the flesh, the adversaries, and the devil, together with all the gates of hell (cf. Matt. 16:18), are raging. "For He spoke, and it came to be" (Ps. 33:9). But it is difficult for us believers to break through; for all the fury of Satan is devoted to this one thing, namely, that he may separate us from the Word, and that we, exhausted and broken either by the multitude or the long duration of our tribulations, may forsake and reject the Word. Accordingly, these two are joined: the omnipotence of the Word and the weakness or the inomnipotence, so to speak, of the human heart, which must hold out, bear, and endure until the Word is fulfilled.

Bernard says concerning the faith of the Virgin Mary when it had been announced to her by the angel that she would be the mother of Christ that the strength of faith of the Virgin who could believe the words of the angel was no less a miracle than the incarnation of the Word itself.[43] Therefore the greatest things in the histories of the saints are the words which God speaks with the saints. Although their virtues and deeds should be praised — and God requires these too — yet they, like the feet, should be put in the lowest place. But the head in the life of the saints is the speaking of God itself. Yet the fact, as it appears, that everything happens contrary to what God promises in His Word, this takes place through the power of the devil and because of the weakness of our flesh, which has doubts about the perpetuity and the truth

---

[42] The Weimar text has *memorabilis,* but we have followed other editions and read *memorabilia.*

[43] Cf. Bernard of Clairvaux, *In nativitate Domini sermo II,* 4, *Patrologia, Series Latina,* CLXXXIII, 121.

of the promised Word. Thus we shall see below that a violent attack is launched against these exceedingly powerful and rich promises, which say: "I will be with you; I will guard you, etc."

We, who do not live in perils and difficulties like those with which Jacob was afflicted, read this carelessly and casually, and we think that it is easy and unimportant. But if we were in his place, we would feel otherwise. For we, who believe God when He promises and have been redeemed by the blood of Christ, see that among Christians everything happens as though it were a matter of hopelessness and impossibility, so that man, together with the flesh and all wisdom and reason, must simply be mortified and must depend on the Word alone, as can be seen in the case of the saintly patriarchs. He who does not prefer the Word to his own counsels, yes, to his own life, farewell to him, and let him become a heathen and an Epicurean. For he will never bear fruit either for himself or others, since he wants to control impossible and incomprehensible matters with his wisdom and counsel. Consequently, it is all over with him. Therefore all things will not flow according to our wish and rule. This one simply has to learn and conclude.

When we are absolved from sins, we have the Word, which is founded and stands firm on the promises of God. But do we not experience the very opposite and undergo very great conflicts against the devil, death, hell, and our understanding? Although this pains the flesh very much, yet in the meantime God faithfully fulfills His promises for those who believe and wait in patience, as is stated in the Epistle to the Hebrews: "Through faith the saints conquered kingdoms, enforced justice, received promises" (cf. 11:33). Thus consolation was especially necessary for the patriarch Jacob both during this exile and later, when he was severely afflicted by Laban. Yet he could not retain it without a great conflict, even though God promises clearly and definitely: "I will not leave you until I have done what I have spoken to you." Thus the disciples completely forget Christ's words and every consolation at the time of the Passion. He had preached to them at length, as that sermon is described in three chapters when He says: "I have spoken these things to you that when the hour comes you will not be offended" (cf. John 16:1, 4). But what benefit these remarkable words of comfort and exhortation produced appeared when He was crucified. Then they recalled nothing at all of what they had heard and seen Christ speaking and doing. But this is placed before us in this way in order that we may learn what a great thing faith is, that it is not a cold and lazy quality, as the papists dream.

16. *Then Jacob awoke from his sleep and said: Surely the Lord is in this place; and I did not know it.*

This appearance or vision did not come to him when he was awake, as most appearances to the saints are. Thus above (Gen. 18:1) the Lord appeared to Abraham in Mamre through angels. There are appearances to men who are awake, and they are more definite than those that occur in dreams. Yet if these, too, do not have their counterparts, or stirrings of the heart, and faith, they are not true. But I cannot easily discuss dreams, for they are common among the godless and the godly. Thus in the histories of the heathen there are descriptions of the dreams of Julius Caesar, Galba, Brutus, Cassius, and others.[44] The dreams they had were of such a nature that the truth and the thing itself followed; and not only did the outcome agree with the dream, but they also understood their dreams after they had awakened. Similar to these are the dreams of Pharaoh and Nebuchadnezzar that are recorded in the sacred histories.

Therefore we shall make the following distinction between dreams: Some are political or private, that is, dreams pertaining to private or public affairs. These have their own type and their own forms. Accordingly, they must be referred to their own class. We shall not speak about these here. Some dreams concerning which Holy Scripture speaks pertain to ecclesiastical and eternal matters. These are true dreams, and it is necessary to speak about them here.

Pharaoh's dream pertained to the years of sterility and fertility. Therefore it is political and private. Thus Nebuchadnezzar's dream was also physical; it pertained to that kingdom. There are many dreams of this kind. God scatters them among the nations, just as He scatters many other gifts, according to the statement in Acts 14:17: "He did good and gave you from heaven rains and fruitful seasons, satisfying your hearts with food and glad-

[44] Cf. *Luther's Works*, 7, pp. 120—121, on Luther's knowledge of Roman thought about dreams.

ness." In this way He has scattered kingdoms and crowns among the godly and the godless alike. Yet one must observe in general concerning political dreams that they also have to have an analogy with the present state of affairs and produce such an impression that the dreamer is moved and stirred. They are not melancholy dreams that have no bearing on reality. Concerning these Ecclus. 34:4 says: "From an unclean thing what will be made clean? And from something false what will be true?" Here all dreams are called unclean, and he who believes them is deceived. And there is also extant a saying of Cato: "Pay no attention to dreams." [45]

But in regard to dreams there has always been a discussion about whether one should or should not believe them. False prophets are wont to praise their dreams. Accordingly, God often forbids us to believe them. For if a dream does not have its analogy, he who believes it is defiled, and the dream is deceptive. Nevertheless, it is certain that dreams that are true and have congruous meanings are also sent to secular men. Concerning these dreams men have handed down definite rules.[46] In the first place, they must not be vague and vanishing images or thoughts but must have an analogy with the present state of affairs. In the second place, they should move the heart in such a way that the dreamer is troubled and disturbed. Thus Daniel says to Nebuchadnezzar: "To you, O king, as you lay in bed came thoughts of what would be hereafter, etc." (2:29). He points out that the king was anxious and concerned in his dreams about the kingdom and the state of affairs after his time. Therefore there must be some anxiety, and then there must be very great agitation or a very strong impression by which the dreamer is moved and influenced. But I am not discussing this. For we must consider the dreams of which Moses is speaking, since at other times he condemns dreams (cf. Deut. 13:3).

For this is what the Lord says to Aaron (Num. 12:6-8): "If there is a prophet among you, I the Lord make Myself known to him in a vision, I speak with him in a dream. Not so with My

---

[45] Cato, *Disticha*, Book II, distich 31 (also quoted below, *Luther's Works*, 7, p. 122).

[46] See also the earlier discussion in these *Lectures on Genesis*, *Luther's Works*, 3, pp. 10—12.

servant Moses; he is entrusted with all My house. With him I speak mouth to mouth." This means: "If anyone presides over the government of church affairs, I shall speak to him by word of mouth or through a vision or through a dream." But He says that He is speaking to Moses in a far different and loftier manner, not through the word of a preacher or a disciple of the prophets, not through a vision or images or through a dream. No, He says: "I speak to him mouth to mouth." Yet here God confirms His revelations, first a verbal revelation; then a vision like the one described in Is. 6:1 ff.; and, in the third place, a dream. These three types God approves, but in the prophets, that is, in those who discharge an ecclesiastical office, and especially if the dreams have a bearing on the Word and agree with the Word. Here one must observe whether they influence the dreamer, whether they have their counterpart and do not conflict with the Word. And there is just as much validity as if the Word itself were presented either through a vision or through the voice of those who are awake. Thus Jacob has the Word and something that is certain. For he received the blessing and was called by God to a patriarchate. He was appointed bishop, lord, and governor of the church and his house by the Word of God through the blessing of his father Isaac. When this foundation has been laid, one should look at the dream to see whether it agrees with the foundation or not. One must see whether stubble or gold is built on the foundation, as Paul says in 1 Cor. 3:12.[47]

In the same manner a foundation has been laid in the matter of discharging a political duty. Although the heathen do not have the Word, they have the actual thing and the calling by which they have been appointed to govern and rule in war and peace. If a dream now comes to a heathen commander or leader — a dream which has a counterpart, that is, agrees with the thing itself and with his thoughts — it should by no means be regarded as worthless. Accordingly, one should regard Jacob's dream much more as true and meaningful because it has been preceded by his appointment and a manifest divine calling to the priesthood and the primogeniture, and the true foundation is the promise. But he is troubled about the future completion of the whole structure above the foundation, since many misfortunes present them-

[47] The original has "2 Cor. 3."

selves, so that it appears that the whole building will fall in ruins. Here his heart begins to waver and have doubts about the success and fulfillment of the promise. Therefore God is present and sends a very clear dream which agrees with the fact and is in harmony with the foundation. In addition, he is agitated. Thus the text says (v. 17): "He was afraid"; that is, he was impelled to reverence when he saw that the dream was in agreement with the foundation.

These are true and meaningful dreams which, like the Word itself, never depart without accomplishing their purpose. They also bring with them the true foundation and the agitation of the heart—the agitation which is in agreement with the foundation—and at the same time faith, which agrees with both, is added. But if they are worthless dreams—like those the false prophets boast of—one will have to pay attention to the analogy, whether your heart has in fact been smitten and agitated. Although Satan, too, can bring this about, yet you must compare your dream with the Word. If your dream differs from what the Word itself states, you must remember that it is false and vain. But this dream of Jacob is in very beautiful agreement with the divine Word which he hears being sent down from heaven: "I am the Lord, etc." Therefore the godless err in their interpretation and understanding of dreams, just as they talk nonsense when they explain signs and prodigies; for they neither observe nor have the Word. This is what happened to the Anabaptists at Münster, who had seen a bow in the clouds and next to it a bloody hand.[48] This they seized for themselves as a sign of victory, even though destruction was threatening them, as the outcome showed. But they erred in their interpretation because they paid no attention to the foundation or the calling. For they had neither the Word nor the power of the sword, since they were not administering the government in accordance with the divine ordinance and calling. If something of this kind had occurred either because of a prodigy or a dream during the rule of Alexander or Julius Caesar, an interpretation would have been easier; for they had the Word and the ordinance of God. Accordingly, political dreams that are vague and without a foundation—that

---

[48] A reference to the tragic events of the revolution in Münster, culminating in its siege and capture on June 24, 1535.

is, when the person is not a public functionary or in the government, and when the agitation and the analogy are not added — are good for nothing.

But dreams pertaining to the church—dreams that have the Word, that have the true foundation and analogy—are more certain. Thus a Christian relies above all on the fact that he has been baptized. If the dream agrees with this foundation and pertains to the strengthening of the godly and the frightening of the godless, one will be able to embrace it without danger. Thus Jacob is strengthened by a dream which has an analogy with his blessing. He knows that he has been blessed and that, according to the Word of the promise, God will be his Father and Protector. But because his heart is troubled and alarmed by the fear of plots and death, the Lord appears to him amid such great grief and speaks to him through a dream which agrees with the actual fact and has a true analogy; for the same Lord speaks with him and says the same things that he had previously heard in the blessing. It is the same Lord, the same Word that he had heard in his father's house.

But the conversation is much more magnificent than the one he had with his father. Therefore when he awakens from his sleep, he marvels and says: "I thought that the Lord was only in my father's house. Therefore up to this time I heard the Word of God in my father's church. But I find God in this place too. For the same Lord whom I heard being praised in my father's house is speaking to me here. Indeed, this conversation is far better. Consequently, it seems that the house of God is here rather than in the house of my father. Yet this place is in the midst of enemies." Accordingly, Jacob learns that the church of God is also in the midst of enemies, as is stated in Ps. 110:2: "Rule in the midst of Thy foes!" This is surely remarkable. For the church of God must be where we think that there are innumerable devils. Thus the place where Jacob falls asleep is in the neighborhood of Jerusalem, where the Canaanites and the power of Satan ruled. Consequently, it seemed to be anything but the house of God. And Jacob only thought: "If I can remain here one night safe and sound, I shall be satisfied. Tomorrow morning I shall rise and flee." Nothing else could have entered his mind than the fact that he was sleeping in the midst of enemies, where the ruler of this world (John 16:11) and the god of this world (2 Cor. 4:4) reigned. "But behold, God is here," he said, "and I did not know it. For I did not think that God is anywhere else than in the house of my father Isaac, where he is the pastor and where the blessing was given to me. But I am really seeing and experiencing that God is fulfilling His promise in a wonderful manner—the promise in which He said: 'I will give you this land.' And now I understand that I will be the lord of this land in which I am lying, and in such great terror and grief I had never hoped that this would happen." In this manner God richly consoles Jacob through this dream. And Jacob, who had been terrified and agitated by the dream which had an analogy and was in agreement with fact itself, is wonderfully strengthened. Therefore it is a true dream.

There are further discussions about where this place Bethel was.[49] For it is very famous in the prophets and in all Holy Scripture, especially in Hos. 12:4, where we read: "He[50] found Him in Bethel," Later it was always praised and honored among the people of Israel, so that Jeroboam, a very wise and exceedingly industrious man, chose this as the place at which to set up the one golden calf near Jerusalem, just as he set up the other calf in Dan, toward the north (1 Kings 12:28-29). For the king fashioned these two gods or idols in conformity with a plan that was very wise according to reason, and he placed them at the two farthest limits of his province. Later the calves of Samaria were added to these.

Bethel is at the farthest limits of the kingdom of Israel, in Ephraim; and the temple at Jerusalem, which was built by Solomon, was 12 boundary stones distant from Bethel, that is, three short miles. Accordingly, Jeroboam reasoned astutely as follows: "I will institute idolatry in two places in order that the people of my realm may have worship and a definite place on both sides, to keep them within the boundaries of the kingdom." He stirs up this great cause of offense at a very convenient place near Jerusalem—a place to which people, abandoning the Word and the temple of God, often came to get away from the crowds. Yet even among the Israelities many held it in contempt. But the prophets were in continual conflict with those idolaters up to the destruction and overthrow of the kingdom. "Do not go to Gilgal, to Bethel,"

---

[49] Lyra *ad* Gen. 28:16 lists the several interpretations.

[50] The Weimar text has *inveni*, but we have followed other editions (as well as the Vulgate) and read *invenit*.

they cried, "to Beth-aven" (cf. Hos. 4:15). For this is what they called Bethel. For here they sought special forms of worship, sacrifices, burnings of incense, and invocation only in order that the temple and the worship in Jerusalem might be held in contempt. Concerning the temple God had said: "Here I will dwell" (cf. 2 Chron. 7:16).

But they guarded their idolatry with a wonderful show of sanctity. For they boasted that such a glorious apparition had come to the patriarch Jacob in this place, that the ladder had been seen here, and that God had spoken with Jacob in this place, not in Jerusalem. Accordingly, the prophets, and Hosea in particular, opposed and condemned this idolatry with great zeal; but they achieved nothing. Thus when we inculcate the doctrine of justification by faith alone so often and so clearly, our adversaries present their Beth-aven, their church, and the authority of the fathers; and this is certainly no small trial by which many are led astray from the true knowledge of and zeal for the Gospel.

Moreover, Bethel means the house of God. God dwells here. God's house. Gotta.[51] That glorious title and extraordinary name moved the people in a wonderful manner, so that they said: "You see that this has actually come to pass in this way, for Moses himself corroborates it. This place is Bethel and the house of God. Jerusalem is not the true place for worship. For here God appeared and spoke. Therefore He must be worshiped here just as Jacob worshiped Him and promised solemnly that he wanted to set up worship and tithe." This was a great offense, and the prophets, Hosea in particular, complained bitterly about it. In the papacy we have nothing like it, nothing that makes such a show.

But nearly all commentators disagree with this view. They say that this place Bethel is Jerusalem, yes, the temple itself. Thus concerning Mt. Moriah, of which mention was made above in chapter 22, they say that this very place is Bethel, where Shem and the other fathers worshiped and sacrificed, and where later the temple was built. Therefore before the time of the patriarch Jacob it was Bethel and the house of God where the fathers worshiped and sacrificed, where Abraham wanted to sacrifice his son Isaac. Nor is there any doubt that this place was chosen for meetings of the church. But they will not find it easy to persuade us that

---

[51] This appears to refer to the Saxon city of Gotha.

this place was the city of Jerusalem itself, and so far as the histories and the prophets testify, it was situated outside Jerusalem and was 12 boundary stones distant from the city. Lyra quotes two verses containing eight names of the city of Jerusalem:

*Solyma, Luza, Bethel, Hierosolyma, Hiebus, Helia,
Urbs sacra Jerusalem dicitur atque Salem.*[52]

But I have my doubts about Luz and Bethel, and this is my view concerning this discussion. The changes of the cities are strange and varied. If the opinion of those who assign this name to the city of Jerusalem is true, then I surely concede that for a time this city was called Bethel, in such a way, however, that it did not retain this name, but that the name was transferred to the city of Jerusalem, or that it was called Bethel with a common noun, not with a proper noun. For the description of the places in Joshua disagrees with this. Joshua points out that Ai and Bethel were neighboring cities (8:1, 9), provided that this city of Bethel remained up to the times of Joshua. And it seems that it was a small village near Ai. As has been stated above, Abraham pitched his camp between Bethel and Ai (Gen. 12:8). Therefore if Jacob called Jerusalem Bethel, he did so with a common noun, not with a proper noun. It is as though he were saying: "Here God dwells." Otherwise I am not able to bring the opinion of the others into agreement with the prophets. The accounts in Judges and Joshua also agree that Mt. Moriah was a place in Bethel. Consequently, there is agreement with the statement of Jacob: "This is the house of God." Otherwise it is certain that the names of cities are often changed in various ways.

But I pass over this. I would like to think that this place was Mt. Calvary itself, where the Lord Himself slept. If I could not do this with thoughts that are sure and firm, they would still be godly thoughts. The tree of the forbidden wood is also said to have stood in the same place.[53] Therefore it was God's will that Christ should be crucified and die here, and that the place where Jacob saw the ladder should be the same place where Christ, the true Jacob, slept in the sepulcher and rose again and the angels descended and ascended. Thus this place should prop-

---

[52] Lyra *ad* Gen. 28:19, quoting "all the doctors."
[53] Cf. *Luther's Works*, 1, p. 310, on the identification of Paradise with Calvary.

erly and truly be called Bethel. But this is only a thought. If it is not true, it is at least harmless. Nor is there any danger if we do not have definite names for the places. At the time of Abraham and Joshua, Jerusalem and Bethel were three miles apart. Whether proper nouns have been changed into common nouns or not is of little importance. Those eight names which Lyra quotes have the same meaning, for the Lord was seen there in a vision of peace.

This I leave to the grammarians. It is sufficient for us to know that Jacob was strengthened here in his faith in the promise, that here he saw the same Lord God, heard the same Word, and in his dream saw the same church he had heard and seen at home. Yet he is alone here, and besides him there is no one else, in order that we may learn that God's church is where God's Word resounds, whether it is in the middle of Turkey, in the papacy, or in hell. For it is God's Word which establishes the church. He is the Lord over all places. Wherever that Word is heard, where Baptism, the Sacrament of the Altar, and absolution are administered, there you must determine and conclude with certainty: "This is surely God's house; here heaven has been opened." But just as the Word is not bound to any place, so the church is not bound to any place. One should not say: "The chief pontiff is at Rome. Therefore the church is there." But where God speaks, where Jacob's ladder is, where the angels ascend and descend, there the church is, there the kingdom of heaven is opened.

17. *And he was afraid, and said: How awesome is this place! This is none other than the house of God, and this is the gate of heaven.*

This is a very wonderful speech. All Holy Scripture has nothing like it either in the Old or in the New Testament. For this place is called the house of God and the gate of heaven, and this is stated only in this one passage and nowhere else. This is nothing else than calling it the kingdom of heaven and heaven itself, for the place where God dwells is the house of God. But where does God dwell? Does He not dwell in heaven? Therefore he joins the earth with heaven and heaven with the earth. He sets up a heavenly habitation and the kingdom of God at that place on the earth and says: "The kingdom of heaven, the gate to heaven, is where the approach to heaven is open and also where the exit from the house of God is open." For he distinguishes between heaven and earth, that is, between the present and the future life; for after this life he promises himself eternal life and the kingdom of heaven, which begins in the present life. Indeed, Jacob already feels that he is and lives in that kingdom. Accordingly, the prophets undoubtedly drew very many outstanding revelations from this speech. From it have flowed those promises in Daniel and elsewhere where Jerusalem is compared to the kingdom of heaven. Dan. 8:10 states: "It grew great, even to the host of heaven; and some of the host of stars it cast down to the ground, and trampled upon them." For here nothing else is meant than the church and the teachers and hearers in it.

Then the church is defined here, what it is and where it is. For where God dwells, there the church is, and nowhere else; for the church is God's house and the gate of heaven, where the entrance to eternal life and the departure from the earthly to the heavenly life are open. But where God has not spoken or dwelt, there the church has never been either. Today we are engaged in a great struggle with the completely corrupt papists concerning the church. They confidently arrogate its name and title to themselves and boast that the church is among them and indeed in their doctrines and ceremonies. But although we acknowledge that the church is among them—for they have Baptism, absolution, and the text of the Gospel, and there are many godly people among them—yet if they want the addition that the pope and their pomp is the true church, we will by no means concede this. We confront them with this text, that God's house and the church of God are the same, according to the statement in John 14:23: "If a man loves Me, he will keep My Word, and My Father will love him, and We will come to him and make Our home with him." His commandments must be there, and it is necessary to love them. For God does not make His abode unless we have His commandments. If the church is to be the house of God, it is necessary for it to have the Word of God and for God alone to be the Head of the household in this house.

But we do not accept that addition of the papists, who cry out: "You have the Keys from us, the Sacrament of the Altar, the calling, and the ministry, which are the marks of the true church. But one thing is lacking, namely, that you refuse to acknowledge that the pope and the cardinals are the church." With regard to this, therefore, there is a conflict between us and the papists. We refuse to admit the enemy along with the Head of the household, for Christ and Satan cannot rule the same house at the same time. For "what accord has Christ with Belial?" (2 Cor. 6:15.) Accordingly, if the pope should be honored, it is necessary for us to deny Christ. For He does not allow Satan to reign in His house. If we want to have a church, it must not be polluted and commingled with any satanic doctrine. But the papistic traditions are godless and in conflict with the Word of God, and it is for the sake of this Word alone that God wants to make His abode with us. Therefore those traditions must be shunned, for Belial and Christ cannot be lords or heads of one house.

Therefore this passage and others like it should be carefully observed, in order that we may learn from them that the pope and his adherents are not the church. But if the objection is raised: "Yet they have Baptism, the Lord's Supper, etc.," I reply: "Those who [54] have the pure Word and Baptism belong to us and to the true church. But those who have pomp in addition are not the church. Even though they have Baptism, the text of the Gospel, etc., yet they have these in vain, because Christ and Belial are not in accord. For the bed is narrow. Consequently, one of the two falls out, and the short cloak cannot cover both, as Is. 28:20 says: 'The bed cannot bear them; nor is it possible to cover both at once.'" And the only thing they strive for is to introduce their abominations secretly and defend them. Therefore one must always confront them with these words (1 Kings 18:21): "How long will you go along limping with two different opinions? If the Lord is God, follow him; but if Baal, then follow him." The Lord and Baal are not in agreement. Nevertheless, Ahab was eager to bring them together. He wanted to serve God in the pure Word and at the same time to mingle human traditions with it. But opposites cannot exist together; they cancel each other.

Accordingly, this is what Jacob says: "This place in which I am sleeping is the house and church of God." Here God Himself has set up a pulpit, and He Himself is the first to preach about the descendants and about the uninterrupted continuance of the church. But Jacob, together with the descendants in his

[54] The Weimar text has *quia,* but we have followed other editions and read *qui.*

loins, is the listener. Likewise the angels in heaven. For if there is even one person who hears the Word together with the angels who are present along with him, it is sufficient.

But he describes the glory of this church in a very magnificent manner by saying that here the entrance to the kingdom of heaven is open. For God governs us in such a way that wherever He speaks with us here on earth, the approach to the kingdom of heaven is open. This is truly extraordinary consolation. Wherever we hear the Word and are baptized, there we enter into eternal life. But where is that place found? On earth, where the ladder which touches heaven stands, where the angels descend and ascend, where Jacob sleeps. It is a physical place, but here there is an ascent into heaven without physical ladders, without wings and feathers. This is how faith speaks: "I am going to the place where the Word is taught, where the Sacrament is offered and Baptism is administered." And all those things that are done in my sight in a physical place are heavenly and divine words and works. That place is not only ground or earth; but it is something more glorious and majestic, namely, the kingdom of God and the gate of heaven. "Here one goes to the stars," as is stated by the poet.[55] There is no reason for you to run to St. James's[56] or to withdraw into a corner or to hide yourself in a monastery. Do not seek a new and foolish entrance. But look in faith at the place where the Word and the sacraments are. Direct your step to the place where the Word resounds and the sacraments are administered, and there write the title THE GATE OF GOD. Let this be done either in the church and in the public assemblies or in bedchambers, when we console and buoy up the sick or when we absolve him who sits with us at table. There the gate of heaven is, as Christ says (Matt. 18:20): "Where two or three are gathered in My name, there am I in the midst of them." Throughout the world the house of God and the gate of heaven is wherever there is the pure teaching of the Word together with the sacraments.

But we should look at the external place not only with the eyes of the flesh and in the manner of beasts; nor should we think that the Word itself is an empty sound. Of course, it is a human voice, and he who speaks the Word is a human being. The temple

---

[55] Vergil, *Aeneid,* IX, 641.
[56] Cf. *Luther's Works,* 4, p. 130, note 31.

itself is built of stones and wood, and it is our temple. When assemblies are not held there, it is not the temple of God unless this term is used in a relative sense. But when sermons are delivered there, when the sacraments are administered and ministers are ordained to teach, then say: "Here is the house of God and the gate of heaven; for God is speaking, as 1 Peter 4:11 states: 'Whoever speaks, as one who utters oracles of God; whoever renders service, as one who renders it by the strength which God supplies.'"

But the blindness and stupidity of our minds has been put before our eyes like a cloud, so that we do not see such great glory. It is great honor and majesty, however, when one says: "This is the Word of God." I hear a man's voice. I see human gestures. The bread and the wine in the Supper are physical things. At ordination the hands of carnal men are imposed. In Baptism water is water. For the flesh judges in no other way concerning all these matters. But if you look at that addition with spiritual eyes, namely, at whose Word it is that is spoken and heard there, not indeed the word of a man — for if it is the word of a man, then the devil is speaking — but the Word of God, then you will understand that it is the house of God and the gate of heaven. The wooden house or the land per se does not deserve this name; but the land where the Word resounds is the land of God, not of the Creator but of the Ruler of His church, who governs His saints in such a way that they enter into the kingdom of heaven. Thus the water that is poured in Baptism is not the water of the Creator; it is the water of God the Savior.

But I see another law in my members fighting against faith (cf. Rom. 7:23). For I know that this is true, yet I am not able to assent with certainty and full confidence. I am not able to believe as much as I would want to believe. This is surely how it is. But not even the angels are able to grasp and perceive what a great thing it is that is being done and said here. Consequently, they cannot look at and consider it enough. But I would desire to grasp as much as I would want to grasp now. But not even this is possible. For flesh and blood, or that weight, mentioned in Heb. 12:1, and the sin surrounding us, resist. This depresses the spirit, which would gladly take hold of those things and drink them to the full, so that it would be inebriated. But it is necessary to be content with a little, provided that the tongue is refreshed.

In the meantime, however, we must accustom ourselves to be able to make that addition which Jacob and the angels in heaven make at this place. For the flesh fixes its eyes only on the water, on the bread, on the wine, and on the ground where Jacob slept; but the spirit must see the water, the hand, the Word of God, and God in the water. The flesh sees so keenly that it judges that the water is water and excludes God, as the Sacramentarians and the Anabaptists do. Therefore one must learn contrary to the view of the flesh that it is not a simple word and only an empty sound, but that it is the Word of the Creator of heaven and earth. Thus the imposition of hands is not a tradition of men, but God makes and ordains ministers. Nor is it the pastor who absolves you, but the mouth and hand of the minister is the mouth and hand of God.

Therefore we should acknowledge and make much of the boundless glory of God by which He has revealed Himself to us in His church. For it is not the kind of house in which He creates as He created all things in the beginning out of nothing. No, it is a house in which He speaks with us, deals with us, feeds us, and cares for us when we are asleep and when we are awake. But how few there are who believe this! This is true, and it is a very great Word, in which the angels in heaven take delight. When they hear it, they are filled with joy and gladness because of this knowledge of the church. Yet they cannot look at, consider, and admire it enough. For the church includes God, who dwells with us in such a way that He quickens, guards, and heals us; and by this dwelling together He brings it about that in this life there is the house of God and the gate of heaven.

These matters are assuredly immeasurable and wonderful. Therefore we should learn to enlarge on and make much of the glory of the church as it deserves. We should not hold it in slight esteem or put its true worth in things that are absurd and of no value, as the sacrilegious papists are wont to do. They imagine that the church should be a physical congregation devoted to drink, food, clothing, etc., although our church also has much that is physical and external, like bread, water, land, etc. But there is a great difference between the physical things of which the papists boast and those we have. For the former have been taken up and employed contrary to God, not for God or according to God's Word. Therefore their church is only empty pretense, imagination, and a false show. On the other hand, it is an exceedingly important thing when Jacob declares specifically that God's house is found where God dwells with us, where we are the household, yes, the sons and daughters, and He Himself is our Father, who speaks and deals with us and brings it about in the most intimate way that the church is also the gate of heaven. For He dwells with us in order that we may enter into the kingdom of heaven. And, what is most delightful, He comes first and appears to us on the ladder. He descends and lives with us. He speaks and works in us.

Thus the church is established among men when God dwells with men, with this end in view that it may be the gate of heaven and that we may pass from this earthly life into the eternal and heavenly life. Who can adequately marvel at or comprehend this, namely, that God dwells with men? This indeed is that heavenly Jerusalem which comes down out of heaven from God and has the splendor of God, as is stated in Rev. 21:2. This is the definition of the church in its essence: "The church is the place or the people where God dwells for the purpose of bringing us into the kingdom of heaven, for it is the gate of heaven." From this it follows most properly that in the church nothing should be heard or seen except what God does, according to the statement (1 Peter 4:11): "Whoever speaks, as one who utters oracles of God; whoever renders service, as one who renders it by the strength which God supplies." But if I am uncertain about the Word or the administration of God, I must be silent. But whenever I minister, that is, baptize or absolve, I must be certain that my work is not mine, but God's, who works through me. Baptism is a work of God; for it is not mine, although I lend my hands and my mouth as instruments. Thus when I absolve you or call you to the ministry and lay my hands on you, you should not doubt that, as Peter says, it is God's strength. This, then, is the complete definition of the church, which is the habitation of God on earth. Not that we should remain on earth, but the sacraments are administered and the Word is taught in order that we may be led into the kingdom of heaven and through the church may enter into heaven.

Jacob saw this, his descendants also saw it, we too, and all who are now the church or will be the church after us see it, namely, that the church is the house of God which leads from earth into heaven. The place of the church is in the temple, in the school, in the house, and in the bedchamber. Wherever two or three gather in the name of Christ, there God dwells (cf. Matt.

18:20). Indeed, if anyone speaks with himself and meditates on the Word, God is present there with the angels; and He works and speaks in such a way that the entrance into the kingdom of heaven is open. On the other hand, God does not dwell in human traditions; for He does not speak there. For one must always pay attention to the fact that Jacob hears God speaking and working. And the services the church performs are truly those that lead into the kingdom of heaven. But the papal church is not the kingdom of heaven; for it seeks gold, silver, kingdoms, and crowns of the world. These are their keys (cf. Matt. 16:19): "Whatever you bind on earth, that is, when you depose kings, take away kingdoms, etc." There is the way to hell. Accordingly, let us, together with the patriarch Jacob, hear the words of God, not of the pope, not the voice of human traditions. For when He speaks, then the gate and entrance to the kingdom of heaven is open.

18. *So Jacob arose early in the morning, and he took the stone which he had put under his head and set it up for a pillar and poured oil on the top of it.*

19. *He called the name of that place BETHEL; but the name of the city was Luz at the first.*

מַצֵּבָה. For a pillar or a setting up. The same word is found in Ps. 2:2: "The kings of the earth set themselves." He set up the stone in order that it might stand like an altar or a column, not lie. But whether Jacob slept in the city of Luz or on the plain outside the city I cannot state with certainty. Some say that he slept on the plain; others think that he slept in the city of Luz, as the text almost seems to state.[57]

Bethel, however, means the place that was called Moriah above. It had this name, "house of God," from the beginning. Therefore it is likely that it was often laid waste by the devil and was immediately restored, because perpetual war is waged between the devil and God. Now God throws the devil out and routs him; now, when the doctrine has again been corrupted, Satan substitutes a den of robbers for the church and befouls the place of the temple of God. In the time of David, Araunah the Jebusite

---

[57] "The place where Jacob slept was at that time outside the city, but later it was included," Lyra *ad* Gen. 28:19.

(cf. 2 Sam. 24:18 ff.) had possession of this place. There he had constructed a barn or threshing floor in which he threshed wheat. This had been done at the instigation of Satan, out of hatred and contempt for this place, just as he had often defiled it before. But David bought it after the pestilence which had raged against the people, and there he built a temple or altar and offered sacrifices to the Lord, because his prayer had been heard, as is stated in 2 Sam. 24:21 ff. For I think it was the place where Jacob slept; and God loved it in a special way for the sake of the fathers, for the sake of Shem, who preached and performed miracles there, and for the sake of others before and after Shem, namely, Abraham, Isaac, Jacob, and Christ Himself.

But the devil is a proud spirit. Therefore he gladly seizes places that are holy and clean, as this one was. The statement of Jacob, who says: "How awesome is this place!" bears witness to this. It is as though he were saying: "Moriah is a place to be venerated on account of the worship and veneration of God, who was worshiped at this place and still is." And for this reason he named it Bethel. Formerly it was called Moriah, because God appeared there. In the meantime, however, while Jacob lived in Egypt with his household, and later, too, throughout the time of the judges, it was occupied by heathen and the devil until it was restored by David and the temple was built there by Solomon. Yet it could have happened that this very place where Jacob sank into sleep was completely laid waste, since Hosea and the Book of Judges clearly show that the city of Bethel was 12 boundary stones distant from Jerusalem. Accordingly, if Moriah is the place where Jacob slept, it lost its name at that time, and later another place was called Bethel. Yet I take Bethel as a common noun meaning "Here God dwells."

But from what source did he have the oil which he poured on the top of the stone? I answer: If there was a city in that place, as the text points out, it was easy for him to find people from whom to buy it. But by pouring out the oil he wanted to point out nothing else than that he dedicated and consecrated this place as the future house and habitation of God; for the Lord spoke there, and the angels were His hearers. But because there were no people to hear and learn this, he thought that on his return from Mesopotamia he would build a chapel there or erect an altar and celebrate such an extraordinary and glorious appearance of God. The oil signifies the anointing or consecration by which kings and priests were anointed, likewise the vessels and the clothing, in order that they might be set apart from profane to sacred use. As a result, our papistic apes have also employed oil, but without the Word. Jacob, however, did not choose this very place but came upon it by chance, and there he heard the Word of God. Accordingly, the place was consecrated by God Himself, whom it pleased to dwell there. Therefore Jacob proclaims that this place is holy, and in order to leave his testimony to his descendants he pours oil on it and promises that he will consecrate it as the house of God if he brings his pilgrimage to a successful conclusion. He was not moved to do so by an impulse of his own or by the tradition or counsels of men. No, he did so because he fears, that is, worships, God here in this place, which was awesome and to be honored on account of the Word of the Lord which he had heard there. I omit the allegory about the spiritual consecration.[58]

20. *Then Jacob made a vow, saying: If God will be with me, and keep me in this way that I go, and will give me bread to eat and clothing to wear,*

21. *so that I come again to my father's house in peace, then the Lord shall be my God,*

22. *and this stone, which I have set up for a pillar, shall be God's house; and of all that Thou givest me I will give the tenth to Thee.*

The last part of this chapter is Jacob's vow, concerning which Lyra disputes at length.[59] First of all, however, one asks why the very saintly patriarch has doubts, or at least speaks in the manner of one who doubts, saying: "If God will give me food, if He will bring me back, etc." Should he not, after receiving the promise, have been certain and persuaded that he would never be without all these things? For God, who promised descendants, cannot lie. But if he is to be the father of many nations, it is necessary for him to live. For the dead cannot be or become parents. There-

[58] Lyra *ad locum* compares Jacob's vow to that of a monk or nun.

[59] Lyra *ad* Gen. 28:20-22, discussing the relation of the vow to "what is necessary for salvation."

fore if he must live, it is also necessary for him to have food and other necessities for this life. But why does he speak as if he had doubts about all this? Indeed, he was strengthened by that glorious vision when God repeated the promise, saying: "I will not leave you until I have accomplished everything I have said." What, then, is the source of such great doubt after those utterly certain promises of God?

I omit more sublime matters that could be adduced here and shall stick to what is on a lower plane. For I have often stated above [60] and elsewhere that it pleases me greatly and is salutary for us to hear of the weaknesses of the saints, for these examples of weakness are more necessary for us and bring more consolation than the examples of that heroic and very great fortitude and other virtues. Thus the fact that David killed Goliath, a bear, a lion, etc., does not edify me much. For I cannot imitate such things, since they surpass my strength and all my thinking. Although they commend the saints in their strength and heroic fortitude, they do not concern us; for they are too sublime for us to be able to match or imitate them. But when examples of weakness, sins, trepidation, and trials are set forth in the saints — as when I read David's complaints, sobs, fears, and feelings of despair — they buoy me up in a wonderful manner and give great consolation. For I see how they, fearful and terrified though they were, did not perish but buoyed themselves up with the promises they had received; and from this I conclude that there is no need for me to despair either. For in this struggle with hell, in fears and struggles of conscience, they feel and speak as if they had no promises at all. Nevertheless, they are finally preserved and sustained by the Word.

For look at Paul, who says about himself (1 Cor. 2:3): "I was with you in weakness and in much fear and trembling." Likewise (2 Cor. 7:5): "Fighting without and fear within." Do you speak this way, Paul? This does not behoove that chosen instrument (cf. Acts 9:15) who has the promise that he should carry Christ's name before the Gentiles, does it? Where are you going, Paul? Into the prison of hell, fear, and despair? Where are we going to remain if you have doubts and are almost diffident concerning your completely certain calling? But this is how it must

---

[60] Cf. *Luther the Expositor,* pp. 75—77.

28:20-22
[W, XLIII, 604, 605]

happen even with the greatest saints. For the divine promises are not given to make us smug; but, as Paul says in another place: "A thorn was given me in the flesh, a messenger of Satan, to harass me" (2 Cor. 12:7). Why? "Lest the magnitude of the gifts of the grace and mercy of God elate me." Therefore God sends wrestlings, trials, and struggles in order that from day to day we may understand and cling to the promises of God more clearly and certainly. This would not happen if the saints always practiced that heroic fortitude. Indeed, in the end they would become smug and lose the promise and every expectation. Therefore they must be disciplined, in order that they may retain faith, hope, and the expectation of the promises. And it is precisely this that edifies and consoles us, when we see that the patriarchs and the prophets were like us, that they were tried by weakness, by doubt, and almost by despair and the loss of faith.

What can be set forth to us that is more useful and more suitable for consolation than the example of Peter? He advances on the water to meet Christ. And when he stepped out of the boat, he first walked on the water to come to Jesus. As the evangelist says, he ran with great impetuosity, with heroic and special spirit, because he knew that Christ was there; and he had the Word and the promise of the Word for his petition: "If it be Thou, bid me come to Thee on the water" (Matt. 14:28). But soon, when a little wind blows, he wavers and sinks. What now? Where is that great spirit? Why did you doubt? But it pleased Christ that he should be tried in this way. For if he had not been tried, he would have been puffed up. But it is better to be tried than to be puffed up. For in this way the promises are retained, and in this way we learn to understand those sobs of the saints, as in Ps. 6:1: "O Lord, rebuke me not in Thy anger." For David, too, was such a great man that God gave him the testimony: "I have found in David, the son of Jesse, a man after My heart, who will do all My will" (Acts 13:22; cf. 1 Sam. 13:14). Yet he prays in this way and struggles with the trials of unbelief and despair.

In this way we, too, have been called, and we have promises that are much clearer and more glorious than those the fathers had. Thus Peter praises this good fortune of ours when he says (2 Peter 1:19): "And we have the prophetic Word made more sure. You will do well to pay attention to this as to a lamp shining in a dark place." Grace and eternal life have been promised and offered to us in a much more glorious way than to them. For the Son has come, and all the promises have been fulfilled. We hear the Son Himself; we have the sacraments and absolution; and day and night the Gospel proclaims to us: "You are holy. You are holy. Your sins have been forgiven you. You are blessed, etc." But what do we do? We still tremble, and we cling to our weakness throughout our life. But why are we not aroused by the example of the patriarchs, who believed to complete perfection? I reply that they, too, were weak, just as we are, although we have richer promises than they had. But it comes to pass as God's voice says to Paul: "My power is made perfect in weakness" (2 Cor. 12:9). For God could not retain and fulfill His promises in us if He did not kill that stupid, proud, and smug flesh in us.

To this end the example of Isaac and Rebecca has been set forth above (Gen. 27; 28:1-2). They, too, were afraid, and they were compelled by fear to send their son into exile. Yet this conflicted with the promise and the blessing given to them. But God should not have been tempted, and the son should not have been hurled rashly into danger in spite of the fact that the promises were firm and certain. For in this way I, too, have been absolved through the Word and have partaken of the Sacrament of the Altar. Surely, then, I am not going to say: "I will not work. I will sit in idleness. If I must live, I will live, etc." This would be tempting God. Indeed, you must use the things given and granted to you by God in His kindness. You must rule, work, and strive not to tempt God. You must not throw yourself headlong into danger or go into the Elbe without paying any attention to the bridge because you have the promise that God does not want to forsake you. For Isaac and Rebecca did not want to tempt the Lord either; but since the promise is completely sure, they follow the advice which God had inspired. For God fulfills His promises with definite means. One should not join those fanatics [61] — who conclude that everything is foreknown — and say: "If I have been predestined, I shall be saved; if not, I shall perish. If it is necessary to die, care of the body and life will profit nothing. If I am destined to be learned, I shall become learned even without books, etc." But God has not given His promises with this arrangement. For Rom. 8:30 says: "Those whom He predestined

[61] Cf. p. 50, note 46.

He also called, and those whom He called He also justified." He does not want to fulfill the end of His promises without means; He wants to do so through means. He has given us the use of the creatures, and these must be used by Christians until we come to the end of the divine promises. Thus Jacob, who is surrounded by promises, nevertheless makes use of the place, the time, and the persons.

I am mentioning this for the sake of an example with which it could perhaps be possible for someone to excuse the very saintly patriarch by saying that he did not want to tempt God. But I do not want to excuse him, just as I do not want to excuse other saints, as though they never doubted or sinned. For it is a salutary example for us and one that is full of consolation; it is far more pleasing than if the heroic deeds of Samson or David concerning which they had no promises were pointed out. But they had a heroic spirit of faith.

Now it is necessary to speak about Jacob's vow. For the papists adduce this passage and the example of Jacob against us, who oppose the monastic vows: Jacob made a vow and kept it. Therefore he who has made a vow must keep it. They add the statement in Num. 30:2: "When a man vows a vow to the Lord, or swears an oath to bind himself by a pledge, he shall not break his word; he shall do according to all that proceeds out of his mouth." Likewise Deut. 23:21-22: "When you make a vow to the Lord your God, you shall not be slack to pay it; for the Lord your God will surely require it of you, and it would be sin in you. But if you refrain from vowing, it shall be no sin in you." These and many other passages and examples the monks adduce against us in order to establish and confirm the abominations of their vows.[62]

But in order that we may be able to refute these abominations, one must first of all hold fast carefully to this rule, that justification, the forgiveness of sins, grace, or mercy, come first and are the cornerstone, so to speak. All of this is simply free and is not obtained because of any works. This rule we should always have in view, namely, that we are not justified by reason of works or by reasons of the Law but gratis, since grace comes

---

[62] Cf. Nicolaus Herborn, O. F. M., *Locorum communium adversus huius temporis haereses Enchiridion* (1529), XXXIX, ed. by Patricius Schlager, *Corpus Catholicorum*, 12 (Münster, 1927), 134, quoting Deut. 23:21-23, Num. 30:2, and other passages in support of monastic vows.

before all our works and merits. Thus it is said in Isaiah (65:1): "I was ready to be found by those who did not seek Me." This should be the cornerstone, and God should be the beginning of our salvation—God, who manifests and reveals Himself to us in order that we may learn to know Him. This is the principle and the foundation that is set forth in all Scripture. First of all, it is God's Word itself, just as the creature itself is the oral Word by which all nations should know God, as Rom. 1:19 says. Something, either a word or a deed, must precede which moves us, and this first impulse must be from God. This is certain: The person becomes acceptable first, acceptable, I say, by justifying grace and the gift of the Holy Spirit, by which man knows God as such a Savior. This is truly the first grace,[63] where we do nothing but are only passive. We hear God speaking the Word, and we feel Him working through the oral Word and the sacraments, through which He awakens in us knowledge of Him.

Now that what is sure and first has been established, the second proposition follows, namely, that of necessity good works are nothing else than a thanksgiving and glorification, no matter what kind of works they are, whether alms or vows or sufferings or finally death itself. All those works should be reckoned as a sacrifice of thanksgiving; for we can give nothing to God, merit or achieve nothing that would lead to the justification of our persons. Now monastic vows are only of a piece with a work that has been performed.[64] For I and all the monks make a vow of chastity, poverty, etc., to God. Why do we do this? Because we want to merit the remission of sins and be saved. Accordingly, these vows conflict with the article of justification as the worst abominations and blasphemies, and all the vows of the monks are godless and sacrilegious. For the monks belong to the number of those who seek God, whom God condemns. On the contrary, He says through Isaiah (65:1): "I was ready to be found by those who did not seek Me." Likewise: "Take your sacrifices away, and eat them. I do not want your sacrifices. I do not care about your vows. 'Do I eat the flesh of bulls?'" (Ps. 50:13). What house are you going to build for Me? Where did I dwell before I created heaven and earth? But this is what I said: 'Hear My voice. All Judah, hear the

---

[63] Cf. also *Luther's Works*, 13, pp. 130—131, on *prima gratia*.

[64] The phrase is *opus operatum;* cf. *Luther's Works*, 26, p. 122, note 38.

word of the Lord. Let My Word be among you that I may be the beginning of your salvation. For I have been found by those who did not seek Me, in order that you may know what free justification or the remission of sins is. It is because of this that the person is acceptable, not because of some work, no matter what kind of work it is." Today the Jews torment themselves to an extraordinary degree in an effort to find the grace of God and to placate God's wrath, but they accomplish nothing. This is now sufficiently certain and established.

Accordingly, there is a very great difference between the vow of Jacob and the monastic vows. Jacob's vow is not a vow of justification or the remission of sins. Indeed, if the person were not acceptable before and a child of God through the remission of sins, he would not become righteous through a vow. In fact, he would not even make a vow. A vow does not make a tree, just as the fruit of a tree is not a tree. No, a vow is a fruit of faith. For this reason we condemn monastic vows in general and all sacrifices, even those that had been prescribed under the Law and Moses. For concerning these GOD also says: "I do not want your sacrifices." Why? "Because you make a hysteron proteron; you want to seek and placate Me with your sacrifices. I will not stand for anything that is done to placate Me. But acknowledge Me as Him who justifies and gives. Then your work will be pleasing, if it is done either as an act of thanksgiving or for the benefit of your neighbor and as a good example. But if you want to feed Me with the flesh of bulls and goats, or with your offerings, then you will labor in vain. For I will not eat your flesh or accept your acts of worship because of which you want Me to give you My grace. For grace must be free or offered gratis. It must be free; otherwise it is not grace. Afterwards I will accept your sacrifices, burnt offerings, and oblations; for you do not offer them for the purpose of placating Me but to acknowledge that I, who bestow and justify, have given you everything gratis. Therefore I shall accept them because you are grateful to Me and glorify Me." Thus Paul says in Rom. 1:21: "The Gentiles knew God but did not glorify Him as God." God has revealed and given it to them; but when they should have given thanks and praise, then they did something else: ἐματαιώθησαν ἐν τοῖς διαλογισμοῖς. The first gift is knowledge of God. Thanksgiving and praise must follow this. But they became foolish in their counsels, and in their idolatry they made for themselves other gods to whom to give and bring offerings, not to receive from them. This is making an idol, abandoning the true God, and glorifying oneself, not God. For this is how they think: "God will give me eternal life in return for my merits, for my cowl, and for my works of supererogation." This is horrible blasphemy.

Therefore this text shows that Jacob did not make such a foolish and godless vow, but that it was a vow of thanksgiving. For he says: "If I come again, etc." It is as though he were saying: "I shall now obligate myself to pay a debt, and I shall make satisfactory reparation when I return. What? I shall build a school and a church here, and I shall give a tithe of bulls and goats and fruits for its establishment and upkeep, likewise a tenth part of the milk and the butter." Of course, God does not need these things. For He does not eat bread or drink wine, as He says in Ps. 50:13: "Do I eat the flesh of bulls?" What, then, are you doing? I answer that Jacob is already righteous. Accordingly, he does not make a vow to placate God by making it; but he wants to do this to give thanks, to glorify God, in order that He may conduct him and bring him back according to the promise. Who will receive these tithes? Not the angels, not the sun, not the moon. But he will perform that extraordinary and glorious work for the purpose of preserving the ministry and founding churches and schools, where the prophets and the sons of the prophets, who are hungry and thirsty, naked and wretched, may live and be supported. Thus one can see today how few there are who are touched by that wretchedness and how grudgingly men who abound in wealth give for the education and training of the youth who are to take the place of those who are now teaching. For this reason I have taken great pleasure in the statement of Henry, the illustrious Prince and Duke of Saxony, who has succeeded to the rule after the death of his brother George and has given special orders that decent stipends be set up for schools and churches. This is what he says: "After all, I must give my pastors something to eat and drink." [65]

But there are very few, whether princes or private citizens, who either make or follow this most praiseworthy statement. Therefore the schools and churches are in great danger, since

[65] On the significance of this comment for the dating of these lectures see our Introduction, p. x.

there will be none to befriend and support the schools and the churches. Accordingly, this vow made by Jacob was not only praiseworthy; it was necessary. This is how Moses should be understood when he says (Deut. 23:21): "When you make a vow to the Lord your God, you shall not be slack to pay it." What does it mean to make a vow to God, or whom is Moses addressing when he says: "The Lord your God"? It means to give tithes to the disciples, sons, and wives of the prophets, to the poor and needy. These are the ones who are to be supported by the tithes offered to God, and through these tithes God is supported. For God says: "Whatever you give to the children of the priests and prophets through whom the doctrine is propagated you must regard as given to Me, not that I may justify you through this work, but it should be a thanksgiving and a sacrifice of praise because I have justified you and have also blessed you in temporal matters. In addition, I shall bless you even more if you give ear to, support, and cherish the poor sons of the prophets."

It is important that Scripture so often repeats in Moses, Solomon, and the Psalms that if you vow anything, you must pay it (Deut. 23:21; Ps. 76:11; Eccles. 5:4). This commandment pertains most to the priests, in order that the ministry may be preserved. If you vow or promise to support the schools, see that you pay it. Christ says (Matt. 26:11): "You always have the poor with you," especially in the time of the revelation of the Gospel. For the Word of God and those who teach it have the same experience that all the other arts have. As the German proverb states: "Art goes begging." Therefore "blessed is he who considers the poor!" says the divine promise (Ps. 41:1). "For you have the first grace and have been justified gratis. Acknowledge this, and be grateful. Then I shall bless you, enrich you, and give you increase in such a way that you will realize that you have been abundantly satisfied." This should be a special exhortation for us to be glad to give assistance to the efforts of pupils and teachers; for in this passage those alms are called tithes given to God, not to them. And Christ has said (Matt. 25:40): "Truly, I say to you, as you did it to one of the least of these My brethren, you did it to Me."

The priests and Levites in the Law of Moses had no part and inheritance with Israel and received nothing from the possession of their brethren. "I am your portion and your inheritance among the people of Israel," says the Lord (Num. 18:20). But what did the Lord have, or how was He their portion? He had the vows, the sacrifices and the tithes. "These," He said, "I give you in order that you may be able to sustain and support yourselves and your household and that you may have time for My ministry, to teach, learn, and preserve My Word." Therefore the priests had no possession and no part among the Children of Israel. They themselves had nothing to eat from their fields or possessions, but they ate with God; they ate with our Lord God from God's tithes. And these are called a divine offering and divine vows, as if our Lord God Himself should eat them or otherwise would have died of hunger.

Therefore if you give anything to scholars, you have given it to God Himself; and you should know that you have done God a most pleasing service and have brought a sacrifice adorned with this glorious and very high title that it is called a vow to God. He who believes and does this should know that it is a special gift of God. For the world does not trouble itself about it. Therefore the Turk comes and seizes what we scrape together and refuse to give to those to whom we should have given it. For God wants to eat with us or to leave nothing of what we possess. Or is it not a glorious honor to be desired by all that I support and feed God Himself whenever I support a teacher or a pupil? For then you are giving tithes for God's house, which cannot be preserved without schools and scholars. Thus on this journey Jacob saw the children of Shem dwelling near Mt. Moriah. They had sons, daughters, grandsons, granddaughters, paternal and maternal aunts who were poor and needy. For since this mountain had previously been laid waste by tyrants, perhaps Eber restored it; and if after Eber's time Abraham and Isaac saw that it had been laid waste, they also restored it and built it up. Jacob now sees that the sons and daughters of the patriarchs are hungry and in need in a desert place. Therefore he vows that if he is brought back safely by the Lord, he will give tithes, that is, will restore the school of the patriarchs by contributing what is necessary for its support. Legal vows like those of the Nazarites were in a class by themselves and superfluous. But a vow that follows justification is a true vow and can be called a vow of love, as this vow made by the patriarch Jacob was. For the highest and chief vow is contained in the First Commandment, where we make a covenant with God that He wants to be our God and we want to believe in God the Father. This is the covenant of the First Table. It is pictured by those Levitical vows and sacrifices, and it is a vow of grace and righteousness. But the vows concerning which it is stated (Deut. 23:22-23) "But if you refrain from vowing, it shall be no sin in you; but if you vow, pay it" are vows of love and are natural and continuous. We are not obliged or compelled to observe a definite way or prescription when making a vow. But if the ministers of the church are not supported, then this vow becomes a natural and moral precept, namely, that everyone [66] should help the preservation of the ministry in his place. Thus the illustrious prince, John Frederick, Elector of Saxony, contributes annually 3,000 golden guldens for the upkeep of the University of Wittenberg.[67] This, in very truth, is Jacob's vow. For although he does not say in express words that he is giving, or making a vow, to God, yet it actually is a vow to God by which he pays as much as is needed to support the pastors, the masters of arts, and the professors of the faculties. And he is obligated to pay this. Although it is not a vow *de facto,* yet it is a vow *de iure;* for we are all bound by virtue of the Christian religion to pledge to give to the schools, even if we do not make a vow *de facto.*

Lyra says that what is necessary is not classified as a vow, but that a vow is spontaneous.[68] Thus the monks vow obedience, chastity, and poverty, which, of course, are not necessary before the vow but become decidedly necessary after the vow. A vow of this kind is the vow of love by which I promise 10 guldens to some poor man who needs them. Here I am obligated to keep my promises. Indeed, I am bound in other respects when I see that a poor neighbor is in need of my help. For I must not let a Christian be hungry, be naked or in need.

In this manner, then, Jacob vows that he wants to restore the school at Moriah and to give the disciples and children of the prophets the necessities of life. "If I return," he says, "I will give you children of Eber tithes for the sake of the house of God,

---

[66] The Weimar text has *singulo,* but we have followed other editions and read *singuli.*

[67] The University of Wittenberg had been reorganized in 1536, with a set budget that included this stipulation of support from the Elector.

[68] Cf. p. 253, note 59.

who has blessed me and has shown me this vision and the gate of heaven."

Hence in the Psalms vows are frequently called acts of thanksgiving, which in other respects are necessary works and have been enjoined upon all men. And they are not only works in words, but they also consist in deeds and true services. Thus it is said (Prov. 3:9): "Honor the Lord with your substance." This must be understood not only of words and of the worship of the mouth or genuflexion but of the deed itself. Thus honoring our parents not only demands that we uncover the head, address them respectfully, and be obedient, but that we also support them and honor them in actual fact. Paul says (1 Tim. 5:17): "Let the elders who rule well be considered worthy of double honor." Likewise in Gal. 6:6: "Let him who is taught in the Word share all good things with him who teaches." Therefore when God wants to be honored, then He wants sacrifices to be offered, not only sacrifices of the mouth but also the reverence of the heart, yes, the deed itself. He wants us to help the ministry, and He wants everyone to contribute for the purpose of supporting the studies of the pupils and of propagating the doctrine. Then God is truly praised and glorified there. Make a vow there, and say: "I promise that I am willing to contribute something for the assistance of the churches." That is St. Jacob's vow.

Therefore a twofold vow has been [69] pictured by the vows of the Law. The one is the vow of faith, to God, who makes a covenant with us that He wants to be our God, as we have stated above concerning the vow of the First Commandment. The other is the vow of love. Although it is free according to the commandment and the Word when I do not know that there is need or when my neighbor does not need my help, it becomes necessary when he has need of my help and others refuse to provide it. Even though I have not introduced the name of the Lord, yet help must be given because Christ enjoins (Luke 6:30): "Give to everyone who begs from you."

The world not only neglects these duties and vows, but it even robs and despoils the churches and schools of the tithes contributed by others, and it wants us to suffer dire hunger and need. Therefore this example should be diligently inculcated,

---

[69] The Weimar text has *et*, but we have read *est*.

namely, that Jacob vows tithes, not in order that God Himself may eat or be enriched; but he gives them to the poor ministers and to those who are always the least of the brethren or disciples of Christ on earth. For all other arts are gainful and have their profits. This profession alone is in need of bountiful giving. We must live from the altar, as Paul says (1 Cor. 9:13). Accordingly, he who is godly and loves the Word of God contributes something. He who hates the doctrine along with those who teach and learn it robs and despoils.

Otherwise God has so ordained that we should live from the vows, sacrifices, and alms that are owed to us by divine right. When the godly see the poverty and need of the ministers of the church and the school, they make vows and obligate themselves to give tithes, as Jacob gave them. He had an excellent understanding of the greatness and the dignity of this office. For he saw that at that time the church was afflicted, forsaken, unsettled, and often troubled and torn by tyrants, while Shem and others also proclaimed the promise there about the Seed who was to come. Jacob knew that this was the line and the succession from which Christ was to descend. Thus above in Gen. 10:21 Shem was called "the father of all the children of Eber," because Christ was to be born from the descendants of Eber. For Eber had two sons, Peleg and Joktan. But Joktan had 13 sons, and Shem was called the father of all of them. Many of these grandsons of Eber became priests who taught the schools and the churches about the Seed who was to come, although these were often scattered, as is clear in the example of these patriarchs, Abraham, Isaac, and Jacob, who are compelled to move so often and sojourn now in Gerar, now in Egypt, now in Canaan. Thus the churches and schools in the world always wander about like nomads. Therefore they had need of sacrifices, tithes, alms, and other services; and when Jacob saw that these were missing in this gathering, he vows and promises that he will give tithes when he returns. Below, in Gen. 35:1, he is ordered by God to return to this place and to erect an altar here to God.

CHAPTER TWENTY-NINE

1. *Then Jacob went on his journey, and came to the land of the people of the east.*
2. *As he looked, he saw a well in the field, and lo, three flocks of sheep lying beside it; for out of that well the flocks were watered. The stone on the well's mouth was large,*
3. *and when all the flocks were gathered there, the shepherds would roll the stone from the mouth of the well, and water the sheep, and put the stone back in its place upon the mouth of the well.*

So far Moses has conducted the very saintly patriarch through those more sublime and truly ecclesiastical exercises of faith and the Word of God, and this topic is most noteworthy in all the histories of the saints, namely, when they hear the Word of God, believe it, and are exercised in faith by many tribulations and annoyances. For although they are weak in faith here, yet they are plainly divine and heavenly men, utterly pure and saintly. In short, they live and act in the sight of God, not of men.

This is the true dignity and sublimity in the saintly fathers. Thus in our life, when we are exercised by the Word in the church and use the sacraments, we are also plagued by various trials, and our faith is tested like gold in a furnace. This is the true saintliness because of which we are called and are saints. For the Holy Spirit sanctifies through the Word taken hold of through faith, and He mortifies the flesh by means of sufferings and troubles, in order that the saints may be quickened and may present their bodies "as a living sacrifice, holy and acceptable to God," as Rom. 12:1 says. This is the highest stage of the life of the saints.

But lest we lose heart if we heard that the saintly fathers are set forth only in the highest stage and kind of life, God leads them back from heaven to earth and describes them as completely worthless and as men of the lowest sort, so that nothing more common or worthless could be mentioned, except that their sins are not praised. Otherwise they are described in a completely meager manner, as though they were crawling in the dust of domestic and political life. For they are engaged in and busy with works that seem to be of no importance at all and without any saintliness, while the papists, on the contrary, seek and admire only the kind of life that is utterly withdrawn from and alien to secular occupations, domestic and political cares. That withdrawal from physical and secular duties they call sanctity and righteousness. But they are completely mistaken in every respect. For we should seek faith and righteousness in such a way that we pay tithes of mint and dill. Thus Christ says in Matt. 23:23: "These you ought to have done, without neglecting the others"; that is, because we dwell and live in the flesh, for this reason the flesh must be cared for, but without sin. The state and domestic affairs must be administered, since we are not yet in Paradise. Nor are we like the angels; but we live in the flesh, in a natural life which has need of food, drink, clothing, house, offspring, and agriculture. There is also need of political government and of protection against evil men. Therefore it is necessary to retain those two parts of this life. They are support and protection. The home supports and cherishes children and the household. The state defends and protects all these.

Accordingly, the saintly fathers, are described in a lowly and carnal manner in this lower stage of life, than which in the eyes of the papists there is nothing more sordid or worthless. Thus they say that nothing else is set forth than that they married wives, procreated offspring, milked cows and goats, etc., which are completely secular and heathenish works.[1] But the Lord has given us a true understanding, for which we should be thankful; for we can look into these matters more deeply than the papists, who see nothing else here except those carnal works. But these works are not so carnal as their own works, which are governed by the devil and are done without the Holy Spirit. For even though they fast, abstain from marriage, and murmur in the churches, yet

---

[1] This is a recurring theme of these *Lectures on Genesis;* cf. *Luther's Works,* 3, p. 43, and passim.

there is no spirit in their prayers, no feeling, no worship of God. Everything is full of greed, idolatry, empty glory, and contempt for GOD.

But we teach that first of all the person must be looked at, whether it is just and godly, which takes place through the Word he believes. Then, however, it carries out its ministry in the church: teaches, exhorts, prays, learns and hears the Word, bears the cross for the sake of the Word, and is mortified in the flesh. That person is saintly, alive, and well-pleasing to God. It proceeds to other external offices after it has heard the Word, believed, prayed, and discharged its duty in the church. Thus after David has done this, he proceeds to the administration of the kingdom, hears lawsuits, wages war, draws up his army, attacks the enemy, kills, and sheds enemy blood. Properly speaking, these are not duties of the church; they are political. Accordingly, if anyone says: "Then David is not saintly, for he is a soldier and bears the sword," that person judges, too grossly, as the papists do. For who is that man David who sheds blood and wages war? He is a person who has been justified in the church by the Word and faith. But later he has the political administration entrusted to him. Therefore he judges, condemns, justifies, administers the state, punishes the guilty, and wages wars. Nevertheless, he remains a man of faith and a good tree. But that spilling of blood is pleasing to God, although the world, the monks, and all other hypocrites are violently offended, because they look only at the external mask of the works. They do not see the Word, faith, the spirit, and the impulse of God, who governs the person not only in sublime duties but also in those that pertain to the state and the household. For David was called by God to do this, as is stated, "that he should do My whole will," [2] which also orders him to humble the Philistines, the Damascenes, the Amalekites, the Ammonites, etc.

"But what does this mean?" the papists say. "He had to pray, sacrifice, and bring offerings in the temple." Right indeed! He also performs the works of the church in accordance with his place and rank. In the morning he prays, meditates on the Word, believes, sings psalms, and carefully discharges the duties that pertain to the church. Afterwards he also administers political and

---

[2] This appears to be an allusion to Acts 13:22, which is a reference to David.

household affairs, procreates children, takes care of the household, eats, and drinks. Thus David goes along in a godly and saintly manner through all three hierarchies: the church, the state, and the household.[3]

In the same manner our life, too, must be arranged, so that we are found in the rank and station which is pleasing to God according to His Word. Above all, you should believe in the Word, confess it, and be prepared to suffer and die for the Word. Later, whether you are a magistrate or the head of a household, you should serve your calling in your place. Such a life pleases God and is honored by God with many great rewards and successes.

Accordingly, the lives of the fathers must be treated and looked at in such a way on that sublime plane, lest the lowest, carnal, and sordid examples in the domestic and political sphere be despised. For these examples are not sordid. Nor are they cheap and worthless when they are done by a person who believes, is acceptable to God, saintly, and divine, by one who knows that whatever he does is pleasing to God, yet in such a way that the order is not disturbed, but that he remains and lives in faith. Afterwards the works of one's calling are also pleasing.

In this manner Moses describes how the patriarch Jacob came to Haran and found there the daughter of his uncle, loved the maiden, took her as his wife, procreated children, and pastured the flocks. All these things are foolish and carnal. No things more carnal can be found among the heathen themselves. For no one sees the essential difference, which is very great, between a heathen and this patriarch Jacob. For Esau and Ishmael also cultivate the fields, pasture sheep, milk cows, have a household and provide pasture for their cattle. All these works are similar to those done by the saints. Yet they are not holy works. Why? Because there is a great and incomprehensible difference between the works of both. Here with Jacob there is faith and the Word; there no Word is found, only unbelief. Accordingly, the works of Jacob are as different from the works of Ishmael and Esau as heaven from earth, no matter how much they seem to be the same works in outward appearance.

Thus Erasmus gives high praise to the virtues of the heathen, those of Socrates, of Cicero, of Atticus, etc.; and he makes a com-

---

[3] Cf. p. 139, note 38.

parison. "Among Christians," he says, "you would scarcely find men who did what Pomponius Atticus or others did. Indeed, among Christians many are found who are openly evil and infamous. These heathen were better by far than they are."[4] But one must reply: Philosophically and materially they are alike, that is, in respect to the kind of life, but not in respect to the distinguishing characteristics and the difference. For if either Cicero or Socrates had sweat blood, he would nevertheless not have pleased God for this reason. Nor is it a question of what works and what great works Alexander the Great, Hannibal, Julius Caesar, and Scipio did. It is certain that these men did things that were greater than those any Christian ever did. For you will not easily find in any Christian king such military strength, likewise such patience and endurance of misfortunes and hardships, no, not even among the kings of the people of Israel, like David or the others. Why, then, do you not extol them and prefer them to all Christian kings, to David and the others?

I answer that if I had a choice, I would select the most sordid and most rustic work of a Christian peasant or maid in preference to all the victories and triumphs of Alexander the Great, Julius Caesar, etc. Why? Because God is here, and the devil is there. This is the essential difference. The material of the works is the same, but the distinguishing characteristics and the difference are infinitely diverse. For God says: "The works and domestic duties of this woman, namely, that she sweeps the house and obeys the housewife, please Me." For "He has regarded the humility of His handmaiden" (Luke 1:48), where there are no great and glorious works except that at home she humbly discharges the duties of a maid, whether in the kitchen or among the cattle. These two, Leah and Rachel, were maids of this kind. They pastured the flocks of their father, drove them to water, and milked the cows and goats. These works were pleasing to God. But Hannibal, Alexander, Scipio, and Cicero do not please God. Why? Because, although they are alike in respect to the kind of works they do, or rather surpass in this regard, they are surpassed in respect to the distinguishing characteristics and the difference.

Not all men are able to understand this. Not even Erasmus saw

[4] Cf. *Luther's Works*, 26, p. 123.

it. Only believers understand the worth and importance of the works of Christians. But faith and the Word make their works important and give them the greatest worth. For God Himself and the Spirit are in the Christian who does the works. But men, who are like horses and mules (cf. Ps. 32:9), are powerfully moved by the outward appearance. Formerly, when I was a monk, I, too, was far saintlier than I am now so far as the external mask is concerned. I prayed more, kept vigils, practiced abstinence, and tormented my flesh. In short, my whole life was altogether showy in the eyes of others, although not in my own eyes; for I was intensely crushed and distressed. But now I eat and dress in the regular and usual manner. Nothing special or extraordinary stands out in my life in comparison with others. At that time, when I was a monk, I did nothing else than waste my time and ruin my health. Indeed, I wounded my conscience with those acts of righteousness, with the result that even now it can scarcely be restored. For beyond nature, in which glorying about works is implanted, I also acquired the disposition and custom of paying attention to my works and my worthiness. But I know for certain that now one reading and one Our Father avails more and is more acceptable to God than all those prayers I mumbled for 15 whole years,[5] for I know that I am heard. There is no need of any vigils or of special fasts and of abstinence, for God gave me "a messenger of Satan" (2 Cor. 12:7) together with other difficulties and the crosses of this world which plague me more than all those things.

So far we have treated this subject, that the very saintly patriarch is described so simply and meagerly that he does not differ in any respect from the lowest and most worthless man among the heathen. But from this the reader [6] should learn the difference between a Christian and a heathen and their works. For if he is a Christian, see whether he honors, hears, and earnestly loves the Word, or whether he is also plagued by a cross and troubles. If this is so, he will come to church, gladly hear the Word, take delight in it, believe from the heart, pray, give thanks, and have

---

[5] These 15 years would seem to date from Luther's entry into the monastery on July 17, 1505.

[6] Here, as elsewhere, the reference to "the reader" is an indication that these lectures have been prepared for publication by an editor; cf. also Introduction, p. xi.

a good conscience. If you see this, then conclude with certainty that he is a saintly man who is pleasing to God. And admire him as such. And whatever he does later, whether in the government or in the management of household affairs, you must say that it is pleasing to God and that God will reward it not only in this life but also in the life to come. Thus it is stated in Revelation (14:13): "Their deeds follow them," not only the works pertaining to the church but also those pertaining to the state and to domestic matters. But the works of the godless and the heathen are not pleasing to God. Therefore they do not follow them; but they die without glory, without being remembered, without admiration. Our works, however, have the glory and the inspection of God and His angels, and they follow us into the life to come.

But let us look at the text. "HE LIFTED HIS FEET" is a common way of speaking in the Hebrew language. For it the translation in the Vulgate has *profectus est*.[7] But note how different the preparation for this journey is from that previous legation, when Abraham sends his servant to bring a wife for Isaac, his son and the heir of the promise. For at that time the servant is sent equipped with gold, silver, gems, camels, and a distinguished retinue. Why is the same preparation not granted to his son Jacob, since he, too, after receiving the promise and the blessing, was appointed as the heir? He enters upon his journey on foot, without a retinue, without camels, and without any expense. He barely has provisions for the journey. "He lifted his feet," *hat seine fuss auffgehaben,* set out on foot; he did not tarry on the way but proceeded in haste, μετὰ σπουδῆς, as is said of Mary when she went through the hill country (Luke 1:39).

Thus he depicts Jacob, the very saintly patriarch and heir of the blessing, as altogether poor, downcast, and lowly. Yet Jacob alone is now the pope, as it were, in the world. For Eber, who was still living during the preceding year, has grown old. Isaac is blind and useless for governing. His son Jacob alone is now the bishop and ruler in the house. But he is sent away with the height of contempt, with danger and great wretchedness, so that he flees on foot, alone, and without a retinue. Although servants, camels, gold, and silver were not lacking, he has to be very poor

---

[7] Reflecting the Vulgate translation, the Douay Version renders these words with "Then Jacob went on in his journey."

and very miserable, and have nothing in his purse but provisions for the journey. What is the reason? It is the reason we have heard above (ch. 27). Rebecca, his mother, said: "Listen, my son, and flee." Flight is the cause of this, likewise the fury of his brother, who was threatening him with death. Therefore Rebecca acted wisely by fitting him out secretly and equipping him with provisions for the journey in order that he might be able to steal away without the knowledge of his brother and the whole household. He had to steal away in secret. "Say nothing," she said, "and go secretly; flee as quickly as you can." This flight and the danger in which he found himself did not allow extensive preparation and a retinue, lest he be hindered by the slowness of the pack animals and the camels and be caught by his angry brother.

Here the Jews prattle irrelevantly and say that it is not likely that Isaac sent his son away with less honor than Abraham sent his servant away above (Gen. 24:10). Therefore they invent the story that Eliphaz (Gen. 36:4), Esau's oldest son, pursued Jacob with a band of armed men, caught him, and robbed him of everything he had.[8]

Lyra approves of this. But these are pure Jewish fables. For Jacob has not been sent by his parents with a retinue as Abraham's servant was sent. The servant was safe and in no danger. He was not fleeing. But Jacob flees secretly. None of his relatives know anything about it. He does not bid farewell to his brother, who does not know that he is fleeing. His brother hated him and was pursuing him. Therefore it is stated: "He lifted his feet; he fled, etc." It was surely a very wise plan on the part of his mother. She was concerned more about the life and safety of her son than about pomp and a magnificent retinue, lest she hurl her son rashly into danger. Jacob is careful to obey his mother. He does not refuse or delay. No, he proceeds on his way in haste.

We have said above that this must be emphasized against all those bold and rash persons who say: "If I have the promise, I will have what is promised, even though I do nothing." [9] Such thoughts must be rejected and condemned on the basis of this example of Jacob, who listens to his mother and flees, even though he has the promise. He does not say: "I have the promise. There-

---

[8] Lyra *ad* Gen. 29:1-3, referring to Gen. 24:10.

[9] Cf. p. 50, note 46.

fore I will be safe and sound, even if I do not follow the advice of my mother." For promises are not given for the purpose of snoring, loafing, and sleeping, or for doing what is in conflict with the promise. No, they are given for working, being watchful, and bearing fruit. Thus I am not baptized, do not partake of the Lord's Supper, and am not absolved for the purpose of sleeping and snoring at home in idleness. But if you have the promise, Baptism, and absolution, remember that you have been called to be watchful and to be anxiously concerned about the things that pertain to your faith and calling. "How can we who died to sin still live in it?" says Paul (Rom. 6:2). We are not absolved from sins in order that we may live for them and serve them, but in order that we may fight against them and stoutly persevere in the promise, in order that I may chastise and mortify my flesh and bear it with a calm mind when God imposes a cross, in order that we may be purged and bring forth richer fruit. "By this," says Christ, "My heavenly Father is glorified, if you become My disciples," (cf. John 15:8); that is, if you suffer as I did, and if you become like Me. For he who is not a "Crosstian," [10] so to speak, is not a Christian; for he is not like Christ, his Teacher.

This, then, is the first thing, namely, that the very great patriarch, who at that time was the only bishop and a burning light in the whole world, has the blessing, the promise, and the Word yet lives and acts as if he had nothing at all. Why? Because here he is not a man of the church but a man of the home and very wretched. He performs his common domestic duties, concerning which God prescribed nothing in His promises, just as He prescribed nothing about how He would help and guide him or about the outcome. Thus He has not given us a promise that there will be peace this year and a rich yield of grain. Accordingly, I should not say: "I do not know what will happen. Therefore I will do nothing." Indeed, God rather says: "Do your duty, and leave the rest to Me." He did not say: "Everything will turn out successfully." No, He said: "Do your duty. You do not have to know how things will turn out or what will happen. You have been justified. Go, then, and exercise your faith in the household and in the state." For this knowledge of God's will and this vocation thanks

---

[10] With this neologism we have sought to reproduce the play on words between *Christianus* and *Crucianus*.

must be given to God that a man of the church, that is, one who has the Word and faith, knows that he pleases God even in the lower stations in the kind of life that has to do with the state and the household, whether he is a servant, a maid, a magistrate, or a subject. If he can only be a part of the political and the domestic sphere, he should give thanks to God and know that he has a God who is well-disposed and propitious toward him.

Furthermore, this serves to console us when the examples of the very saintly patriarchs are set forth not only in sublime and heroic virtues but also in the most insignificant and least important deeds, in those sordid and despised works connected with domestic life, lest we despair or think that we are cast off and spurned by God when we are occupied with these duties of life. But we should know that all things are sanctified by the Word and faith. Yet the world does not see this sanctity; but when it hears that these common duties are related even about the saintliest men, it thinks that every exertion is wasted and that good time is poorly invested when one reads these legends. For the world is not worthy of seeing the glory of God, as the well-known statement puts it: "Away with the wicked, lest he see the glory of God!" [11] Only believers see and understand the works of God. Therefore these works are precious in our eyes, yes, in the eyes of God.

Nor should you reflect or wonder why the Holy Spirit takes pleasure in the description of these servile and despised works. But listen to St. Paul when he says (Rom. 15:4): "Whatever was written in former days was written for our instruction, that by steadfastness and by the encouragement of the Scriptures we might have hope." If we believed firmly, as I do, even though I believe weakly, that the Holy Spirit Himself and God, the Creator of all things, is the Author of this book and of such unimportant matters, as they seem to be to the flesh, then we would have the greatest consolation, as Paul says. Indeed our hearts would be able to glory in this and to be proud that God deigns to be mindful of and to remember these patriarchs, that He did not want to forget them. He wanted not only their heroic virtues but also the sordidness of their works to be praised, to be adorned

---

[11] The traditional formula cited by Luther here and elsewhere is *Tollatur impius, ne videat gloriam Dei.*

with these descriptions as with gems and gold, and to be set forth to the whole world in order that they might be spread abroad, read, and become known. To the believers, therefore, all things work together for good (cf. Rom. 8:28), yes, for glory, even the things that are least important, most sordid, and most despised. For they see that God takes pleasure in these things, so that He sings psalms not only about the glorious and extraordinary virtues of the saints but also about their most insignificant little works, because they are works of God. Therefore God takes pleasure in His works, whether they are very great or very small. He takes pleasure to our very great consolation, as it is said (Ps. 147:11): "The Lord takes pleasure in those who fear Him." And in Ps. 56:8 David says: "Thou hast put my tears in Thy sight. Thou hast kept count of my tossings."

What then? It is not true, is it, that God has nothing else to do than to keep count of David's tears and tossings? Is He not occupied with the governing of the world and with hearing the choirs of the angels, who praise and bless Him without end? What can be said that is more wonderful? Yet it is true. To keep count of the tears and tossings of David is also care that is incumbent on God. Thus another psalm says: "He who avenges blood is mindful of them; He does not forget the cry of the afflicted" (9:12). Likewise (Ps. 116:15): "Precious in the sight of the Lord is the death of His saints." And Moses says to Pharaoh (Ex. 10:26): "Not a hoof shall be left behind"; that is, "Not only the men, women, children, and beasts of burden will go out of Egypt; but whatever we have, even the most insignificant hoof, we shall not leave behind." Accordingly, not only the heroic virtues and the glorious works He does through us, likewise the blood, death, and very grievous conflicts of the saints, are precious in the sight of the Lord, but even the meanest hooves themselves are precious. Yes, listen to Christ. He does better than this. He says (Matt. 10:30): "Even the hairs of your head are all numbered." You shall not lose a hair. What, I ask, is more trifling in value and more despised in the human body than a hair, a whisker, a nail? Yet all these are numbered and cared for by the Father who is in heaven.

This is how these examples of the trifling and sordid works in the saints are to be dealt with, in order that they may teach and console us. For we do not deny that they are mean and of trifling value if we look only at the instrument in which they are done. But one must also consider God Himself, the Author. For whether you see the sordidness or the gems of the saints and their works, yet they are pleasing to God, who is the Author of trifling and noble works alike; for they are works of God, and God cooperates. Therefore this is great and immeasurable consolation for those who believe. And these things are described in order that we may see how tenderly God loves and embraces us, and what great and anxious concern He has for us. So closely does He look at me that He is afraid I may lose a hair. But if He numbers and cares for hairs, He has far greater concern for the body, the soul, the blood, and all sufferings.

But these things are too sublime. Therefore we do not believe. The more worthless and sordid the works are, the less we believe. The very filth and meanness of the works is a hindrance to our faith. Otherwise we would magnify without end the mercy of God in these very small and unimportant works, and our faith would be strengthened very much. For so great is God's concern and solicitude for us that He cannot forget one hair, one little tear and one little worry, so to speak. And when the Holy Spirit goes along so weakly in describing His saints, He means that the most insignificant of all the works of the saints please God very much. A Christian is something precious. There is nothing so insignificant in him that it does not please God. To shed one's blood, to die, to sweat, to fight and struggle against the devil is in reality something great and decidedly pleasing to God. Therefore conclude as follows: When you are a believer, then even physical, carnal, and animal duties are pleasing to God, whether you eat, drink, are awake, or sleep. These are purely bodily and animal things. So great a thing is faith.

First of all, therefore, see to it that you become a Christian and a person pleasing and acceptable through the Word, through Baptism and the sacraments. If the person believes and adheres to the Word, and does not persecute the Word but gives thanks for it, then you should do nothing else than what Solomon says (Eccles. 9:7-9): "Go, eat your bread with enjoyment, and drink your wine with a merry heart; for God has already approved what you do. Let your garments be always white; let not oil be lacking on your head. Enjoy life with the wife whom you love, all the days of your vain life which He has given you under the sun, because that is your portion in life and in your toil at which you toil under the sun." What more will you require? What could be said more pleasantly, more delightfully, and more clearly?

It is true, of course, that even in the godless diligent application to duty is pleasing to God; but unbelief and vainglory prevent them from relating their works to the glory of God. For the fault and sin is in the person who does not please God. Therefore although the good works even of the godless merit their rewards in this life, yet they are not kept count of, not collected in a bottle, according to what is stated in Ps. 56:8. But the tears of the saints, their flights, their trials, and their smallest and greatest works are kept count of to be praised and celebrated forever.

Therefore what Paul points out in Rom. 15:4 when he says that nothing has been written in Holy Scripture in vain is exceedingly sweet consolation. For it is certain that these very mean and insignificant works are set forth in order that God's good pleasure in His saints (cf. Ps. 147:11) may be pointed out. For the remission of their sins and their acceptance always remain, and they live under the cloud and shadow of God's wings and under His protection as long as they are in grace. This we should also apply to ourselves. For if we are Christians and truly godly, we know that we are like those very great saints, if not in the highest rank of the greatest virtues, nevertheless in these meanest and sordid deeds of this life, and that so far as the care and protection of God are concerned, we are loved no less than they are. As a sure pledge of this most tender and burning love we have God's Son, for whose sake the Father loves us and makes us sit in the heavenly places, as Paul says (Eph. 2:6). We should know that what is stated very sweetly in Ps. 37:23-24 also applies to us. There we read: "The steps of a man are from the Lord, and He establishes him in whose way He delights; though he fall, he shall not be cast headlong, for the Lord is the stay of his hand." Let us only believe, and give assent to, this promise. For just as parents guard their little ones with all care, lest perchance they fall, lest they stumble somewhere or offend, and, if they see a spot or mucus smeared on their cheeks, dry it and wipe it off—which an enemy or a stranger does not do—and if a feather sticks to their hair, comb and adorn it, so great also is God's care, love, and true fatherly feeling toward all who believe in Him.

These things in the main have been stated concerning what is taught in this chapter. What follows pertains simply to domestic matters. We shall scan it and examine the grammatical points. "He came to the land of the people of the east"—in Latin one would say: "He came to the land of the Orientals" or "into the Orient"—is a common expression in the Hebrew language. For in this way one who is to be killed is called a child of death, and an arrow is called a child of the quiver. A child of pride is a designation for a proud man. Be children of fortitude, that is, be brave. A child of Belial means an evil and worthless man.

Accordingly, the very saintly patriarch Jacob set out for the land of the people of the east, or the Orientals. With this general name for the whole region Holy Scripture indicates in a veiled manner that although this seemed servile and trifling, it was nevertheless an arduous and difficult work born of the Word and faith. For it was necessary to travel in an unknown region. Nor is the name of this region mentioned. For he does not call it Haran; he calls it the east. It was not yet known to or inhabited by the Arabs and the Syrians. There was nothing here except Babel. Therefore he simply says that he set out for the east, that is, for an unknown and desert chaos, as it were. Thus above Abraham departed from Chaldaea without knowing where he was going or where he should settle. He risks it in reliance on our Lord God. Therefore his traveling seemed to be a servile act. In reality however, it is a work of great and burning faith; for he does not know into what chaos of men or localities he is being brought. He has no knowledge of the people, the places, or the byways. He does not know where he will have suitable lodging from night to night. Thus it was an exceedingly dangerous and troublesome journey. In the meantime he struggled in faith with death and the devil throughout the journey. He was uncertain about where he was going or with what fortune he would arrive at his destination.

By chance, however, he espies a well in the field and makes his way to it. This, too, is a servile act, except that here consolation begins to be shown to him when he comes to a place in which he is safer and less apprehensive. In addition, he hears about his uncle Laban. I have nothing more to say. Therefore I shall add nothing. For I take no pleasure in allegories, because the letter instructs us with greater certainty and fullness than an allegory does. It is sufficient for us to know that these sordid and servile works of the saints meet with the approval of God. Consequently, when we are in our calling, we have no doubt at all that whatever we do or suffer is pleasing to God to such an extent that God wanted this to be put into this book and all these works of the saints to be praised. He did not allow these things to be consigned to oblivion. The letter of the text itself is clear per se. Allegorically, they take the three herds at the one well to mean the Trinity and the large and heavy stone to mean Moses.[12] But this does not concern me. I leave it to others.

4. *Jacob said to them: My brothers, where do you come from? They said: We are from Haran.*

5. *He said to them: Do you know Laban the son of Nahor? They said: We know him.*

6. *He said to them: Is it well with him? They said: It is well; and see, Rachel his daughter is coming with the sheep!*

7. *He said: Behold, it is still high day, it is not time for the animals to be gathered together; water the sheep, and go, pasture them.*

8. *But they said: We cannot until all the flocks are gathered together, and the stone is rolled from the mouth of the well; then we water the sheep.*

Haran is a city of Mesopotamia where Crassus was later conquered by the Parthians in a great massacre.[13] Laban, however, is Nahor's grandson, not his son. Nahor had already died. Bethuel, Nahor's son, was the father of Laban and Rebecca. But Nahor is mentioned because he is the father and head of this household. Jacob asks: "Does he have peace?" That is, "Is he well?" This is a Hebraism.

The grammarians raise a question concerning the stone of the well.[14] They ask whether legal precautions had been taken, lest someone move the stone away and water his flock before all had come together, or whether the size and weight of the stone was so great that the combined strength of two or three men was

---

[12] *Glossa ordinaria ad* Gen. 29:1-3: the well represents Baptism, and the three flocks the Trinity.

[13] See p. 211, note 17.

[14] Lyra *ad* Gen. 29, *Additio*.

needed to remove it. I do not think that the removal of the stone was forbidden by any law, but I think that the size of the stone was so great that one or two men were not able to remove it. But because there was no large supply of water in Mesopotamia, they guarded the wells carefully and covered them with large stones. Furthermore, the shepherds of the flocks were not all strong men, but young men and maidens like Rebecca [15] were employed to tend the flocks and hold them in check. They assembled at the fountain and waited for stronger men to roll the stone back, just as Jacob approaches and removes the stone without anyone's help. This, I think, is the reason why the help of many was needed. Yet others have a right to their own opinion.

9. *While he was still speaking with them, Rachel came with her father's sheep; for she kept them.*

10. *Now when Jacob saw Rachel the daughter of Laban his mother's brother, and the sheep of Laban his mother's brother, Jacob went and rolled the stone from the well's mouth, and watered the flock of Laban his mother's brother.*

11. *Then Jacob kissed Rachel, and wept aloud.*

12. *And Jacob told Rachel that he was her father's kinsman, and that he was Rebecca's son; and she ran and told her father.*

The commentaries of the Hebrews have noted—and the text seems to indicate the same thing—that when the Holy Spirit rushed upon the patriarch Jacob, he was so strengthened by that impulse of the Holy Spirit that he was able to roll away the stone without the help of anyone.[16] Then, when in his exile he found Rachel, his blood relation, he took courage and gained great hope that at last he would obtain what he had in mind and what his father had commanded him with respect to taking a wife. Therefore he is immediately inflamed with love at first sight, and natural desire toward his kinswoman comes to the fore, so that the twofold impulse of faith and love made his body and heart more animated. For he wanted to show himself as a man of strength

---

[15] The text has "Rebecca," but "Rachel" seems to be meant.
[16] Lyra *ad* Gen. 29, *Addito.*

and agility—in order that he might capture the maiden's heart and entice her to fall in love with him.

And these things, too, are only natural. But they are recorded by the Holy Spirit in order that no one may think that they are disgraceful or forbidden. For it is a Christian and godly thing to love a girl to join her to you in marriage, since there is a natural desire and inclination of sex to sex. Although this is not completely without sin, yet God does not want it to be despised as dishonorable. For it is a work of God created in man's nature, and it should not only not be despised or vilified but should even be honored. For God wants to be glorified in all works, both small and great. He does not want to be despised even in the smallest work. Thus Christ says (Matt. 25:40): "As you did it to one of the least of these My brethren, you did it to Me." So we should not cast aside or trample underfoot even the smallest precepts and ordinances of God. If you want to drink water, good. Drink, and give thanks to God. If it does not please you to drink it, do not despise it.

Accordingly, these carnal, childish, and womanish things are nothing but filth. Yet they are recounted by the Holy Spirit, not to provoke lust, not to kindle disgraceful love affairs in the hearts of youths, but to nourish the hope and the dignity of marriage, and that the Holy Spirit may testify that neither marriage nor the love of a husband and wife is displeasing to God, since God has created and ordained this love. Therefore you should not blaspheme it as disgraceful and forbidden, as the monks have said that marriage is an impure and dangerous kind of life.

Therefore I think that at the hour at which Jacob espied his kinswoman he was carried away, so to speak, and strengthened in spirit to such an extent that he was able to roll the stone away without help. Otherwise the strength of four or five boys would have been needed for this. He wanted to do this favor and service for the maiden in order that she might be able to water her flocks at the proper time. But she does not yet know that he is her kinsman. After he has rolled the stone away, he approaches the maiden, and kisses her. He is unknown and a stranger before he greets her. This also seems disgraceful, and according to these ways of ours, it is neither customary nor proper. But previously he heard the other shepherds say: "Behold, Rachel is coming, etc." Therefore he knew that she was a blood relation of his, and among those people it was customary to add kisses when they met and greeted one another. This is a custom today in Belgium [17] and also in other lands. Our people only hold out the hand, and they embrace maidens or matrons modestly and shyly. There are as many customs as there are lands. It was, therefore, an indication of love toward his kinswoman and future wife which he demonstrated with this kiss, just as if he had stretched out his hand or had offered her some gift.

This was the source of that strength when he moved the stone away. It sprang from affection for his kinswoman, then from love toward his spouse, who, as he saw, had been chosen and presented to him by God. In the third place, special joy was added, because he saw that he had finally reached port after such a difficult and dangerous journey. But the Holy Spirit increased and confirmed all this. Lastly, Jacob is called the brother of Rachel's father according to the custom of the Hebrews, who call a sister's son a brother, as Moses himself will explain when he says that "Laban heard the tidings of Jacob, his sister's son."

13. *When Laban heard the tidings of Jacob his sister's son, he ran to meet him, and embraced him and kissed him, and brought him to his house. Jacob told Laban all these things.*

You see that these things have been described as altogether pastoral and after the manner of shepherds. Yet in these matters the Holy Spirit is so wordy that He causes the irreligious reader distaste and loathing. Other histories about very great events —about the burning of Sodom, about the sacrifice of Isaac—He has described with very few words and has summed up in barely five or six verses. But when He comes to these sordid, carnal, and foolish matters, He is wordy beyond measure, in order that we may know that the Lord takes pleasure in those who fear Him (Ps. 147:11). For if we believe and are sure of the freely offered mercy of God, we should not doubt that everything we do pleases God very much and that He has numbered even the hairs of our head (cf. Matt. 10:30), yes, that the kisses and embraces are pleasing to Him, likewise the removal of that stone. All these things are recounted in this passage as very great and extraordinary works in the eyes of God and the angels. God could not forget them but wanted them recorded for our instruction and consolation.

[17] See also Luther's *House Postil* (W LII, 665).

Therefore although we are harshly plagued in this life and subjected to many disasters and finally to death itself, we should know nevertheless that it is all precious, according to the statement (Ps. 116:15): "Precious in the sight of the Lord is the death of His saints." We should have the same thought about other works, whether we eat or drink or sleep or are awake. Thus Paul says in Col. 3:17: "Whatever you do, in word or deed, do everything in the name of the Lord Jesus, giving thanks to God the Father through Him." And we should be exercised in these lower matters in order that we may gradually proceed and become accustomed to matters more sublime. But faith, which works great and heroic things, lowers itself even to domestic and servile things, pastures flocks, leads them to water, milks goats; for God has made both: the fool and the wise man, the small and the great, what is precious and what is of trifling value. Therefore the works of a manservant or a maidservant and a master, of a woman and a man, are equally pleasing. Only believe, and honor God above all things in the church. See to it that you remain in His Word. "If you abide in Me," says Christ, "and My words abide in you, you will bear abundant fruit, and your fruit will remain" (cf. John 15:7, 8, 16).

Therefore faith and the person who is in grace must be considered. For such an abundance of divine goodness has been poured out on us that God numbers and observes even the least of our works. Whatever they are or of whatever nature they are in the end, they are all praiseworthy and pleasing because the person is pleasing. Nor does the judgment of the flesh have a place here. The flesh says that these matters pertain to some profane writer, as though they were unworthy of the sacred chronicles, yes, that not even the Greek or the Latin authors would think it fit to celebrate such matters concerning their heroes; for they do not understand what a life of godliness is, what things are pleasing, and what things are displeasing to God, as the well-known saying puts it: "Away with the godless lest he see the glory of God!" [18]

Therefore we should read this with reverence and thank God that we know we are pleasing to God even when we sleep, eat, drink, marry; when husbands, children, and wives live to-

---

[18] Cf. p. 275, note 11.

gether; when we manage the household; when we milk goats. We should exercise ourselves in these matters; for they are just as great and wonderful as those sublime works, because they are done by a great person who believes and is an heir of the kingdom of heaven. If it pleases God, some day or hour will come when we will also do great and heroic works.

God has also depicted this will and good pleasure of His in the feelings of parents toward their children. For in the domestic sphere we see that father and mother are moved and delighted more if a little son or a little daughter brings a little flower or some other little thing than if a servant or maid brings a sack or a great beam. Those little works that would be despised in servants and maids are delightful and pleasing in children. Therefore describing the legends of hypocrites and monks is different from describing the legends of those who are truly saints. The former ridicule the works and the whole life of the latter as impure, and they dream that they can placate God with their self-chosen and monstrous works. But these works have been condemned by God, for they are not done by a person who is pleasing and acceptable. Therefore let us look at the rest. It is no less foolish and carnal in the judgment of hypocrites. Now a new section follows, namely, how Jacob became a bridegroom.

14. *And Laban said to him: Surely you are my bone and my flesh! And he stayed with him a month.*

The beginnings are favorable, as usually happens in the case of hypocrites. For throughout the history Laban will be described as a greedy and grasping man. And the name Laban agrees beautifully, for it means "white." Hypocrites, you see, have a great show of godliness, discipline, and morals, so that nothing seems saintlier, nothing more honorable, and nothing more religious than they are. But it would have been more appropriate if the word had been turned around and he had been called Nabal.[19] Accordingly, he displays great piety and love toward his cousin. But in the meantime he thinks: "Behold, I have obtained a very good

---

[19] The name Nabal appears in 1 Sam. 25:3 ff., whence it has come to mean a stingy person. Here Luther is reproducing the play on words between "Laban" and "Nabal"; he repeats it several times in these *Lectures on Genesis,* including *Luther's Works,* 8, p. 92, where note 20 should be corrected accordingly.

and useful servant who will be compelled to do and bear everything according to my will, for he is a fugitive and an exile who has been able to find no other place to which to withdraw. He is poor, starving, and naked. In this prison and with sufficiently strong bonds he will be detained in my house. For without me he would have to perish of hunger."

Yet at first he fawns on him, as hypocrites usually do. "You are my bone and my flesh," he says. He runs to meet him, embraces and kisses him, as if he loved him in earnest and truly. But soon he betrays his hidden and faithless heart, just as in other circumstances a fish and a guest often become worthless after three days, as is commonly said.[20] Accordingly, Laban is described as a very pretentious hypocrite so far as external works and words are concerned. Inwardly, however he maintains idolatry, pride, greed, and contempt for his neighbor. He considers only his own advantage. With such a fellow the good and saintly man Jacob has to live. And observe, I ask you, how insignificant the beginnings of such great honors and of the dignity of this most eminent patriarch are — this patriarch from whom so many kings, so many prophets, Christ Himself, and the apostles sprang, in whose possession was the whole majesty of eternal life, who was a king and a priest, and who obtained the whole blessing from his father. He is exceedingly poor and altogether downcast, to such an extent that he has nowhere to set his foot. Indeed, this is creating a man out of nothing.

15. *Then Laban said to Jacob: Because you are my kinsman, should you therefore serve me for nothing? Tell me, what shall your wages be?*

Jacob was with Laban for one month, and during this time he surely was not supported by him for nothing. Undoubtedly he was not lazy. No, he did the work of a godly and faithful man not only because he was impelled by poverty and need but also because the Holy Spirit was in him — the Holy Spirit, by whom saintly men are moved to do honorable and godly service of every kind. God also blesses these men in order that they may be useful to many. Joseph is an example. Although he had nothing but food and

---

[20] Cf. Plautus, *Miles gloriosus*, 741.

clothing, yet he enriched his master, and that without any expectation of reward. It is undoubtedly such men about whom Paul says in Col. 3:23: "Whatever your task, work heartily, as serving the Lord and not men." Servants of this kind who serve so faithfully that they do not please men but please God are very rare. But Jacob was a servant of this kind during that month and as long as he served Laban. He was not lazy, but he attended to his domestic duties of his own accord and with the greatest diligence. He pastured the flocks, provided them with water, and took care of all similar tasks as faithfully and as diligently as he could. But it pleased greedy Laban very much when he saw that Jacob devoted so much zeal and energy to his duties as a servant. Therefore he immediately makes an agreement with him regarding wages. This is the highest commendation of Jacob's diligence and industry coupled with outstanding faithfulness.

And it is truly an outstanding and very rare virtue, especially among blood relations and kinsmen, where you would find very few who think that they should serve their kinsmen faithfully. For they think they have some right to devour, rob, and squander the property of their kinsmen. In-laws and kinsmen like Jacob and Joseph, or like Naaman at the court of the king of Syria, are very rare. To such a man you could entrust the care and administration of household affairs. Accordingly, Laban saw that he had acquired a servant to his heart's liking, one who was industrious and busy, by whose efforts the best provision would be made for the cattle, the household would be put in order, and very fine discipline would be restored in the house, together with a great increase of all the property. The statement which follows bears this out. "You had little before I came to you," he says (Gen. 30:30). At the same time God's blessing for the sake of the faithful servant was added. This servant was really the salvation and the pillar of the household. "Therefore I do not want you to serve me for nothing," says Laban. For he sees that Jacob is no lazy beast like the servants and maids we have today, but that he did more for the profit and advantage of his uncle than had been commanded. Accordingly, the reward for such faithful service follows.

16. *Now Laban had two daughters; the name of the older was Leah, and the name of the younger was Rachel.*

17. *Leah's eyes were weak, but Rachel was beautiful and lovely.*

18. *Jacob loved Rachel; and he said: I will serve you seven years for your younger daughter Rachel.*

19. *Laban said: It is better that I give her to you than that I should give her to any other man; stay with me.*

20. *So Jacob served seven years for Rachel, and they seemed to him but a few days because of the love he had for her.*

But this is altogether childish and carnal. For what does it mean that the very saintly man, who was adorned by God with such great promises and to whom [21] God Himself appeared in a very clear vision, becomes young again at this age and nearly returns to boyhood? He sees two maidens, and one more beautiful than the other. Of these he loves the one who is outstanding because of her beauty; the other one he does not love. This does not seem proper for the octogenarian Jacob, does it? For it is certain that at this time he had reached the age of 80 or at least 78. But at this age he begins for the first time to dally like a youngster and to love. Why, pray, does the Holy Spirit record such things and set them before us to be read, as though we should be edified by such a disgraceful deed? For, what is more, it will be stated below that Jacob loved his son Joseph because Joseph was born when Jacob was an old man (Gen. 37:3). This time was not more than 14 years distant. Nevertheless, it is called Jacob's old age. Therefore it is not proper for such a saintly man to be so foolish and lustful that he looks at a maiden's beauty and loves a beautiful one more than he loves one who is ugly. For one cannot say that he did so out of love for offspring, since for the most part ugly women are most fertile, as is clear in the case of Leah. But by no childbearing could she bring it about that she was loved as much by Jacob as Rachel was loved. Therefore he cannot be excused on the pretext of seeking offspring, but it is simply droll and ridiculous to love a maiden because of her beauty, not for the sake of offspring.

By rights, of course, we should love the female sex simply for the sake of offspring and procreation. It was created by God to

---

[21] The Weimar text has *cum*, but we have followed the Erlangen and other editions and read *cui*.

serve this purpose, not for us to misuse it merely to satisfy lust. The structure of a woman's whole body bears this out. It has its own organs and members with which to conceive, nourish, and carry the fetus. But few consider this, and Jacob, too, strays from this purpose. For he loves Rachel because of her beauty, and he does not love Leah, who is less beautiful. Yet it is less seemly for old men than for youths to look at beauty.

But this should be taught and dealt with in the church, lest we shrink from marriage. Thus the papists have debased and condemned this with their irrational babbling. For the Holy Spirit records this to give evidence that God does not reject and condemn even those who look at beauty in a wife, and that such a choice is without sin. Therefore no one should think that he is committing a sin if he prefers a beautiful woman to one who is ugly. Thus this, too, teaches and edifies us. Furthermore, Jacob hoped for offspring from a woman of outstanding beauty and strength of body. For when contracting marriages the strong should be chosen and united with the strong, the industrious with the industrious. Thus this distinction is observed among dumb brutes, among oxen, horses, sheep, roosters, and all other animals. Because of the corruption resulting from original sin it does not happen this way among men. For this is why it happens that some are born strong, others weak. Sometimes they are leprous, sometimes blind, and sometimes feeble-minded, because of the fault and guilt of the parents. Therefore one must bear it that strong persons are united with those who are weak on account of original sin, and this evil must be counteracted with the remedy of matrimony shown by God, no matter how they are united or who they are.

Thus all animals also have their fixed times for procreation. As a result of the poison of original sin man alone has irregular and unfixed impulses, which could not be taken care of in any other way than by means of this union, where he who can have a wife who is beautiful and whose strength is unimpaired should have her by all means. He who cannot have a choice should marry the one who is offered, whether she is beautiful or not. Furthermore, after original sin marriage is decidedly troublesome and burdensome to the flesh because the union is indissoluble. For although passion and the love of sex for sex remains, yet that bond concerning which Moses says that a wife should be an inseparable companion for life in the eyes of her husband is very hard and difficult. For no matter what calamity befalls either their bodies, their property, or their offspring, that firm and indissoluble bond remains. And every choice is removed; nor is any change, any rejection or repudiation, permitted. On top of this, the devil, the foe of all the ordinances of God, puts in his appearance. He troubles and torments married people in various ways. Because of so many great troubles and difficulties of marriage it is not wicked if one chooses a beautiful woman with her bodily strength unimpaired in order that he may be able to endure this bond of marriage with all its troubles longer and more easily. Nor is it advisable to choose a woman who is odious and troublesome at the very beginning, for Satan is wont to alienate and tear apart even those whose beauty is outstanding and who embrace each other with the greatest love.

Here the Holy Spirit teaches that such a choice has not been condemned by God. For He commends it, or rather yields to the wish of this very saintly patriarch in order that he may love a beautiful woman more than one who is ugly. He lets it happen. For marriage is the kind of life that has need of the remission of sins and the indulgence of God, so that God not only connives at such lust, provided that it is lawful through marriage, but also at the mistakes and offenses of domestics, of children, and of married couples which are wont to occur in the management of household affairs. For just as it is necessary for the state and the church to be under the remission of sins, so the life of married people is also under the indulgence of God and the remission of sins. God does not want those conjugal matters to be condemned, namely, that a husband chooses and loves a beautiful wife. Although in the beginning this is not difficult in the first fervor of the love with which bridegroom and bride are mutually aglow, yet it gradually cools down. Indeed, at times it degenerates after a month into exceedingly sharp hatred at the instigation of the devil, who bewitches the hearts of married people in various and strange ways.

Accordingly, this, of course, is not an excuse for this sin, which the hypocrites censure in this patriarch. But it is praise of the indulgence of God; He does not condemn the rejection of Leah, who is less beautiful, and the choice of the other, who is more beautiful. The papists explain it as wantonness, but they do not see what reason has driven him to matrimony. For concern about descendants weighs on Jacob, who has the promise. Therefore he is apprehensive about getting a suitable and pleasing wife rather than about finding a fixed abode and house. This is contrary to all the reasonings of the philosophers and the precepts of wise men. Hesiod says: "First a house, a wife, and an ox for plowing." [22] Here our Jacob is concerned about none of these, not about a house, not about an ox, not about other necessities; but first of all he chooses a wife.

Furthermore, the papists do not even see that outstanding chastity is concealed under this youthful love. For the Holy Spirit not only does not condemn the mutual love of the bridegroom and the bride per se, but at the same time He points out especially how chaste Jacob was. Or is this not outstanding chastity when a man lives continently and chastely up to his eightieth or eighty-fourth year? For Jacob became a husband for the first time when he was 84 years old. He lived for so long a time as a celibate after the first flower of his age up to the years of his old age. For 14 years later he will be called an old man (Gen. 30:30). Therefore if the papists look at the fact that he chose a beautiful maiden, why do they not also see that he lived continently up to his eighty-fourth year? At that time nature was stronger and more perfect, so that a man was capable of procreating when he was about 15 or 16 years old. To endure and conquer that wickedness of the flesh and law of the members—which is called lust—from that year on and in the very flower of one's age is certainly a great miracle and a very fierce fight against the flesh. Few have withstood it. Therefore the papists stray very far from the truth if they think that the fathers lived a carnal life, as they surely do think. For it is their opinion that no one but the celibate monks and nuns lives a chaste life, and it offends them very gravely that the patriarchs were married. They have no understanding whatever of the exceptional chastity of those men. It would not have been strange if during such a long period of continence Jacob had completely mortified his flesh and destroyed his innate power to procreate. For the years of his boyhood, youth, and manhood have now elapsed, and now he is 84 years old. He has struggled with

---

[22] Hesiod, *Works and Days,* 463, recited by Luther (or inserted by his editors) verbatim according to the original Greek.

his flesh for 68 years. Yet desire remained in him, and the inclination toward sex, toward the young maiden, and indeed toward the more beautiful one, whom he, an old man with gray hair, prefers to the one who is less beautiful.

Therefore these examples of chastity surpass all our continence, and especially the altogether impure celibacy of the papists in the monasteries, which are now mere brothels. Or even if they have preserved chastity, it is not to be compared to the chastity of the fathers, in whom the flesh was mortified in such a way with great faith and spirit that the natural inclination toward and the affection for the other sex were nevertheless not extinguished. Thus Jacob loves his bride with a true love and to an extraordinary degree, so that those seven years barely seemed to equal a period of three or seven days. Furthermore, what is most important of all, after he has become a bridegroom, he waits seven years until he is united with his bride. If today anyone had to wait so many years for his wedding day and in the meantime had to serve as a pauper and beggar, he would surely abandon both his bride and his father-in-law. But those papal swine do not consider this. Nor do they see the illustrious and invaluable example of chastity which at the same time is coupled with wonderful patience which for seven whole years endures this servitude and a delay that certainly would be intolerable for any other man. Besides, he is wretched and poor. He has nothing of his own, not even a shoestrap or a thread. He does it all out of love for a maiden — love by which he was captivated to such an extent that those seven years seemed to be only days, that is, as if they had been no more than seven days.

Augustine also admires this patience and waiting, searches for the reason, and asks how Jacob was able to show such patience, since it is contrary to and beyond man's nature.[23] For all descriptions of love and lovers bear out what he says: "I love impatiently." And deferred love in particular disheartens men and makes them impatient. Love songs complain that days and months are too long, as that man in the poet says: "If I do not find this day longer now than a whole year."[24] But Augustine replies that

---

[23] Augustine, *Quaestiones in Heptateuchum*, I, 88—89, *Patrologia, Series Latina*, XXXIV, 570—571.

[24] Vergil, *Eclogues*, VII, 43.

this time and these years seemed so short because his chores were not burdensome and difficult. For love is all-powerful, just as, on the other hand, he who hates can endure nothing. Love does for nothing what in other circumstances a man could not be induced to do for any reward or in response to any plea. Thus harlots or adulterers often suffer more than a respectable wife or husband would endure. So great is the power of mad love. Therefore pure and honorable love does and endures much more.

But this reply is not adequate. For one must add that here it is pointed out how this love of the bridegroom is governed by the Spirit of faith in Jacob. But under that Governor everything is good and easy. For if God is present and dwells with us in all things with that chief and principal consolation, then "I can do all things," says Paul, "in Christ, who strengthens me" (cf. Phil. 4:13). Therefore no matter how carnal and juvenile these things are, yet they are approved in the very saintly man as an example for us and for our consolation. For he had the promise of descendants, and of this he was chiefly mindful. Therefore it was necessary for him to take a wife.

Now we shall explain the things that pertain to grammar. The text says that Leah's eyes were רַכּוֹת, which we have translated with *ein blöd gesicht*, "weak of sight"; and I think it has been rendered well enough. For what others say, namely, that she had rather long eyes, is false.[25] It seems to me that she was an honorable maiden with good morals and unimpaired strength, but not beautiful, especially not in the eyes, which are man's greatest adornment. Thus Pliny calls the eyes the king among the members of the human body,[26] and they surely are the outstanding part of the body. Therefore charm and beauty of the eyes is a rare gift in man. Flashing eyes, however, which men commonly call falcon eyes, are especially praised. Concerning maidens it is said: "She sees like a falcon." For they are very keen and vivacious eyes and almost gleaming, "very clear and bright." And both vice and virtue of the heart can be detected from the eyes. Therefore beautiful eyes are a miracle, as it were, in the human race; for they signify excellence of character and nature. Below (Gen. 49:12)

[25] Sebastian Münster, *En tibi lector* (Basel 1546), p. 63, note "d" *ad* Gen. 29:17, suggesting that a letter had dropped out of the Hebrew.

[26] Pliny, *Natural History*, XVIII, 43.

it will be stated about the Messiah that "His eyes shall be red with wine," will be like dark-red wine. Such eyes adorn the face very much and give it life, so to speak, and a kind of cheerfulness. On the other hand, small and dull eyes, which are not sharp and alive, darken and deform the whole face. Leah had eyes like this, with which she did not have sharp vision. Because of her tender or weak eyes, therefore, she was not in favor. For the Hebrew word רַכּוֹת means "weak," as is stated above: "Abraham took a tender calf" (cf. Gen. 18:7), a delicate one. I disregard the mystery which some deal with here [27] and follow the historical meaning. For this is the simple and plain reason why Jacob was rather unfriendly to Leah, for she had eyes less sharp and charming.

But Rachel was beautiful. The meaning in the Hebrew word תֹּאַר is properly referred to the fourth species in the category of quality, to the figure which contains the form and the proportion of quality.[28] Rachel's eyes had the right shape, and her forehead, her cheeks, and her whole body had the proper arrangement and symmetry of its members. There is true beauty and charm when the face has a suitable and symmetrical proportion of the eyes, the forehead, the cheeks, and the other parts. So far Moses has described this bridegroom and lover Jacob in a manner that is childish enough. Out of love for a charming and beautiful maiden he endures such a long and hard servitude, and from this one can gather how great his love is. And one should note that Holy Scripture does not condemn but praises this love in the bridegroom. But what follows is an outstanding and brilliant example of Jacob's patience in this servitude and in his love for the maiden.

21. *Then Jacob said to Laban: Give me my wife that I may go in to her, for my time is completed.*

He calls her his wife, even though she is a virgin. For Scripture does not distinguish between a wife and a betrothed woman, as can be seen in Moses and Matthew, where betrothed virgins are called wives. Therefore Jacob regards Rachel as his lawful

---

[27] As Luther indicates elsewhere in his comments on this chapter, the contrast between Leah and Rachel had been taken, in the monastic exegetical tradition, as a "mystery" or allegory of the active and contemplative life.

[28] Cf. Aristotle, *Metaphysics*, Book V, ch. 14, on the meaning of "quality."

wife, and he burns with true marital love toward her, as young men and bridegrooms are wont to do. But the ardor of the bridegroom is strongest when the time for embracing and copulating draws near. In this patriarch of ours, however, this very pure and ardent love toward his wife Rachel is most shamefully disturbed, as is stated next.

22. *So Laban gathered together all the men of the place, and made a feast.*

The scoundrel would deserve to be cursed into the abyss of hell. Moses does not say: "He called and invited men to the nuptial feast," which is customarily done solemnly and in an honorable manner, but that he gathered together, "raked together," not for the glory and honor of the bridegroom and the bride but to deceive and make sport of the very pious and saintly man, and in order that he might hold him captive with his tricks, lest in any way he be able to repudiate and exchange the woman with whom he cohabited that night, even though he had been deceived and deluded. Therefore he suddenly collects a number of witnesses. And Scripture seems to hint that Laban did not have a good reputation among his pious and honorable neighbors, who undoubtedly understood his evil wiles and the wrongs he inflicted on pious and faithful Jacob during those seven years. Therefore he collected fickle people who would not disapprove of this imposture. This means that he was an exceedingly evil old fox completely ruined by greed. Jacob, however,[29] joyful and aglow with love toward his Rachel, suspects nothing wrong or evil; but full of hope and joy he waits for his very charming bride in order that he may have pleasure in the joy he has hoped for and desired for such a long time.

23. *But in the evening he took his daughter Leah and brought her to Jacob; and he went in to her.*

24. *(Laban gave his maid Zilpah to his daughter Leah to be her maid.)*

25. *And in the morning, behold, it was Leah; and Jacob said to*

[29] The Weimar text has *ad*, but we have followed other editions and read *at*.

Laban: What is this you have done to me? Did I not serve with you for Rachel? Why, then, have you deceived me?

This is that example of patience. Therefore let him who can learn patience do so. I certainly cannot. For it is intolerable and inimitable. The very pious and saintly man loves the maiden so ardently that he does and endures everything for seven whole years. Indeed, he enriches that greedy old fox Laban with the stipulation and condition that he give him his daughter Rachel in marriage. But in return for such faithful service Laban thanks him by secretly taking away from him his wife, the virgin whom Jacob loved and had sought and desired for so many years, and at that in the very hour of the marital joy he had longed for most. Laban not only snatches her away—which, of course, is very annoying in itself—but he also thrusts on him another, who is revolting to him, and in this way puts a perpetual burden on his neck. It is surely a horrible and exceedingly disgraceful imposture. Jacob knows nothing else than that he has his most charming bride in his embrace, and behold, he has a substitute. If someone should take your money, gold, silver, and cattle, it is a small loss; but to take a virgin, a beautiful and beloved wife from whom you expect offspring with your whole heart and from whom you hope for the seed of the promised descendants, this is surely a wrong and insult that surpasses all wrongs. For this whole hope and expectation of Jacob suddenly collapsed. Nor could any other thought enter his mind than that he would be deprived forever of the love of Rachel, his bride, and that she would no longer be his wife. Thus the exceedingly pleasant hope and that very fond expectation of the love and embrace of his wife which has lasted for seven whole years to the boundless joy of both is cheated. But they did not suffer this wrong without tears and great grief. It is an evil too dreadful and cruel, and the patience is incredible. I surely would not have endured it but would have disputed with Laban and would have summoned him to court, in order that he would have been compelled by the laws to give my wife back, and I would have rejected the other one and sent her back to her father. For not Leah but Rachel had been betrothed to him, and this had been publicly reported and was undoubtedly known throughout the whole town.

I think. however, that those whom Laban gathered together

as his guests were fickle and worthless fellows, good-for-nothing rascals, who were compelled to approve and excuse this crime to please Laban. But the separation is very hard and is intolerable. Indeed, even if I were older than Methuselah himself, I could not bear it; for this separation is contrary to nature and to every human feeling. What great commotions those who snatch virgins and women have stirred up in all histories! How often have very flourishing kingdoms clashed in battle with one another because of wrongs of this kind! Because of the abduction of Helen the Greeks stirred up almost the whole world. The Sabines went to war against the Romans because of the abduction of their daughters. And below in chapter 34 the Shechemites are slain by the sons of Jacob because of the abduction of Dinah. For the feeling of love in a bridegroom is most tender and impatient, especially at the very moment of marriage, when the embrace and the nuptial joy are at hand. Therefore he can endure nothing less than to have his bride torn away from him—his bride with whom he is madly in love and whom he holds dearer than gold and silver, yes, than his eyes and life itself. Furthermore, Jacob had sought and chosen this bride at the order and in accordance with the wish of his father for the sake of the promised descendants he hoped for from his beautiful and young bride. But this hope collapses in one moment. So does the joy that has been so long hoped for. Therefore if anyone can magnify and execrate such outstanding and unheard-of malice, let him do so. For it is too great to be expressed in any words. Indeed, reproof and indignation seem to be indicated in the text. For it is not said that Laban brought Leah to Jacob as his wife, as he later informs us concerning Rachel, namely, that he gave his daughter Rachel as his wife. Moses does not regard it as proper to call Leah a wife. No, he says: "He took his daughter Leah and brought her to Jacob."

But terrible cupidity impelled greedy Laban to commit such a great crime, not so much in order to foist his older daughter on Jacob as to detain him for seven more years. For he was aware of wonderful success and of the increase of his property. Therefore it was shameful and horrible for the very pious man to be detained by such a monstrous crime in order to satisfy the greedy desires of this old fox. But he must suffer the derision, which is really altogether too hard. How Rachel herself felt is not told, but it is reasonable to suppose that her indignation was not less.

For she undoubtedly knew that she was the bride, and it was known to the whole neighborhood that Jacob was serving for Rachel during those seven years. Therefore she was disturbed by this wrong just as much as the bridegroom himself. Indeed, she could endure and overcome much less; for the nature of her sex is weaker. She was sure that she was the bride and that she was to be led to the bridal chamber. But in the very hour in which she thinks she will enjoy love and the bridegroom she has longed for, she is most shamefully deceived, not without great grief, not without tears and wailing.

Accordingly, this is a sad and mournful marriage. For the bridegroom is wretchedly deceived; but Rachel, the bride, is rejected. Undoubtedly she could not conceal her completely justifiable grief and indignation and gave evidence of this with her tears and her voice; and she expostulated with her father, saying: "Why are you taking from me my bridegroom whom you yourself promised me?" But the cruel father was not at all moved. Perhaps he even restrained her with threats. Leah knew that she was not the bride but the bride's sister, and perhaps she offered some resistance to the wish of her father. Yet out of human affection she allowed herself to be taken away and to be forced to commit this wrong. Indeed, she congratulated herself on this act of violence in order that she might become the mother of the promised descendants who, as she heard, were awaited by Jacob. And below in chapter 30 it seems that Rachel manifested not a little feeling and hatred toward her sister Leah for this very reason. Therefore this was an unfortunate marriage for Jacob and Rachel because of the unexpected deception, and in the case of the very saintly patriarch Jacob an example of exceptional chastity and of a cross and the greatest patience is set forth. For I do not know whether anyone of the saints, not to say the heathen, would have been able to bear this cross with such great patience. It is too high and too terrible.

But the question is asked what kind of nuptial rites there were among those people, for Jacob alone sleeps with her alone in the bedchamber and on the same bed. Yet he does not realize that Leah has been substituted for Rachel. For he has lived in this house for seven whole years, and here he undoubtedly saw his bride occasionally and sometimes spoke with her. And if he could not have discovered this by touching her in the bed, yet he could have recognized and distinguished her voice. According to our customs, we act far more cautiously. For we lead the bride both to the church and to the nuptial chamber not in darkness but with trumpets and torches, and we also bring witnesses along, so that there can be no room for any imposture. One gathers from the account that this custom was not in vogue among these people, for otherwise Jacob would not have been deceived in such a shameful manner. Besides, it was customary at that time for the men and the women to have separate dwelling places. They did not live so close together as is customary among us. Young men lived with their fathers, and maidens lived apart with their mothers. But Jacob had his bride with him in the bedchamber. He surely could have conversed freely with her. He could have discovered even by touching her that it was not Rachel. From this one gathers that in this age there was the greatest modesty, or at least in the case of the patriarch Jacob. Or Leah was certainly instructed by her father to be completely silent or to speak softly. Nevertheless, Jacob's modesty must have been very great. Consequently, he neither spoke with her nor touched her but only embraced her with marital love, out of exceedingly great joy that finally he had been able to enjoy the love of his very dear bride. Scripture commends this outstanding modesty and chastity, that he entered the bridal chamber without suspicion, without lasciviousness, without lewd desire, and with simple and marital affection. For what Lyra says, namely, that he was continent for three nights, I pass over.[30] Consideration should rather be given to his great frankness in not discovering by any sign at all that the woman to whom he came was a stranger. For one should not look at the fathers as the papists do. It is their opinion that the fathers indulged madly in lust, as they themselves do. But in Jacob there was very simple chastity and completely pure love toward his bride. Nor did he have any reason to suspect that another woman had been substituted; for both parents and the bride herself are very well known, and in all of them the greatest candor and the purest sincerity have always been seen. Nevertheless, he is deceived.

But this is what I think, and I excuse Jacob, as I said above about Lot when he lay with his daughters.[31] For it can happen

[30] Lyra *ad* Gen. 29:21.
[31] See *Luther's Works*, 3, pp. 308—310.

that at times a man is so absorbed in strong imagination and in the application of his mind that he does not hear, see, and feel anything at all, even though he hears with open ears and sees with open eyes. For a strong and intent thought of the heart withdraws the mind from the senses, so that a man sees and feels nothing on the outside. This is precisely what happens in the case of the stronger emotions, whether in anger, in grief, or in love. For these emotions make a man senseless and irrational. Hence in battles you may often see men thunderstruck and dismayed and soldiers completely stunned by trepidation and fear. Thus Lot, overwhelmed more by the drunkenness of grief than by that of wine, and absorbed in the sadness resulting from the hellish burning of Sodom, felt and noticed nothing. But whatever he did, he did unwittingly and with the heart of someone else.

This is strange. But it is customary, and in the case of melancholics it is natural when they give serious attention to some endeavor or to thinking about something. From a melancholic you could often take away all his property without his knowledge, even though he himself were present. In the same manner, Jacob's heart was occupied with and absorbed in love and joy, and he gave thanks to God because he had a bride from whom he was hoping for descendants. He was drunk, not with wine but with love for Rachel, whom he had sought and desired for such a long time. This drunkenness of love is certainly great insensibility. Stupefied, as it were, by this, he could not notice or feel the deceit. For he suspects nothing evil but is completely absorbed in thought and in love. He is sure that his bride can no longer be taken from him. Therefore nothing was further from his mind than that the old fox felt obliged to take his bride away from him and to substitute Leah.

This is how I spoke above concerning Isaac when he blessed Jacob instead of Esau. Although he recognized Jacob's voice, and although his heart felt beforehand that deceit and trickery were at hand, nevertheless, since he was occupied with the desire to pronounce a blessing, he gives no thought even to the things he feels and hears. Such examples occur often in life when hearts fall back from the external senses into the thoughts with which they were previously occupied, and when they think that it is impossible for them to be deceived or to suffer any harm; for they trust their hearts more than their eyes and ears. Therefore we must think that Jacob, too, drunk as he was with love, was stupefied and carried away, as it were, so that he thought of nothing less than that he could be deceived. That powerful ardor of love blinded him.

This is what has come to my mind about the imposture of this old fox, namely, how Jacob was deceived by it. At the same time, however, that outstanding and rare example of modesty should be noted, and the chastity of the patriarchs should be enlarged on over and above all the chastity and celibacy of the monks. For here the exceedingly ardent impulses of love and lust are overcome or at least repressed both in Jacob and in Rachel. Although Rachel was the true bride, yet she is excluded from the marriage chamber for which she has hoped and which is her due, and she is compelled to pretend that she is not the bride and to comfort and assuage the wretched love and longing for the bridegroom with her tears.

Furthermore, one can see here how great paternal power was among those people. For Leah is compelled by only one word and nod from her father Laban to take the place of Rachel and herself to become the bride even contrary to the plighted troth. For before that time Jacob had not exchanged a single word with Leah about getting married. No love, no pledge, no agreement had intervened; but without consent, agreements, and discussion the daughter is seized by the father and placed on the nuptial bed of Jacob. The father does not try to find out what his daughter wants; he does not hear her answer. If these were the customs of those people, they certainly were very bad. For it is certain that no betrothal was concluded between Leah and Jacob and that no witnesses were summoned. But everything is attended to suddenly by the tyranny and violence of the father, who seizes his daughter and brings her in to Jacob. Therefore this is a very bad example by which we see that Leah becomes a bride by the sheer tyranny and cruel boldness of her father. Although it is reasonable to suppose that she consented readily to become the mother of the saintly posterity and is therefore excusable, the tyranny of the father is completely detestable. And although the saintly man tolerates this wrong, yet it is a detestable example and one that should by no means be imitated.

Here Lyra and others ask whether there was a true marriage

that night between Leah and Jacob.[32] I reply that there was not. Then was it adultery? By no means! What then? A monstrosity! For if you look at the deed itself, Jacob is not Leah's husband; but he taints and defiles a woman who was not betrothed to him. Yet he is without guilt; but this guilt clings to faithless Laban, who deceives the bridegroom and the bride and tears the marriage asunder by uniting Jacob with another woman than the one he had promised in marriage. Accordingly, he can neither be called an adulterer, nor does he deserve to be regarded as one. And if the question is asked whether Jacob sinned by lying with a strange woman, one must reply that although the deed itself is manifest defilement and not a marriage, yet he did not sin; for he has been deceived by another's treachery, which he could not even suspect. For who would fear that a father would defraud his very own daughter of the joy hoped for for such a long time? The daughter had no other thought than that this night she would become a bride to be united with her very dear bridegroom. And Jacob entered with true marital love, without any doubt that he would embrace Rachel as his wife. For the treacherous rascal Laban had promised this and had pretended for seven whole years. But in one moment he destroys the marriage that has been pretended for such a long time. This is plain rascality.

Therefore we shall reply to the proposed question by saying that there was no marriage between Jacob and Leah, for the willing consent of both was lacking. She had not been betrothed to Jacob, and Jacob was not Leah's bridegroom. But a mistake was made, and it was a case of invincible ignorance in a political matter.[33] This, as the jurists say, excuses one completely. For they distinguish between gross, careless or negligent, and invincible ignorance. Where there is ignorance of the deed, the person, the circumstances, and all things, this is not a crime but is simply innocence in political matters. In theology, however, this has no validity, although some have also related it to theology.[34] But its place is only outside theology, in the political sphere. It should

---

[32] Lyra *ad* Gen. 29:25, citing the principle that consent is necessary for a true marriage.

[33] Apparently a reference to the legal axiom, *Ignorantia legis non excusat, sed ignorantia facti excusare potest.*

[34] "It is not imputed as a sin to a man if he fails to know what he is unable to know. Consequently, ignorance of such things is called *invincible,* because it

not be adduced before the court of God. Otherwise all men would be saved. Thus the fact that the Jews crucified the Son of God is a mistake and irrefutable ignorance on their part, as Paul testifies in 1 Cor. 2:8.[35] For reason does not understand it. Yet this does not mean that they are excused before God. Therefore invincible ignorance should be placed outside theology. But in the political sphere it is a complete excuse. Thus this union of Jacob and Leah is not a marriage, and the deed per se is a defilement. But it is excused on the ground of invincible ignorance. Leah is also excused; she should not be regarded as a harlot. She is excused on the ground of the authority of her father, who said: "I bid, compel, and order you as your parent. You, Leah, are a bride on the strength of my authority and will." Therefore she goes forth in simplicity and in pure filial obedience; and although it is probable that she allowed herself to be brought without reluctance, yet she is excused on the ground of paternal power and filial obedience.

But it is very hard and shameful for the father to compel her with his tyranny. And she herself does not dare refuse. Accordingly, all guilt should be cast on greedy Nabal, whose aim it was to foist both daughters on the very pious man. No sin and guilt adheres to Jacob, but this is a case of pure ignorance. For without his knowledge and against his will he is defrauded of the love of the very charming bride whom he hopes to embrace that night. Thus the Roman historians excuse their Lucretia.[36] Although there was no invincible ignorance here, yet Lucretia suffered violence. For adultery was committed, since two persons who are married come together and violate the laws of both marriage beds. Nevertheless, Tarquin alone is an adulterer, not Lucretia; for she was compelled by the power of the sword to prostitute her body. The weak woman suffered the adulterer's force and violence which she could not drive away.

---

cannot be overcome by study [or effort]. For this reason such ignorance, not being voluntary, since it is not in our power to be rid of it, is not a sin. Hence it is evident that no invincible ignorance is a sin." Thomas Aquinas, *Summa Theologica*, I—II, Q. 76, Art. 2.

[35] Here the original correctly has "1 Cor. 2," but the Weimar editors, for some reason, have suggested the correction "2 Cor. 2."

[36] Lucretia is discussed at greater length in connection with the story of Joseph below; cf. *Luther's Works*, 7, pp. 90 ff., esp. p. 90, note 46.

Thus it is related about Lucia that when the judge threatened to drag her to the altars of the idols and to the brothel, and the youths who were to defile her had already been assembled, she replied: "If you seize my hand to offer incense to an idol, you are an idolater, not I. And if I am led to a brothel, I will not be a harlot on this account, but I will get a double crown of chastity." [37] In the same manner we must free the patriarch Jacob from guilt. He enters the marriage chamber out of simple marital affection, and he thinks that he will find his Rachel there. But contrary to every thought and wish he is united with Leah, who had not been betrothed to him.

But after his complaint there will be a true marriage when God grants a dispensation for this union and confirms it by giving offspring: Simeon, Levi, Reuben, etc. Then it must be called well done, in order that everything the saints do may work together for their good (cf. Rom. 8:28). Otherwise it is neither a marriage nor adultery; it is simply a monstrosity. Nor should this example be imitated by us. Children should not be forced to love and marry those from whom they recoil. Besides, enough and more than enough happens in the way of dangers and trouble, even if those who are aglow with love for each other are united, as daily examples show. Nor has this patience been set forth for us to imitate; for it is too hard and completely heroic, namely, to endure and suffer with equanimity that one's bride is snatched away in the very hour and at the very moment of the nuptials. Therefore one will have to admire and praise this example rather than imitate it.

But Moses proceeds to describe how Jacob felt when he discovered the deceit. Undoubtedly he was greatly dismayed when as the sun rose in the morning he saw that a strange woman had been united with him. Not only was he terrified to see that he had been imposed on and that his dearly beloved bride had been snatched away from him, but terror of conscience was also added because of the defilement or incest.[38] For he was a godly and saintly man who grieved more about the sin than about the wrong.

---

[37] On Lucia cf. Aldhelm, *Tractatus de laudibus virginitatis, Patrologia, Series Latina,* LXXXIX, 142.

[38] Cf. *Luther's Works,* 45, p. 7, where Luther declares: "I am forbidden to marry . . . my wife's sister, while my wife is still alive."

Nor could he understand at once how this exchange had happened. But he throws the blame on Laban and attests his innocence by asking: "Why have you done this to me? Have I not served you for Rachel? Why have you deceived me?"

26. *Laban said: It is not so done in our country, to give the younger before the first-born.*

On top of all this, the scoundrel makes fun of him. On top of such a great injury and the shameful disturbance of the nuptial joys, treacherous Nabal taunts him. "This is not done," he says, "in our country." Why, then, did you not say this before, when Jacob said: "I will serve you for seven years for Rachel"? Aha, is this speech of yours just being born? as the man says in the comedy.[39] Why did you not bring up the custom of your nation before this? Now the old fox finally comes with it. It is not enough for him to have duped his most honorable son-in-law. In addition, he even makes fun of him with words. Yes, by fraud and deceit he heaps up another seven years of servitude, merely in order that his property may be increased and grow by reason of another's toil, even by means of lying and trickery. Accordingly, he deserved to be cursed by God for enriching himself with another man's sweat and toil. But here, too, the common saying held true: "The worse the rogue, the better the luck." The more worthless a person is, the more fortunate he is. But the Hebraism in this passage should be noted. "One does not do it." In the Hebrew language an impersonal verb often has an active or a plural meaning. "They do not do this," that is, "This is not done." Luke 6:38 says: "They will put good measure into your lap."

27. *Complete the week of this one, and we will give you the other also in return for serving me another seven years.*

"Of this one," namely, of Leah. There it is. Laban saw that his domestic establishment has been increased through the servitude of Jacob. Consequently, he thinks about deceiving him and retaining him for seven more years. For this is how he reasoned: "If I give him my daughter Rachel, he will soon go away, and he will leave my house, which has increased beautifully thanks

---

[39] Terence, *Adelphi*, V, 3, 19.

to his presence and fidelity. Therefore I shall have to detain him longer, whether rightly or wrongly—not that I do not wish him well; for if I had more daughters, I would give them to him—but to keep him with me longer—in order that I may become rich through his faithful service." What a scoundrel he is! Jacob had now satisfied his father's command, by which he had been ordered to marry a wife from this family; and he had now served for seven years according to the agreement with his father-in-law. Therefore he was thinking of returning home with his wife. Then the devil confronts him with this trouble and thus not only disturbs and prevents his nuptials but even adds another period of seven years.

Accordingly, Jacob must serve for 14 years. For he has not served for Leah. This certainly was a heavy and troublesome burden. Now he has two wives. Yet he has nothing of his own. He serves with empty hands, and this is very hard and troublesome. Greedy Nabal appropriates everything. His sole aim is to enrich himself through the diligence and the good offices of this very pious man. But now he in turn should have been good to Jacob and given him a dowry. Yet he makes fun of him and foists on him two maids and the daughter from whom Jacob recoils. Look at what greed does! Therefore he is a plunderer, a robber, a thief, and a brigand. He gets rich on the blood and sweat of a very pious man and of his daughters, as will follow below. He has grabbed everything for himself. This is how the exceedingly filthy slave of mammon is described. Consequently, it is no wonder that the whole world execrates him. He goes beyond the rapacity of all thieves and robbers, and no rhetoric can elaborate sufficiently on this avarice.

28. *Jacob did so, and completed her week; then Laban gave him his daughter Rachel to wife.*

Jacob accepts the condition offered by his greedy and unjust father-in-law. In this way the whole business is settled. But the question is asked, why Jacob consents. For although Laban mentions the custom of the country—and perhaps it was the custom in that region for the older daughters to be given in marriage first—yet this is a futile argument. It is strange that Jacob was ignorant of this custom and that he did not see any example of nuptials that accorded or disagreed with that custom, since during a period of seven years one can easily observe the customs of any region. But as soon as he hears this custom mentioned, he consents. He would have had every right to reject Leah and say: "No matter what the custom is, you pledged Rachel to me, and in accordance with our agreement I have served you seven years for her. I will keep her and no other."

But what should the saintly man do? He lets it pass. He bears this wrong with equanimity in order that he may obtain Rachel, who was his one true bride; and he sees that he cannot obtain her except on the completely unfair condition that he keep Leah, whom he did not love. For he thought: "What am I to do? Leah has been deceived on the authority of her father, just as I have been deceived by his crafty scheme. If I forsake her, she will be forsaken forever. She has been defiled by me and deprived of her best dowry, namely her virginity. Or all men will suspect that she has lost her chastity, even if I had abstained from her." Thus Jacob is persuaded by mercy, love, and patience not to repudiate Leah. This is an outstanding example of the special mercy and virtue because of which he keeps with him the woman who, as he knows, has been substituted for his bride.

But a question is asked about lawfulness, whether it was permitted and whether such mercy is not condemned by the Law of Moses, which says that one should not marry two sisters.[40] The person is excused on the ground of mercy and love, but concerning the deed there is doubt. Indeed, the Law orders him to get rid of the one or the other. Therefore this example should not be taken as a precedent: Jacob keeps Leah and regards her as his lawful wife, although he would have been glad to forsake her. For the law and custom of the fatherland stood in the way. Then, too, there was the defilement that had been committed. But because Jacob consents he begins to be guilty and by his consent to confirm the crime. What, then, shall we say?

I reply: Some examples are heroic; others pertain to customs.[41] Laws and customs must simply be observed, and no transgression should be tolerated, lest confusion arise. The heroic examples are those that do not agree with the laws. For it often happens that a heroic man, whom God has endowed with special power,

---

[40] A reference to Lev. 18:18; cf. also p. 304, note 38.
[41] Cf. *Luther's Works*, 13, pp. 154—166.

bursts through and breaks the rule but does not leave an example behind him. Customs, laws, and rights should be observed and examples should be followed. But in the case of heroic men there is no precedent. No example is valid unless it is similar in all respects. If you are similar to Jacob, and if such a case, such an occasion and necessity, arises, then you will be permitted to do what Jacob was permitted to do. If you are not similar to Jacob in all respects, you will have to adhere to the law and the common customs.

One must not burst through rashly and set an example and a precedent because of some heroic case. The grammarian says that nouns ending in *a* are of the feminine gender, that those ending in *um* are neuter. But if you adduce *auriga* or *Glycerium* as examples, they will not square with the rule, although they have the same ending.[42] For they are heroic words, that is, exceptions. They are not subject to the rules, but the rules are subject to them. A poet does not care about a rule. The same thing must be observed in medicine and in jurisprudence. If a physician always proceeds according to the rigor of the rules, he kills many. Although rules must be followed, they should not be followed rashly. For some case can occur which refuses to be under the rule. Then geometrical proportion must be applied.[43]

The monks have followed arithmetical proportion in their rules, one like the other. As much as the one works, eats, drinks, and sleeps, so much should the other work, eat, and sleep. But this arithmetic equality pertains to the marketplace, to buying and selling, not to governments. Thus many monks, inasmuch as they were not able to bear matching or equal burdens of the order, have been killed. One can be content with seven hours' sleep, another with three; for another man 10 hours are not enough. Therefore Augustine spoke wisely and admirably when he said: "Not all in the same way, for all of you are not equally strong." [44] This statement is also praised by the Bishop of Worms.[45] For

---

[42] *Auriga*, "charioteer," is masculine, despite its ending; Glycerium, the name of a character in the *Andria* of Terence, is feminine, despite its ending.

[43] This seems to be a version of Luther's more usual distinction between mathematical and physical accuracy; cf. *Luther's Works*, 13, p. 120, note 68.

[44] Augustine, *Regula ad servos Dei*, I, *Patrologia, Series Latina*, XXXII, 1378.

[45] Apparently a reference to Johann von Dalberg (1445—1503), who is cited

it agrees with geometric proportion, which does not balance or compare one thing with another, as is customarily done in the marketplace; but it compares the persons and arranges the matter according to them. But in the market arithmetic proportion enforces everything without respect of persons. Whether it is a woman or a man or a child, it sells bread for one, two, or three cents. But in eating, the proportion of the persons is observed. One man in the monastery is content with one cake; another man is not.

I am mentioning this as an example. But one must be much more cautious [46] in theology, lest someone argue as follows: "Jacob breaks the custom and the Law of Moses. Therefore I shall be permitted to do the same thing." I deny that this is a precedent, and the reason is that Jacob is not bound by customs but is a heroic person who is led by a heroic custom, not by a custom that is legal. Therefore he should not to be imitated. No, he should be observed and admired. You should not imitate Achilles when he slays Hector; or if you try this, Hector will slay you. You must not carry heaven or the pillars of Hercules, since you are barely equal to the carrying of one stick. They are the fools in the state who want to imitate the heroic men whom they see going along above and outside the rules. "Such a great man acted and thought this way. Therefore I shall follow the same course." But you have another mirror to look into, namely, the common custom, likewise the common right and law. Do not transgress this, before God calls you and orders you to be a hero or a Jacob. Otherwise such people become apes who invite destruction for themselves and for others. Thus when a well-known incendiary who was pusillanimous by nature became an ape and wanted to imitate the illustrious deeds of other heroes, he revealed his folly and brought destruction on himself.[47] For stupid men of this kind accomplish nothing else than the destruction of states and the confusion and disturbance of the world.

These examples, then, should be treated in such a way that the customs which should be followed remain intact. We should

---

in connection with this same quotation from Augustine's *Rule* later in these *Lectures on Genesis* (*Luther's Works*, 8, p. 173).

[46] The Weimar text has *canendum*, but we have read *cavendum*.

[47] Apparently an allusion to the story in Suetonius, *Lives of the Caesars*, "Vitellius," ch. 15, 17.

look at heroic examples and admire them, but we should not imitate them. Paul hurls a viper clinging to his hands into the fire (Acts 28:5). Follow his example. There is the story of a certain physician who had lifted up a child from Baptism and had heard the words of Baptism pronounced there together with the prayers and statements of Scripture by which it is pointed out that we are freed from the kingdom of the devil and transferred into the kingdom of God's Son. Then he wondered at the greatness of the promises and the blessings that are conferred in Baptism and said: "If I knew that I, too, had been baptized in this way and that the same words had been pronounced for me, I would never dread the devil." When he had been reminded and persuaded by others that he, too, had been baptized into these words, he received such great faith that he determined positively never to fear the devil. Finally, however, a specter confronted him, and the devil appeared to him in the form of a billy goat. But so little was he terrified by this that he tore off one horn, broke it, and brought it back to his companions from whom he had departed. One of his companions saw this. Although he did not have the same faith, nevertheless, impelled by his admiration of this miracle, he boasts that he, too, has been baptized and that he would not dread any specter no matter how horrible. Accordingly, he proceeds to the same place, and that specter of a goat with horns returns. But when he wanted to take hold of its horns, the devil twists his neck and kills him.[48] Why, then, did the former escape the danger and not the latter? Because the latter was presumptuous and did not have true faith. He thought that he was able to conquer Satan with his own power and strength. He did not have true faith.

Therefore everyone should examine his gift. For just as we are unequal in our bodies, our talents, and our property, so we are unequal in spiritual gifts. Everyone should remain in his place in the moral law and the common right until God calls or compels him to do something special. Jacob did not do this by his own counsel, but he was seized and compelled by the will of God to do this contrary to his own opinion and will. Therefore God later

---

[48] This anecdote, which recurs several times in Luther's writings, apparently comes from hearsay rather than from the *Lives of the Fathers*, which was the source of other such stories.

confirms this deed with the blessing of offspring, and Leah becomes a mother of patriarchs.

In this way, then, the fathers should be excused. But their examples should not become precedents, lest confusion and destruction of the laws and the common customs ensue. But we should remain within the limits of the laws unless a special vocation or heroic inspiration calls us away. But if some fanatic is induced by Jacob's example to argue as follows: "Jacob married two sisters; therefore I am permitted to do the same thing," I reply: I deny that this is a precedent, for one must distinguish between persons in civil life and heroic persons who have special impulses and inspirations. For God is the Manager and Governor of all. If He inspires someone to do what is contrary to the common rule, the rule should not be broken or set aside by this. No, one must stay with the common right and permit God Himself to except those whom He wishes. For only He can rightly say: "This is what I command; let My will be the reason." [49] He can change the laws. If He excepts a person, that person is excepted; otherwise not.

Thus Münzer, a stupid man, read the histories of the kings and the judges, the achievements of Joshua, Samson, and David; and from the pulpit he impressed their examples on the peasants. "You are the people of God," he shouted. "Therefore you should follow the examples of the saints, of Samson and Joshua; and by killing the princes you should change the political state of affairs." [50] But the conclusion is false, for heroic men who have special impulses are excepted from the rule. We, too, who are under the rule, neither can nor should imitate them.

29. *(Laban gave his maid Bilhah to his daughter Rachel to be her maid.)*

30. *So Jacob went in to Rachel also, and he loved Rachel more than Leah, and served Laban for another seven years.*

After the description of heroic and wonderful deeds the Holy Spirit descends to weaknesses and to customs. For although a

[49] Juvenal, *Satires*, Book VI, line 223.

[50] Cf. his "Sermon Before the Princes" of July 13, 1524, in Carl Hinrichs (ed.), *Thomas Müntzer: Politische Schriften mit Kommentar* (Halle, 1950), pp. 1—28.

heroic man is excepted from the rule, yet one must observe the rule, as in grammar. Even though the Latin word for poet is not of the feminine gender according to the ending in *a*, yet it is declined according to the rule of nouns ending in *a*. It is necessary for him to be so heroic in order that he may not break the customs. Indeed, he should rather preserve, defend, and guide them. Even though he himself for his own person has been excepted in a special manner, yet he must descend to the first declension and the rule. Concerning Hercules the poets say that he broke the oars on the ship of the Argonauts.[51] Yet everything turned out successfully according to his plans. Thus although heroic men break the laws, they do not tear states apart.

Accordingly, this pious man Jacob is now described as a fool; for because of his love for Rachel he is involved in servitude for seven more years. A heroic man would not have done this but would have said: "I have served you for Rachel; I want her to be handed over to me as my bride." Furthermore, he would have threatened blows or abducted by force the maiden promised to him. He certainly would have had every right to do this. But the great man lowers himself and stoops to the utmost servitude; he serves double servitude for Rachel alone. For he had made no agreement on account of Leah. Previously he had been exalted to heaven, and before God he dared what would have been permitted to no one else. Now, humbled again, he stoops to servitude.

But we are glad to read these examples by which the Holy Spirit wants to commend Holy Scripture to us and to show carnal and weak things in heroic men. For it is a greater consolation to see carnal things in the saints than those sublime and great things which we cannot imitate. Therefore the Holy Spirit does not want these domestic and common affairs of human life to be neglected but commends them so much that at times He even relates imperfections and faults in order to point out that He is patient and forbearing, that He bears the ways of the weak, that He does not reject infants because of pimples, filth, and troubles, provided that they persevere in faith and love, as Paul says (cf. 1 Tim. 2:15). He has patience in many infirmities. Thus Heb. 4:15 [52]

[51] Cf. *Luther's Works*, 13, pp. 199—200.
[52] The original has "Heb. 5."

states: "We have not a High Priest who is unable to sympathize, etc."

This pertains to the consolation of the church, in which one does not always find heroic men, or at least not many. But these, too, are declined in the feminine gender, even though they are of the masculine gender. Thus God allows Jacob to be cast off and to be subject to servitude that is disgraceful and unworthy of a free man. And this is done out of carnal love for the bride for whom that old lover has a passionate affection. And he is so foolish that although he now has his Rachel by every right, he hands himself over to servitude for seven years to please the young woman. Above he stated that because of his great love those seven years seemed to him like a few days. Now, when he has gained possession of the wife he loved so much, he again hurls himself into that workhouse of slavery for seven more years. Was it not childish, carnal, and patently foolish to subject himself to servitude of his own accord and to put off the care of a household for the sake of the maiden who had been betrothed and handed over to him by every right? For to give thought to your own roof and to the arrangement of your own house is right and necessary if you have taken a wife. Here Jacob casts this care completely aside to please the maiden. Meanwhile he serves an infamous monster, a greedy and ungrateful man.

Such people, accordingly, are the heroic men, and they are described this way as an example for us in order that we may know that they were men like ourselves, now strong and resolute, now abject and weak. In sublime and heroic matters they are invincible and incomparable lions; in domestic matters they are foolish and weak. But God has regard for and approves both, the one who does sublime deeds as well as the one who does deeds that are humble.

31. *When the Lord saw that Leah was hated, He opened her womb; but Rachel was barren.*

These are decidedly carnal things. The Lord must look into the matter. Does God have no other occupation left than to have regard for the lowliness of the household? If He has such an abundance of leisure He will find something to do against the devil, the god of this world (cf. 2 Cor. 4:4), or with the monarchs and princes of the world. What does He do with the maiden Leah? I reply: Everyone should know that God cares for him in his calling. For God cares about little, mediocre, and big things. He is the Creator and Governor of everything. But who would believe that God cares for Leah? Surely all men should conclude firmly that God has regard for and cares for them, no matter how small, abject, and lowly they are. For this is why Moses so carefully depicts the condition of Jacob's household affairs and sets it before our eyes.

Jacob has possession of his wife for whom he has had such a great desire. In addition, he has Leah, whom he did not love or care about. Rachel understands this, and she has the keys and the management of the whole household. She is always close to Jacob and is the dear girl. But the whole house and the neighborhood attend to the lady of the house, and they knew that Leah is despised and neglected even by Jacob. For his fondness for her springs from mercy, not from marital ardor and the love of a bridegroom. It is only the giving of alms. Therefore wretched Leah sits sadly in her tent with her maid and spends her time spinning and weeping. For the rest of the household, and especially Rachel, despises her because she has been scorned by her husband, who prefers Rachel and is desperately in love with Rachel alone. She is not beautiful, not pleasing. No, she is odious and hated, שְׂנוּאָה. There the poor girl sits; no one pays any attention to her. Rachel gives herself airs before her; she does not deign to look at her. "I am the lady of the house," she thought, "Leah is a slave." These are truly carnal things in the saintly fathers and mothers, like the things that usually happen in our houses.

But we must not think that Leah endured this contempt without great grief, without tears and wailing. For the female sex is a weak vessel which has an ardent desire to be loved, or at least does not want to be despised, especially not by her husband or by the household. Therefore Leah was greatly grieved by the fact that she was being cast aside and scorned to such an extent in the house and that Rachel, together with the household, was in charge and was behaving insolently toward her. For no one cares about her; no one has any regard for her, not even Jacob himself. But the LORD alone must look into the matter, must break and crucify Jacob's disposition, and must also break Rachel's spirit. The Lord has regard for her, and in such a way that He crucifies Jacob's love and disposition, and breaks Rachel's pride by exalting Leah, who is odious and despised. In this way one must learn that God sees and governs all things but has regard solely and in a special manner for what is despised and cast off, just as Christ Himself was on the cross. For what the world and even saintly people like Jacob and Rachel throw away, this he gathers up, and it is altogether sacred to Him.

This is wonderful and great consolation for the afflicted and wretched, who should rouse themselves to faith and hope, since they hear God described and defined as He who is always pleased with the prayer of THE HUMBLE AND THE MEEK, as Judith 9:11 says. The sobbing, yes, the death, of those who are downcast is precious in the Lord's sight. He who can believe this is undoubtedly pleasing and acceptable to God. For it is certain that He neither wants nor is able to bear contempt for His creature, whether it is small or great. He does not want the great ones to boast or to be proud that they have the means with which to protect and defend themselves. But He does not want those who are downcast to despair, for they have One who has regard for them and receives them. Therefore God, who has regard for the lowly things in heaven and on earth, should be blessed.

He Himself is also a very great hero and is subject to no rule. Yet He bends down, or lowers Himself, in such a way that there is no place where He sees so sharply as He does if He looks at what is downcast and lowly. For thus Leah was completely downcast and was unwelcome and odious to all. If she gave any orders to the household, they said: "Why do you give me orders? Rachel and Jacob do not care about you." Perhaps Rachel also added to this disobedience in the household by her pride, so that Leah was scorned by the master, the lady, and the whole household. But this disturbed and distressed her heart greatly. For it is very sad for a saintly wife if she sees that she is being neglected by her husband. She can more easily overcome wrongs done by others if her husband embraces her in love. For a husband's love is the life of a wife, and I want this to be understood of good and honorable women. When the husband is sad, morose, difficult, and angry, this is harsher for a godly woman than death itself. For she wants to be gladdened by her husband, and she fears contempt just as she fears darkness and the worst evils.

Poor Leah was harassed by these sorrows and this grief; she

was sad and pained that she was despised by her lord. But listen to Moses, who says: "THE LORD SAW, etc." No one else sees it. God has regard for and blesses the downcast, weeping, odious, and saddened woman; but He humbles the one who is proud. Therefore another light arises here for her who is sitting in darkness. For Jacob is crucified in his love, and Rachel is crucified in her glory. The Lord closes Rachel's womb and lets her be barren, which was no smaller cross. Indeed, it was death itself for Rachel, as she will complain bitterly later on. But He honors the one who is cast off by opening her womb and making her a mother. For this is what closing or opening the womb means, namely, giving offspring and fruit, just as the earth is opened when it sprouts forth.

שְׂנוּאָה points out the contempt suffered by those who are despised and cast off, and observe carefully that God is called One who has regard for the שְׂנוּאִים, that is, for those who are scorned and cast off. Only let them not despair. The Holy Spirit writes this for the consolation of the afflicted, namely, that God blesses and exalts Leah, so that she conceives and gives birth.

32. *And Leah conceived and bore a son, and she called his name Reuben; for she said: Because the Lord has looked upon my affliction; surely now my husband will love me.*

Yet the poor woman, who had weak eyes that were also tormented by the tears resulting from such anxiety, believes that God has regard for her. "The Lord has seen that I am odious," she says. She brings up no merits—only this, that the Lord has had regard for the שְׂנוּאָה. For this is the title and the most proper definition of God: "He who regards the despised and the humble." He also has regard for the proud and the great men in the world. But they have no need of His grace and mercy; they despise His regard. Therefore He must disregard them, as it is stated in Ps. 138:6: "The haughty He knows from afar." Moreover, it seems that the verse in Mary's song (Luke 1:48)—"He has regarded the low estate of His handmaiden"—was taken from this source, because they are the same words that are found in this passage.

We cannot translate the Hebrew word עֲנִי properly enough. In Num. 12:3 Moses is said to have been a man עֲנִי, most wretched, completely despised, the most miserable man on earth, as Paul says in 1 Cor. 15:19. In Latin it is *miseria;* in German it is *Elend.* Thus Mary sings: "He has regarded my wretchedness; He has seen my wretchedness." For Mary was deprived of her parents, was an orphan and forsaken, was in servitude to others. Then God has regard for the handmaiden who is so wretched. And Leah says in this place: "Jacob has had no regard for me, with the exception of what he has done out of mercy. Rachel has plainly despised me. Therefore I am wretched and downcast, שְׂנוּאָה. But the Lord has had regard for me and has given me a son." Therefore she gives thanks, praises God, and adds: "Now my husband will love me. Now his hatred and contempt will be changed into love and honor, for thanks to God's blessing I have become a mother. This has not happened to my sister. Therefore I am far more fortunate than she is, not because I have deserved it but because the Lord has had regard for me."

The fruitfulness and childbearing of women has always been regarded as an outstanding blessing even among the heathen, and for this reason women were held in honor. In Rome men were forbidden to wear gold, but women were permitted to do so.[53] Therefore Leah is now a great lady, for she is fruitful and gives birth before her sister does, who, as all wished and hoped, would give birth first. But when Rachel heard this, she was undoubtedly impelled to envy and hate her sister, and the whole household was also amazed at this wonderful change. But God did it. He has regard for what is lowly and cast off.

Therefore although these things are purely carnal and matters of domestic economy, and show nothing whatever that is spiritual, yet they are actually completely spiritual, as is apparent from Leah's words, which contain wonderful consolation. For God oversees and governs not only the angels but also the domestic economy and everything that pertains to the domestic economy. He is able to change the hearts and judgments of men in such a way that those who shortly before were completely rejected become altogether pleasing. For this reason Leah adorns her son with this name Reuben as a public testimony against those who despised and hated her. It is as though she were saying: "Now you see that I have not been cast off by God. God has not despised me as you have despised me. רְאוּ, see; רָאוּ, they have seen the son.

---

[53] This may be a reference to Livy, *History,* Book XXXIV, chs. 1 ff.

Behold, you have the son; observe him. For God has had regard for me. To you I was שְׂנוּאָה. I am naming him Reuben in order that you may cease from hatred and contempt. He is a son of vision. God sees. I see. You see that I am not cast off, as I formerly seemed to you." In this way the Lord comforts the wretched and detested Leah; and she herself confesses, gives thanks, and taunts all those who despised her. This undoubtedly displeased Rachel, who was loved very much by Jacob and was always regarded as the true mother of the house. Yet she remains barren. Indeed, three additional sons are given to Leah, as we read in what follows.

33. *She conceived again and bore a son, and said: Because the Lord has heard that I am hated, He has given me this son also; and she called his name Simeon.*

Previously the Lord saw; now He also hears. For I still think that she was treated in a haughty manner by Rachel and that no attention was paid to the birth and God's regard for her. "What is this?" Rachel and the household asked. "Who knows whether she will give birth to more sons? It can happen that this son dies in a short time and that Rachel, as the true mother of the house, also gives birth." Thus Leah has not yet broken down the contempt and overcome it. But violently and contrary to common sense they still despise the blessing of God and His regard for Leah. Therefore she repeats her prayer to God: "Lord God, I have given birth to a son, but they pay no attention at all to this birth. I am not yet sufficiently acceptable because of the one son. Give me another son, in order that finally I, too, may be regarded as the mother of the house." Although Jacob did not altogether despise her, yet he did love her. But the hatred of the household and that of Rachel has not yet been overcome. "This first-born son," she said, "should have won me favor and authority, but I am still despised."

Accordingly, the Lord hears this prayer and gives a second son, Simeon. She names him Simeon because she has been heard. But then Rachel wavers and begins to be humbled and to die, so to speak, as will appear below when she says: "Give me children, or I shall die!" For she is still barren. And Leah has already conceived her third son.

34. *Again she conceived and bore a son, and said: Now this time*

my husband will be joined to me, because I have borne him three sons. Therefore his name was called Levi.

This is what Leah wants to say: "Now, after my husband has loved me, he will also leave Rachel's tent. For so far he has been living with her as his beloved wife and has not come in to me except out of mercy. But now he will also be united with me after leaving Rachel, who is barren. Although I know that I am loved more by him than I was before, yet he has not yet joined me to himself as the companion of his table and his couch. So far Rachel has enjoyed this kindness and honor. But now he will be united and dwell with me." Therefore she calls her son Levi, that is, a joining or uniting, as though she were saying: "I will bring it about that he becomes the companion of my couch and table." But this was most annoying to Rachel, and she thought: "Now I will be the שְׂנוּאָה. My husband will be indignant and say: 'Although you have been my beloved wife, yet the Lord is not blessing you but is blessing Leah, and He wants me to love Leah.'" This is surely a strange state of affairs, yes, a change, in the house of Jacob.

35. *And she conceived again and bore a son, and said: This time I will praise the Lord; therefore she called his name Judah. Then she ceased bearing.*

It is as though she were saying: "I was content with one, two, but especially three sons. In addition, however, I am getting a fourth. Now I praise and thank the Lord. Indeed, now I shall be praised, preferred, and loved as the mother of the house. I have been lifted up from my humility and wretchedness, and my sister has fallen from her honor and loftiness." Now Rachel will desire to die from indignation and impatience, and she will say to her husband: "Give me children, or I shall die!"

So far we have heard how Jacob, after the nuptials with Leah and Rachel, begot four sons from that despised and neglected Leah. With this example God shows that He is propitious and favorably disposed toward those who are humble, afflicted, and cast off, so that all who labor and are heavy-laden (cf. Matt. 11:28) have no grounds for complaint, especially if they believe in God and are not overcome by impatience and indignation. For it is much better to be afflicted and troubled when God laughs and is favorably disposed than to be fortunate when God is angry. For what is the world with its favor, joy, and pleasures in comparison with the favorable and kindly regard God has for the humble? But the flesh does not let us understand or believe this. Indeed, it frequently murmurs because of the evils that are present, and it tries to hurl disturbed hearts down from faith and consolation and to impel them to murmur and rage against God. For so many various misfortunes break and beat us down severely in our weakness.

But would that we could learn and could accustom ourselves to that battle against the flesh — the battle about which Paul teaches! For if one could not take hold of and do everything the spirit wishes, yet we would realize that God does not want to forsake us or let us be conquered and overcome by the flesh. I surely would be glad to rejoice, glory, and triumph with Paul in death, in the cross, and in sufferings. But the spirit is willing; the flesh, on the other hand, is weak (cf. Matt. 26:41). Therefore let it suffice for us and be our consolation that God pardons and that the Holy Spirit helps our infirmity (cf. Rom. 8:26), in order that the spirit may triumph over the rebellious flesh, lest it bend to the one side or the other, either to smugness or to despair and impatience. This is our glory, namely, God's pardon, which could impute to us the wickedness of our flesh. But because the spirit resists, it does not impute this wickedness to us. No, it mercifully forgives and pardons. And this is how the Holy Spirit buoyed up and comforted Leah. He had regard for her humility (cf. Luke 1:48) and heard her prayer. Later He added courage, so that she said: "I will thank the Lord, etc." All these are words and statements of the spirit which rebels and resists, even though it is not yet triumphant. Nevertheless, it does not yield and does not agree with the infirmity and wickedness of the flesh.

Lyra — whether he took it from the Jews or discovered this distinction by his own ingenuity — distinguishes the trials of Leah piously enough according to four points: she was despised by Rachel, neglected by her husband, regarded as a foreigner and an outsider by the neighbors and the household, and finally cast off by God.[54] This division pleases me well and agrees with the experience of those who are afflicted. For when one evidence

[54] Lyra *ad* Gen. 29:31-35.

of sorrow is presented, the person who is tried immediately draws one conclusion from another conclusion. For because Leah is despised by Rachel, she reasons inevitably that her husband is rather hostile to her and that for this reason not she but Rachel is the true mother of the house. In the third place, the reproach from the neighbors and the household was added. From them she heard that she had been forced in by trickery and deceit and that she deserved to be despised by Rachel, who had been lawfully betrothed to Jacob. Satan undoubtedly inculcated and augmented all this, and in this way he aggravated the trial to an extraordinary degree and even suggested that God Himself had been alienated from her.

But against these four evidences of sorrow and despair God gives Leah four other evidences of consolation, namely, four sons. In the first place, against Rachel's contempt He has regard for her humility. Secondly, because she was being neglected so far by her husband, He hears her prayer. Thirdly, lest she seem to be a stranger and completely excluded, God grants that her husband is joined to her and clings to her. Fourthly, she triumphs victoriously over all trials. She is no longer looked down on and despised, but she praises God and gives thanks. We, too, should follow this example and learn that after a trial God is wont to grant liberation and consolation in rich abundance. In this way all sorrow and disturbance is overcome. But it is hard for the flesh to wait for consolation from God. Therefore such examples of faith are set forth in order that we may see how Leah cried out, believed, waited, and bore every wrong and vexation from her sister in faith and hope. And finally God had regard for her as she hoped in Him, and He comforted her richly.

CHAPTER THIRTY

1. *When Rachel saw that she bore Jacob no children, she envied her sister; and she said to Jacob: Give me children, or I shall die!*

THIS is one of the most obscure chapters of this book so far as the words, the meaning, and the history are concerned. Accordingly, many questions pertaining both to the grammar and especially to the history present themselves. The latter are far more difficult than the former. But lest we seem to pass them by completely, let us do what we can. In the first place, this question arises in the eyes of carnal and Epicurean men who regard these histories as examples of extreme baseness. For Jacob marries two sisters and, in addition, two of their maidservants. Thus he is the husband of four wives. Therefore they judge Jacob according to their own character and represent him as exceedingly lustful and completely devoted to the love of women day and night, since he could not be content with one wife but married four. As a result, they are greatly offended and seize the opportunity to blaspheme and to praise their own celibacy in opposition to the licentiousness and lusts, as they think, of the saintly patriarchs, especially of Jacob. But these judgments of theirs are like those a pig or an ass would pronounce on some illustrious lutenist. They are the kind of people who are completely abandoned to lust, whoredom, and adultery, who dream day and night only of their sexual fun and imagine what they would do if such license were granted to them that they would be able to change wives every night and have fun with them according to the flames and ardent desires of the flesh as they have fun with their harlots. They do not distinguish the saintly life of married people from their own whoredom.

But Lyra works very hard here in defense of Jacob.[1] But one should reply to those insipid and lustful swine by saying that the chastity of Jacob, who has four, five, or 100 wives, is greater than the chastity one finds in all their celibacy, even if they abstain from harlots. Let us imagine someone who is a true celibate and completely continent. Nevertheless, it is certain that Jacob is 100 times more chaste. For that celibate burns and seethes with lust day and night. When he is asleep, he experiences pollutions; when he is awake, he feels the itch again. What kind of chastity is this, to live and burn in the midst of flames and lust? Whenever he looks at a beautiful woman, he is completely inflamed; and although he checks himself and abstains from the act, yet that flame causes pollutions for him not only when he is asleep but also when he is awake, as Gerson testifies.[2]

This, then, is not free and voluntary chastity; it is forced. For he would prefer to break through and be mad about women. He cannot check the flames. I am speaking about men who, like Bernard and Bonaventure, were continent and fought against lust. Although they were saintly and good men in other respects, yet they could not be free from the itch. Indeed, Jerome complains about the dreams in which he dreamed that in Rome he was dancing among girls.[3] Ambrose and Augustine also point out cautiously that although they both abstained from the female sex, they were not free from the itch and nocturnal pollutions.[4] But if this happened to those very pious and saintly men, why must we spend time on the hypocritical celibacy and on the judgments of these swine who think that the fathers behaved toward their wives as they themselves would do if they were permitted to dwell with so many wives?

But what follows and what has been stated above about Jacob's continence gives evidence that he lived in complete chastity. For is it not continence to live as a celibate up to the eightieth

---

[1] Lyra *ad* Gen. 30:24.

[2] Cf. Jean Gerson, *De vita spirituali animae,* Lectio prima, Septimum corollarium, *Oeuvres complètes,* III (Paris, 1962), 122.

[3] Cf. Jerome's letter to Eustochium, Epistle XXII, *Patrologia, Series Latina,* XXII, 398—399; see also *Luther's Works,* 22, pp. 266 ff.

[4] Augustine, *Confessions,* Book X, ch. 30; cf. Ambrose, *Exhortatio virginitatis,* IX, 58, *Patrologia, Series Latina,* XVI, 369.

year of one's life and to practice continence, not out of compulsion but because the spirit wants it? Do the same thing from your earliest years up to old age, and we will praise your celibacy. Therefore there is no glory in papistical celibacy if it is compared with the chastity of the patriarchs.

Later, however, we shall hear how Jacob complains about his difficult and troublesome kind of life, when he expostulates with Laban. "By day," he says, "the heat consumed me, and the cold by night; and sleep fled from my eyes" (Gen. 31:40). Here he describes his whole way of life, which he did not spend in ease without cares, toils, and troubles. He did not loaf in idleness at home near the fire and play with Leah, but day and night he was compelled to be away from home, to pasture the cattle, and to carry out all the duties connected with the cattle. He suffered cold and heat under the open sky and very seldom came to his tent. This should drive away the itch even when one is young. Therefore Jacob lived most continently with so many wives, and far more chastely than anyone else with one wife. For to burn by day, to freeze by night, and to be overwhelmed by toils in foreign and difficult servitude under an unfair and greedy master is surely a great and intolerable burden.

Therefore Lyra rightly excuses Jacob for living continently and for associating temperately with his wives and maidservants. For he associated with them only out of love for offspring. This is also apparent in those anxious wishes of the women. For see how anxiously they make advances to their husband in order that they may be able to have offspring. Therefore he was very seldom in the tents of his wives, and he lived with his wives in the purest love of offspring. And we see that it is for the sake of offspring that he loves Leah, who previously was hated and despised, and that he associates more with her than with Rachel after he notices that she is fruitful. This, then, is how we shall reply to the first question of this passage to stop the mouths of the exceedingly filthy people who judge the marriages of the patriarchs according to their own lusts and impure celibacy.

The second question had been dealt with previously, namely, that beside the two sisters he also marries two maidservants.[5] Although I make no positive statement, yet in that age it seems

[5] Cf. *Luther's Works*, 3, pp. 42 ff.

[W, XLIII, 652, 653]

to have been the custom of that region for barren wives to hand their maidservants over to their husbands. Thus Laban adds a maidservant to both of his daughters, perhaps to the end that in case the daughter did not give birth, the maidservant might take her place and that the house might be built from her. Thus above (cf. Gen. 16:2) Sarah gave a maidservant to Abraham, not a strange maid but one from her own house and domestics. Isaac did not follow this custom. Nor would Jacob have employed it if he had not been deceived by Laban and the women had not demanded it so emphatically. For one must also consider that at that time fertility was regarded as an extraordinary blessing and a special gift of God, as is clear from Deut. 28:4, where Moses numbers fertility among the blessings. "There will not be a barren woman among you," he says (cf. Ex. 23:26). We do not regard this so highly today. Although we like and desire it in cattle, yet in the human race there are few who regard a woman's fertility as a blessing. Indeed, there are many who have an aversion for it and regard sterility as a special blessing. Surely this is also contrary to nature. Much less is it pious and saintly. For this affection has been implanted by God in man's nature, so that it desires its increase and multiplication. Accordingly, it is inhuman and godless to have a loathing for offspring. Thus someone [6] recently called his wife a sow, since she gave birth rather often. The good-for-nothing and impure fellow! The saintly fathers did not feel like this at all; for they acknowledged a fruitful wife as a special blessing of God and, on the other hand, regarded sterility as a curse. And this judgment flowed from the Word of God in Gen. 1:28, where He said: "Be fruitful and multiply." From this they understood that children are a gift of God.

Furthermore, this example or deed according to which maidservants were handed over in place of wives who were barren should not become a precedent. No one should say: "Jacob did this. Therefore it will also be permitted to me," as has been stated about Münzer, who urged the peasants to slay their princes according to the example of Joshua and Samson.[7] But remember that you must abide by this rule: "Each man should have his own

---

[6] The Weimar text has *quidem,* but we have followed the Erlangen and other editions and read *quidam.*

[7] See p. 311, note 50.

wife" (1 Cor. 7:2). If you want to be like Joshua and Samson, see to it also that all the circumstances impel you to change the civil administration and slay the magistrate, just as those heroes were moved by a special call. Otherwise the example has no validity. For you have more and greater examples which testify that one should not slay a magistrate, should not change the civil administration. Accordingly, you, like the other subjects, must be obedient to the government; for you have not been excepted from the rule. Therefore remain in obedience. Do not become a hero like Münzer and others.

Accordingly, this is handed down not as an example but in order that we may abstain from the example and from imitating it. We should admire but not imitate it. For there are some things which we should imitate and some things which we should admire. Hope, believe, pray, just as Leah did. But you should not marry four wives, as Jacob did. For this pertains only to Jacob and to those whom God wanted to be exempted from the rule. We should exercise ourselves in the faith, patience, and hope set forth in the fathers, and we should abstain from those heroic examples. These are the questions that had to be examined at the beginning of this chapter. Now let us also look at the text, which is also obscure. "She envied her sister," or "She was jealous against her sister." For the verb קָנָא means "to be envious," "to be jealous"; and קַנָּא is "one who is jealous."

But the question is asked whether those very saintly women, who called upon God in true faith, also labored under envy and hatred. The text indicates this clearly. Lyra distinguishes between two kinds of envy: the one because of which I envy another person his good fortune, the other because of which I am displeased and angry on account of my wretchedness.[8] Properly speaking, however, this is not envy. We, as we are wont to do at other times, excuse it by saying that the saintly fathers and mothers were still under the flesh, just as we, too, have the flesh opposing us and making us captive to the law of sin (cf. Rom. 7:23). Furthermore, it is characteristic of all trials, and especially of those that are sublime, to take away almost every feeling of godliness. Thus he who is oppressed by a cross and disaster feels no patience. He who is tried in faith and hope feels no faith and hope. To him

[8] Lyra *ad* Gen. 30:1.

it does not seem that he believes or hopes, but he thinks that he is altogether godless. He who is harassed by despair and by raging against God when God manages something in a way that is different from what we had prescribed feels the height of aversion and indignation toward God and seems to have no spark of faith and hope.

These are wont to be the thoughts of afflicted people in the very paroxysm of trials. Otherwise, when there is no trial, when I argue or speak about faith and about hope, nothing seems easier than this. But when the paroxysm comes, everything suddenly vanishes. Thus in other kinds of trials — in impatience, wrath, and lust — one sees and feels a burning desire for vengeance. It is true that such feelings are not faith, hope, and love. No, they are the flesh itself. Thus Rachel had the trial of envy because of which she wished that it could come to pass that her sister would not give birth, even though she did not succumb to it. But what Paul said happened to her: "What I do not wish, I do; what I wish, I do not do" (cf. Rom. 7:19). He who is tried by doubt experiences an ineffable sighing by which he wishes that he were not troubled by doubt. Yet he feels that doubt has greater power and makes him captive to the law of sin and unbelief (cf. Rom. 7:23). But in opposition to this sighing a secret sighing is aroused through the Holy Spirit — a sighing which, on the other hand, murmurs against it, contradicts it, is angry with unbelief, and says: "Shame on you, wretched unbelief! Do not say: 'Who knows? It is a lie, etc.'" This takes place with a small sigh and an ineffable sobbing which sustains the tried heart, lest it become wicked and despise God. This is what the Epicureans are wont to do; in every trial, no matter how light it is, they bid a long farewell to faith and hope.

But this battle is exceedingly annoying to the flesh, which would prefer a faith that is not tried or assailed but kills lions and bears, as David, Samson, or others did. But my faith is so small and weak that it could very easily be devoured by a lion or a bear. Yet the bruised reed and the dimly burning wick (Is. 42:3) are present. So is God, who understands the sighings, who knows what the Holy Spirit demands for us. Therefore before God there is a great fire. Indeed, it is hotter and greater than heaven and earth. Accordingly, the saints should be excused according to this statement of Paul (Rom. 7:23): "I see in my members another law at war with the law of my mind and making me captive."

Likewise: "According to the flesh, I serve the law of sin" (cf. Rom. 7:25). For in this way the saintly mothers were human beings who lived in the flesh but did not walk according to the flesh—an example for us, lest we despair or yield to the flesh. Although Rachel envies her sister and is jealous of her, the spirit wars and struggles against the jealousy of the flesh. She would have been glad to have the blessing with which her sister was presented; yet she checks herself, lest she wish that her sister become barren.

But from this it is clear that the very saintly women were not lustful but were desirous of offspring and the blessing. For this was the cause of envy in Rachel, who, if she had been like other women whom our age has produced in large numbers, would have said: "What is it to me whether I bear children or not? Provided that I remain the mother of the household and have an abundance of all other things, I have enough." But Rachel demands offspring so much that she prefers death to remaining sterile. I do not remember reading a similar statement in any history. Therefore she is an example of a very pious and continent woman whose only zeal and burning desire is for offspring, even if it means death. Thus above (Gen. 16:2) Sarah also showed a similar desire for offspring. And in both this feeling is decidedly praiseworthy. "If I do not have children, I shall die" says Rachel. "I prefer being without life to being without children. And if my flesh is worn out and barren, nevertheless let my husband beget children from my maidservant. If children from her are also denied, it is my wish that GOD would call me out of this life." There was no small reason for this desire, for Jacob undoubtedly proclaimed to both that he had the promise that the Blessed Seed would be born from him, and because of this proclamation the desire for acquiring offspring was kindled, especially in Rachel. The less hope she had, the greater her desire was. Consequently, she determines either to bear children or die. Thus later she dies in childbirth. This desire and feeling of the godly woman is good and saintly, but it is so strong that she falls into a paroxysm of envy and jealousy toward her sister. Nor should this be regarded as a disgraceful example, as the papists accuse these saintly people of lust. For they did not look at the shameful and wretched pleasure of the flesh in marriage. No, they looked at the blessing of offspring for the sake of the Promised Seed.

2. *Jacob's anger was kindled against Rachel, and he said: Am I in the place of God, who has withheld from you the fruit of the womb?*

Jacob is angry because of this violent struggle. "I am not at fault," he says. "Nevertheless, you are the wife whom I love most and with whom I have dwelt more frequently than with your sister. I am not God, who could grant you fertility and the power to bear children."

All this is decidedly insignificant and sordid; and even though it is praised, yet it is human, carnal, and womanish. One wonders why the Holy Spirit busies Himself with it, namely, how Rachel envied Leah, how the one bore children and the other was barren, likewise that Rachel almost blasphemed and struggled too violently for offspring from her husband, with the result that Jacob is angry with her in a carnal manner and actual dissension arises between the spouses. Is this not childish?

We have dealt with this question above, and one should always present and inculcate it. Why does the Holy Spirit, whose mouth is completely pure, speak about these things with such zeal? The very saintly pope, together with the altogether chaste monks and nuns, does not even deign to think about them, since such things are completely sordid and carnal. For they walk about in the great wonders of their celibacy. But this filth about conception, about childbearing, and the quarrels of married people they regard as not worth reading. "In accordance with His holiness, the Holy Spirit could have spoken about heavenly and other more sublime things," they say, "not about insignificant and carnal things. He should have become a monk or a nun, but He merely recounts what the state of Jacob's household management was and how his marriage fared. These matters offend us angelic men who walk above the clouds in the wisdom and religion of the angels (cf. Col. 2:18)."

But because those men have a loathing for these small things, the Holy Spirit in turn hates such proud and boastful saints, does not acknowledge them as His own, leaves them in their glory, pride, and vanity, and descends to His creatures, cares for them, and honors them. For He Himself has created the world; He has created male and female and has blessed them that they might be fruitful. He has subjected the world to them and still sustains everything; He gives nourishment and provides milk for the mother to support and suckle her child. These creatures He does not despise; He does not disdain His work. Yet He does not regard celibacy reproachfully; for it, too, is a gift of God, and we commend both in their order and measure. We do not praise marriage in such a manner that we disparage or reject celibacy. This the papists do not do, for they extol celibacy in such a way that they treat marriage with reproach. Nor do they praise continence as a gift of GOD. They praise it as their own work. This is a doctrine of demons (1 Tim. 4:1), as is also clear from the fruits that have arisen from this source. For because they have wanted to glory in the works of the flesh, they live in a most disgraceful manner and surpass all pimps and harlots in shamelessness. Why? Because they have not praised continence as God's work but have praised it as their own work; and they have despised and disparaged marriage, which is a work and ordinance of God.

Accordingly, God delights in describing such lowly matters to give evidence that He does not despise, abhor, or withdraw from, the management of a household, from a good husband, from a wife, and from children. Why does He do this? Because He is the Creator and He governs and preserves them as His creation, even though the flesh has been corrupted by sin. Nor is the flesh of celibates uncorrupted, and they themselves have also been born from the same source. Why, then, do they disparage it and prefer their impure chastity to marriage? Therefore the Holy Spirit wants to teach us and to give evidence by dealing with these lowly, human, and common matters, in order that we may know that He wants to be with us, to care for us, and to show that He is our Creator and Ruler. This the papists do not see; they despise it. Therefore they pay the proper penalty for their contempt.

In the second place, they do not see with what pure and maternal hearts these women ask for children. These feelings and words of Rachel show that her heart was altogether alien to lust. This they do not see. Why? Because it is written: "Away with the godless man, lest he see or hear what God says, what He does and works!" [9] They are not worthy of seeing God's glory. Thus they hear us today as we cry out, as we teach and sing the Word

---

[9] Cf. p 275, note 11.

of God. They see the works of God. Yet they do not see. Why? Because they are not worthy. Thus they do not see either that Rachel is set forth as an example of very beautiful and motherly affection and chastity. The only thing she seeks is offspring from her flesh. Likewise Leah. They hear that these people give utterance to nothing else than "The Lord has given; the Lord has blessed!" And below (Gen. 31:53), when they quarrel: "The Lord will judge between me and you." All their conversations are about God, about His blessings and works. Yet the papists regard all these things as sins, and they consider the saintly matrons as unworthy of having their examples set forth in the church.

What better and more useful thing can be taught in the church than the example of a godly mother of a household who prays, sighs, cries out, gives thanks, rules the house, performs the function of sex, and desires offspring with the greatest chastity, gratitude, and godliness? What more should she do? But the pope, the cardinals, and the bishops should not see this, for they are not worthy. The Holy Spirit allows them to walk in wonderful and superheavenly things and to admire their chastity, which is worthy of brothels. But they should by no means see these things. In the meantime He governs the saintly women in such a way that He gives evidence that they are His creation and that He wants to rule them not only according to the spirit but also according to the flesh, in order that they may call upon and adore God, give thanks for their offspring, be obedient to their husband, etc.; that is, to hand down these sordid things to the churches to be read, in order that God may show His magnificent and wonderful works in the church, how He works heavenly and spiritual things in things that are carnal and earthly. But godless men see the carnal things; they do not see the spiritual and divine things.

Thirdly, they do not see with what hardships and troubles the wretched women were afflicted; but they dream that they lived in luxury, in idleness, and pleasures. This is the kind of life they themselves live. They think that Jacob was a great lord and that he enjoyed his wives in grandeur, that Rachel was loaded with the greatest splendor and with riches after the fashion of a queen. For these men desire such a life and such wives, and many of them enjoy these advantages. But look at the history, and you will find that Jacob was a poor and needy man who did not have even a few cents of his own. Thus the women, too, were very poor, as Rachel and Leah complain below (31:14-15): "Is there any portion or inheritance left to us in our father's house? Are we not regarded by him as foreigners? For he has sold us, and he has been using up the money given for us." But if the daughters were poor beggars, it is much more likely that the maidservants were in need.

Accordingly, the greatest poverty was coupled with exceedingly hard labor, which they sustained day and night. In addition, they endured hunger, thirst, and cold. You, too, should imitate this — you who accuse very saintly people of incontinence! You should marry four wives and serve a greedy and ungrateful master for 14 years. But no one sees or considers this. Nor is there anyone today who would be willing to marry even one wife, let alone four, with the stipulation that he be only a servant and by his toil and sweat increase another man's goods, but not see from what source he may support himself and his wife.

Therefore the fact that Jacob marries so many wives in the hope that God will alleviate his poverty and support him and his whole household is incredible confidence. Although it is very easy to marry a wife, it is very difficult to support her along with the children and the household. Accordingly, no one notices this faith of Jacob. Indeed, many hate fertility in a wife for the sole reason that the offspring must be supported and brought up. For this is what they commonly say: "Why should I marry a wife when I am a pauper and a beggar? I would rather bear the burden of poverty alone and not load myself with misery and want." But this blame is unjustly fastened on marriage and fruitfulness. Indeed, you are indicting your unbelief by distrusting God's goodness, and you are bringing greater misery upon yourself by disparaging God's blessing. For if you had trust in God's grace and promises, you would undoubtedly be supported. But because you do not hope in the Lord, you will never prosper.

In this manner we see that in these sordid matters the greatest virtues shine forth, namely, outstanding faith, completely certain hope, and unconquerable patience toward God and toward men. Neither the papists nor others will easily see this unless the circumstances are carefully considered. But away with those who do not care at all and do not believe! Let them remain exceedingly filthy pimps! We should learn that a believing husband and a believing wife are needed not only for the church and the state but also for the management of a household. For an unbeliever never does anything right or successfully. I remember that Staupitz told me a story about a prior in a certain monastery who continually complained that the income of the monastery was too slender for him to be able to procure the food and necessities for the monks from this source. Finally Staupitz demanded from him a statement of the income and the expenditures. Here he saw that the property of the monastery had been notably increased every year. Therefore after summoning him to his presence he removed him from office, saying: "You are not a man of faith. Consequently, it is impossible for you to further the interests of the monastery." [10]

All government and all life rests on faith. But Jacob's example serves in a wonderful manner to awaken and strengthen this faith. For he did not have even a cent, and yet he had to support four wives in this servitude, from which he has nothing else than food and clothing. With this he was content for 14 years. No one of us will easily imitate this by marrying even one wife, let alone, two or four. For no one is willing to live and suffer want for even one week without a fixed income. How is anyone going to serve for 14 years only for daily food? Indeed, we should not be compared to those men; but we are completely without faith. Therefore when the Holy Spirit speaks about insignificant and despised matters, He simultaneously enfolds most precious gems of the greatest virtues, which these swinish papists do not see. For they see only the carnal things, and instead of honey they suck poison from the rose. For in these examples of the fathers they carp at them for indulging in the sport of love, because they have many wives, and for giving themselves up to lustful coition, as they think, when Rachel or Leah desire offspring. They do not think about how they called upon and glorified God, how they were endowed with faith and incredible patience.

But how would people lost in idleness and luxury, as the canons and the cardinals are, judge otherwise? These men spend their lives without toil and without any trials. Therefore we should read Holy Scripture in another and better way, and for this reason

---

[10] Luther's mentor, Johann Staupitz, had been the vicar-general of the Augustinians from 1504 to 1520, when he withdrew from office.

I repeat and emphasize so often that we should regard these insignificant and completely carnal matters not with the eyes of the flesh but with the eyes of the spirit. Then we shall see wonderful counsels of the Holy Spirit in descriptions of this kind more than in the greatest and most spiritual matters.

3. *Then she said: Here is my maid Bilhah; go in to her, that she may bear upon my knees, and even I may have children through her.*

"To bear upon the knees" is a Hebrew expression with which Rachel points out that she wants to become a mother, and with these words she adopts the offspring from her maidservant; for they indicate the duties of a mother, since a mother holds an infant on her knees. Thus it is stated in Is. 66:12: "You shall be dandled upon her knees." The mother has the child on her lap. Therefore she thought: "Though I cannot have a son from myself, yet I will become the mother of the Blessed Seed through my maidservant." From this one can see a most ardent desire for the Promised Seed, likewise the piety and outstanding faith with which they clung to the promises concerning the Christ which had been made to Jacob. Furthermore, the women had to be endowed with remarkable probity, since they could be wives of such a poor man and serve in their father's house as maidservants. This was incomparable saintliness and wonderful faith, patience, hope, and love. The delicate daughters of our citizens or peasants could never have shown anything like this.

4. *So she gave him her maid Bilhah as a wife; and Jacob went in to her.*

No woman will do even this, for she will rather do without offspring than concede the glory of motherhood and the bed to a maidservant. This is a wonderful state of mind. A similar example has been described above (Gen. 16:2) in the case of Sarah, namely, that they yielded their conjugal honor to maidservants. No woman will do this according to the flesh; it is a work of the spirit by which she was aroused. She thought: "I, too, want to be a mother, even though I must give up all the glory of the couch and of motherhood for a time."

5. *And Bilhah conceived and bore Jacob a son.*

6. *Then Rachel said: God has judged me, and has also heard my voice and given me a son. Therefore she called his name Dan.*

These are not the words of a wanton harlot. For she gives thanks to God because she has been heard. She mentions God as a judge and assigns to Him the gift of fertility. "I have cried out," she says, "and I have prayed. But blessed be the Lord, who has judged me and has heard my voice!"

It is a most beautiful thanksgiving. Yet she still clings to the flesh. Therefore she says: "God has judged me and pleaded my cause." It is as though she were saying: "Although my sister is not the real wife, yet she has been proud toward me, just as above (Gen. 16:4) Hagar was proud toward Sarah, because she has excelled me in fertility. But the Lord has judged me too." But why, dear Rachel, are you so happy? In spite of all he is not your son. He has not been born from your flesh. Your womb and your breasts do not know this son. What of it? Nevertheless, she congratulates herself that she has an adopted son from her maidservant. So great was her admiration of fertility.

Dan means judgment. "For God has seen my wretchedness and reproach." Thus she says below (v. 23): "God has taken away my reproach." For sterility was regarded as a reproach because of the statement (Gen. 1:28): "Be fruitful and multiply." "But God has judged"; that is, "He has fought and exerted Himself for me. Now I, too, shall amount to something, although a son has been born for me from a maidservant." For this is how she prayed: "Lord God, since Thou dost not want me to be a mother, even though I am the mother of the household and the chief wife, at least grant offspring from my handmaiden if I am not worthy. For why dost Thou condemn, reject, disturb, and despise me?" This was the prayer she spoke with many sighs and tears, and she points out that it was heard. Accordingly, even though these things seem to be carnal and wanton, yet they are all done in the highest spirit, in faith and wonderful patience, then also with praise to God and with thanks that God liberated her from the reproach of sterility.

7. *Rachel's maid Bilhah conceived again and bore Jacob a second son.*

8. *Then Rachel said: With wrestlings of God I have wrestled with my sister, and have prevailed. So she called his name Naphtali.*

But now Rachel's joy increases with the birth of the second son. Among the Hebrews, however, it is asked what Naphtali means. The grammarians are at loggerheads, and the case is still before the judge.[11] Santes Pagninus and Münster translate: "With wrestlings of God I have wrestled"; that is, "With mighty wrestlings I have wrestled with my sister." [12] They add this reason, that in the Hebrew language all magnificent things are called divine. Hence Nineveh is called a city of God (cf. Jonah 3:3), that is, a magnificent city. Likewise a cedar of God (cf. Ps. 80:10), that is, lofty and large. Although I do not arrogate to myself the power of judgment in the Hebrew language, yet I hate the boldness of resorting to distortion in matters that have been stated simply. As though Nineveh were not also a city of God among the uncircumcised, but only those who are circumcised were God's people. All this flows from the pride and arrogance of the Jews, who put up with calling nothing magnificent except what pertains to them. But who has given this power of interpretation to the grammarians of the Hebrews that they explain a wrestling of God as meaning a magnificent wrestling? Accordingly, I shall follow the simple grammatical sense.

פָּתַל means "to change," "to pervert." In Ps. 18:26 we read: "With the pure Thou dost show thyself pure; and with the crooked Thou dost show Thyself perverse." If someone turns away from God and does and teaches otherwise than God teaches and does, wants to do something that is better and more excellent, yet perverts everything, then God is also perverted and changed, with the result that He does not follow what the perverse man has prescribed but leaves him to his own thoughts. Hence Naphtali means "one who has been changed." A change has taken place. Thus Rachel says: "Blessed be the Lord, for a change has taken place between me and my sister." And it appears that she spoke these words after Leah had ceased bearing when the fourth son

---

[11] Horace, *Ars poetica*, line 78; cf. also *Luther's Works*, 4, p. 192, and 8, p. 278.

[12] Sebastian Münster translated this verse with *Luctationibus divinis luctata sum cum sorore mea, et praevalui, En tibi lector* (see p. 293, note 25), p. 64.

had been born. Then Rachel gets children through her maidservant, namely, Dan and Naphtali. Therefore she said: "A change or alteration has taken place. My sister has stopped bearing; but I am beginning and continuing to obtain offspring, not at my own pleasure or wish but because of the grace and the gift of God, who has heard my prayer."

But now the question arises how Jacob could beget 12 children in seven years. For in the first seven years he served for nothing, without a wife and offspring. In the second seven years he married two sisters, and Joseph seems to have been born in the last year of the servitude, after all the other sons, that is, in the fourteenth year. For this is how the order and sequence of the account has it in the text. But how could this have happened, since in the first four years Leah alone bore four sons? Accordingly, the remaining eight must have been born in three years, which is impossible. I answer: Moses has employed anticipation, that is, the figure which rhetoricians call hysteron proteron, as we shall explain later.[13] From this one will understand what kind of change this is in consequence of which Rachel gives the name to her son. For this is the source of this difficulty and obscurity, since it appears that all these patriarchs were born during the second period of seven years. But if this is explained, the name Naphtali will also be clearer.

But in order that this may happen one must add to the second period of seven years the six years during which Jacob served for the cattle. For this is the actual sequence of the account. During the first four years the four sons of Leah were born: Reuben, Simeon, Levi, and Judah. Then Leah ceases to bear, and Dan is born to Rachel from her maidservant. He is Jacob's fifth son, and this is the fifth year, during which Leah does not give birth. But Bilhah, Rachel's maidservant, fills this year by bearing her son Dan. And then Rachel congratulates herself on her fertility, and in addition a second son, Naphtali, comes along in the sixth year, during which Leah did not bear either. Therefore the son is called Naphtali. It is as though Rachel were saying: "My sister has ceased bearing during these two years, the fifth and the sixth. Now my circumstances are changed and altered for the better," as has been stated previously concerning the etymology of the

---

[13] See also *Luther's Works*, 4, p. 300.

word on the basis of Ps. 18. And the word is found in the same meaning in Proverbs: "There is nothing perverse in the words of wisdom" (cf. 8:8); that is, God's Word is not changed, not perverted; it is simple and right. "But here a change takes place," says Rachel, "which is a change made by God. For when my sister ceased bearing, I obtained offspring, because I prevailed; and now I am making progress, growing, and flourishing, while she is drying up." Thus the godly woman gives thanks to God because He has heard her prayer and has given offspring, at least from the flesh of her maidservant. But this great desire for children should not be regarded as disgraceful concupiscence and lust. No, in both of these women there were very chaste longings for offspring, so that they also handed over to their maidservants the right to motherhood and to the blessing in consequence of which Jacob's descendants were destined to gain possession of the land of Canaan. Jacob diligently inculcated this promise. Therefore both wanted to be the mother of the Blessed Seed and of the descendants.

Up to this point Moses has kept the historical line or sequence in the description of the six years. But now it is changed, and a case of hysteron proteron occurs. Unless this figure is carefully observed in reading the sacred histories, yes, all histories, it often occasions great obscurities. For now, according to the historical sequence, Joseph's birth should follow, after Naphtali. But Moses postpones it until the third paragraph and returns to Leah — who in the two years, and also in the year in which Joseph will be born, did not give birth at all — by the figure known as hysteron proteron, that is, putting the last first, by which very obscure passages in the histories are often explained. In the sixteenth book of his *City of God* Augustine calls it anticipation and recapitulation.[14] It is one of the rules that are necessary for the understanding of Holy Scripture.

Joseph should have been first and should have been placed after Naphtali. But he becomes the hysteron. Leah, together with her maidservant Zilpah, should have been the hysteron, and they become the proteron. For in the histories different events have often happened at the same time but in different places,

---

[14] Augustine, *City of God*, Book XV, ch. 21, perhaps in combination with Book XVI, ch. 40.

one in Rome, another in Greece. Then they are not described in a definite order, but one history must be carried through to the end. Later the same time must be repeated, and the narrative of the other history must be completed. For the times are the same, but the things which happened at the same time are different.

Accordingly, one should state it in a table as follows: The first four years belong to Leah. The fifth and the sixth belong to Rachel's maidservant. The seventh is the year of Joseph's birth; for below (Gen. 41:46) he says to Pharaoh that he was 30 years old, which agrees excellently with the reckoning of the years. In the seventh year after Jacob's marriage to Rachel, Joseph was born, as is very clear. But Moses is silent about this, and before speaking about the birth of Joseph he mentions the rest of the sons born to Leah and her maidservant. They are born during the six years that are added to Jacob's servitude for the cattle. For below the text says that after Joseph's birth Jacob wanted to depart to his fatherland, but that he once again entered into an agreement with Laban with regard to six years. Accordingly, the circumstances demonstrate clearly that Joseph was born before these last six years, namely, in the seventh year, and that he was nourished and brought up for six years in Mesopotamia. Benjamin was born seven years after Joseph in the land of Canaan. His mother died in childbirth. Thus it is clear that Jacob served his father-in-law for 20 years, 14 for Laban's daughters and six for the cattle. All these years must be added together in this reckoning.

But because Leah ceased bearing for three years, she wanted to imitate the example of Rachel. She thought: "Behold, my sister has given birth to a son, Joseph, and for this reason she is loved by my husband as his chief wife, from whom he is hoping for true descendants. And now he regards his son Joseph as the first-born. Joseph is the light and the leader because he is the son of the queen and mother of the house." Therefore Leah was envious and was concerned about how she might change the mind of her husband and alienate him from her sister. So she made the plan to give him her maidservant. From her Jacob obtained Gad, his eighth son. But in the ninth year Asher, his ninth son, is born. Then Reuben, the first-born from Leah, a boy of eight or nine years, goes out into the field. There he happens to find mandrakes, and he brings them home. After taking them Rachel enters into an agreement with Leah that she should sleep with Jacob that night. For such domestic quarrelling and dislike arose between the women for a most honorable reason. Accordingly, Leah conceives and bears Issachar in the tenth year and Zebulun in the eleventh year. In the twelfth year Dinah is born. Thus in 12 years Jacob begot 11 sons and one daughter, namely, Dinah.

But it offends the reader that after the birth of the 11 patriarchs the birth of Joseph is described last, although he was born six years before Moses mentions this. But this is clear from the rule which I have mentioned and of which very frequent use is made in the books of the kings and the prophets, yes, even in the histories of the heathen. This is done in order to continue uninterruptedly one account with which other, different accounts are coincident.

A table copied from Dr. Luther's work on chronology which illustrates the historical sequence in an excellent manner [15]

Leah bore		Rachel bore
Reuben	1	0
Simeon	2	0
Levi	3	0
Judah	4	0
0	5	Dan ⎫ from Bilhah
0	6	Naphtali ⎭
0	7	Joseph
from Zilpah { Gad	8	0
{ Asher	9	0
Issachar	10	0
Zebulun	11	0
Dinah	12	0
0	13	0
		Benjamin

The household management of these people was extraordinary. For we see that the women had the power to give their maidservants to their husbands and to take them away again. For after Rachel has given birth to Joseph, her first-born, she no longer grants her maidservant admittance to her husband. Nor does Leah do so after Gad and Asher have been born to her maidservant. From this it is evident how chaste they were. For Jacob was not

[15] Although Luther (or his editors) referred to his "Computation of the Years of the World," first published in 1541, throughout these *Lectures on Genesis*, this is the first explicit admission of borrowing from it; cf. Introduction, p. **ix**.

permitted to lie with the maidservants to satisfy his lust, but only when his wives wanted and permitted it, which adulterers and fornicators are not wont to do. The lust of the flesh was mortified in Jacob and was kept within its limits; it did not wander forth to where it wished and desire drew it. These two things, the figure known as anticipation and the fact that the chastity of the very saintly men is praised, must be carefully noted. Otherwise no one will easily understand this history.

Furthermore, God's presence in this most humble kind of life should be recognized. Like the other kinds of life, it is full of vexations and troubles. For God rules and protects the saints even in menial matters, so that people whose lot is lowest do not despair and those who have been placed in the highest station do not become proud. For God governs the world in such a way that He casts down what is high and raises what is low. He confounds the wisdom of the wise and the understanding of the prudent (cf. Is. 44:25; 1 Cor. 1:19). These changes are made by God. The church has been subjected to servitude in the world. Indeed, it has been given up to death, as Paul says (cf. 2 Cor. 4:11). Yet if the world were without the church, kings and princes with all their power would perish. For it is completely subject, and it rules and bears the world. For the godly sustain the world. Nevertheless, they are servants, as is stated in the Greek verse: "The master is the only slave of a house." [16] The father of the household is the only servant in the house. The mother of the household is the only maidservant. The only subject in the state is the magistrate. The others, who seem to be servants, enjoy the advantages, the peace, and the tranquility of the state, the realm, and all empires. He who rules is a servant of servants.

God regulates the world in such a way that all things—those that are highest, those in the middle, and those that are lowest—serve Him. The highest things are the lowest, and the lowest are the highest. Therefore Duke Frederick, the Elector of Saxony, stated wisely and brilliantly to Staupitz that when he made a mental survey of the whole world and all ranks of men, it seemed to him that the peasants, who occupied the lowest place in the state, were the happiest, because they alone enjoy peace and true

---

[16] Manander, *Monostichoi*, 168; like the quotation from Hesiod referred to on p. 291, note 22, these words are quoted verbatim in the original Greek.

tranquility and are not tormented by the cares and dangers of the state. In summer they cultivate their fields; in winter they sit by the fire and enjoy their possessions. Although they lack royal magnificence, they nevertheless enjoy the greatest blessings, namely, tranquility and ease, and live more safely and happily within their own enclosure than kings and princes within their citadels or fortifications.[17]

This is God's wonderful governance or changing of things. For the things that seem to be lowest and most wretched are the greatest and most prosperous. Nothing in the world is more wretched than the church. Hence arise those complaints of the church: "Why hast Thou turned Thy face away? Why dost Thou forget me? I preach, I confess, I do and endure everything that God enjoins; but no one is more afflicted and forsaken than I am." But then the Lord replies: "I do not forget you," as is stated most sweetly in Is. 49:14-15: "But Zion said: 'The Lord has forsaken me, my Lord has forgotten me.' Can a woman forget her sucking child, that she should have no compassion on the sons of her womb? Even these may forget, yet will I not forget you."

But God's care and concern for us does not appear to be so great. Therefore one must learn, and accustom oneself to, that changing and alteration of things and men in the world. The heathen have learned in one way or another by experience that a servant is the master in the house and that the master is a servant. Indeed, the monks made the same complaint about their servants. For they had brothers whom they called lay brothers. To them the kitchen and domestic works were entrusted. But these also ruled over the others, so that the proverb "The master has turned" came into use from the words of the Gospel (Luke 22:61): "The Lord turned and looked, etc." By this they meant to say: "The one who turned is our Lord who rules us."[18] Thus in our management of household affairs the maidservants rule their mistresses, and the children rule the whole house and the domestics who serve them. By means of examples of this kind God teaches that He is present and cares for us, that He does not forget us, no matter in what kind of life we live. The church is

---

[17] Cf. also *Luther's Works*, 7, p. 193.

[18] *Conversus* was the title for a lay brother who, though he lived in the monastery, had not taken a monastic vow.

the queen in the world; but nothing is less apparent, since the world reigns and exercises dominion. But if the church did not sustain the world by its praying and teaching, all things would perish in one moment. The world does not see or believe this. Indeed, the Turk and the Frenchman think that they rule and sustain the world, that is, until they fall into ruin and are confounded in their counsels and endeavors. Then they will finally find out that they are nothing. But it will be too late.

9. *When Leah saw that she had ceased bearing children, she took her maid Zilpah and gave her to Jacob as a wife.*

10. *Then Leah's maid Zilpah bore Jacob a son.*

11. *And Leah said: Good fortune! So she called his name Gad.*

Here the birth of Joseph should have been related, but by employing the figure called hysteron proteron Leah's sons are mentioned. But one must remove all suspicion of promiscuous lusts and fornication from these saintly people. For Jacob does not desire the maidservant. Nor does he plot against her chastity, as fornicators are wont to do; but he would have been content with the love of Rachel alone, with whom alone he was desperately in love. In compliance with the order of his wife, however, he goes in to the maidservant, to whom she has yielded the marriage couch because she gives up hope that offspring will be born from her body. For she has been barren for three whole years. Nor is she glad to hand over the maidservant to her husband; but if she had had hope of conceiving later, she would never have done this. This will be clear from what follows, when she again gives birth, removes the maidservant, and does not want her to bear any more children from her husband. Thus after the birth of Joseph Rachel also does not want her maidservant to be joined to her husband again.

The saintly mothers certainly had a very ardent and anxious desire for offspring. Therefore after Leah has been barren for three years, she grieves that her husband is being estranged from her; and because there is no hope that offspring will be born from her body, she joins her maidservant to him. For Rachel is puffed up more by the birth of Joseph alone than Leah is by the birth of four sons. The father, the mother, and the whole household look at this son alone and are filled with admiration; for he was born from Rachel, who was the beloved chief wife, from whom the master of the house and the heir of the kingdom and the priesthood was expected. Therefore Leah is troubled. She thinks: "Wretched woman that I am! Now I have been humiliated a second time. My offspring is neglected. Besides, my husband has become estranged from me." Thus she expostulates with Rachel later when she says: "You have taken away my husband." Surely these seem to be manifestations of carnal hatred and envy; but God mercifully tolerates them, and without paying regard to them He blesses both Leah and Rachel. Therefore Leah came to the following resolution: "My husband will surely have to be brought back into my tent. I see that Joseph is the sole care and delight of his father, because he was born from my sister, who was preferred to me. But I shall give him Zilpah in order that I may draw him away from Rachel and gain him for myself." Accordingly, one can see wonderful eagerness and love for offspring in the saintly women, not lust.

Whenever the Manichaeans and the papists come upon these passages of Holy Scripture, they stop their ears and close their eyes. In their judgment these carnal matters are so filthy that they barely deign to read and become acquainted with them. In his *Confessions* Augustine reports that the Manichaeans inveighed against the very saintly patriarchs with the most virulent reproaches for having many wives and children. "When I was a Manichaean," he says, "I derided them as completely lustful men. But you in turn, dear Manichaean, derided me when I devoted myself to your prodigious nonsense, so that when plucking an apple or a pear from a tree I believed that the tree wept." [19] Thus while the papists look down from on high on that zeal in parents for procreating children, meanwhile they themselves are involved in loathsome lusts. Indeed, Gerson, Bonaventure, Hugo, Origen, and Jerome were no less offended by these examples. Consequently, they pass them by and do not deign to look at them with a deeper insight. The significance they attach to them is only allegorical.

They do not see that it is stated very clearly in the text how the very saintly women cry out, pray, give thanks, and trust in God.

---

[19] Augustine, *Confessions,* Book III, ch. 12.

Likewise that God heard them, that God had regard for them and brought about a change. God, who was invoked, who heard, and who was praised and blessed, is in the midst of these accounts. Therefore they should not have regarded purity, innocence, and chastity in accordance with their own judgment as concupiscence and lustful acts befitting pimps. It is certainly remarkable that no one among the fathers ever saw this; and, what is more, it is stated in the text: "Leah gave him her maidservant to wife." Therefore they were not harlots. No, they were lawful wives given to Jacob for the purpose of procreating offspring.

But I have often declared that I greatly abhor allegories and condemn the fondness for them. For the examples and the footsteps of the fathers frighten me. By means of their allegories they obscure doctrine and the edification of love, patience, and hope in God when by those speculations of their allegories they divert us from the doctrine and genuine meaning of the words. Jerome and Origen are especially devoted to this. Indeed, Augustine, too, would have been brought to do so had he not been withdrawn from it by his controversies and disputes with the heretics. But because I admired these men as very great theologians, I followed the same course at the outset. When I read the Bible, I did not follow the literal sense; but according to their example, I turned everything into allegories.

Accordingly, I urge students of theology to shun this kind of interpretation in the Holy Scriptures. For allegory is pernicious when it does not agree with the history, but especially when it takes the place of the history, from which the church is more correctly instructed about the wonderful administration of God in all stations of life, in the management of a household, in the state, and in the church. Inasmuch as such interpreters overlook these things in the histories, they necessarily transform everything into allegories and a different meaning. Thus in this example, because they do not see the counsels of God and His governance, which is hidden under this ordinary outward appearance of household management and marriage, they attach to it a foreign meaning concerning the contemplative and active life.[20] For these are their theses to which they, for the most part, refer everything. Rachel, they say, signifies the contemplative life; but Leah sig-

---

[20] *Glossa ordinaria* ad Gen. 30:1, as the "moral sense."

nifies the active life. This, of course, is that outstanding wisdom with which they have covered and enveloped with the densest darkness the necessary doctrine of the church concerning marriage and concerning household economy and what belongs to it.

Rachel, they say, is loved by Jacob because she has beautiful eyes. To her they apply the contemplative life. But to Leah they apply the active life, since she is not loved but is neglected by Jacob. They do so for the purpose of elevating themselves above every other kind of life. For the active life is characteristic of people who are engaged in household and political activities, who sweat in the field and in the house. This is a most troublesome life; it is ugly, just as Leah had weak eyes. But the contemplative life is found in the monasteries, in the associations of the priests who are free from household and political annoyances, who sit at leisure and speculate about God, pray, fast, and have their visions, revelations, and illuminations. And finally the satanic madness and illusion of the allegory concerning the speculative life proceeded so far that no one seemed to be a monk in the true sense of the word unless he had special revelations. This was especially true of the Minorites.[21] They dreamed of nothing else than the mutual discussions of Christ, the angels, the saints, and Mary with the souls. There is still extant a book about the revelations of Brigit which contains a conversation between Christ and the souls.[22] But they are satanic illusions pure and simple by which I myself had almost been taken in when I was still a monk had I not been withdrawn through Staupitz, who drove me to the public profession of theology when, at his advice and order, I had been declared to be a doctor of theology.[23]

Therefore the life of the monks was called the beautiful and beloved Rachel, but domestic and political activity was compared to ugly Leah. Indeed, in the monasteries the priests, in turn, were also distinguished from the lay brothers. To the latter

[21] Apparently a reference to the Spiritual Franciscans and Fraticelli, who carried on and cultivated the visions of Joachim of Fiore (d. 1202).

[22] St. Brigitta or Bridget of Sweden (d. 1373), whose *Revelationes* were published in 1492; writing in December, 1545, Luther says that he had heard of the prophecies "of the insane Brigitta" 40 years earlier (*W* LIV, 398).

[23] Staupitz gave Luther this advice in September, 1511, in a conversation under a pear tree near the Black Cloister (cf. *W. Tischreden*, III, 187—188).

the active life was assigned, and to the former the contemplative life. But in this way we will become like the Turks and the Tartars, not like Leah and Rachel. For in Turkey there are also many religious who make it their one aim to interpret the Alcoran of Mohammed allegorically in order that they may gain greater admiration. For an allegory is like a beautiful harlot who fondles men in such a way that it is impossible for her not to be loved, especially by idle men who are free from a trial. Men of this kind think that they are in the middle of Paradise and on God's lap whenever they indulge in such speculations. At first allegories originated from stupid and idle monks. Finally they spread so widely that some men turned Ovid's *Metamorphoses* into allegories.[24] They made a laurel tree Mary, and Apollo they made Christ. Although this is absurd, nevertheless, when it is set forth to youths who lack experience but are lovers and students of literature, it is so pleasing to them at the outset that they devote themselves completely to those interpretations.

Consequently, I hate allegories. But if anyone wants to make use of them, let him see to it that he handles them with discretion. For first of all the historical sense must be sought. It gives us correct and solid instruction; it fights, defends, conquers, and builds. If this is genuine and pure, an allegory may be sought later, not a monastic allegory or one concerning the speculative life but one that is in agreement with the history and embraces the sacred matters pertaining to the holy cross, that is, the doctrine of the cross, of faith, of hope, of love, and of patience, not a monk who sits and speaks with Christ and boasts of visions and of having heard the voices of angels or the voice of Blessed Virgin Mary. For he sits in idleness without a cross and trial. Such a speculative life is cursed and damned.

Therefore an allegory should agree with the history, and on it as on a foundation one should build precious stones, gold, and silver (cf. 1 Cor. 3:12). Otherwise an allegory is pernicious and produces only errors; or, if it is exceptionally good, the result is merely stubble and absurdities pure and simple. And one must

---

[24] Probably the best-known of these Christian allegories on the *Metamorphoses* of Ovid was that of a French Franciscan, sometimes called "Chrétien Légouais"; it seems to have been composed between 1316 and 1328, and ran to about 70,000 lines.

distinguish carefully between the foundation or the doctrine itself and the building which is constructed on it. The allegory should not be the foundation. No, it should be the upper side, whether it is gold or gems or even straw, provided that it rests on the foundation. Otherwise they are diabolical allurements if they disagree with the foundation. For God will not give special revelations to everyone; He will not promulgate a new Decalog, but He has bound us to this commandment which resounded from heaven: "HEAR HIM" (Matt. 17:5). Likewise: "They have Moses and the prophets" (Luke 16:29). He wants us to hear the Word and to believe it. Here you have speculations in sufficient abundance; you have been withdrawn not only from outward affairs but also from the thoughts of your intellect and reason, so that you keep the Sabbath here and your opinions and your judgment cease.

But the active life is love, or faith working through love, likewise patience under the cross. These are the exercises of both the contemplative and the active life, not only in the monasteries among the monks and the lay brothers but also in the domestic and political sphere among all men who live in faith and are exercised by deeds, no matter how obscure and sordid these deeds are. But human nature does not want to be content with the usual doctrine and Word of the Gospel or to be satisfied with the sacraments which have been handed down through the Son of God and the apostles and have been propagated through their successors; but it demands something special. Then the devil comes and speaks with you. Therefore unless you will be able to reply: "This is what God's Word says; you say things contrary to the Word. Get behind me, Satan! (cf. Matt. 16:23)" you will be overthrown immediately.

I teach this with special zeal and indignation because I have seen that this passage has been so disgracefully defiled by the wild ravings of the Manichaeans. The monks and papists have become like the Manichaeans in all respects and have filled the church with Brigittian and other books with which they have reviled the domestic and the political sphere, although, of course, they could never do without these. But if you look a little more deeply into this history, you will see examples of the greatest chastity in marriage — such chastity as there has never been among those who have boasted of the state of virginity and chastity, with the exception of the special and miraculous examples of the Baptist, Mary, and others like them. In the others there remains the burning rage of lust. Therefore no chastity can be compared to the examples of these women. For they are described and adorned with very beautiful words; how they pray, sob, cry out, believe, and await offspring from God in marriage. But lust does not think about God, does not call upon Him, does not give thanks. No, it is blind and insane. But these women pray and weep, saying: "O God, give offspring, etc." These are not the words of a lustful woman; they are the words of a very chaste and honorable matron.

Therefore the examples of these women are most useful and especially necessary for the churches, for they give evidence that God presides over, governs, and protects the domestic kind of life, in comparison with which your celibacy, your monastic and contemplative life, stinks before God, yes, even in your own conscience. The monks also pay the penalty they deserve for this contempt of marriage on their part. Because they laugh at these and similar examples and God's works are filthy in their eyes, they themselves in turn have also been cast off and despised by God until they have fallen into monstrous shamelessness and lust.

The rabbis quarrel about the etymology of the noun גָּד and have various interpretations of it.[25] But I think that it is most correctly rendered with "girded," "armed," "equipped for war." From it we have גְּדוּד, "soldier," "highwayman." Jerome translates it with "skirmishers in the army," that is, "soldiers equipped for war." But we have translated it in this way advisedly and knowingly, even though I know that sometimes it means "a cutting" and sometimes "success" and "good fortune," as Münster and others have translated it. This we readily grant them. For Augustine, too, has interpreted it in the same way. We do not oppose their view, but we do not follow it. Thus in Is. 20 and 65 we have also adopted a different view. Here the Vulgate and the translation of others has: "You set up a table for good fortune." We have translated with "You set up a table for Mars." For the Jews also worshiped Mars in imitation of the Greeks. We have kept to the root of the word, which means "to be girded."

---

[25] In Is. 65:11 ("who set a table for Fortune"), Luther simply transliterates "Gad." The reference to Is. 20 is not clear.

And Moses confirms this interpretation of ours below in chapter 49:19 in the blessing of the sons of Gad, where it is stated: "Girded, he will engage in battle." This authority is sufficient for us in opposition to the quarrels of the rabbis. Gad shall be in the forefront, shall be in the lead. Therefore we have translated with "Prepared for war. There will be success." He who wants to follow others may surely do so. When Naphtali was born, Rachel had said: "I have prevailed. I have conquered." Here Leah says: "I shall prevail; now I have the conqueror. There is a stout beginning; for I, too, have a warrior who shall be victorious and propagate my line."

Thus there was a contest and some jealousy between the saintly mothers with the result that out of excessive zeal both give up their maternal honor and assign it to a maidservant. For it was a great honor to conceive children from Jacob, who had the promise of the Blessed Seed — the promise which he undoubtedly impressed diligently and constantly. "Thus Abraham, Isaac, and God Himself told me that the Savior of the whole world will come from my descendants." Such a godly and saintly husband did not conceal from his wives the things that pertain to the household and to his descendants. By this preaching the very saintly women were inflamed with a burning faith, so that they sought, not lust but offspring for the sake of the glory of their future descendants. For if intercourse had been the only thing they desired, they would not have been so concerned about offspring and would not have handed over their maidservants to their husband. Rachel would have said: "What is it to me? Even if I do not bear children, I shall nevertheless enjoy intercourse with my husband. This is enough for me." But it is pointed out clearly how they despised the pleasure of intercourse and were aflame with the desire to become mothers of the Promised Seed. About this they contended with each other to the point of envy. But the papists pay no attention to this, for a godless person will not see the glory of God.

12. *Leah's maid Zilpah bore Jacob a second son.*

13. *And Leah said: Happy am I! For the women will call me happy. So she called his name Asher.*

Zilpah bears a second son for Leah, and on him she again

congratulates herself to an extraordinary degree. For only offspring was sought. Accordingly, examples of chastity must be sought in this history, not examples of lust. Leah wishes to please her husband with her fertility, which is a most praiseworthy virtue in a wife who desires to dwell with her husband and not to follow a stranger, yes, to be anxious to please this husband alone, to have the favor of him alone, but especially such a great man, to whom the Savior of the world was promised. Therefore these are truly and most especially manifestations of marital love full of godliness, chastity, and obedience, not of lust, as the Roman sow and many of the fathers and monks have interpreted it. Asher means "blessed." "Now I will be blessed and happy," she says, "and all wives and daughters will call me fortunate. I will be a beloved mother of the house for Jacob, so much so that it will be said that Jacob loves Leah and despises the other woman as barren."

14. *In the days of wheat harvest Reuben went and found mandrakes in the field, and brought them to his mother Leah. Then Rachel said to Leah: Give me, I pray, some of your son's mandrakes.*

15. *But she said to her: Is it a small matter that you have taken away my husband? Would you take away my son's mandrakes also? Rachel said: Then he may lie with you tonight for your son's mandrakes.*

16. *When Jacob came from the field in the evening, Leah went out to meet him, and said: You must come in to me; for I have hired you with my son's mandrakes. So he lay with her that night.*

Reuben was a lad eight or nine years of age when this happened. He was not a married man, and he could not have been more than nine years old. Accordingly, he went out to his father while he was pasturing the flocks of Laban or working in the field, as boys are wont to do. Perhaps he was even sent by his mother. Because it was the time of the wheat harvest, he happened to find דּוּדָאִים. The lad did not understand what he found and brought to his mother. But it seems that it was a beautiful fruit and that he was captivated by its color. But it is not certain what kind of fruit or flower it was. The Vulgate and other interpreters have translated it with "mandrake," which, as is commonly supposed, is produced from the urine of hanged thieves. Thus authors tell many other foolish stories in their descriptions of these mandrakes, but these stories are nonsense pure and simple which may have originated among the Jews.[26] But the boy did not go to a gallows; he went into the field.

But it must have been a fruit which usually ripens about the time of the wheat harvest, which is rather late, like nightshade or the winter cherry, the dewberry, and the raspberry.[27] Many others also think it was nightshade, which has fruit that is beautiful in color and pleasing to the taste and is often used as medicine. Or they must have been blueberries, which are very sweet and pleasing to the taste. But I leave this to the grammarians and the physicians, for every nation has its special and peculiar fruits and herbs. The color was pleasing to the lad; and when he returned home, the women quarreled about the mandrakes. Rachel is so delighted with the mandrakes that she hands over her husband to Leah and yields her right for the sole purpose of taking them away from the lad.

But this is ridiculous and puerile beyond measure, so much so that nothing more inconsequential can be mentioned or recorded. Why, then, is it recorded? I reply: One must always keep in view what I emphasize so often, namely, that the Holy Spirit is the Author of this book. He Himself takes such delight in playing and trifling when describing things that are unimportant, puerile, and worthless; and He hands this down to be taught in the church as though it redounded to the greatest edification. But were there not at that time other more illustrious achievements among the kings of Egypt, Babylonia, Persia, and Palestine, etc. — achievements which would have been more worth reading? Of what consequence is it to relate how a lad brings mandrakes and two sisters quarrel about their husband and exchanging the bed?

Undoubtedly many more important things happened than

---

[26] The "mandrake," widely supposed to be an aphrodisiac, is the subject of many practices and stories in Near Eastern folklore and religion, some of them quoted by Lyra *ad* Gen. 30:14.

[27] Cf. Luther's manuscript notes for the translation of this passage (*W, Deutsche Bibel, III,* 199—200), revealing his research into the German botanical equivalents for various Hebrew names of plants.

those that are described here. But these inconsequential matters abound in consolation and doctrine. The others do not. Nor should they be passed by, much less disparaged as sordid and worthless, as the papists do. Well, let these things be inconsequential. Furthermore, let the deeds of other men be very great and splendid; let them be kings, pontiffs, cardinals, etc.—the Holy Spirit and God the Creator deigns to play, to jest, and to trifle with His saints in unimportant and inconsequential matters, not in the resurrection of the dead or in other miracles but in the quarrel of Rachel and Leah about the mandrakes; and He wants these matters set before the churches.

But what are the histories of the heathen written by Vergil, Homer, Livy, or others, no matter how much they are decked out with words? They are histories of the Greeks, of Alexander, and of Hannibal. But they lack the magnificence, the glory, and the crown of the Word and promise of God. This diadem they do not have. Therefore they are records of things that have no value rather than actual histories. For what is history without the Word of God when the Lord says: "This is My will, My glory; this is pleasing to Me; with this I am delighted; I dwell here"? Accordingly, no matter how puerile and sordid these things are, yet they have immense and unlimited weight, namely, the Word of God. Although the histories of Alexander, Julius Caesar, etc., are outstanding and very splendid, they lack the true adornment. Therefore they are like chaff scattered by the wind and destitute of true weight; they are glory only of the belly and the flesh.

Therefore we should attach the greatest value to these histories and console ourselves with them, even though we are lowly, abject, and despised, as we certainly are. For there is nothing more despised and abject than a Christian man who believes the Word of God. All others are princes, lords, and happy men who do all things as they please. Only that nation which has the Word and believes in God is a child of the cross and vexation. If the world is not there to crucify it, yet the devil, together with his angels, is not absent. But this is our consolation, that the most ordinary home life of Christians with wife, with children, and with domestics—which has the appearances of being a mere trifle—presents true and divine histories adorned with the glory of the Word of God.

But we should take hold of and firmly retain the Word, and

we should bear in mind that we have been baptized, absolved, and taught by the Word of God. Therefore let us give thanks to God and be joyful. Whether heaven or the whole world crashes in ruins and, in addition, hits us on the head, we are nevertheless certain that our games and most wretched misfortunes have been adorned and crowned with divine glory and splendor, namely, with the Word of God. For this reason these histories are called sacred and are common to all men who have the Word of God and in whom God works, and does so with good pleasure, with His mercy, and with His grace. He does not deal in this way with Alexander, Scipio, Cicero, Hannibal, etc. Therefore we should rejoice and be grateful and happy to find rest in God's good pleasure, and we should bear with equanimity whatever troubles confront us. And no matter how unimportant, servile, womanish, and full of wretchedness our works are, we should nevertheless add this title: THE WORD OF GOD, because of which everything we do becomes glorious and will remain forever, while, on the other hand, the histories of the world are eternally wretched.

In this way we shall understand that this has not been set forth in vain by the Holy Spirit to be read, taught, and believed. The pope, together with his supporters, proudly despises it and dreams in the meantime that he now has his exalted seat in heaven next to St. Peter. Thus Tetzel, the well-known preacher of indulgences, boasted that because of the countless number of souls he had saved through indulgences he would not change places with St. Peter.[28] This, however, is vain and diabolical boasting. But God has regard for what is lowly on earth (cf. Ps. 113:6). He says: "I created this woman and joined her to a husband. United they produce offspring and endure the troubles of matrimony. Therefore they please Me by rendering service to marriage and My ordinance." Even among the heathen married people are far more acceptable than all the philosophers who indulge in wonderful speculations about celibacy. How much more acceptable they should be among us, who have been baptized, taught, crowned

---

[28] Together with the more familiar boast that "as soon as the money rings in the chest, the soul springs from purgatory to heaven," this statement was attributed to Johann Tetzel, the indulgence peddler —with how much historical accuracy, it is virtually impossible to determine.

and adorned with the glory of the Word of God, who have the angels as guardians!

Therefore let us glory and rejoice in these puerile and domestic matters, since the Holy Spirit deigns to describe them in order to point out that He is with us, who believe and have the Word, and that even those trifles about the mandrakes and the foolish quarrels of the women are pleasing to God. Only let us not despair, but let us remain in faith. Then let the devil go his way and do what he cannot stop doing. We are in a spiritual calling. We have the Word, Baptism, and absolution. We are certain that God is with us and for us. *I would rather be in hell with God present than in heaven with God absent.*[29] "For even though I walk in the midst of the shadow of death," says David, "I will fear no evil; for Thou art with me" (cf. Ps. 23:4). And "if I descend into hell, Thou art there" (cf. Ps. 139:8). If I have Thy Word, I do not care about the fire of hell. On the other hand, I would not like to be even in heaven if Thou wert not with me. For where God is, there the kingdom of God is. Where the Word is, there Paradise and all things are. Therefore we should give thanks for the Word, because we are already in Paradise and under the good pleasure of God, to whom all things are acceptable, whether we eat mandrakes or vegetables or milk; for we are in the Word.

One should take this teaching from this passage. It is surely outstanding, and it is necessary for the church. One must also say something about the quarrel of the women. For these histories should not be looked at in the way the papists regard them, namely, as the fun of harlots. The saintly women desire nothing else than the natural fruit of their bodies. For by nature woman has been created for the purpose of bearing children. Therefore she has breasts; she has arms for the purpose of nourishing, cherishing, and carrying her offspring. It was the intention of the Creator that women should bear children and that men should beget them — with the exception of those men whom God Himself excepted. Matt. 19:12 speaks about these. Otherwise the creature has been created to be fruitful. Therefore one can see in these women how they fight, not out of lust but out of love and desire for offspring, to which end they know they have been created.

---

[29] The italics are in the original.

Therefore they want their womb, breasts, hands, and all their members to serve God.

Although they already had children before, yet they bore in mind that children are mortal and that it could happen that they would be deprived of them. Therefore if one woman had had even a hundred children, still she would always have desired more, for they had in view the promised descendants to whom the preaching they had heard from their husband pertained. Thus the saintly women should be praised, and one should stop the mouths of the papists, who appraise the chastity and the marriages of the patriarchs according to their own lusts. Thus even Augustine was induced by the error of the Manichaeans to think that their life was lustful. But here we hear that Leah prayed, cried out, and sobbed for offspring and was heard by God. This is not characteristic of a lustful woman, but it is typical of a chaste and saintly matron who has an aversion for lust and desires the birth of children.

17. *And God hearkened to Leah, and she conceived and bore Jacob a fifth son.*

18. *Leah said: God has given me my hire because I gave my maid to my husband. So she called his name Issachar.*

The fifth son of Leah was born in the tenth year. Leah gives thanks, and just as she prayed and wept, so she now praises God with a joyful heart. The grammarians of the Hebrews argue about how the name Issachar should be read.[30] It makes no difference whether you read Isaschar or Issachar.

19. *And Leah conceived again, and she bore Jacob a sixth son.*

20. *Then Leah said: God has endowed me with a good dowry; now my husband will honor me, because I have borne him six sons. So she called his name Zebulun.*

All these words and works are characteristic of very saintly matrons, namely, to pray, to weep, to give thanks; they are typical

---

[30] In his own translation Luther followed the pointing of the Masoretic text and wrote Isaschar; English versions, following the Septuagint and the Vulgate (and perhaps an earlier pointing of the Hebrew), write Issachar.

of honorable women, not of harlots and disreputable women. What more can we do before God that is greater than these two services—the services of prayer and thanksgiving? In the first place, one must hear the Word, which is given to us by God. Here we do nothing, but we only take hold of what has been offered. In the second place, one must pray and implore God's help after the Word has been heard and taken hold of, and after getting this help one must give thanks and offer sacrifice. But we pray not only with the mouth or the voice but also with sobbing of the heart, with all our strength and members. This is prayer without ceasing (cf. Acts 5:12; 1 Thess. 5:17).

The word זְבָדַנִי occurs nowhere else in Holy Scripture. In accordance with the example of others, we have translated it with "has endowed me." But I am not sure that this is the true interpretation, for it cannot be illustrated with another example. She wanted to say: "God has given me something good," whether you take this to be a dowry or a gift. But we see nothing else than the greatest piety and the most saintly use of the female sex and of marriage. Virgins do not have such glory and praise either in the Old or in the New Testament.

21. *Afterwards she bore a daughter, and called her name Dinah.*

So far Moses has enumerated the offspring of Leah: six sons and one daughter, likewise two sons from her maidservant. Now the birth of Joseph from Rachel follows.

22. *Then God remembered Rachel, and God hearkened to her and opened her womb.*

23. *She conceived and bore a son, and said: God has taken away my reproach.*

24. *And she called his name Joseph, saying: May the Lord add to me another son!*

Above it has been stated that the sequence of the history must be observed and that Moses employed recapitulation or anticipation. For Joseph was born in the seventh year. Therefore his birth should have been described much earlier. But because Moses has postponed it to this last place, he now returns to the proteron, which has become the hysteron. For it is clear that Joseph was born in the seventh year of the servitude, since Jacob serves for six years after his birth. Therefore four sons and his daughter Dinah were born after Joseph in that six-year period, although in the history they have been mentioned first. This anticipation often makes narratives somewhat obscure. Therefore one should carefully observe it when reading the histories, lest an inattentive reader be deceived or hampered.

Once again, however, the Holy Spirit not only excuses but even praises these very saintly women, who were aglow with a boundless desire for offspring, not with lust. And the chastity of Jacob's marriage is praised for us in such a way that one sees in it almost nothing that is carnal. Yet it is impossible for nothing carnal to be in marriage. But Jacob is adorned in such a way by God that it seems that his marriage was not infected by original sin but was wholly angelic. For consider what exercises of godliness and of the highest worship of God were there. Rachel prays, sobs, and weeps up to the sixth year, and during this time she was well troubled and exercised with great patience. For it was a great burden and a very heavy cross to endure the reproach of sterility for such a long time. How many women she sees bearing children in the meantime! Indeed, she sees her own sister Leah honored with the glory of motherhood, that she abounds in offspring and has four sons. But I think that she was consumed with grief to such an extent that she easily banished not only lust from her heart but also all joys. Laughter or jests gave her no pleasure; but she spent her days and nights in perpetual sighings, sobbings, tears, complaints, and prayer. Accordingly, the marriage of Jacob and Rachel is described as completely chaste. Whenever Rachel wanted to live with her husband, she did so only for the purpose of becoming a mother and increasing the house of Jacob, who had the promise. She is an example of a very saintly woman who implored the mercy of God in faith and patience, waited for consolation, and endured the trial and the exceedingly burdensome grief.

Therefore Moses has employed a significant word: "The Lord remembered." It is as though he were saying: "She had almost despaired within herself, and she was convinced in her heart that God would never remember her, yes, that He had forgotten her forever." "I shall not be a mother," she thought, "but I am the most wretched of all women. I should have been the mother of the house, but God has forgotten me." In this way she was led down into hell, where no hope of help seems to be left. In despair she takes hold of her maidservant and hands her over to her husband, which she would not have done if she had not given up all hope. Yet she despairs in such a way that she retains a spark of faith. In her despair she retains that sobbing which Paul calls ineffable (cf. Rom. 8:26), but this is so deeply buried and covered with impossibility and contrary emotions of the heart that she is barely conscious of that sobbing or sighing.

Thus Hannah, the mother of Samuel, also despaired of offspring and could not be conscious of her sobbing and of that desire for offspring in the inmost depths of her heart. But God, who searches the heart, understands the ineffable sobbing, which can neither be felt nor expressed with any words. Augustine also tells the story of his mother Monica, who lamented for nine years and deplored the downfall of her son because he had gone over to the sect of the Manichaeans. But her only request from God was that her son might be converted and become a Christian, and for this reason she wanted to betroth a Christian wife to him in order that he might be brought back on the right way by being associated with and admonished by a godly woman. She would have been content if he had only been converted to sound doctrine from the heresy of the Manichaeans. But the Lord seemed to deny her this, as Augustine says. Nevertheless, He heard what was most important and the deep desire of her heart, namely, the ineffable sobbing.[31]

But just as the prayer and the sobbing are ineffable, so the hearing and the joy are inestimable and ineffable, as Paul says (Eph. 3:20): "Now to Him who by the power at work within us is able to do far more abundantly than all that we ask or think." He does not give what His saints seek on the surface of their hearts and with that foam of words, but He is an almighty and exceedingly rich Bestower who gives in accordance with the depth of that sighing. Therefore He lets prayer be directed, grow, and be increased; and He does not hear immediately. For if He were to answer at the first outcry or petition, prayer would not increase but would become cold. Therefore He defers help. As a result, prayer grows from day to day and becomes more efficacious.

[31] Augustine, *Confessions,* Book III, ch. 11.

The sobbing of the heart also becomes deeper and more ardent until it comes to the point of despair, as it were. Then prayer becomes most ardent and passionate, when it seems that now the sobbing is nearly at a standstill.

But if He heard immediately, prayer would not be so strong, so alive, and so ardent; but it would be only a superficial and pedagogical sobbing which is still learning to pray, to sob, and to desire, and is not yet a master of prayer. But when the point of despair has been reached and the afflicted heart thinks: "Alas, nothing will come of it; all is lost!" yet a spark and a dimly burning wick remain (cf. Is. 42:3), then be strong and hold out. For this is the struggle of the saints who think that the rope will now be torn yet who continue to sob. Then, therefore, prayer is perfect and strongest.

Here it is said about Rachel: "God remembered, etc." It is as though Moses were saying: "The only feeling Rachel had was that all her prayers and tears had been in vain and useless, and that she had been utterly obliterated and deleted from the heart and the memory of God." But you should not come to this conclusion, my dear Rachel; for you are making a big mistake. That feeling of yours is carnal; it is not yet the spirit that is sighing and the ineffable sobbing, but it is the flesh that is feeling and is weak. God has never forgotten you, but from the beginning, when you began to ask for offspring, He immediately heard and marked all the words of your sobbing. But your prayer was not yet ardent and strong [32] enough. Therefore it had to grow and become strong, and for this reason God put matters off until the second, third, fourth, and fifth year. Then for the first time He gave consolation through your maidservant. But your sobbing did not yet find rest. God still seemed to be turned away. Therefore God remembered, although He had never forgotten you for one moment. But this was finally the time for Him to hear your sighs, when you thought that they had been completely buried, covered, and forgotten.

This is how we, too, should learn to ask and hope for help whenever there is misfortune and faith totters. For we have the promise of the Gospel; we have Baptism, absolution, etc., by which we have

---

[32] The Weimar text has *foris,* but we have followed other editions and read *fortis.*

been instructed and strengthened. We have the command by which we are ordered to pray; we have the spirit of grace and of prayer. But as soon as we have begun to pray, our heart is troubled and complains that it is accomplishing nothing. Therefore one must learn that if you accomplish nothing by asking, you should add searching, that is, you should seek; if that, too, seems to be useless, and God conceals and hides Himself even more, add knocking, and do not cease until you storm the door by which He has been confined (cf. Matt. 7:7-8). For there is no doubt that our prayer is heard immediately after the first syllable has been uttered. Thus the angel says to Daniel: "At the beginning of your supplications a word went forth, and I have come to tell it to you" (9:23). But the fact that God does not immediately give what we pray for—this happens because He wants to be sought and to be taken by storm by insisting beyond measure, as the parable of the unrighteous judge teaches in Luke 18:2 ff. For then He comes and liberates the elect and gives more abundantly than we have prayed, sought, and knocked. But He defers in order that our praying may increase and that our sobbing may become stronger. This sobbing seems very feeble to us while we are sighing, but it is actually most ardent. Thus Paul calls it a shouting (cf. Gal. 4:6). For we not only recite words by forming a sound with the tongue and the lips or even let our prayers have a clear sound, but we simply shout out. There is no sound or voice of the mouth, but there is an outcry of the heart and ineffable sobbing; it is under the left breast, when the heart sobs and sighs as it almost fails for distress. Then indeed prayer is perfect and efficacious.

This should be frequently stated and repeated, lest we cast aside all hope and confidence with regard to our praying. Even though this praying is cold at the outset and does not immediately obtain help, yet we should know that help is postponed in order that prayer may become more perfect and stronger. For there is wonderful power and omnipotence in prayer. Thus when Rachel seemed to be altogether despised and scorned by God and nevertheless still remained a dimly burning wick (cf. Is. 42:3), it was impossible for God not to be awakened when called upon, sought, and stormed. But in the same manner He also helps all who call upon Him, and He helps so richly and liberally that they are compelled to acknowledge that they never hoped for any such thing. Thus Monica could say: "I did not ask for this, and I never had the courage to hope that my son would ever become such a great doctor of the church." Therefore we should never lose heart; but we should persist in praying, wishing, and seeking until hope and the awaited liberation appear.

Furthermore, Rachel herself points out sufficiently what her cross and trial was. For she says: "He has gathered up my reproach." For five or six years in succession she bore reproach and disgrace on account of her sterility, and in her own judgment and in the judgment of others she was regarded as the most wretched of all women. For she saw that her sister was fruitful; she saw that the maidservants, her sister's and her own, and all other women bore children and for this reason were praised, loved, and held in honor. "But I alone," she thought, "am regarded as rejected and cursed. The Lord, however, has seen all this manifold and burdensome reproach and disgrace which I have borne, and He has gathered it up and removed it from me. Now I am the wife and mother of the house." Thus her desire was fulfilled, and her sobbing was heard after it had been tested and increased by a delay that lasted so many years. It is also clear from this passage, where Rachel says that the Lord had gathered up her reproach, that at that time sterility in a woman was commonly regarded as disgraceful, especially in that line from which the promised descendants were expected. In the New Testament it was not regarded as a reproach; for virginity was most highly commended, especially in the ministry of the church. But among the fathers it was a very heavy cross and an exceedingly great disgrace. And this verdict flowed from the Word of God in Gen. 1: "God created male and female, and blessed them and said: 'Be fruitful and multiply, and fill the earth'" (cf. vv. 27–28). These words Adam transmitted to his descendants and diligently inculcated in them. Therefore it was handed down to his descendants that every sterile woman was rejected and cursed before God. The fact that the curse of God was simultaneously included in that passage was by far the hardest thing to bear. Sterility per se is a heavy burden and a great calamity, but it becomes far heavier when, in addition, a sterile wife is under a curse and does not please God, or when even though she pleases Him, she is nevertheless despised and scorned among the rest of the women of the people of God.

Therefore Elizabeth, the mother of John the Baptist, also gives thanks in nearly the same words when she says (Luke 1:25):

"Thus the Lord has done to me in the days when He looked on me, to take away my reproach among men." And the angel says to Mary: "Elizabeth . . . who was called barren" (Luke 1:36). It is as though he were saying: "Who is in ill report and in the greatest disgrace because she is not fruitful." Accordingly, in those times sterility was not only a special plague and cross among men but was even connected with a curse of God. Today many who are in prosperous circumstances and illustrious by birth are very much annoyed if they are deprived of this [33] blessing, and they have a very great desire for offspring, since they have the means with which to support it. But this cross is more tolerable for them because the New Testament does not add that they are condemned and rejected by God for this reason. The rest of the populace is more wicked than even the heathen themselves. For most married people do not desire offspring. Indeed, they turn away from it and consider it better to live without children, because they are poor and do not have the means with which to support a household. But this is especially true of those who are devoted to idleness and laziness and shun the sweat and the toil of marriage. But the purpose of marriage is not to have pleasure and to be idle but to procreate and bring up children, to support a household. This, of course, is a huge burden full of great cares and toils. But you have been created by God to be a husband or a wife and that you may learn to bear these troubles. Those who have no love for children are swine, stocks, and logs unworthy of being called men or women; for they despise the blessing of God, the Creator and Author of marriage.

25. *When Rachel had borne Joseph, Jacob said to Laban: Send me away, that I may go to my own home and country.*

26. *Give me my wives and my children for whom I have served you, and let me go; for you know the service which I have given you.*

Observe how respectfully the patriarch begs for his release. Nor does he demand anything but his wives and children. Yet he hints that he has deserved well of Laban and that he has earned

---

[33] The Weimar text has *hoc*, but we have followed other editions and read *hac*.

something as a reward. For this is why he says: "You know the service which I have given you." It is as though he were saying: "It is fair for you to think that I have served you not only for my wives and children but also for a marriage portion, for wages, or for some gift with which you might honor me, yes, also your daughters and grandchildren, for my faithful and generous service." Jacob wanted to point this out modestly and cautiously. But why does he do this? Because Laban was a filthy and greedy man. He was a dog, etc., a monster of that happy age. For because of his outstanding wickedness he should more properly be living in this last age, which is completely ruined by avarice and all vices. Accordingly, one should note this carefully on account of the deed of Jacob which follows and which we shall excuse for this reason.

For the very pious man had served for 14 whole years in extreme poverty. Servitude of this kind, coupled as it was with poverty, no one could endure today. For he served during the first seven years for Rachel; but he was most shamefully disappointed in his hope, and he received no reward at all from Laban, who thought: "He is a stranger and an exile. Therefore I shall use his services as long as I can; for he serves faithfully and increases my property." What miseries, therefore, shall we think he endured! For Laban — or rather Nabal, by turning the word around [34] — did not acknowledge the faithfulness and the diligence of the very saintly man, and now he is planning to let him go without a reward. For previously Jacob acquired no property; or, if he did, it was very small. He had nothing besides food and clothing, and yet that was very slender. The godly man has been serving a real dog. And below the daughters will complain about their father's rapacity by which Rachel was moved to steal the idols from her father. For he did not regard them as daughters but treated them like slaves whose services, the spinning and the hardships, he turned to his own profit and advantage. But now, when he makes an agreement concerning wages, he is eager to cheat him again, lest he have to pay something to his son-in-law and his daughters for the servitude by which he had been enriched.

These wrongs inflicted great grief both on Jacob himself and on his wives, and they often complained in secret about the

---

[34] Cf. p. 285, note 19.

poverty and need to which they were reduced by the fraudulent practices and the rapacity of their father. For this the circumstances point out clearly when they are considered more carefully, and there is execrable wickedness foreign to all human feeling and nature. For otherwise fathers love their daughters more because they are the weaker sex. Loveless and cruel Nabal, however, even plunders his daughters on top of this and torments them with the harshest servitude. But when a reward is discussed, he meditates anew on tricks and wiles. Jacob does all things sincerely and candidly, but that imposter devises only acts of robbery and cunning. Thus Jacob complains below (31:7): "You have changed my wages 10 times." Therefore Laban's lovelessness, cruelty, and avarice cannot be sufficiently stressed.

Accordingly, it must be brought to light and emphasized in every way, for it shows the reason for Jacob's deed, which will be recounted below when he deceives Laban again, lest this be regarded as wicked or criminal,[35] as it appears to be to one who looks at it in passing. But it was a necessary deception on account of the unjust rapacity of his father-in-law.

But now he seeks permission to depart. "I have served you 14 years," he says, "the first seven years for nothing. Deceived by your stratagems, I have added a second period of seven years, and now I have fulfilled this. Hereafter, therefore, I must also look out for myself, my household, and my home. But you should remember how faithfully I and my wives have served you. Yet you pay no attention to this, for you have paid me no wages for serving for 14 years. Therefore it is right and good for me to leave and to take care of my own affairs. Give me my wives and my children." It is as though he were saying: "If you pay me nothing, there will come a time when God will take vengeance and punish you for your ingratitude."

27. *But Laban said to him: If you will allow me to say so, I have learned by divination that the Lord has blessed me because of you.*

You holy pope! You pious Bishop of Mainz,[36] can you also

---

[35] The Weimar text has *ad*, but we have followed other editions and read *aut*.

[36] The German *B. von M.* refers to the Cardinal Archbishop of Mainz, Albrecht (1490—1545).

speak of God? Laban brings up the name and the blessing of God. But if you are speaking the truth and feel that you have been increased and enriched by the blessing of God on Jacob's account, why do you not give thanks? But you are planning to despoil, defraud, and deceive him in order that he may serve you longer. This, of course, is what hypocrites and all greedy and godless men usually do. They use the Lord's name, but in vain. Therefore Moses uses a remarkable word, נִחַשְׁתִּי , from the word for serpent, and it seems that at the same time he had regard for this meaning. The word also means auguries and divinations. Num. 24:1: "He did not go . . . to meet with omens." But it was customary to take auguries by means of serpents. Therefore Moses wanted to point out that Laban was an augur. "I have taken auguries," he says. "I thought. I have a foreboding. My heart has a presentiment of this. I have surmised as if by some divine sign that God has blessed me on your account." But he does not want to confer this honor on Jacob. He does not want to thank him. Nor does he give the glory to God. "I seemed to conclude," he says, "that God has blessed me through you." He does not want to seem to be a man who is unworthy of having his household increased by God, although it was very poor before Jacob came.

Moses wanted to say this with a remarkable and significant word. But such men are deceitful and double-tongued. They say one thing and think something else, like the cleft tongue of a serpent. He does not say simply: "I experience, I understand, I am sure that I have been blessed and enriched on your account." For if he had acknowledged this, he would have been compelled to open his coffers and to pay something to his son-in-law, his daughters, and his grandchildren. But he does not affirm this; but he calls it in question and argues, in case Jacob should want to demand wages from him. He wants to have a reason for declining under some pretext. Therefore he says: "I have learned by divination. It is possible that the Lord has blessed me through you." This is one of the tricks of the jurists, namely, to use ambiguous words which can be bent in both directions as one pleases.

But afterwards we shall hear that Laban was also an idolater. Perhaps, therefore, he took auguries or consulted idols and persuaded himself that he had been increased by this good fortune as a result of the worship of idols. But I am not discussing this. It is certain that he used God's name in vain. For he is eager to accommodate himself to the character and customs of Jacob. He sees that Jacob is a godly man. Therefore he employs the same words that Jacob was accustomed to employ.

28. *And he said: Name your wages, and I will give it.*

The Hebrew word נָקַב means "to perforate." In Hag. 1:6 we read about "a bag with holes, נָקוּב ." It also means "to name," and in this meaning it is also used in Lev. 24:16: "He who blasphemes the name of the Lord." He who has named the name of God and has blasphemed. He who swears by God's name. And this is how we have translated it in this passage. Moses could have used another word, but he points out that with a special and religious word Laban wanted to prevent Jacob from demanding too much pay, as though he would offend God by making an unjust demand. For all his words proceed from a heart thoroughly corrupted by avarice and cupidity, and they aim to defraud and despoil Jacob. But he adds: "And I will give it." This is not true. He does not plan to pay even a cent, just as later he will devise a new deception to avoid keeping the pacts and agreements about the wages to be paid. Here we shall see that he was not only greedy and godless, but that he was greed itself.

29. *Jacob said to him: You yourself know how I served you, and how your cattle have fared with me.*

30. *For you had little before I came, and it has increased abundantly; and the Lord has blessed you wherever I turned.*

Jacob repeats his former words with a severe censure of Laban's greed, godlessness, and augury, as though he were saying: "There is no reason for you to take auguries or to be in doubt about whether you should refer to me or to you the blessing that has been received. The fact itself says that you were blessed when I stepped in, that is, when I entered. For previously you also took auguries. Therefore if anything had been added because of an augury, it would also have been added in my absence. But the fact shows that your property was not increased until I undertook the care of your house." Accordingly, he refutes the godless and inept reply concerning an augury and praises his own services. "You know," he says, "how diligently and faithfully I have served you, and this the fact itself declares, even though you deny it or I say nothing about it. For how much cattle was handed over to me? Perhaps 1,000 sheep, which Rachel alone, your daughter, pastured, so that you needed neither a servant nor a shepherd, so small was the number. Why, then, do you have to take auguries, you greedygut?" For this is how Jacob could have upbraided the filthy and greedy man more properly and more sharply. The herd which a girl drives to pasture cannot be numerous. But that small number has been increased, or has broken out. For this is the force of the Hebrew word. "With me in charge of the pasturing, your cattle have been multiplied and increased as though by force. Because of their great number, they have broken out of the fences and the folds. Accordingly, God blessed you when I stepped in and arrived, not because of your auguries and idols."

This is a sufficiently sharp confutation and rebuke with which he censures the exceedingly greedy man who is reluctant to pay just wages to a very faithful servant who deserved very well of him by being a slave, not for one but for 14 years, for which he gave nothing but grabbed and raked together everything to himself. Besides, he defrauded his son-in-law and his daughters and left them nothing for their very severe hardships. But a little later an example of God's justice against abominable rapacity will follow. For he who sows sparingly reaps sparingly (cf. 2 Cor. 9:6).

This is an example completely conformable to our customs. For we see that the princes, the nobles, the peasants, and the citizens all play the part of Laban against poor Jacob. Yet what happens here will happen to all. For no matter how they snatch, rake together, and heap up, God still blesses Jacob, who is despoiled. And from him who snatches everything He, in turn, snatches everything. For thus it is stated in Ps. 39:6: "Man heaps up and knows not who will gather." And it is surely a very great misfortune that the world does not let itself be persuaded of this but wants to feel and experience the divine judgment. For when men seek, heap up, and snatch by fair means and foul, then they think that they are happy and that they have the things for which they have longed so eagerly. But the psalm replies: "He knows not for whom he gathers them."

Thus many states and princes collect a huge amount of money and are insane in their usury and greed. But for whom do they gather it? For the godless soldier, Brother Veit,[37] who a little later plunders and destroys everything. This is what almost happened to us recently in the disturbance which arose between the dukes of Saxony near the town of Wurzen.[38] If God had not prevented it, how soon Brother Veit would have come and torn everything to pieces in one day! Pope Clement plundered the church at Toledo and seized from it a large sum of money which easily equalled the wealth of three kingdoms. He did so under the pretext that he wanted to pay it into the treasury of the Church of St. Peter.[39] For he was a remarkable master of the art of plundering and raking together, and it seemed that the whole world did not satisfy his cupidity. But he was also gathering up treasure for the godless soldier who later destroyed and pillaged everything. The same thing will happen to all others who grow rich on usury and interest and rake together without measure and without end. Whenever they are admonished to leave something for the poor or to collect something with God's blessing, they do not listen but think as follows: "Money must be sought first; after money comes virtue."[40] "If I have amassed a sum of money, I shall enjoy it later. Yet I will keep it, no matter by what right or by what wrong I have procured it." But this will by no means happen, for the psalm says: "He knows not for whom he will gather it."

But how much more blessed it would be to fear God and to do something with God's blessing, as Ps. 37:16 states: "Better is a little that the righteous has than the abundance of many wicked"! But the story is told to those who are deaf.[41] For they must gather up and rake together in such a way that they have a פָּרִיץ, a robber, to plunder it. Therefore we should observe the common saying: "Let it go as it goes, etc." The world does not

---

[37] *Bruder Veiten,* also called *Bruder Landsknecht* (*Luther's Works,* 22, p. 521, note 16).

[38] On April 7, 1542, Luther addressed an "admonition to peace" to the Elector John Frederick and to Duke Maurice (*W, Briefe,* X, 32—36); on the significance of this allusion for the dating of these lectures, see Introduction, p. xi.

[39] A reference to the "sack of Rome" of May 6, 1527, in which Pope Clement VII, who had entered into the "holy league" of Cognac a year before, suffered a humiliating defeat.

[40] Horace, *Epistles,* I, 1, 53.

[41] Terence, *Heautontimorumenos,* II, 1, 10; cf. also *Luther's Works,* 4, p. 400.

want to be told; it wants to find out. While Laban strives to gather up and collect everything and defrauds his son-in-law and his daughters of their wages, he loses everything. He who wants to have too much gets nothing. I myself, who am now 60 years old, have seen very many examples of Labanites whose great wealth has suddenly been dissipated. I could mention the examples of certain men even in the small town of Mansfeld, which is my native land. And in other cities — in Leipzig, Freiberg, and many other places where there are mines — outstanding examples are reported of men who plundered and amassed treasure in our time. But now not even a cent of their most abundant wealth remains. This is gathering up into a sack with holes, as Haggai says (1:6). Why does this happen? "Because I have blown upon it," says the Lord. When He blows, wealth is scattered, even though the whole world were full of gold and silver.

Even though we accomplished nothing among godless and irreligious hypocrites, yet this must be inculcated on the chance that it may influence some. Laban cared nothing about this. Nevertheless, Jacob taught his wives and his household, and he also warned Laban himself about God's wrath against godlessness and greed. "See," he said to his household, "how great my father-in-law's greed is. He neither fears God nor pays any attention to our servitude. For he not only pays no wages, but he even despoils and robs his daughters and his grandchildren. What am I to do? If I mention wages, he will invent another trick with which to defraud us." For to such people robbing, deceiving, and defrauding is a joy. They devise nothing else than deceits and wiles, and if they can fleece a man of a heller, they think they have gained a gulden. They are an execrable class of people, hateful to God and men.

All translate the last part with "when I came in or entered," *ad ingressum sive introitum meum.* But, the fact itself states that Laban did not become rich as soon as Jacob entered. Therefore it is more correctly rendered into Latin with *ad pedem vel ad cursum meum* and into German with *durch meinen Fuss.* This points out at the same time Jacob's indefatigable zeal and his exceedingly severe hardships. It is as if he were saying: "Day and night I ran hither and thither. I did not ride on a horse or in a chariot; but I was exhausted by running in various directions to the field, to the pasturegrounds of the cattle, and to the house to serve you properly and faithfully. During the day I was exhausted by the heat and during the night by the cold. The Lord has blessed you in consequence of that running and toil of mine."

But now when shall I provide for my own household also?

This is a very sharp rebuke. Jacob wants to say: "You are my father-in-law. Therefore by the very law of nature you should have urged me to take care of my household immediately after the birth of my four sons. If you had a godly or honorable heart, you would deal with me as follows: 'My dear Jacob, I see that our offspring is now being increased by the birth of four grandsons. I will give you 1,000 sheep from which to acquire property for yourself and [42] your household.'" For who would not help a daughter and an honorable son-in-law, especially one who serves his own advantages? But Laban does not do this. Therefore Jacob's complaint about his poverty is completely just. "When am I going to provide for my own house? I have two wives, just as many maidservants, and seven sons. You enjoy the labors and the acquisitions of all these, and you seize what should have fallen to our advantage. Or do you not think that according to divine and natural law I must at one time look out for my own house?" Below he will say to Laban: "If God had not been with me, you would have sent me away empty-handed even now" (cf. Gen. 31:42). Or is it not unfair and cruel to snatch the bread from the mouths and the jaws of your daughters, your grandsons, and your son-in-law?

For this is the force of these words, which contain a sharp rebuke, even though they are set forth respectfully and modestly by Jacob. "I am the husband of four wives, the parent of so many children. But for these I do not toil. Nor do I benefit them. But I support you and your house. You devour and seize what has been acquired by our labors. If you had even a grain of reason and common sense, or even of shame and kindness, you would not let us wander about this way, naked and in need of everything." This amounts to stealing the holy cross and the gold from the feet of the saints. It amounts to killing starving Lazarus with hunger.

Accordingly, this is an incredible example of unheard-of greed,

---

[42] The Weimar text has *ex*, but we have followed other editions and read *et*.

which we should emphasize in order that we may learn to condemn and detest the world, together with its monster, which is greed, and to announce the future punishments for the dissipation of unjustly acquired property. Proverbial statements of all nations testify to this. "The third heir does not rejoice in ill-gotten gains." [43] One day you young men will see the children of greedy men in want and begging and, on the other hand, the promise of the Holy Spirit fulfilled: "I have not seen the righteous man forsaken or his children begging bread" (Ps. 37:25). But again: "I have not seen a godless man preserved," as is stated (Ps. 37:35-36): "I have seen a wicked man overbearing, and towering like a cedar of Lebanon. Again I passed by, and, lo, he was no more; though I sought him, he could not be found." Experience agrees beautifully with Holy Scripture. Thus Laban will be cursed as a plunderer and robber of his daughters and his grandchildren, and his goods will be scattered.

But Jacob's speech is completely honorable, and the reason for which he asks for his release is altogether just. "I have been ordered," he wants to say, "to provide for my household according to the divine and natural law." Thus Paul says (1 Tim. 5:8): "If anyone does not provide for his [44] relatives, and especially for his own family, he has disowned the faith and is worse than an unbeliever." But Laban hears nothing and is not influenced by the honesty and the need of his son-in-law. Thus there is a saying which states: "The belly has no ears."

31. *He said: What shall I give you?*

He asks the question with sufficient trepidation. It is as if he were saying: "If you need 100 guldens, I ask you to demand only four." Or, on the other hand, should he not immediately have burst out into these words: "I acknowledge your faithfulness and diligence. There is no need of words. Of my own accord I am rendering every service to you, and whatever, as I understand it, will be to your advantage I will readily do for you, my son-in-law and son"? But observe what greed does. He still asks: "What shall I give you? Beware of demanding too much." Ah,

---

[43] Cf. p. 66, note 57.

[44] The Weimar text has *tuorum,* but we have followed other editions and read *suorum.*

you miserable dog! Jacob is your son-in-law, they are your daughters and grandsons; and you ask how you should serve them. Moses gives an excellent description of such a remarkable Euclio; he describes him better and more accurately than any Apelles could have painted him with colors.[45]

But what is Jacob to do? He sees that his father-in-law is completely devoid of all kindness and godliness. Therefore he thinks that these matters should be entrusted to the divine judgment. Surely no greedy men ever escape the vengeance of God. Indeed, they perish because of the growth and increase of their property; for they grow only to be cursed and destroyed, not to be blessed. Therefore as often as you see a greedy man, you see a man perishing and ruined. But Jacob understands his deceptive and cunning heart. Consequently, he thinks: "Even if I demand money and you promise to give it, yet you will give nothing. You will invent some fraud by which to elude whatever agreement has been entered into with you. Now you will give some loss of property as a reason, now other difficulties with which to bind me from time to time." For the excuses of those who are reluctant to pay are numberless. Therefore he offers another condition.

Jacob said: You shall not give me anything; if you will do this for me, I will again feed your flock and keep it.

"I do not want any of your property to be lost. You may certainly keep what has been acquired so far because of my work and diligence, and I will remain with you and pasture your flocks with the same faithfulness. Nor do I demand fixed wages, but I will wait for the blessing of the Lord and be content with whatever He gives." This speech was very pleasing to greedy Laban, since he heard that for the present no money had to be paid out by him and that he could have longer use of such a faithful servant. Accordingly, the pact between Laban and Jacob follows.

32. *Let me pass through all your flock today, removing from it every speckled and spotted sheep and every black lamb, and the spotted and speckled among the goats; and such shall be my wages.*

[45] Cf. *Luther's Works*, 4, p. 364, note 57.

33. *So my honesty will answer for me later, when you come to look into my wages with you. Every one that is not speckled and spotted among the goats and black among the lambs, if found with me, shall be counted stolen.*

The property and resources of Laban were sheep, she-goats, lambs,[46] he-goats, etc. But because the passage is rather obscure, one must first of all gather a definite meaning from it. For Jerome complains that it has been rendered in a most confused manner by the Septuagint and that he has never seen anyone among the Hebrew or the Latin interpreters who has explained it with sufficient clarity.[47] Burgensis makes almost the same complaint.[48] Lyra satisfies me in a way, although he is still at a loss with respect to certain matters where the grammar causes obscurity and the words are elliptical.[49] For the most part the difficulty is found in six verses. But the gist is this: "We shall make a pact," says Jacob. "I demand nothing from you, but I shall be content with whatever falls to me by the blessing of the Lord. Therefore let us pass through your flocks and separate from them everything that is spotted and mottled, so that those of one color remain on the one side and those that are mottled are placed on the other side." But there are four kinds, namely, rams, ewes, she-goats, and he-goats. But by synecdoche sometimes only one kind is named, sometimes more. All are not always counted. This is the source of the difficulty. But after the flocks have been distributed, Jacob gets those of one color. But those with spotted pelts are given to Laban. Jacob presents the condition to his father-in-law that everything born spotted and marked from among those of one color should come to him as wages, but that the rest of the young of one color, whether white or black, should fall to his father-in-law.

Laban gladly accepts this condition. He suspects no hidden deceit or guile, since for so many years he has seen Jacob's faithfulness and integrity. Therefore he opens his mouth for new

---

[46] The Weimar text has *agri*, but we have followed other editions and read *agni*.

[47] Jerome, *Hebraicae quaestiones in libro Geneseos, Corpus Christianorum, Series Latina,* LXXII, 37.

[48] Paulus Burgensis *ad* Gen. 30:32-33.

[49] Lyra *ad* Gen. 30:27 ff.

booty. He laughs and wonders silently at the artlessness of Jacob, who has chosen the smaller number and has left the young of one color to himself. There would undoubtedly be a larger number of these. For it is natural for white young to be born from white and for black to be born from black. But it happens very rarely that spotted young are born from those of one color, unless nature is imitated by human skill and diligence, as will be stated later. Therefore Laban congratulated himself not only that his property was not diminished, but that it was even increased. For nature is on his side.

But with this itself he again reveals his execrable avarice, for instead of accepting such an unfair condition he should have admonished his son-in-law not to defraud himself. For he chose for himself only the white or black animals, from which, according to nature, young like them had to be born, not young that were mottled. "What are you doing, my son-in-law?" he should have said. "You are defrauding yourself of the wages owed to you when you separate the spotted animals for yourself in place of wages." It is an unfair pact and contrary to nature. But nothing of this kind enters his mind. Indeed, he rather rejoices that another opportunity has been given him to deceive and make fun of this fool, and he hopes that if it ever happened at other times, he will be increased and enriched most of all by this pact. The heinousness of greed is so great that it makes men utter strangers to all godliness, kindness, and mercy, and clothes them with cruelty and diabolical wickedness. For here Laban is described as a man who is made so wild with greed, so cruel and loveless, that he is not willing to yield even a hoof from the whole herd to his son-in-law and his daughters.

This is the meaning of this pact, in which at the same time the monstrous greed of Laban should be emphasized and censured. Now let us look at the text, which, as I have said, is rather obscure because of the omission of words. First he says that he will separate all the marked animals, even though they have only one mark, if, for example, a black animal has one white mark on its forehead or elsewhere, or a white animal has one black mark on any part of its body. With this term he seems to include in a class, as it were, or by synecdoche, all the animals marked not only with one mark but with more, and indeed with little spots or marks. For the Hebrews call these animals נָקֹד (speckled).

Then he calls the spotted animals טָלוּא, which we have properly translated with "mottled." For this is how these two terms are distinguished. The former are marked with larger and broader spots of two colors, white or black; the latter are marked with smaller spots. Thirdly, he says that he will separate the reddish animals among the lambs. He means the reddish lambkins. But there is a difference between שֶׂה and כֶּבֶשׂ. The former is the name of a class and is applicable to all other cattle. The latter means a lamb a year old or younger. When it is more than a year old, it is no longer called כֶּבֶשׂ. We call it a paschal lamb, an Easter lamb. Fourthly, he also separates those that are spotted and marked in the herd of goats, just as among the sheep. But from the lambkins he selects only the reddish ones.

Then the words "and such shall be my wages" follow. Here there is an ellipsis, and one must supply the words "whatever will be born from them that is like them and whatever is spotted from the white ones." For it seems to me that only the herd of the white animals was left to Jacob, although others think that the black animals were also added. The meaning is: "Whatever will be born from the white animals that is mottled and has a spotted skin will be mine. But whatever will be born that is white will belong to you." Accordingly, it is an altogether unfair condition, since it is contrary to nature for reddish or spotted animals to be produced from white goats or sheep. Nevertheless, he presents this condition to the greedy man. For then [50] he says: "My justice will give me the answer"; that is, "I will be just. For this agreement depends on fortune and chance, in case it should happen that spotted animals are born to me from the white ones, lest you suspect that something is done deceitfully or fraudulently by me, although I have never done you an injustice. Furthermore, whatever will be found with me that is not mottled but is of one color and white, you shall say it has been taken from you by theft, and you shall be free to charge me with stealing."

This was an exceedingly hard obligation for a man so saintly and fair to assume toward a most infamous scoundrel. It appears from this that Laban often reproached Jacob whenever his cupidity and avarice were not satisfied or Jacob's household slaugh-

---

[50] The Weimar text has *tu,* but we have followed other editions and read *tum.*

tered and ate sheep, goats, etc., from the flock. Or, at all events, with such rebukes and reproaches he wanted to threaten Jacob and take precautions, lest Jacob turn anything to his own advantage, although Laban could have no doubt about Jacob's faithfulness and diligence.

34. *Laban said: Good! Let it be as you have said.*

It seems that Laban still doubts and mistrusts Jacob. "Would that what you have said may happen!" he says. "Come, let us try it, until I see whether the results of the breeding come up to my expectation!" Although he sees that everything conforms to his avarice, he does not yet accept it as settled, but he does so with the condition that he may be able to change and rescind the agreement when and as often as he wishes. Thus we shall hear below (Gen. 31:41) that Jacob's wages were changed 10 times. Accordingly, the loathing of Laban's avarice increases more and more, for he still snarls when his son-in-law offers him a completely fair condition that is altogether unfair to himself. He does not come out with a clear assent, not because he concluded that the acceptance of this agreement would not be useful to himself, but in order that he may retain the power to retract or renounce it, no matter what the outcome may be. Do you see what avarice does?

Therefore it has been admirably said by the poet: "Accursed craving for gold, to what do you not drive mortal hearts?" [51] For in this way men are changed, so that they retain nothing human but become statues and images without any feeling of humanity. Here what is said in Ps. 115:4, 8 [52] fits in well: "The idols of the nations are silver and gold. . . . Those who make them are like them; so are all who trust in them." Usurers, robbers, and greedy-guts are not human. They have eyes, and they do not see. They have ears, and they do not hear. In Ecclesiasticus 10:7 it is written that there is nothing more abominable than a greedy man. For they are loveless, monstrous, and cruel men. If they could pay for the life of all men with a heller, they would not pay it. Accordingly, they are robbers and murderers; for they snatch and

---

[51] Vergil, *Aeneid*, III, 56—57; cf. also *Luther's Works*, 27, p. 61, note 47.
[52] The original has "Psalm 113."

devour what should serve for the enjoyment and the support of others.

But if there had been even a tiny spark of humanity left in Laban, he should have been moved to humane conduct and to kindness by the virtue and generosity of his son-in-law and thought: "I see that my son-in-law is endowed with a good and honest character and is so concerned about my affairs that he is offering me a condition that is not only tolerable but even most profitable. But God forbid that I should accept it! He has my daughters as wives with whom he lives honorably and lovingly, and he has served me faithfully for 14 years. Truly, I would be crueler than any beast if I were to procure advantages from his disadvantages." But he does not even dream of any of these things; for his greed extinguishes all humanity, modesty, and man's very nature, and makes idols of silver and gold, etc.

Therefore the story of the poets about King Midas pleases me very much. They write that everything he touched was changed [53] into gold, just as he had wished it to happen. Surely such greedy men are like statues of silver or gold without any feeling of humanity. And elsewhere it has been admirably said that a greedy man does nothing well except when he dies.[54] For they are useless, yes, harmful, burdens of the earth, and they should be removed from all well-established states; for they are plagues of human society and examples, yes, horrible monstrosities, of inhumanity, cruelty, and impudence.

35. *But that day Laban removed the he-goats that were striped and spotted, and all the she-goats that were striped and spotted, everyone that had white on it, and every lamb that was black, and put them in charge of his sons;*

36. *and he set a distance of three day's journey between himself and Jacob; and Jacob fed the rest of Laban's flock.*

Here Moses uses other terms than those he has previously used. Above (vv. 32 ff.) he mentioned the reddish animals among

---

[53] The Weimar text has *vera,* but we have followed other editions and read *versa.*

[54] Cf. Publilius Syrus, *Sententiae* (see *Luther's Works,* 4, p. 61, note 54), maxim 23.

the lambs, likewise the spotted ones among the sheep and the goats. Here he mentions the he-goats to point out the great and insatiable cupidity of Laban, who separated even those animals that were not mentioned in the agreement. For although we have stated above that this is done by synecdoche, yet it seems that he did not exchange the previous designations with different designations without design. The עֲקֻדִּים are the larger he-goats which go in front of the flock, just as the תְּיָשִׁים are the smaller he-goats or bucks which are raised for food, not for breeding.

I do not know the etymology of the word עֲקֻדִּים. עָקַד means "to bind." Therefore some explain it to mean he-goats with a white ring on black feet, or, on the other hand, as a ring with which their feet seem to be bound, as it were.[55] Or, what pleases me more, he means those which have rather long marks all along the back, a long stripe, as nearly all he-goats have. As a result, this, too, serves to emphasize the greed of Laban, who was most careful to separate even those whose spots could hardly be noticed. For this is why he says: "Everyone that has white on it and everyone among the sheep that has black on it." It is as though he were saying: "When he had already separated the animals with spotted skins, he also took care to look carefully even at the hair on the feet or in the beard of every animal of one color, to see whether any were marked by a different color." He resorted to such an anxious and careful separation toward his daughters and his son-in-law to show that his completely sordid heart deserved the hatred of all mortals and of God. So much about the agreement.

37. *Then Jacob took fresh rods of poplar and almond and plane, and peeled white streaks in them, exposing the white of the rods.*

38. *He set the rods which he had peeled in front of the flocks in the runnels, that is, the watering troughs, where the flocks came to drink. And since they bred when they came to drink,*

39. *the flocks bred in front of the rods, and so the flocks brought forth striped, speckled, and spotted.*

We have heard that Laban longed avidly and anxiously for

---

[55] Lyra *ad* Gen. 30, *Additio.*

new plunder. But what happens? God shows Jacob a special artifice with which to correct and change nature. For he takes rods from three trees and peels them, not that he pulls off the bark completely, but in order to vary the colors, namely, white and black, in such a way that on the one side the white appears because the bark has been peeled off and on the other side the black appears because the bark has been left on. These he places in the runnels, so that the sheep have the rods before their eyes and conceive while looking at them. It was an ingenious philosophy or magic art by which he brought it about that in the heat of passion the sheep begot mottled offspring while looking at the mottled rods. And in this way multicolored and spotted offspring were born from the white or black herd. In Hebrew "they conceived" is יֶחֱמוּ, from יָחַם. The sheep warmed themselves near the rods; that is, they copulated. In Ps. 51:7 we read: "In sins יֶחֱמַתְנִי my mother glowed with love, my mother conceived me"; that is, I was conceived in the heat of passion and the shameful desire of the flesh. The heat that procreates is meant. Before the Fall it was pure and was created and necessary for procreation. But now it is corrupted by original sin. It is not a harmless heat, as it was in the beginning; but it is corrupted by lust and concupiscence. Therefore in this way, by skill and ingenuity, or by natural magic, Jacob foils the skill, or rather the wickedness, of Laban. This magic the fathers learned either by rather long practice or as a result of the instruction of their ancestors. For Jacob was undoubtedly taught by one of the patriarchs or by divine inspiration through the Holy Spirit. It is an established fact and in agreement with the teaching of physicians, who state that in the conception of all living beings, not only of dumb animals but also of human beings, special forms or marks are imprinted on the young, both as a result of a mental image and as a result of various objects that appear to the heart or the eyes, not only in the very heat of conception but also after impregnation has taken place.[56]

Jerome and the naturalists relate the example of a queen who gave birth to a child with the form and face of an Ethiopian as a result of a strong mental image of an Ethiopian painted on a tab-

[56] Luther seems here to reflect both the folklore he had learned as a child and the theories of prenatal influence he heard from his medical colleagues at Wittenberg.

let near her bed.⁵⁷ They also tell that another woman who was accused of adultery because, although she herself was ugly, she had given birth to a beautiful infant unlike both parents and the whole relationship. She would have been condemned, they say, had Hippocrates not obtained her liberation by giving the advice to ask her whether in her bedchamber she had had a painted tablet which had given her pleasure when she looked at it. When this had been found, she was absolved by the judges.⁵⁸ Thus we sometimes see bloody spots or spots of another color scattered on the face, on the eyes, on the cheeks, and on the neck of infants, namely, when pregnant women have been suddenly excited by the sight and the fear of something unusual and have moved their hands to those members. Here at Wittenberg we have seen a citizen with a face like a corpse who stated that while his mother was pregnant, she was suddenly confronted by the sight of a corpse and was so terrified that the face of the fetus in her womb took on the form of a corpse.

The same custom is carefully observed when cattle and beasts of burden are mated. Thus Jerome states that among the Spaniards horses of the noblest stock are placed before the mares when mating takes place, in order that foals like them may be produced.⁵⁹ Therefore there should be no joking with pregnant women, but they should receive careful attention because of the fetus. For there are countless dangers of miscarriages, monsters, and various deformities. Therefore a husband should live "considerately" with his wife at this time most of all, as Peter says (1 Peter 3:17). I remember that when I was a boy at Eisenach, a beautiful and virtuous matron gave birth to a dormouse. This happened because one of the neighbors had hung a little bell on a dormouse in order that the rest might be put to flight when the bell made a sound. This dormouse met the pregnant woman, who, ignorant of the matter, was so terrified by the sudden meeting and sight of the dormouse that the fetus in her womb degenerated into the shape of the little beast. Such examples are all

---

⁵⁷ Jerome, *Hebraicae quaestiones in libro Geneseos, Corpus Christianorum, Series Latina,* LXXII, 38.

⁵⁸ This anecdote is cited from Jerome by Lyra *ad* Gen. 30:37-42, but both Jerome and Lyra refer to Quintilian rather than to Hippocrates.

⁵⁹ See note 57.

too common when pregnant women are often excited by sudden emotions and fears at the risk of their life.

Accordingly, one must be on guard, lest they experience both bodily and mental disturbances that are rather violent. For those who pay no attention to pregnant women and do not spare the tender fetus become murderers and parricides. Thus some men are so cruel that they vent their rage on pregnant women even with blows. Of course, they are brave and full of courage against the weak sex! Otherwise, however, they are complete cowards. We heard recently that a certain prince, noted for many other crimes and outrages, drew his sword against his wife when she was sick and bedfast.[60] Truly an outstanding hero and a mighty soldier! But this is by no means heroic; it is outrageous and most disgraceful. For if you are a man, you will find your equal with whom you may clash. Heroes are brave against the brave and weak against the weak. For why is it that you stir up a fight against a child or a pregnant woman? Even in the company of temperate husbands this sex has dangers enough and more than enough in other respects from neighbors, from the devil, and from various apparitions and pictures of dumb animals. It is an outrage if they are increased by your cruelty.

Indeed, even the heathen have praised this virtue in their heroes, namely, that they were gentle and pleasant toward their wives. For the description of Achilles and Hector, etc., in Homer bear this out. Armed Hector kisses his little son.[61] Thus they were women with women, so much so that nothing seemed more womanish than those heroes in the company of their wives. But in battle Achilles conducts himself differently against Hector from the way he conducts himself when he amuses himself with Briseis.[62] Therefore those who are brave and pugnacious against the unarmed and weak sex are worthy of hatred. We men are born not to harm but to defend the weaker sex. For a woman has a body created for pregnancy, for the nourishment of the fetus, and she is exposed to very many dangers. Therefore she must be treated with wisdom and moderation. So far the first

---

[60] During 1541 Luther was highly critical of Philip of Hesse, but it is not clear whether this anecdote refers to him or to some other German prince.

[61] Homer, *Iliad,* VI, 466—481.

[62] Homer, *Iliad,* XIX, 282 ff.

part of this text has been explained, and one activity of Jacob has been described.

40. *And Jacob separated the lambs, and set the faces of the flocks toward the striped and all the black in the flock of Laban; and he put his own droves apart, and did not put them with Laban's flock.*

41. *Whenever the stronger of the flock were breeding, Jacob laid the rods in the runnels before the eyes of the flock, that they might breed among the rods;*

42. *but for the feebler of the flock he did not lay them there; so the feebler were Laban's, and the stronger Jacob's.*

43. *Thus the man grew exceedingly rich, and had large flocks, maidservants and menservants, and camels and asses.*

The other activity has to do with conception in the spring and in the autumn. For Jacob employed his artifice at the first conception, that is, in the spring when the sheep are stronger; then he placed the rods in the runnels in order that the stronger young that belonged to him might become mottled. But in the autumn and at the late mating the sheep are weaker because they lack the heat of the sun, which they have in the spring. Therefore he did not lay the rods. He wanted the lambs that belonged to Laban to be born of one color, according to nature.

But the spring matings are better because they take place when the sun is in the ascendant, when the heat returns, and the strength of all the plants and animals is increased. Therefore Jacob took care to have the better and stronger sheep, those born in the spring, just as those born in the autumn and late are called late and winter sheep. But this activity was sufficiently ingenious. Indeed, it was an act of shrewdness and almost of villainy. Yet here, too, Jacob observed such fairness and moderation in order that he might not cause his father-in-law to suspect that he was being deceived by cunning. At the winter mating he made no change, in order that Laban, too, might retain a part and not be completely despoiled. Accordingly, Laban was brilliantly circumvented and could not understand how it happened that the spring lambs were born with spotted skins and the autumn lambs followed nature. He thought that this happened by chance or by the blessing of God. Therefore he changed the agreement 10 times, as will be stated below, where, if ever before, he sets forth the most notorious and detestable example of his avarice. For because he saw that the spring lambs were better and stronger, he rescinded the agreement and chose the mottled lambs. Then, since Jacob did not correct nature by means of his artifice, lambs of one color were born, and the better lambs fell to Jacob's lot a second time. Therefore Laban was deceived again, and again he changed the agreement for the third, fourth, yes, the tenth time. O disgraceful avarice! It should be spit on by everybody!

Our rabbis, however, flog me because, as they say, I have rendered this passage poorly in my German translation.[63] For they add a third activity from what is stated, namely, that Jacob combined the separated flock with the sheep in Laban's flock, etc. They interpret it by saying that he drove the spotted lambs into one flock and made them go ahead of the flock of Laban's sheep in order that the sheep that followed might give birth to other spotted young by looking at the mottled lambs in front of them. But this has come from the exceedingly wicked and greedy rabbis, who measure the very saintly patriarch according to their own character, as though he had not been content with that magic but even brought the spotted sheep in sight of the flocks of one color in order that the young might become mottled not only because of the mottled rods but also as a result of looking at the mottled flock, although Moses speaks only about the rods and means the very opposite, namely, that Jacob removed the mottled flock to another place. For he speaks of the lambs which he separated. Thus today they also separate the lambs when they lead the dams to pasture. And the two flocks were separated by the space of a three days' journey. Therefore both flocks, Jacob's and Laban's, could not be together in one place.

Moses writes that Jacob became very rich by this activity, or, as it says in the Hebrew: "That man burst forth"; [64] that is, he was increased beyond measure. This seems to me at least to

[63] The notes of Luther and his colleagues on the translation of this passage are contained in W, *Deutsche Bibel*, III, 200—201.

[64] All the editions have *dirupit* here; but we have conjectured the reading *erupit*, which suits both the sense and the grammar.

be the true and actual meaning of this very obscure passage. It agrees with the judgment of all Catholics and is taken from a comparison with what follows, which, of course, will illustrate and confirm this meaning even more, also on the basis of a careful consideration of all the circumstances.

But the question is asked whether this deed of Jacob's can be excused, namely, that he deceives his father-in-law by manifest cheating.[65] For it has some semblance of greediness, or rather of theft and robbery. For why does he not observe the order of nature at both times, in the spring and in the autumn? I reply: From what has been stated above and what will follow below one can take an excuse that is different and honorable. In the first place, he is excused by human right, which concedes to those who serve greedy and unjust masters, if they pay no wages but only plunder, despoil, and rob, the right to snatch in their turn what is owing to them in wages. But this must be done in the proper way, lest it be done to the detriment of the master. In this way the Children of Israel despoiled Egypt, and for their undeserved servitude they received the wages which the Egyptians had not yet paid.

In the same manner Jacob had served for 14 years and had been afflicted with many miseries, difficulties, and troubles. Yet he was defrauded of his just wages. Therefore what he seized belonged rightfully to him, even against the will and without the knowledge of his master. This is one reply.

Secondly, even though it is guile and deceit, yet Jacob does this by divine authority; for an angel appeared to him and showed him this natural and permissible magic. Accordingly, Jacob learned this from the angel or from the saintly fathers, who had great experience with and knowledge of these things. But when God orders saintly and believing men to do something, this is undoubtedly saintly and permissible.

Thirdly, he will say below (Gen. 31:42) — for this chapter cannot be understood without the one that follows — "God saw my affliction and the labor of my hands." There we shall hear by what traits he was impelled to devise this fraud. "What was lost by theft," he will say, "I was forced to pay. If the God of my father Abraham and the fear of Isaac had not been on my side, you would

---

[65] Lyra *ad* Gen. 30, *Additio*.

have sent me away empty-handed now too." Because of the insatiable greed of his father-in-law the very pious and faithful Jacob had no hope of laying up and gathering together any property. It certainly was no small calamity by which he was moved to this robbery, especially since the divine authority by which he was ordered to do this was added. "For Laban has experienced more profit from you," said the angel, "than you could seize from him. Therefore you can rightfully use skill and deceit to take something away from him, not what has been seized but what has been conceded and given by God Himself." Therefore Jacob was excused by both human and divine right and by extreme necessity.

But this example will not have to be imitated by anyone except in a similar situation. For otherwise the eyes of scoundrels look only at the deed itself; they disregard the circumstances and rashly adapt it as an example to other acts of robbery. But you should by no means follow it unless you are like Jacob in all respects and all circumstances in a similar situation impel you. For he increased the property of his father-in-law and rendered such hard service to exceedingly greedy and rapacious Laban, who did not even give him enough food. He endured sleeplessness, hunger, thirst, heat, and cold by night and by day without any compensation or reward. Indeed, over and above this, Laban planned to despoil him of the wages agreed on, since he retains the right to change the agreement as often as he wishes. These circumstances should be carefully looked at and weighed. Then Jacob will not be accused of avarice, nor will anyone readily want to imitate this example; for it is heroic, just as many other examples in the lives of the patriarchs are. But we have spoken above about heroic deeds.[66] Sometimes heroes accommodate themselves to rules; sometimes they do not. Here, however, Jacob does not sin against the rule; for natural and civil law comes to his aid, and Christ says: "The laborer is worthy of his hire" (Matt. 10:10).

[66] Cf. p. 307.

INDEXES

Index

By WALTER A. HANSEN

Aaron 237
Abecedarians 24
Abel 74
Abimelech 30, 39, 51, 52, 55, 59, 63, 64, 81, 83, 84, 85, 87, 92
Abner 35
Abraham 3, 9, 10, 15, 16, 17, 18, 19, 20, 21, 22, 23, 26, 27, 28, 29, 51, 52, 55, 59, 61, 63, 72, 73, 74, 76, 78, 81, 83, 84, 90, 91, 93, 95, 105, 134, 136, 137, 143, 146, 149, 161, 165, 191, 197, 201, 202, 204, 207, 209, 209, 210, 217, 224, 226, 228, 229, 231, 236, 242, 243, 244, 252, 262, 265, 272, 273, 279, 294, 325, 350, 385
Absalom 145, 165, 206
Absolution 45, 46, 140, 141, 149, 183, 197, 205, 244, 245, 256, 274, 355, 360
Abstinence 3, 271
Achilles 309, 382
Ad ingressum sive introitum meum 370
Ad pedem vel ad cursum meum 370
Ad replendam civitatem 189
Adam 18, 24, 27, 44, 49, 74, 119, 149, 153, 163, 165, 203, 217, 222, 229, 362

Adelphi, by Terence 38 fn., 120 fn., 305 fn.
Adulterer(s) 29, 41, 51, 293, 302, 303, 341
Adultery 28, 37, 39, 41, 51, 52, 86, 190, 193, 214, 302, 303, 304, 322, 381
Aeneid, by Vergil 132 fn., 172 fn., 247 fn., 377 fn.
Afflictions(s) 5, 6, 12, 22, 57, 65, 88, 166, 171, 177, 385
Agriculture 267
Ahab 12, 246
Ahitophel 145
Ahuzzath 81
Ai 243
Albrecht, Cardinal Archbishop of Mainz 265 fn.
Alcoran 79, 221, 347
Aldhelm 304 fn.
Alexander the Great 239, 270, 353, 354
Alexandria 96
Allegory 88, 216, 223, 253, 279, 294 fn., 345, 346, 347, 348
Altar(s) 78, 80, 81, 83, 251, 252, 265, 304
Amalek 152
Amalekites 268
Ambrose 91, 220, 323
Ammianus Marcellinus 191 fn.
Ammonites 171, 268
Amorites 91
Anabaptists 239, 249

Aner 52
Angel(s) 20, 21, 23, 34, 50, 61, 62, 63, 70, 71, 125, 160, 161, 196, 215, 216, 217, 218, 219, 220, 221, 222, 223, 224, 229, 230, 234, 236, 243, 244, 247, 248, 249, 251, 252, 260, 267, 272, 276, 283, 317, 329, 346, 353, 355, 361, 363, 385, 386
Anger 12, 76, 82, 152, 169, 172, 173, 174, 221, 255, 300
Anointing 253
Anticipation 337, 341, 357, 358
Antipater 160, 161
Antiphrasis 35, 36
Antiquities of the Jews, by Josephus 160 fn.
Antony, St. 3, 4, 13
Ape(s) 309
Apelles 373
Aphrodisiac 352 fn.
Apostles 11, 15, 19, 25, 43, 44, 52, 90, 131, 138, 204, 216, 227, 286, 348
Apostles' Creed 46 fn.
Apparel, fine and precious 125
Apparitions 382
Aquinas, Thomas 36 fn., 72 fn., 205 fn., 303 fn.
Arabia 55
Arabians 155, 159
Arabs 279

Arannah 251
Argonauts 312
Aristotle 112 fn., 294 fn.
Arius 96
Arrogance 92, 93, 121, 122, 124, 180, 182, 336
Ars poetica, by Horace 336 fn.
Artesian well 64 fn.
Asceticism 33 fn.
Asher 339, 340, 351
Ass(es) 73, 76, 322
Attic Nights, by Aulus Gellius 182 fn.
Augur 366
Auguries 366, 367, 368
Augustine, St. 11, 12 fn., 24 fn., 30 fn., 37, 40, 65, 88, 91, 103, 104, 111, 158, 180, 217, 292 fn., 308, 309 fn., 323, 338, 344, 345, 349, 356, 359
Augustinians 333 fn.
Auriga 308
Aut nihil, aut totum 105 fn.

Baal(s) 12, 246
Babylon 160
Babylonia 352
Babylonians 208
Bait 150
Balaam 207, 209
Baptism 21, 22, 43, 131, 141, 145, 149, 183, 196, 205, 244, 245, 246, 247, 248, 250, 274, 277, 280 fn., 310, 355, 360
Bark 380
Basemath 93
Bear(s) 254, 327
Beauty 29, 41, 112, 288, 289, 290, 293, 294
Beer 133
Beer-sheba 61, 69, 73, 209
Begegnet 211
Belgium 283
Belial 246, 279

Believer(s) 17, 214, 223 fn., 234, 271, 275, 276, 277
Belly 6, 14, 36, 208, 353
 has no ears 372
Benjamin ix, 339, 340
Bernard, St. 3, 71, 133, 220, 221, 222, 234, 323
Besold, Jerome ix
Beth-aven 242
Bethel 241, 242, 243, 244, 251, 252
Bethlehem 220
Bethuel 280
Betrothal(s) 193, 301
Bible 79, 345; *see also* Divine Scripture, Holy Bible, Holy Scripture(s), Scripture(s), Word of God
Bibliander, Theodore 79 fn.
Bilhah 337, 340
Billy goat 310
Birthright 113, 148, 151, 152, 153, 154, 155, 157, 167
Bishop(s) 90, 122, 123, 155, 192, 199, 238, 272, 274, 331
 of Mainz 365
 of Worms 308
Bishoprics 192
Black Cloister 346 fn.
Blasphemy 11, 12, 43, 45, 206, 215, 258, 260
Blessed Seed 226, 328, 334, 338, 350
Blessed Virgin 20, 347
Blessing(s) 10, 18, 19, 21, 37, 43, 57, 59, 60, 64, 65, 76, 77, 78, 82, 84, 86, 87, 89, 94, 95, 99, 105, 108, 109, 110, 111, 112, 114, 116, 117, 118, 127, 129, 129, 132, 133, 134, 136, 138, 139, 140, 141,

142, 143, 144, 145, 146, 147, 148, 149, 150, 151, 152, 153, 155, 156, 157, 158, 159, 160, 161, 162, 163, 164, 167, 168, 169, 170, 173, 175, 176, 177, 178, 181, 182, 183, 184, 187, 196, 197, 198, 199, 200, 201, 202, 203, 204, 205, 206, 210, 217, 225, 226, 228, 230, 231, 232, 233, 238, 240, 241, 272, 274, 286, 287, 300, 310, 311, 317, 318, 325, 328, 331, 332, 338, 342, 363, 366, 367, 369, 373, 374, 384
Blueberries 352
Boils 156
Bonaventure 36, 221, 323, 344
Book of Judges 153, 252
Books of the Kings 138
Bread 7, 13, 16, 21, 38, 49, 54, 61, 137, 139, 143, 144, 183, 197, 202, 232, 248, 249, 260, 277, 371
Breeding 376, 379
Bride 290, 291, 292, 295, 296, 297, 298, 299, 300, 301, 302, 303, 304, 307, 312, 313
Bridegroom 285, 290, 291, 292, 293, 294, 295, 297, 298, 301, 302, 314
Briefe, by Luther 369 fn.
Brigit 346
Briseis 382
Brothel(s) 292, 304, 331
Brother Veit 369
Bruder Landsknecht 369 fn.
Bruder Veiten 369 fn.
Brutus 236
Bucks 379
Burgensis, Paulus 374

INDEX

Cain 163, 177
Calf 294
 golden 241
Calling 6, 50, 130, 238, 239, 245, 254, 269, 274, 280, 314
Calvary, Mt. 243
Calves of Samaria 241
Camels 272, 273
Canaan 94, 139, 143, 198, 210, 224, 225, 226, 265, 338, 339
Canaanites 10, 182, 193, 240
Canonries 192
Canons 333
Cardinals 35, 195, 245, 331, 333, 353
Carlstadt 109 fn.
Carmina, by Horace 16 fn., 66 fn.
Caro . . . angelificata 222 fn.
Carrhae 211 fn.
Carthusians 13
Cassia 136
Cassius 236
Castigations 13, 157
Catastrophe 113, 117, 119
Catholics 385
Cato 237
Cattle 3, 4, 6, 7, 8, 13, 54, 55, 58, 59, 60, 132, 152, 269, 270, 287, 296, 324, 325, 337, 339, 368, 370, 376, 391
Cause
 efficient 112, 188
 final 112, 113, 188
 formal 112, 113
 material 112, 113, 188
Celibacy 8, 33 fn., 176, 192, 292, 301, 322, 323, 324, 329, 330, 349, 354
Celibate(s) 33, 90, 291, 323, 330
Centurion 125
Ceremonials 20, 109
Ceremonies 80, 97, 110, 125, 135, 136, 245

Chaldaea 279
Chaldean(s) 10, 209, 210
Chapel 78, 252
Charran 210
 battle at 211 fn.
Chastity 27, 28, 29, 35, 40, 54, 60, 124, 164, 195, 200, 233, 258, 263, 291, 292, 298, 299, 301, 304, 307, 323, 324, 330, 331, 341, 343, 345, 348, 349, 351, 356, 358
Childbearing 289, 317, 329
Childbirth 31, 339
Children 3, 5, 6, 7, 8, 13, 14, 16, 27, 29, 31, 38, 58, 66, 67, 71, 78, 86, 89, 90, 93, 99, 100, 102, 107, 108, 112, 114, 115, 124, 132, 138, 140, 146, 150, 160, 163, 164, 165, 166, 168, 169, 174, 175, 185, 189, 190, 193, 194, 200, 202, 203, 261, 263, 267, 276, 279, 284, 285, 290, 304, 318, 319, 325, 328, 329, 330, 332, 337, 338, 342, 343, 344, 350, 353, 355, 356, 358, 362, 363, 364, 365, 371, 327
 of God 199, 229
 of Israel 139, 144, 153, 262, 385
Christ
 genealogy of 216
 kingdom of 26, 28, 88
 knowledge of 43, 223
 priesthood of 140, 142
 suffering of 177
 et passim
Christian(s) 18, 21, 22, 26, 33, 46, 48, 52, 63, 69, 71, 72, 77, 95, 128, 146, 185, 189, 190, 195, 202, 203, 204, 206, 208, 235, 240, 257, 263, 269, 270, 271, 274, 277, 278, 353, 359
Christianus 274 fn.
Chronology 340
Church(es) 3, 9, 15, 24, 25, 27, 28, 31, 33, 38, 41, 52, 53, 70, 74, 78, 80, 84, 87, 89, 92, 94, 96, 97, 102, 106, 109, 111, 112, 113, 114, 115 fn., 116, 122, 123, 132, 138, 139, 143, 145, 147, 155, 156, 159, 161, 162, 163, 166, 169, 173, 174, 175, 182, 185, 186, 188, 189, 191, 192, 196, 200, 201, 202, 204, 207, 208, 209, 214, 216, 223, 224, 226, 238, 240, 242, 244, 245, 246, 247, 248, 249, 250, 251, 260, 261, 263, 264, 265, 266, 267, 268, 269, 271, 272, 274, 275, 284, 289, 290, 299, 313, 331, 333, 341, 342, 343, 345, 346, 348, 349, 352, 353, 355, 362
 of St. Peter 369
Cicero 66 fn., 104, 269, 270, 354
Circumcision 20, 80, 83, 84
Cistern 64 fn.
City of God, by St. Augustine 11 fn., 12 fn., 30 fn., 338
Classics
 Greek x
 Latin x
Clement VII, pope 369
Clergy 80, 195
Code of Justinian 115 fn.
Cohabitation 51
Coition 51, 333
Comedy 119, 120, 121, 305

LUTHER'S WORKS

Comfort 14, 15, 16, 18, 21, 23, 25, 27, 31, 33, 34, 36, 37, 43, 55, 57, 58, 61, 62, 64, 69, 71, 76, 77, 78, 81, 83, 84, 87, 88, 103, 131, 136, 154, 156, 157, 172, 199, 235
   kingdom of 26
Communion 209
   of properties 219
"Computation of the Years of the World," by Luther 340 fn.
Conception 380, 383
Concupiscence 338, 345, 380
Condemnation 18, 50, 52
Confession 41, 86, 122, 154, 155, 157
Confessions, by St. Augustine 103 fn., 180 fn., 323 fn., 344, 359 fn.
Confessors 156
Conscience(s) 26, 33, 37, 66, 88, 157, 254, 271
   evil 145, 190, 191, 194
   good 39, 65, 191, 195, 272
   terror of 304
   timid 47
Consecration 253
Consolation 131, 192, 203, 205, 215, 223, 230, 231, 235, 247, 254, 255, 257, 275, 276, 277, 279, 283, 293, 313, 315, 316, 317, 320, 321, 353, 358, 360
Contempt 10, 14, 43, 45, 95, 107, 114, 138, 145, 148, 153, 166, 179, 200, 241, 242, 252, 268, 272, 286, 314, 315, 316, 317, 318, 321, 330
Epicurean 124
Continence 37, 291, 292, 323, 324, 330

Conversus 342 fn.
Convocations 109
Copulation 4, 37
Cornelius 27, 51, 130
Corpse 381
Corpus Catholicorum 257 fn.
Corpus Christianorum, Series Latina 222 fn., 374 fn., 381 fn.
Corpus iuris canonici, edd. Aemilius Ludovicus Richter and Aemilius Friedberg 154 fn., 188 fn.
Corruption 62, 86, 130, 208
Court devil 181 fn.
Cowl(s) 7, 260
Cows 97, 267, 269, 270
Crassus 210, 211, 280
Crassus, by Plutarch 211 fn.
Creator 35, 146, 184, 191, 192, 197, 222, 248, 249, 275, 314, 330, 353, 355, 363
Credo quia absurdum 129 fn.
Creed 46, 214
Crime(s) 11, 29, 34, 51, 110, 194, 297, 302, 382
Cross(es) 6, 14, 45, 88, 89, 90, 91, 92, 142, 143, 144, 146, 166, 176, 183, 185, 186, 190, 192, 200, 215, 220, 268, 271, 274, 298, 315, 316, 320, 326, 347, 348, 353, 358, 362, 363, 371
Crosstian 274
Crown(s) 110, 184, 206, 237, 251, 304, 353
Crucianus 274 fn.
Cynic 30

Damascenes 268
Damnation 45, 229
Dams 384
Dan 241, 335, 337, 340

Danaides 66
Daniel 94, 125, 171, 237, 245, 361
Daphne 89
David 24, 40, 84, 111, 131, 144, 155, 165, 184, 185, 203, 206, 225, 251, 252, 254, 255, 257, 268, 269, 270, 276, 311, 327, 355
Davus 120
De continentia, by St. Augustine 37 fn.
De excessu fratris Satyri, by Ambrose 220 fn.
De incarnatione verbi, by Bonaventura 221 fn.
De poenitentia et remissionibus 154 fn.
De resurrectione, by Tertullian 222 fn.
De situ et nominibus locorum Hebraicorum, by Jerome 210 fn.
De vita spirituali, by Jean Gerson 323 fn.
Death 4, 5, 18, 19, 21, 22, 23, 24, 25, 26, 27, 28, 39, 41, 48, 49, 50, 53, 55, 60, 63, 74, 75, 76, 77, 78, 100, 130, 131, 132, 143, 146, 148, 151, 154, 158, 163, 164, 177, 185, 186, 190, 191, 206, 219, 221, 228, 230, 233, 234, 235, 240, 273, 276, 279, 284, 315, 316, 328, 341, 355
   eternal 137, 229
Deathbed repentance 152 fn.
Decalog 20, 92, 214, 233, 348
Deceit 113, 128, 150, 199, 300, 304, 305, 321, 370, 374, 385, 386
Deception 95, 106, 110, 111, 113, 114, 127, 129, 298, 365, 367

INDEX

Decretalia Gregorii IX 154 fn.
Decretals 79
Deformities 381
Degrees 109
Demons 22, 130, 142, 143, 185, 218, 222, 330
Denouement 119
Despair 10, 13, 14, 43, 45, 169, 215, 254, 255, 320, 321, 327, 359, 360
Deutsche Bibel, by Luther 352 fn., 384 fn.
Devil(s) 5, 9, 10, 11, 16, 18, 21, 23, 26, 27, 32, 34, 39, 40, 42, 43, 47, 48, 58, 61, 77, 111, 132, 141, 142, 143, 146, 150, 151, 163, 165, 168, 170, 173, 181, 185, 186, 191, 203, 204, 205, 206, 208, 209, 210, 215, 219, 221, 222, 226, 227, 228, 230, 231, 233, 234, 235, 240, 248, 251, 252, 267, 270, 277, 279, 290, 306, 313, 348, 353, 355, 382
  author of all dissensions 33
  kingdom of 310
Dewberry 352
Dialectician(s) 24, 117, 148
Dialectics 24
Diebus unis 177
Diet of Augsburg 115 fn.
Dietrich, Veit ix
Dinah 90, 297, 340, 358
Diogenes 30
Discipline 189, 285, 287
Disobedience 315
Disticha, by Cato 237 fn.
Divination(s) 366
Divine Majesty 132, 187, 196, 218
Divine Scripture 73; *see also* Bible, Holy

Bible, Holy Scripture(s), Scriptures(s), Word of God
Divinity 42, 44, 151, 219, 221, 222, 223
Doctoral candidates 109 fn.
Doctrine(s) 11, 27, 36, 71, 72, 81, 103, 125, 158, 187, 193, 201, 204, 206, 214, 217, 230, 232, 245, 261, 264, 265, 345, 346, 347, 348, 353
  Christian 80, 188
  false 40
  heavenly 79, 96
  of demons 330
  of justification by faith alone 242
  or resurrection of the dead 19 fn.
  of the pope 79
  satanic 246
  sound 80, 83, 97, 208, 209, 359
  true 176, 208
  two kinds of 80
Dog 232, 364, 373
Dogmas 191
Domestics 6, 7, 8, 13, 14, 16, 30, 31, 53, 55, 57, 58, 138, 160, 290, 325, 342, 353
Donatistae 24 fn.
Donatus 24
Dormouse 381
Douay Version 272 fn.
Dowry 306, 307, 357
Dream(s) 20, 103, 122, 139, 212, 215, 217, 238, 240, 241, 244, 323
  deceptive 237
  melancholy 237
  political 236, 237, 239
  private 236
  Roman thought about 236 fn.
  true 237, 239
  unclean 237

Düben 63
Dung 4
Durch meinen Fuss 370

Easter 46 fn., 154, 376
Eber 20, 100, 101, 105, 111, 262, 263, 265, 272
Eclogues, by Vergil 53 fn., 292 fn.
Edom 160, 207
Edomites 155
Egypt 14, 15, 30, 51, 90, 131, 144, 252, 265, 276, 352, 385
Egyptians 150, 159, 385
Eigen wat, gut ist dat 55
Eighth Commandment 40
Eilenburg 63
Ein blöd gesicht 293
Ein' feste Burg 50 fn.
Ein galgen rew 152 fn.
Ein oder zwen tage 177
Ein schwerborn 88
Eisenach 381
Elbe 256
Elihu 207
Elijah 10, 12, 25, 30
Eliphaz 273
Elisha 10, 160
Elizabeth
  Luther's daughter 5 fn.
  mother of John the Baptist 362, 363
Ellipsis 376
ἐματαιώθησαν ἐν τοῖς διαλογισμοῖς 259
Emperor(s) 80, 94, 115, 194
En tibi lector, by Sebastian Münster 293 fn.
Enosh 79
Enthusiasts 39
Envy 6, 58, 68, 86, 221, 222, 327, 328, 344, 350
  two kinds of 326
Ephraim 241
Ephron 211
Epicurean(s) 11, 43, 45, 47, 202, 235, 327
Epistle
  to the Galatians 40

to the Hebrews 142, 154, 156, 235
Epistles, by Horace 172 fn., 369 fn.
Epitasis 113
Er kam on gefer an den ort 211
Er traffe eben an 211
Erasmus 58, 269, 270
Erfurt 88
Erlangen
　edition 7 fn., 27 fn., 37 fn., 43 fn., 100 fn., 288 fn., 325 fn.
　reading 62 fn., 118 fn.
　text 35 fn., 39 fn., 123 fn.
Error(s) 80, 103, 106, 121, 193, 194, 208, 347, 356
Es ist Essig 88
Esau 14, 70, 89, 90, 91, 92, 93, 94, 95, 96, 97, 99, 100, 101, 102, 103, 104, 105, 106, 107, 108, 110, 111, 112, 113, 114, 115, 116, 117, 120, 125, 126, 127, 128, 129, 134, 136, 143, 146, 147, 148, 149, 151, 152, 154, 156, 157, 159, 160, 161, 162, 163, 165, 166, 167, 168, 169, 170, 171, 172, 174, 175, 176, 177, 180, 181, 182, 184, 193, 198, 199, 200, 201, 202, 204, 205, 209, 210, 226, 231, 269, 273, 300
Esauites 176
Esek 65, 67, 68, 69
Eshcol 52
Ethiopian 380
Etymology 88, 337, 349, 379
Eucharist 21
Euclio 373
Euphrates 210
Eustochium 323 fn.

Evangelist(s) 216 fn. 255
Eve 119, 153
Ewes 374
Exhortatio virginitatis, by Ambrose 323 fn.
Experiments 128

Faith 4, 5, 6, 7, 8, 9, 12, 14, 15, 16, 17, 18, 19, 22, 24, 26, 27, 28, 39, 41, 43, 44, 46, 50, 55, 56, 57, 59, 68, 69, 70, 72, 76, 77, 79, 80, 82, 86, 87, 89, 116, 117, 118, 119, 120, 125, 127, 128, 129, 130, 132, 133, 140, 141, 142, 144, 146, 158, 161, 175, 176, 177, 184, 186, 187, 188, 196, 197, 199, 200, 201, 202, 203, 204, 207, 212, 214, 217, 220, 223, 224, 230, 233, 234, 235, 236, 239, 242, 244, 247, 248, 255, 257, 259, 264, 266, 267, 268, 269, 271, 274, 275, 277, 279, 281, 284, 292, 293, 310, 315, 320, 321, 326, 327, 332, 333, 334, 335, 347, 348, 350, 355, 358, 359, 360, 372
　formless 205, 206
　historical 131
　true and living 205, 206
Falcon 293
Fall 222, 380
Famine 9, 10, 12, 13, 16, 41, 53, 143, 170, 200
Fanatic(s) 34, 178, 256, 311
Farmer(s) 57, 136
Fastings 3, 4, 13, 156
Fasts 6, 13, 29, 71, 157, 271
Fetus 75, 289, 381, 382
Feudal privileges 109 fn.

Fides
　historica 131 fn.
　informis 205 fn.
Fiefs 125, 126, 136
Filth 6, 277, 282, 312, 329
First Commandment 115, 125, 262, 264
First Table 80, 94, 114, 115, 120, 125, 263
Fish 150, 286
Fisherman 150
Flesh 3, 4, 14, 17, 21, 22, 23, 27, 33, 37, 39, 45, 47, 48, 49, 54, 59, 61, 62, 63, 71, 72, 93, 113, 119, 129, 130, 131, 132, 133, 141, 143, 145, 163, 164, 168, 183, 184, 185, 186, 187, 188, 189, 191, 192, 195, 203, 204, 205, 207, 208, 213, 215, 217, 220, 221, 223, 224, 227, 229, 230, 232, 233, 234, 235, 247, 248, 249, 255, 256, 266, 267, 268, 271, 275, 284, 286, 289, 291, 292, 320, 321, 322, 326, 327, 328, 330, 331, 334, 335, 338, 341, 353, 360, 380
Flock(s) 269, 270, 280, 281, 282, 284, 287, 351, 373, 374, 379, 384
Flood 91, 100
Foals 381
Fons 64
Food(s) 7, 8, 9, 10, 39, 54, 57, 105, 106, 116, 135, 138, 149 fn., 159, 167, 195, 219, 232, 234, 236, 249, 253, 254, 333, 364, 379, 386
Foolishness 25, 120, 125, 127, 130, 132, 152, 208
Forgiveness of sins 22,

INDEX

141, 153, 155, 196, 230, 233, 257; *see also* Remission of sins
Formula of Concord, Solid Declaration 50 fn.
Fornication 34, 37, 41, 52, 86, 91, 190, 193, 343
Forster, John x
Fourth Commandment 107, 115, 165
Fox 295, 296, 297, 300, 301, 305
Francis 72
Franciscans 35, 346 fn., 347 fn.
Fratricide 201
Fraud 134, 150, 305, 373, 385
Freiberg 370
Frenchman 370
Friedberg, Aemilius 154 fn.
Furies 165

Gad 339, 340, 349 fn., 350
Galba 236
Gallows repentance 152, 155
Gambling 11
Gellius 182
Genesis ix, x, 99 fn., 101
Gentiles 52, 254, 259
Genuflexion 264
George, Duke of Saxony x, 260
Gerar 6, 58, 61, 62, 67, 69, 265
German(s) x, 19, 35, 66, 67, 88, 152, 156, 177, 211, 317, 370
Gerson, Jean 323, 344
Gilgal 241
Ginger 89
Gloriari in Domino 18
Glossa ordinaria 216, 280 fn., 345 fn.
Gluttons 58
Glycerium 308
Goat(s) 97, 267, 270, 284, 285, 310, 376, 377, 379
God
children of 199, 229
foreknowledge of 42, 44
hidden 44, 45, 46, 48, 50
is one and three at the same time 75
is unchangeable 48
kingdom of 33, 90, 138, 156, 157, 230, 244, 247, 355
knowledge of 43, 51, 84, 95, 124, 209, 223, 259
oneness of 72
revealed 44, 45, 46, 48, 50
revelation of 44
shows no partiality 51
unrevealed 44, 45, 46
wrath of 10, 29, 71, 140, 152, 153, 154, 155, 156, 157, 158, 161, 163, 167, 168, 169, 170, 194, 199, 219, 259
et passim
Godhead 74
Godless 7, 10, 11, 12, 74, 77, 171, 183, 236, 237, 239, 240, 272, 278, 284
Godlessness 160, 200, 367, 370
Godliness 6, 39, 41, 51, 52, 58, 80, 86, 163, 176, 178, 192, 207, 221, 233, 284, 285, 326, 331, 351, 358, 373, 375
Godly 10, 12, 27, 47, 48, 56, 57, 62, 77, 84, 121, 138, 147, 171, 189, 200, 203, 206, 236, 237, 240, 265, 341
Goliath 131, 254
Gospel 10, 11, 12, 17, 35, 39, 43, 45, 47, 49, 56, 62, 74, 78, 88, 96, 115, 125, 137, 141, 156, 157, 158, 171, 186, 188, 192, 193, 228, 229, 242, 245, 246, 256, 261, 342, 348, 360
Matthew's 216
of John 217
Gotha 242 fn.
Goths 11
Gotta 242
Government(s) 4, 5, 6, 15, 31, 39, 40, 71, 80, 104, 111, 112, 114, 115, 116, 122, 123, 124, 139, 141, 155, 177, 183, 184, 201, 202, 204, 207, 238, 239, 240, 267, 272, 308, 326, 333
Grace 31, 56, 59, 74, 77, 79, 94, 140, 154, 155, 156, 157, 183, 196, 197, 199, 229, 230, 233, 255, 257, 258, 259, 261, 263, 278, 284, 316, 332, 337, 354, 361
kingdom of 38
Grain 10, 13, 58, 138, 141, 274
Grammar 102, 209, 293, 312, 322, 374, 384 fn.
Grammarian(s) 244, 280, 308, 336, 352, 356
Gratitude 331
Greece 71, 339
Greed 5, 11, 268, 295, 306, 367, 368, 370, 371, 372, 375, 378, 379, 386
Greedygut(s) 368, 377
Greek(s) 24, 291 fn., 297, 341 fn., 349, 353
Gregory 216
Grief 90, 95, 97, 152, 154, 162, 163, 164, 165, 175, 180, 209, 210, 211, 212, 240, 241, 296, 298, 300, 314, 315, 358

Habakkuk 158
Hagar 92, 335
Haggai 370
Hannah 359
Hannibal 270, 353, 354
Haran 209, 210, 269, 279, 280
Harlot(s) 124, 191, 293, 303, 322, 330, 335, 345, 347, 355, 357
Hat seine fuss aufgehaben 272
Hatred 5, 10, 16, 45, 58, 60, 68, 69, 86, 88, 89, 151, 152, 154, 155, 181, 222, 252, 290, 298, 317, 318, 326, 344, 379, 382
Haughtiness 92, 94
Health 271
Heathen 37, 83, 84, 89, 119, 138, 157, 165, 166, 167, 176, 190, 235, 238, 252, 269, 270, 271, 272, 298, 317, 340, 342, 353, 354, 363, 382
Heautontimorumenos, by Terence 119 fn., 184 fn., 369 fn.
Heaven 15, 45, 47, 48, 49, 74, 76, 119, 123, 138, 143, 157, 158, 167, 168, 185, 214, 215, 216, 217, 220, 221, 222, 223, 224, 225, 236, 249, 258, 264, 267, 269, 276, 309, 312, 315, 327, 348, 354, 355
  kingdom of 23, 132, 137, 140, 142, 145, 177, 244, 245, 247, 248, 250, 251, 285
Heavenly spheres 22
Hebraicae quaestiones in libro Geneseos, by Jerome 374 fn., 381 fn.
Hebraism 280, 305
Hebrew(s) 36, 67, 72, 84, 88, 211, 281, 283, 293 fn., 336, 356, 375, 380, 384
Hebron 6, 9, 13, 59, 61
Hector 309, 382
Hecyra, by Terence 95 fn.
He-goats 374, 379
Helen 297
Helios 121 fn.
Hell 19, 21, 24, 25, 26, 27, 32, 48, 74, 130, 132, 142, 143, 149, 151, 158, 168, 191, 202, 206, 219, 220, 221, 224, 231, 234, 235, 244, 251, 254, 295, 355, 259
Henry, Duke of Saxony x, 260
Herborn, Nicolaus 257 fn.
Hercules 309, 312
Herd 368, 375, 376, 380
Heresy 96, 124, 359
Heretics 16, 36, 96, 345
Hermits 4 fn.
Herod 160, 161
Hesiod 291, 341 fn.
Heth 180
Hierarchies, three 139, 155, 269
Hilarion 4, 13
Hinrichs, Carl 311 fn.
Hippocrates 381
History, by Livy 317 fn.
Hittites 96, 97, 102, 146, 167
Holiness 4, 214, 329
Holy Bible 43; *see also* Bible, Divine Scripture, Holy Scripture(s), Scripture(s), Word of God
Holy Roman Empire 115 fn.
Holy Scripture(s) 4, 18, 20, 24, 26, 42, 43, 68, 80, 88, 104, 125, 128, 140, 146, 147, 152, 158, 159, 194, 195, 199, 206, 236, 241, 244, 278, 279, 294, 312, 333, 338, 344, 345, 357, 372; *see also* Bible, Divine Scripture, Holy Bible, Scripture(s), Word of God
Holy Spirit 24, 27, 29, 30, 33, 39, 67, 72, 73, 84, 95, 102, 104, 105, 114, 117, 118, 129, 133, 134, 135, 136, 140, 141, 148, 158, 168, 187, 196, 220, 223, 226, 227, 258, 266, 267, 275, 277, 281, 282, 283, 286, 288, 289, 290, 291, 311, 312, 320, 327, 329, 330, 331, 333, 334, 352, 353, 354, 355, 358, 372, 380
  does not come without the Word 111
  rhetoric of 28
Homer 353, 382
Hope 8, 14, 27, 53, 62, 69, 77, 79, 80, 82, 167, 168, 169, 171, 177, 184, 186, 192, 202, 203, 204, 208, 255, 275, 282, 295, 296, 297, 315, 321, 326, 327, 328, 332, 334, 343, 345, 347, 359, 361, 362, 364, 386
Horace 16 fn., 66 fn., 172 fn., 336 fn., 369 fn.
Horse(s) 121, 208, 271, 289, 370, 381
Hosea 242, 252
Hostia 52
House Postil, by Luther 283 fn.
Household 3, 5, 6, 7, 8, 9, 12, 13, 14, 15, 31, 38, 39, 54, 55, 58, 60, 61, 69, 77, 78, 79, 80, 82, 83, 85, 89, 90, 92, 93, 95, 97, 100, 108, 111,

INDEX 397

122, 124, 138, 139, 141, 143, 144, 160, 161, 163, 166, 167, 168, 171, 175, 191, 192, 194, 200, 201, 202, 210, 245, 246, 250, 252, 262, 267, 268, 269, 273, 274, 275, 280, 285, 287, 313, 314, 315, 317, 318, 320, 321, 328, 330, 331, 332, 333, 335, 341, 343, 345, 350, 363, 365, 366, 370, 371, 372, 376
Hugo 344
Humanity 151, 219, 222, 223, 377, 378
Humiliation 219
Humility 79, 91, 94, 95, 121, 153, 192, 224, 227, 233, 270, 319, 320, 321
Hunger 6, 9, 10, 13, 16, 144, 262, 264, 286, 332, 371, 386
Hunter(s) 102, 167
Husband(s) 3, 14, 30, 31, 32, 35, 36, 37, 39, 41, 51, 72, 73, 77, 94, 100, 101, 102, 104, 111, 112, 113, 114, 134, 176, 180, 191, 192, 282, 284, 290, 291, 293, 302, 314, 315, 317, 320, 321, 322, 324, 325, 328, 329, 331, 332, 339, 340, 343, 344, 351, 352, 354, 356, 358, 359, 363, 371, 381, 382
Hypocrisy 6, 9, 107, 108, 199, 232
Hypocrite(s) 6, 7, 13, 35, 39, 107, 108, 147, 199, 208, 213, 232, 268, 285, 286, 290, 366, 370
Hysteron proteron 210, 259, 337, 338, 343, 358

Idol(s) 36, 241, 260, 304, 364, 368, 377, 378
  worship of 366
Idolater(s) 72, 204, 207, 241, 304, 366
Idolatry 12, 96, 97, 114, 170, 207, 241, 242, 259, 268, 286
Idumaeans 160, 171
Ignorance
  careless 302
  gross 302
  invincible 302, 303
  negligent 302
Ignorantia legis non excusat, sed ignorantia facti excusare potest 302 fn.
Iliad, by Homer 382 fn.
Immortality 73, 77, 78
  of the soul xii
Impatience 5, 13, 14, 30, 59, 163, 215, 319, 320, 327
Imposture 295, 296, 299, 301
Impregnation 380
In constantem virum 42 fn.
In Genesin Homilia, by Origen 58 fn.
In Joannis Evangelium Tractatus, by St. Augustine 217 fn.
In nativitate Domini sermo, by Bernard of Clairvaux 234 fn.
Inangelatus 222 fn.
Incarnation 42, 78, 216, 217, 220, 221, 223, 234
Incense 242, 304
Incest 91, 304
Incontinence 332
Inductions 128
Indulgences 354
Infancy 75, 101
Infant(s) 75, 76, 100, 101, 173, 312, 334, 381
Ingratitude 16, 82, 365

Injustice(s) 65, 66, 182, 376
Inomnipotence 234
Institutes, by Quintilian 118 fn.
Intercession 211
Intercourse 30, 32, 350
Interest 369
Isaac ix, 3, 6, 7, 8, 9, 10, 12, 13, 14, 15, 16, 17, 20, 21, 24, 25, 26, 27, 28, 30, 31, 32, 36, 39, 40, 41, 42, 49, 51, 52, 53, 54, 55, 56, 57, 58, 59, 60, 61, 62, 63, 64, 65, 67, 68, 69, 70, 73, 74, 77, 78, 79, 80, 81, 82, 83, 84, 85, 86, 87, 89, 90, 91, 92, 93, 95, 96, 97, 98, 99, 100, 101, 102, 103, 104, 105, 106, 107, 108, 110, 111, 113, 114, 116, 118, 119, 120, 125, 126, 127, 128, 129, 133, 134, 135, 136, 137, 138, 139, 140, 141, 142, 143, 146, 148, 149, 155, 159, 162, 163, 165, 166, 167, 174, 175, 176, 177, 179, 180, 182, 192, 193, 194, 195, 196, 197, 199, 200, 201, 207, 209, 217, 224, 225, 229, 238, 241, 242, 252, 256, 262, 265, 272, 273, 283, 300, 350, 385
Isaiah 103, 111, 258
Ishmael 36, 73, 93, 94, 105, 165, 199, 269
Israel 12, 94, 139, 144, 157, 161, 184, 209, 219, 241, 261, 262, 270, 385
  kingdom of 160
Israelite(s) 150, 217, 241
Issachar 340, 356
Italy 11, 29

Jacob ix, 3, 10, 14, 17, 27, 61, 73, 89, 90, et passim
James's, St. 247
Jebusite 251
Jeremiah 77
Jeroboam 241
Jerome 40, 52, 84, 88, 111 fn., 162, 207, 210, 323, 344, 345, 349, 374, 380, 381
Jerusalem 160, 161, 240, 241, 242, 243, 244, 245, 250
Jesse 255
Jewish War, by Josephus 160 fn.
Jews 19, 30, 32, 36, 56, 71, 72, 73, 83, 101, 104, 134, 141, 149, 157, 160, 161, 162, 174, 178, 212, 259, 273, 303, 320, 336, 349, 352
Jezebel 25
Joab 35
Joachim of Fiore 346 fn.
Job 14, 30, 203, 206, 207, 209, 215
John 217, 223
John Frederick, Elector of Saxony 263
John the Baptist 161, 349, 362
Joktan 265
Joram 160
Joseph 10, 90, 286, 287, 288, 303 fn., 337, 338, 339, 340, 343, 344, 357, 258
Josephus 160 fn.
Joshua 109, 243, 244, 311, 325, 326
Judah 61, 91, 161, 225, 258, 337, 340
Judas 154
  of Meissen x
Judea 161, 174
Judge(s) 15, 115, 122, 227, 252, 304, 311, 335, 381
  unrighteous 361
Judgment(s) 26, 34, 53, 59, 84, 93, 99, 103, 104, 107, 119, 150, 153, 157, 164, 167, 170, 171, 182, 189, 284, 285, 368, 373
Judith 93
Julius Caesar 160, 236, 239, 270, 353
Jurisprudence 68, 308
Jurists 42, 65, 189, 302, 366
  pettifogging 194
Justice 51, 65, 84, 235, 368, 376
Justification 242, 257, 258, 259, 262
Juvenal 311 fn.

κάθαρμα 52
Keys 21, 142, 145, 185, 196, 245, 251
Kindness(es) 7, 8, 9, 32, 33, 34, 52, 57, 64, 81, 82, 86, 107, 169, 193, 196, 219, 256, 319, 371, 373, 375, 378
King(s) 22, 25, 26, 28, 31, 41, 51, 52, 55, 58, 59, 60, 63, 64, 65, 66, 80, 81, 82, 83, 84, 85 fn., 86, 87, 94, 95, 102, 112, 121, 122, 130, 135, 139, 143, 144, 145, 152, 153, 160, 161, 167, 168, 184, 185, 195, 200, 202, 205, 206, 207, 226, 227, 237, 253, 270, 286, 287, 293, 311, 340, 341, 342, 352, 353, 378
Kingdom(s) 20, 22, 41, 44, 51, 52, 53, 64, 81, 83, 84, 85, 94, 96, 112, 145, 146, 148, 185, 191, 199, 235, 236, 237, 268, 297, 344, 369
  eternal 19, 140
  of Christ 26, 28, 38
  of God 33, 90, 138, 156, 157, 230, 244, 247, 355
  of God's Son 310
  of heaven 23, 132, 137, 140, 142, 145, 177, 244, 245, 247, 248, 250, 251, 285
  of Israel 160, 241
  of wrath 38
Kitchen 270, 342
Koran 79 fn., 222 fn.

Laban ix, x, 144, 173, 179, 182, 192, 193, 195, 207, 209, 231, 235, 279, 280, 283, 285, 286, 287, 295, 296, 297, 301, 302, 305, 306, 324, 325, 339, 351, 363, 364, 365, 366, 367, 368, 370, 371, 372, 373, 374, 375, 376, 377, 378, 379, 380, 383, 384, 386
Labanites 370
Ladder 215, 216, 217, 218, 220, 223, 242, 243, 244, 247, 250
Lambkins 376
Lambs 374, 376, 383, 384
Last Day 22, 37, 90
Last Judgment 38
Latin 24 fn., 35, 225 fn., 279, 317, 370
Laudari in Domino 18
Law(s) 19, 20, 22, 23, 34, 38, 39, 43, 53, 62, 63, 80, 88, 102, 105, 110, 111, 112, 114, 115, 129, 132, 162, 164, 177, 195, 213, 230, 257, 259, 261, 264, 281, 291, 296, 307, 308, 309, 310, 311, 312, 326, 327, 328, 371, 372
  canon 194 fn.
  civil 194, 386
  natural 386
  papal 194
Lawsuits 268

INDEX

Lay brothers 342, 346, 348
Lazarus 371
Laziness 95, 363
Leah 270, 288, 289, 290, 293, 294, 296, 297, 298, 299, 300, 301, 302, 303, 304, 305, 306, 307, 311, 312, 314, 315, 316, 317, 318, 319, 320, 321, 324, 326, 329, 331, 332, 336, 337, 338, 339, 340, 343, 344, 345, 346, 347, 350, 351, 352, 353, 356, 357, 358
Lebanon 372
Lectures on Genesis, by Luther x, xii, 47 fn., 99 fn., 112 fn., 237 fn., 367 fn., 285 fn., 309 fn., 340 fn.
Leipzig 370
Leisure 80, 81, 313, 346
Leo IV, pope 137 fn.
Lethargy 142
Levi 304, 319, 337, 340
Levites 19, 261
Leviticus 19
Liber regulae pastoralis, by Gregory 216 fn.
Licentiate 125
Lie(s) 72, 114, 126, 150, 327
  obliging 40, 41, 110
  of love or compassion 40
  playful 41, 110
  respectable or pious 40
  three kinds of 40
  useful 41
Life 16, 26, 32, 33, 36, 53, 55, 58, 64, 70, 72, 73, 74, 75, 76, 77, 84, 87, 100, 101, 103, 112, 113, 114, 115, 120, 121, 122, 135, 138, 142, 143, 144, 149, 155, 164, 165, 173, 175, 180, 184, 189, 190, 193, 199, 200, 203, 218, 219, 233, 234, 235, 249, 254, 256, 263, 266, 267, 269, 270, 272, 273, 275, 277, 278, 282, 284, 285, 290, 294, 297, 300, 312, 315, 324, 328, 331, 333, 341, 342, 356, 377, 382
  active and contemplative 294 fn., 345, 346, 347, 348, 349
  blameless 83
  blessed 7
  book of 45, 50
  carnal 291
  celibate 91
  chaste 291
  Christian 205
  civil 311
  eternal 4, 17, 18, 19, 50, 78, 89, 110, 132, 137, 140, 142, 155, 177, 183, 186, 187, 191, 192, 195, 204, 229, 230, 245, 247, 250, 255, 260, 286
  future 39, 54, 245
  godly 15, 54
  hard 55
  heavenly 158, 250
  home 163
  household 6
  married 5
  monastic 9, 349
  physical 3, 10, 141
  present 10, 39, 229, 245
  saintly 34, 83, 322
  superheavenly 39
  voluptuous 7
Lion(s) 33, 131, 215, 254, 313, 327
Lives of the Caesars, by Suetonius 309 fn.
Lives of the Fathers 47, 310 fn.
Livy 317 fn., 353
Locorum communium adversus huius temporis haereses Enchiridion, by Nicolaus Herborn, ed. by Patricius Schlager 257 fn.
Lord's Prayer 52, 138, 214
Lord's Supper 21, 23, 141, 246, 274
Lot 207, 299, 300
Love 12, 31, 32, 34, 40, 49, 67, 79, 80, 82, 89, 95, 114, 140, 164, 189, 195, 214, 221, 232, 233, 262, 263, 264, 278, 281, 282, 283, 288, 290, 291, 292, 293, 294, 295, 296, 297, 299, 300, 301, 302, 303, 304, 307, 313, 314, 315, 316, 317, 322, 324, 327, 333, 334, 343, 344, 345, 347, 348, 351, 355, 380
Lucia 304
Lucifer 168, 222
Lucretia 303
Luke 34, 116
Lust(s) 5, 34, 35, 37, 38, 71, 112, 170, 189, 190, 191, 193, 195, 232, 282, 290, 291, 299, 301, 322, 323, 327, 328, 338, 341, 343, 349, 351, 355, 356, 358, 380
Lutenist 322
Luther ix, x, xi, xii, 5 fn., 8 fn., 11 fn., 15 fn., 24 fn., 33 fn., 36 fn., 44 fn., 48 fn., 50 fn., 63 fn., 131 fn., 140 fn., 142 fn., 154 fn., 158 fn., 181 fn., 194 fn., 222 fn., 225 fn., 236 fn., 271 fn., 275 fn., 283 fn., 285 fn., 291 fn., 294 fn., 304 fn., 308 fn., 310 fn., 333 fn., 340 fn., 346 fn., 349 fn., 352 fn., 356 fn., 369 fn., 380 fn., 382 fn., 384 fn.
Luther the Expositor, by

LUTHER'S WORKS

Jaroslav Pelikan 15 fn., 111 fn., 254 fn.
Luther's Works 4 fn., 9 fn., 10 fn., 17 fn., 19 fn., 23 fn., 24 fn., 29 fn., 33 fn., 36 fn., 38 fn., 40 fn., 44 fn., 47 fn., 48 fn., 50 fn., 66 fn., 70 fn., 71 fn., 73 fn., 88 fn., 96 fn., 99 fn., 105 fn., 112 fn., 131 fn., 139 fn., 140 fn., 142 fn., 150 fn., 155 fn., 157 fn., 158 fn., 163 fn., 181 fn., 194 fn., 197 fn., 200 fn., 206 fn., 207 fn., 213 fn., 219 fn., 220 fn., 224 fn., 225 fn., 228 fn., 236 fn., 237 fn., 243 fn., 247 fn., 258 fn., 267 fn., 270 fn., 285 fn., 299 fn., 303 fn., 304 fn., 307 fn., 308 fn., 309 fn., 312 fn., 323 fn., 324 fn., 336 fn., 337 fn., 342 fn., 369 fn., 373 fn., 377 fn., 378 fn.
Lutherans x
Luxury 11, 331, 333
Luz 243, 251
Lyra 25 fn., 30 fn., 36 fn., 56 fn., 101 fn., 111 fn., 113, 134 fn., 149, 160 fn., 212, 216, 241 fn., 243, 244, 251 fn., 253, 263, 273, 280 fn., 281 fn., 299, 301, 302 fn., 320, 323, 324, 326, 352 fn., 374, 379 fn., 381 fn., 385 fn.

Magdalena, Luther's daughter 5 fn.
Mansfeld 370
Many-breasted 197
Magistrate(s) 5, 15, 124, 159, 184, 186, 193, 269, 275, 326, 341

Malachi 135
Mammon 58, 208, 306
Magic 380, 384, 385
Mamre 236
Man muss höher faren 96
Mandrake(s) 352, 353, 355
Manichaeans 103, 144, 348, 356, 359
Manichaeus 228
Marriage(s) 4, 5, 6, 8, 31, 33, 34, 36, 37, 38, 52, 57, 85, 91, 166, 167, 168, 172, 174, 175, 180, 182, 188, 189, 190, 191, 192, 193, 195, 198, 267, 282, 289, 290, 296, 297, 298, 301, 302, 303, 304, 306, 324, 328, 329, 330, 332, 339, 345, 346, 348, 349, 354, 356, 357, 358, 363
  clandestine 194
  is a divine institution 32
  thorns of 196
Mares 381
Mars 349
Martyrs 54, 59, 90, 131, 156
Mary 161, 220, 272, 316, 346, 347, 349, 363
Mask(s) 135, 147, 268, 271
Masoretic text 356 fn.
Mass 137 fn., 157
Mathesius, John x
Mating 381, 383
Matrimony 192, 289, 291, 354
Matthew 216, 294
Maurice x
Meat 6, 137, 232
Mediator 21
Medicine 68, 308, 352
Meinhold, Peter ix, x
Meissen x
Melancholia 133, 134
Melancholic(s) 300
Melanchthon ix, 73 fn.
Menander 341 fn.

Mercy 56, 59, 74, 125, 140, 152, 154, 155, 157, 170, 181, 199, 219, 221, 255, 257, 277, 283, 307, 314, 316, 317, 319, 354, 358, 375
Merits 157, 258, 260, 316
Mesopotamia 99, 175, 210, 252, 280, 281, 339
Messiah 94, 157, 294
μετὰ σπουδῆς 272
Metamorphoses, by Ovid 347 fn.
Metaphor 150 fn.
Metaphysics, by Aristotle 294 fn.
Metellus 182
Methuselah 297
Michal 40
Micio 120 fn.
Midas 378
Miles gloriosus, by Plautus 286 fn.
Mines 370
Minister(s) 10, 11, 23, 49, 71, 130, 145, 192, 216, 229, 249, 263, 265
Ministry 21, 50, 62, 141, 186, 209, 245, 250, 260, 261, 262, 263, 264, 268, 362
Minorites 346
Minucius Felix 44 fn.
Miracle(s) 8, 32, 45, 56, 57, 175, 213, 234, 252, 291, 293, 310, 353
Miscarriages 381
Misfortune(s) 8, 10, 11, 12, 13, 14, 21, 30, 53, 56, 62, 77, 89, 90, 92, 96, 118, 121, 165, 168, 170, 171, 176, 177, 179, 180, 190, 234, 238, 270, 320, 354, 360, 368
Moabites 207
Moderation 32, 116, 382, 383

INDEX

Modesty 30, 37, 193, 227, 233, 299, 301, 378
Mohammed 71, 79, 347
Monarch(s) 94, 313
Monastery 247, 271 fn., 292, 309, 342 fn., 346, 348
Monasticism 4 fn.
Money 13, 17, 38, 55, 58, 59, 61, 140, 197, 296, 332, 354 fn., 368, 369, 373
Monica 103, 180, 181, 359, 361
Monk(s) 3, 4, 5, 6, 7, 8, 9, 13, 14, 35, 36, 71, 80, 92, 114, 138, 139, 157, 193, 210, 253 fn., 257, 258, 263, 268, 271, 282, 285, 291, 301, 308, 329, 333, 342, 347, 351
Monostichoi, by Menander 341 fn.
Moon 6, 7, 91, 97, 260
Morals 11, 20, 28, 29, 86, 104, 124, 187, 188, 285, 293
Moriah, Mt. 242, 243, 251, 252, 262, 263
Mortification 184, 203
Moses 3, 6, 9, 19, 20, 44, 47, 53, 55, 56, 57, 59, 61, 62, 65, 69, 79, 91, 92, 100, 108, 109, 110, 114, 116, 123, 125, 129, 130, 131, 134, 136, 138, 145, 147, 179, 192, 199, 200, 210, 211, 223, 224, 227, 237, 238, 242, 259, 261, 266, 269, 276, 280, 283, 289, 294, 295, 297, 304, 307, 309, 314, 316, 325, 337, 338, 339, 340, 348, 350, 357, 358, 360, 366, 367, 373, 378, 384
Moths 136

Mucus 278
Mulde River 63
Mule(s) 73, 271
Münster 239
Münster, Sebastian 293 fn., 336, 349
Münzer 96, 311, 325
Murder(s) 41, 143, 162, 163, 172, 181
Murderer(s) 41, 164, 177, 181, 377, 382
Mystery 44, 78, 217, 218, 294
Mystics, German 128 fn.

Naaman 287
Nabal 285, 303, 305, 306, 364, 365
Nahor 207, 208, 209, 210, 280
Naphtali 336, 337, 338, 340, 350
Nard 136
Nathanael 217
Nativity 220, 229
Natural History, by Pliny 293 fn.
Naturalists 380
Nature 37, 49, 62, 71, 72, 74, 75, 101, 129, 190, 229, 271, 282, 291, 292, 293, 297, 325, 355, 365, 371, 375, 376, 378, 380, 383, 384, 385
  divine 219, 222
  human 169, 208, 218, 219, 220, 221, 222, 229, 348
  of angels 221
Nazarites 262
Nebuchadnezzar 236, 237
Neighbor(s) 5, 8, 40, 65, 67, 78, 82, 83, 85, 97, 109, 112, 114, 181, 189, 191, 259, 263, 264, 286, 295, 320, 321, 381, 382
Nennen 79
Neologism 274 fn.
Neophytes 47
New Testament 8, 140, 141, 244, 357, 362, 363
Nightshade 352
Nineveh 336
Niphal 228 fn.
Noah 74, 149, 207
Nobles 42, 52, 368
Nomads 265
Nun(s) 48, 253 fn., 329
Nuptial feast 295
Nuptials 304, 206, 319
Nürnberg ix

Obedience 7, 114, 117, 118, 233, 263, 303, 326, 351
Octavian, by Minucius Felix 44 fn.
Office 119, 123, 265, 268, 330
  ecclesiastical 238
  priestly 103, 197
Oil 133, 180, 252, 253
Old Testament 244, 357
Omens 366
Omnipotence 132, 234, 361
Omnis utriusque 154 fn.
On Christian Doctrine, by St. Augustine 88 fn.
On the Bondage of the Will, by Luther 43, 44 fn., 50 fn.
Optative mood 141
Opus operatum 258 fn.
Oracle(s) 102, 104, 200, 248, 250
Orationes Philippicae, by Cicero 66 fn.
Orders 7
Ordination 248
Orient 92, 279
Orientals 279
Origen 58, 88, 344, 345
Ornat 125
Our Father 197, 271
Ovid 347
Ox(en) 73, 76, 208, 289, 291

Pahl, Paul D. 182 fn.
Palestine 14, 15, 352

Palestinians 28
Papacy 48, 71, 91, 125, 154, 156, 242, 244
Papists 5, 7, 33, 36, 52, 90, 137, 199, 213, 214, 236, 245, 246, 249, 267, 268, 289, 290, 291, 292, 299, 328, 330, 331, 332, 333, 344, 348, 350, 353, 355, 356
Parable 56, 158, 361
Paradise 42, 49, 167, 243 fn., 267, 347, 355
Parent(s) 22, 40, 71, 86, 92, 97, 102, 106, 107, 108, 112, 114, 115, 116, 143, 162, 163, 164, 165, 166, 169, 170, 173, 175, 176, 177, 183, 184, 186, 193, 194, 195, 198, 200, 207, 209, 210, 211, 212, 229, 253, 264, 273, 278, 285, 289, 299, 303, 317, 344, 371, 381
first 42, 49
Paris 9 fn.
Parix 225
Paroxismus 113 fn.
Parricides 382
Parthians 210, 280
Passion of Christ 235
Pastor(s) 21, 23, 71, 122, 123, 124, 193, 241, 249, 260, 263
Patience 7, 8, 12, 13, 14, 15, 25, 27, 34, 58, 65, 68, 69, 70, 79, 81, 82, 85, 86, 89, 90, 91, 95, 103, 144, 192, 205, 233, 235, 270, 292, 294, 296, 298, 304, 307, 312, 326, 332, 333, 334, 335, 345, 347, 348, 358
Patriarch(s) ix, 7, 10, 16, 22, 26, 53, 57, 59, 61, 69, 70, 72, 77, 89, 90, 91, 100, 101, 105, 110, 114, 140, 141, 142, 144, 163, 168, 177, 196, 197, 200, 201, 204, 205, 207, 209, 210, 211, 212, 213, 214, 216, 217, 223, 224, 226, 227, 229, 233, 235, 242, 251, 253, 255, 256, 257, 262, 265, 266, 269, 271, 272, 274, 275, 279, 281, 286, 290, 291, 295, 298, 299, 301, 304, 311, 322, 324, 337, 340, 344, 356, 363, 380, 384, 386
Patriarchate 238
Patrologia, Series Latina 133 fn., 137 fn., 210 fn., 216 fn., 220 fn., 234 fn., 292 fn., 304 fn., 308 fn., 323 fn.
Paucis diebus 177
Paul, St. 5, 10, 11, 22, 23, 27, 37, 40, 52, 62, 71, 82, 85, 89, 96 fn., 129, 131, 132, 145, 155 fn., 156, 164, 178, 192, 204, 208, 224, 227, 230, 238, 254, 255, 256, 259, 264, 265, 275, 278, 284, 287, 293, 303, 310, 316, 320, 327, 341, 359, 361, 372
Peace 5, 6, 16, 53, 54, 56, 58, 66, 67, 76, 80, 81, 84, 87, 89, 136, 215, 218, 238, 244, 274, 341
Peasant(s) 121, 270, 311, 325, 334, 341, 368
Peccatum grande 52
Peleg 265
Penance 154
Penitence 153, 162
Pepper 89
Perdition 18, 171, 199
Perez 91, 225
Persecution(s) 15, 59, 186,
Persia 352
Pestilence 10, 252
Peter, St. 11, 20, 25, 27, 31, 40, 51, 104, 116, 130, 186, 204, 250, 254, 255, 381
Church of 369
Phaethon 121
Pharaoh 51, 82, 130, 236, 276, 339
Pharisees 26
Phicol 81
Philip 217
Philip of Hesse 382 fn.
Philistines 58, 60, 61, 63, 64, 65, 69, 88, 131, 155, 200, 225, 268
Philo 161
Philosophers 291, 354
Philosophy 201, 388
Phormio, by Terence 118 fn., 120 fn., 121 fn., 136 fn.
Physician(s) 308, 310, 352, 380
Piety 55, 285, 334, 357
Pig 322
Pilgrimage(s) 233, 253
Pimples 312
Pimps 330, 332, 345
Plague(s) 164, 170, 363, 378
Plautus 88 fn., 286 fn.
Play on words 274 fn., 285 fn.
Pleasure(s) 6, 7, 14, 15, 37, 50, 66, 68, 69, 189, 199, 215, 220, 276, 278, 283, 320, 328, 331, 350, 354, 355, 358, 363, 381
Pliny 293
Plutarch 211 fn.
Poet(s) 66, 172, 292, 308, 377, 378
Poison 23, 164, 289, 333
Pollutions 323
πολύμαστος 197
Pontiffs 353
Pontius Pilate 220
Pope 7, 71, 73, 77, 79, 100, 102, 115, 195, 213, 245, 246, 251,

INDEX

272, 329, 331, 354, 365
Pottage 113, 148, 170
Poverty 8, 183, 258, 263, 265, 286, 332, 364, 371
Praedicamenta 38 fn.
Prayer(s) 3, 6, 109, 119, 122, 123, 124, 153, 156, 157, 165, 167, 171, 192, 196, 197, 199, 217, 252, 268, 271, 310, 318, 320, 321, 335, 337, 338, 357, 358, 359, 360, 361
Preacher(s) 16, 72, 216, 217, 238, 354
Predestination 42, 44, 45, 46, 47, 48, 49, 50, 173, 178
Pregnancy 382
Presumption 124, 175
Pride 6, 94, 95, 104, 105, 112, 279, 286, 315, 336
Priest(s) 5, 58, 81, 84, 92, 112, 113, 114, 125, 136, 143, 167, 168, 175, 176, 184, 185, 192, 202, 205, 207, 217, 226, 253, 261, 262, 265, 286, 346
 high 19, 20, 313
Priesthood 93, 94, 102, 104, 106, 107, 112, 139, 141, 148, 162, 163, 166, 168, 169, 175, 183, 184, 238, 344
 Christ's 140, 142
 Levitical 20
Prima gratia 258 fn.
Primogeniture 92, 93, 94, 95, 96, 97, 99, 102, 105, 108, 109, 110, 111, 113, 114, 116, 150, 170, 200, 215, 238
Prior 333
Procreation 30, 288, 289, 380

Profectus est 272
Promiscuity 34, 51
Promise(s) 8, 9, 12, 15, 16, 17, 18, 21, 22, 23, 25, 31, 41, 43, 46, 48, 54, 55, 56, 57, 59, 60, 61, 62, 63, 69, 76, 78, 79, 80, 81, 83, 93, 94, 95, 97, 101, 103, 104, 106, 113, 116, 128, 131, 134, 137, 138, 140, 141, 142, 143, 144, 145, 154, 159, 160, 162, 163, 167, 173, 174, 175, 177, 178, 179, 182, 183, 184, 186, 192, 198, 200, 201, 202, 204, 205, 206, 207, 208, 209, 214, 215, 216, 217, 224, 225, 226, 229, 230, 231, 232, 233, 235, 239, 240, 241, 244, 245, 253, 254, 256, 257, 260, 261, 265, 272, 273, 274, 278, 288, 291, 293, 310, 328, 332, 334, 350, 353, 358, 360, 372
Promised Land 17
Promised Seed 23, 328, 334, 350
Promovierung 109 fn.
Prophecy 101, 102, 104, 105, 110, 112, 113, 114, 116, 118, 143, 150, 155, 160, 161, 162, 169, 170, 176, 223, 346 fn.
Prophet(s) 5, 10, 12, 19, 25, 26, 42, 52, 73, 79, 81, 84, 85, 86, 88, 131, 153, 185, 209, 216, 229, 238, 241, 242, 243, 245, 255, 260, 261, 263, 286, 340, 348
 false 237, 239
Prophetess 79
Proportion

 arithmetical 308, 309
 geometrical 308, 309
Proselytes 83
Prosperity 56, 175, 201
Pseudo-Dionysius 139 fn.
Pseudolus, by Plautus 88 fn.
Publilius Syrus 378 fn.
Pulpit 246, 311
Punishment(s) 12, 51, 65, 71, 124, 152, 153, 154, 155, 164, 165, 169, 170, 171, 190, 191, 195, 372
Pupil(s) 6, 24, 71, 84, 261, 262, 264
Purgatory 354 fn.
Purity 214, 345
Puteus 64
Pythagoras 22, 23 fn.

Quaestiones in Heptateuchum, by St. Augustine 292 fn.
Quality, category of 294
Quarrel(s) 15, 55, 65, 67, 68, 96, 104, 106, 116, 181, 200, 329, 350, 353, 355
Queen(s) 95, 102, 166, 331, 339, 343, 380
Quintilian 118 fn., 381 fn.

Rabbi Solomon 149 fn.
Rabbis 88, 113 fn., 349, 350, 384
Rabbits 33, 107
Rachel 270, 281, 282, 283, 288, 289, 294, 295, 296, 297, 298, 299, 300, 301, 302, 304, 305, 307, 312, 313, 314, 315, 316, 318, 319, 320, 321, 324, 327, 328, 329, 330, 331, 332, 333, 334, 335, 336, 337, 338, 339, 340, 343, 344, 345, 346, 347, 350, 352, 353, 357, 358, 360, 361, 362, 364, 368
Rahab 40

Rain 138
Rams 374
Rapine 11
Raspberry 352
Reason 44, 45, 72, 73, 74, 129, 130, 132, 174, 186, 190, 194, 202, 213, 219, 235, 303, 371
Rebecca x, 14, 24, 25, 28, 29, 30, 34, 40, 41, 51, 59, 76, 77, 79, 91, 92, 93, 95, 97, 98, 101, 102, 103, 104, 105, 106, 107, 108, 110, 111, 112, 113, 114, 115, 116, 117, 118, 120, 121, 125, 127, 132, 134, 141, 147, 163, 166, 167, 168, 169, 170, 172, 173, 174, 175, 176, 177, 178, 179, 180, 181, 182, 194, 199, 200, 207, 209, 256, 273, 280, 281
Rebellion 161
Recapitulation 338, 357
Red Sea 131, 132
Redemption 18, 196
Reformation x, 109 fn., 115 fn.
Refutation of the Alcoran, by "Brother Richard" 79 fn.
Regula ad servos Dei, by St. Augustine 308 fn.
Rehoboth 69, 76, 80
Religion 3, 7, 43, 80, 96, 97, 108, 115, 176, 208, 263, 329
  Near Eastern 352 fn.
Remission of sins 213, 258, 259, 278, 290; *see also* Forgiveness of sins
Repentance 82, 151, 152, 153, 154, 155, 157, 162, 163
  Esauitic 170
Res gestae, by Ammianus Marcellinus 191 fn.

Resurrection 17, 19, 39, 42, 73, 74, 75, 353
Reuben 90, 304, 317, 318, 337, 339, 340, 351
Revelation(s) 73, 216, 238, 245, 261, 346, 348
  of immortality 77
Revelationes, by St. Brigitta or Bridget of Sweden 346 fn.
Rhetoric 24, 147, 182, 306
  of Holy Spirit 28
Rhetoricians 24, 337
Richter, Aemilius Ludovicus 154 fn.
Righteousness 3, 18, 51, 154, 158, 196, 214, 263, 267, 271
  formal 213, 232
Rods 380, 383, 384
Roman(s) 12, 24, 161, 209, 297
Rome 11, 156, 244, 317, 323, 339
  sack of x, 369 fn.
Roosters 289
Ruffen 79
Rungs 216, 218
Runnels 380, 383

Sabbath 20, 348
Sabines 297
Sacrament(s) 21, 23, 42, 43, 45, 46, 47, 49, 124, 141, 184, 197, 208, 223, 247, 248, 250, 258, 277, 348
  of the Altar 145, 185, 205, 244, 245, 256
Sacramentarians 249
Sacrifice(s) 5, 6, 8, 20, 52, 77, 78, 103, 109, 110, 242, 252, 258, 259, 261, 262, 263, 264, 265, 266, 283, 357
Saintliness 153, 214, 266, 267, 334
  two kinds of 213

Saints 4, 8, 12, 14, 15, 22, 25, 28, 32, 53, 57, 65, 69, 75, 79, 87, 89, 90, 94, 117, 119, 120, 121, 125, 128, 131, 147, 150, 186, 187, 212, 232, 233, 234, 236, 248, 254, 255, 257, 266, 276, 277, 278, 279, 280, 284, 285, 298, 304, 312, 327, 329, 341, 346, 353, 359, 360, 371
Salvation 11, 12, 21, 42, 43, 45, 46, 50, 144, 154, 155, 156, 203, 216, 230, 253 fn., 258, 259, 287
Samaria 241
Samson 131, 257, 311, 325, 326, 327
Samuel 152, 202, 359
Sancti Bernardi vita prima 133 fn.
Sanctification 18
Sanctity 8, 39, 195, 232, 242, 267, 275
Sanctuary 84
Sarah 17, 29, 36, 93, 95, 325, 334, 335
Satan 10, 11, 18, 46, 48, 49, 67, 131, 145, 151, 189, 190, 194, 205, 215, 219, 221, 224, 234, 239, 246, 251, 252, 255, 271, 290, 310, 321, 348
  fall of 222 fn.
Satires, by Juvenal 311 fn.
Satisfaction 162
  papistic 155
Saul 94, 145, 152, 184, 185
Saulites 206
Savior 17, 46, 48, 49, 217, 228, 248, 258, 350, 351
Saxony x, 63, 263, 341, 369
Scepter 110, 161, 184, 185

INDEX

Schick, George V. xii, 182 fn.
Schlager, Patricius 257 fn.
Scholastics 194
School(s) 109, 136, 250, 260, 261, 263, 264, 265
Schradin, John x
Schuldopfer 52
Scipio 270, 354
Scripture(s) 18, 21, 24, 26, 27, 61, 73, 92, 104, 106, 109, 111, 122, 149, 182, 185, 192, 199, 207, 227, 258, 261, 275, 294, 295, 299, 310; *see also* Bible, Divine Scripture, Holy Bible, Holy Scripture(s), Word of God
Second Article of Apostles' Creed 46 fn.
Second Table 80, 94, 114, 115, 120, 125
Sect(s) 96, 97, 103, 123, 359
Sectarians 123
Self-righteous 210
Semen 37
Sententiae, by Publilius Syrus 378 fn.
Septem 88
Septuagint 356 fn., 374
Sermon on the Mount 9 fn.
Sermones de tempore, by Bernard of Clairvaux 220 fn.
Sermons on the Gospel of John 48 fn.
Serpent 58, 153, 366
Servitude 143, 150, 292, 294, 305, 312, 313, 324, 333, 337, 339, 341, 358, 364, 365, 370, 385
Sex(es) 31, 33, 35, 39, 189, 282, 288, 289, 292, 298, 314, 323, 331, 357, 365, 382

Shechem 84
Shechemites 297
Sheep 30, 47, 107, 115, 152, 269, 289, 368, 371, 374, 376, 377, 379, 380, 383, 384
She-goats 374
Shem 15, 20, 101, 242, 252, 262, 265
Shepherd(s) 55, 65, 81, 87, 200, 281, 283, 368
Shiloh 162
Shrew 190 fn.
Shua 91
Sieben 88
Simeon 304, 318, 337, 340
Sin(s) 4, 5, 11, 18, 21, 24, 27, 28, 34, 39, 41, 45, 49, 51, 52, 62, 67, 73, 82, 85, 86, 93, 114, 125, 132, 140, 146, 149, 150, 152, 154, 157, 164, 170, 171, 178, 179, 185, 193, 194, 205, 208, 210, 215, 219, 220, 222, 228, 230, 235, 248, 254, 256, 257, 263, 267, 274, 278, 282, 302 fn., 303, 304, 326, 327, 328, 330, 331
  forgiveness of 22, 141, 153, 155, 196, 230, 233, 257
  mortal 36, 113
  original 22, 23, 30, 33, 35, 37, 42, 44, 157, 165, 190, 204, 289, 358 380
  remission of 213, 258, 259, 278, 290
  victory over 19
Sinner(s) 38, 86, 154, 157, 158, 214, 216
Sitnah 67, 68, 69
Slavery 313
Sleep 74, 75, 103, 127, 215, 229, 240, 252, 308, 324

Smugness 320
Socrates 190, 269, 270
Sodom 34, 283, 300
Solomon 81, 122, 203, 241, 252, 261, 277
Son of God 18, 19, 27, 42, 43, 45, 46, 47, 48, 49, 50, 56, 72, 142, 146, 220, 221, 222, 223, 231, 278, 303, 348
  kingdom of 310
Son of Man 7, 217, 218, 228
Sorbonnists 9
Soul(s) 18, 40, 43, 62, 74, 75, 76, 88, 106, 135, 136, 140, 143, 144, 155, 190, 203, 228, 229, 277, 346
  immortality of xii
Sow 325, 351
Spaniards 381
Specter 310
Speculation(s) 44, 45, 47, 133, 216, 345, 347, 348, 354
Stars 6, 186, 222, 225, 245
State(s) 6, 15, 31, 38, 106, 108, 112, 121, 122, 123, 124, 139, 143, 155, 159, 161, 188, 189, 267, 269, 272, 274, 275, 290, 309, 333, 341, 342, 345, 368, 378
  robe of 110
Staupitz, Johann 47, 333, 341, 346
Stratagems 215, 365
Suetonius 309 fn.
Summa Theologica, by Thomas Aquinas 72 fn., 205 fn., 303 fn.
Sun 6, 7, 8, 91, 97, 121 fn., 176, 186, 260, 277, 278, 304, 383
Sunday 137 fn.
Superstitions 96
Supper 248; *see also*

Lord's Supper, Sacrament of the Altar
Swine 30, 33, 37, 292, 323, 363
Syllogism(s) 73, 128
Synecdoche 374, 375, 379
Syria 91, 143, 287
Syrians 155, 279
Syrus 120

Tabernacle(s) 19, 78, 79, 80, 81, 83, 84
Tamar 91
Tarquin 303
Tartars 347
Teacher(s) 6, 21, 71, 73, 79, 80, 83, 96, 123, 136, 158, 159, 245, 261, 262, 274
  malicious 49
Temptation 207, 215
Ten Commandments 214
Terah 210
Terence 38 fn., 95 fn., 118 fn., 119 fn., 120 fn., 121 fn., 136 fn., 184 fn., 305 fn., 369 fn.
Tertullian 129 fn., 222 fn.
Tetzel, Johann 354
Thanksgiving 109, 258, 259, 260, 261, 264, 335, 357
Theologians 25, 42, 345
  at Paris 9 fn.
Theology 63, 136, 201, 302, 303, 309, 345, 346
  of the scholastics 194
Thomas Müntzer: Politische Schriften mit Kommentar, by Carl Hinrichs 311 fn.
Thunderbolt 121
Tigris 210
Tischreden, by Luther 346 fn.
Tithes 24, 260, 261, 262, 264, 265, 267
Titus Pomponius Atticus 104 fn., 269, 270
Tobias 203, 206

Tobit 77
Toledo 369
Tollatur impius, ne videat gloriam Dei 275 fn.
Tomtit 225
Torgau 46
Tractatus de laudibus virginitatis, by Aldhelm 304 fn.
Tradition(s) 96, 249, 253
  human 79, 97, 246, 251
  monastic exegetical 294 fn.
  papistic 246
Tragedy 119
Trial(s) 5, 6, 7, 8, 13, 14, 15, 16, 46, 47, 48, 49, 53, 54, 55, 56, 57, 58, 59, 60, 61, 63, 64, 69, 70, 76, 77, 80, 89, 90, 144, 145, 146, 166, 175, 176, 183, 199, 200, 202, 205, 210, 212, 215, 231, 254, 255, 266, 278, 320, 321, 326, 327, 333, 347, 358, 362
Tribulation(s) 6, 12, 14, 15, 21, 24, 61, 62, 69, 79, 87, 90, 92, 145, 171, 195, 223, 234, 266
Trick(s) 107, 117, 127, 151, 295, 365, 366, 370
Trinity 39, 73, 78, 212 fn., 280
τροποφορεῖ 34
Truth 4, 11, 38, 41, 48, 49, 71, 73, 74, 80, 144, 145, 177, 208, 213, 236, 291, 366
Turk(s) 12, 22, 23, 27, 43, 70, 71, 72, 73, 77, 130, 170, 199, 262, 343, 347
Turkey 244, 347
Twins 101, 176, 199
Tyranny 130, 150, 161, 209, 227, 228, 301, 303
Tyrant(s) 18, 130, 171, 186, 262, 265

Unbelief 6, 14, 45, 46, 131, 157, 205, 255, 269, 278, 327, 332
Unbeliever(s) 138, 332, 372
Uncleanness 4, 34, 37, 38
Ungodliness 115, 157
Ungodly 10, 121, 143, 171
University of Wittenberg 263
Ur 209, 210
Urine 352
Usury 368, 369
Uz 207

Vainglory 278
Vale of Succoth 84

Vengeance 8, 65, 67, 327, 365, 373
Venice 74
Vergil 53 fn., 132 fn., 172 fn., 247 fn., 292 fn., 353, 377 fn.
Vestments 110, 125
Vice(s) 4, 83, 181, 207, 208, 293, 364
Victory 18, 19, 39, 72, 90, 92, 131, 132, 143, 185, 227, 228, 230, 231, 234, 239
Vigils 3, 4, 6, 271
Villainy 80
Vinegar 67, 88
Vineyards 136, 138
Viper 310
Virgin(s) 35, 36, 40, 294, 296, 297, 357
  foolish 158
Virgin Mary 218, 220, 222, 234
Virginity 307, 348, 362
Virtue(s) 5, 6, 7, 8, 9, 12, 25, 41, 65, 81, 83, 89, 91, 233, 234, 254, 269, 275, 276, 278, 287, 293, 307,

… 332, 333, 351, 369, 378, 382
Vision(s) 71, 211, 236, 237, 238, 244, 254, 264, 288, 318, 346, 347
Vocation 36, 274, 311
Von Dalberg, Johann 308 fn.
Vow(s) 253, 260, 261, 262, 264, 265
  de facto 263
  de iure 263
  monastic 257, 258, 259, 342 fn.
Vulgate 97, 241 fn., 272, 349, 352, 356 fn.

Wages 287, 364, 365, 366, 367, 368, 370, 373, 374, 375, 376, 377, 385, 386
Wagon 121, 215
Wantonness 290
War(s) 10, 124, 131, 150, 170, 230, 238, 251, 268, 297, 349, 350
Warfare 61, 68, 227
Water 8, 49, 58, 59, 60, 64, 65, 68, 82, 137, 150, 248, 249, 255, 281, 282, 284, 287
Wealth 11, 16, 56, 57, 66, 72, 77, 80, 86, 112, 199, 260, 369, 370
Weddings 109
Weimar
  edition 7 fn., 43 fn.
  editors xii, 20 fn., 91 fn., 210 fn., 232 fn., 308 fn.
  text xii, 27 fn., 35 fn., 37 fn., 39 fn., 62 fn., 66 fn., 78 fn., 83 fn., 100 fn., 118 fn., 123 fn., 147 fn., 149 fn., 155 fn., 156 fn., 178 fn., 191 fn., 219 fn., 225 fn., 230 fn., 231 fn., 234 fn.,
241 fn., 246 fn., 263 fn., 264 fn., 288 fn., 295 fn., 309 fn., 325 fn., 360 fn., 363 fn., 365 fn., 371 fn., 372 fn., 376 fn., 378 fn.
Well of the Living and the Seeing 59
West 71
Wheels 121
Whoredom 322
Wickedness 5, 11, 12, 23, 40, 58, 65, 68, 69, 82, 145, 153, 165, 174, 200, 208, 210, 291, 320, 364, 365, 375, 380
Widow 35
Wife 3, 5, 6, 7, 9, 13, 14, 16, 17, 24, 25, 27, 28, 29, 30, 31, 32, 33, 34, 35, 36, 37, 38, 39, 40, 41, 51, 52, 53, 55, 60, 66, 70, 72, 77, 78, 82, 83, 89, 90, 92, 93, 94, 95, 96, 97, 99, 100, 102, 103, 104, 107, 108, 112, 114, 124, 138, 160, 166, 168, 169, 172, 174, 175, 176, 178, 179, 185, 190 fn., 191, 192, 193, 195, 199, 200, 202, 203, 206, 207, 210, 229, 261, 269, 272, 277, 281, 282, 283, 284, 289, 290, 291, 293, 294, 295, 296, 297, 302, 304 fn., 306, 307, 313, 314, 315, 319, 322, 323, 324, 325, 326, 329, 330, 331, 332, 333, 334, 335, 337, 339, 341, 343, 344, 345, 350, 351, 353, 359, 362, 363, 364, 365, 370, 371, 378, 381, 382
Wine 6, 21, 49, 59, 133, 135, 136, 137, 138, 197, 248, 249, 260, 277, 294, 300
Falernian 16
Winter cherry 352
Wisdom 3, 4, 24, 25, 28, 45, 58, 72, 120, 121, 122, 124, 128, 186, 194, 208, 215, 219, 224, 226, 227, 230, 235, 329, 338, 341, 346, 382
Wittenberg x, 35 fn., 63 fn., 194 fn., 380 fn., 381
  University of 263
Wolves 107
Womb 75, 76, 101, 105, 176, 316, 335, 342, 356, 381
Wonders 130
Word of God 3, 4, 5, 6, 10, 11, 14, 16, 22, 23, 49, 51, 54, 70, 72, 78, 83, 84, 86, 88, 128, 129, 144, 145, 156, 164, 179, 183, 185, 186, 192, 232, 233, 238, 240, 244, 245, 246, 248, 249, 253, 258, 261, 265, 266, 325, 330, 348, 353, 354, 355, 357, 362; *see also* Bible, Divine Scripture, Holy Bible, Holy Scripture(s), Scripture(s), *et passim*
Work(s) 3, 4, 5, 7, 13, 14, 42, 47, 49, 70, 71, 94, 103, 115, 118, 122, 132, 141, 142, 149, 157, 173, 175, 214, 215, 223, 233, 247, 250, 257, 259, 264, 267, 268, 269, 270, 271, 276, 277, 278, 279, 280, 282, 283, 284, 286, 330, 331, 334, 342, 349

good 80, 232, 258, 278
human 84
of supererogation 260
outward and showy 6
self-chosen 6, 285
Works and Days, by Hesiod 291 fn.
World 6, 7, 11, 12, 17, 18, 19, 26, 28, 32, 34, 42, 43, 49, 55, 57, 62, 67, 70, 72, 74, 84, 85, 88, 100, 109, 110, 112, 119, 130, 142, 143, 146, 150, 155, 186, 187, 188, 192, 197, 199, 201, 206, 208, 219, 220, 222, 224, 225, 226, 227, 228, 231, 234, 240, 247, 251, 262, 264, 265, 268, 272, 274, 275, 276, 297, 306, 309, 313, 314, 315, 316, 320, 329, 341, 342, 343, 350, 351, 353, 354, 368, 269, 370, 372
Worms 130, 206
Worship 7, 9, 20, 49, 71, 80, 82, 83, 84, 94, 95, 96, 97, 155, 188, 241, 242, 252, 259, 264, 358
of idols 366
Wrath 77, 88, 171, 172, 198, 222, 327
kingdom of 38
of God 10, 59, 71, 140, 152, 153, 154, 155, 156, 157, 158, 161, 163, 167, 168, 169, 170, 194, 199, 219, 259
Wurzen x, 369

Xanthippe 190 fn.

Young 375, 380, 383
Youth(s) 164, 192, 260, 282, 289, 304, 347

Zeal 107, 119, 169, 207, 242, 287, 328, 329, 344, 348, 350, 370
Zebulun 340
Zerah 91
Zeus 121 fn.
Zilpah 338, 340, 344, 350
Zion 342

INDEX TO SCRIPTURE PASSAGES

Genesis
  1:1 — 72
  1:27-28 — 362
  1:28 — 325, 335
  2:18 — 32
  3:5 — 42
  3:12 — 153
  3:15 — 58, 226
  3:24 — 50
  4:26 — 79
  5 — 200
  10:21 — 265
  12 — 40, 143
  12:8 — 243
  12:11 ff. — 28
  14:13 — 52
  15:16 — 91
  16:2 — 325, 328, 334
  16:4 — 92, 335
  16:14 — 59
  17:1 — 197
  17:17 — 29
  18 — 20
  18:1 — 236
  18:7 — 294
  18:12 — 36
  20 — 81
  20:2 — 28
  21 — 88
  21:9 — 36
  21:9 ff. — 94
  21:22 ff. — 81
  21:25-26 — 63
  22 — 19, 143, 242
  22:2 — 161, 202
  22:12 — 202
  22:18 — 17, 84, 217
  23 — 78
  23:7 — 146
  23:8 — 211
  23:16 — 17
  24:10 — 273
  25 — 160
  25:11 — 200
  25:23 — 15, 94, 101, 129, 150, 151, 160, 169, 176
  26:3 — 57
  26:4 — 225, 228
  26:6-7 — 25
  26:8 — 30
  26:12-14 — 56
  26:35 — 166
  27 — 113, 256, 273
  27:1 — 101
  27:23 — 134
  27:32 — 149
  27:33 — 134
  27:34-35 — 149
  27:39-40 — 160
  28:1-2 — 256
  28:11 — 212
  28:12-14 — 216
  28:13 — 225
  28:16 — 241
  28:17 — 239
  28:19 — 243, 251
  28:20-22 — 253
  29 — 280, 281
  29:1-3 — 273, 280
  29:17 — 293
  29:21 — 299
  29:25 — 302
  29:31-35 — 320
  30 — 298, 379, 385
  30:1 — 326, 345
  30:14 — 352
  30:23 — 335
  30:24 — 323
  30:27 — 374
  30:30 — 291
  30:32 — 378
  30:32-33 — 374
  30:37-42 — 381
  31:7 — 365
  31:14-15 — 332
  31:40 — 324
  31:41 — 377
  31:42 — 371, 385
  31:53 — 331
  32:26 — 161
  32:28 — 160
  33:1-3 — 160
  34 — 297
  35 — 200
  35:1 — 265
  35:28 — 201
  36:4 — 273
  37:3 — 288
  38:29 — 225
  49:10 — 161, 162
  49:10-11 — 160
  49:12 — 293
  49:19 — 350

Exodus
  3:6 — 91
  10:26 — 130, 276
  11:2 — 150
  14:15 — 131, 132
  20:2 — 115, 125
  20:16 — 40
  21:17 — 164
  23:26 — 325
  28:2 ff. — 125
  32:6 — 36
  33 — 44
  33:15 — 123
  33:20 — 47
  33:23 — 44

Leviticus
  18:18 — 307
  19:32 — 86
  20:9 — 164
  24:16 — 367

Numbers
  12:3 — 316
  12:6-8 — 237
  18:20 — 261
  23:19 — 135
  24:1 — 366
  27:20, 23 — 109
  30:2 — 257

Deuteronomy
  6:5 — 106
  6:7 — 145
  8:3 — 206
  13:3 — 237
  23:21 — 261
  23:21-22 — 257
  23:21-23 — 257
  23:22-23 — 263
  27:16 — 164
  28:4 — 325
  32:15 — 138
  33:9 — 114
  34:9 — 109

Joshua
  2:5 — 40
  8:1, 9 — 243

Judges
  10:15 — 153
1 Samuel
  2:30 — 84, 148
  13:14 — 255
  15:3 — 152
  15:15 — 152
  15:17 — 94
  15:23 — 153
  16:1, 13 ff. — 184
  16:7 — 107
  16:13 — 202
  19:11 ff. — 40
  25:3 — 285
2 Samuel
  2:14 — 35
  5:20 — 225
  15:25-26 — 145, 206
  24:18 ff. — 252
  24:21 ff. — 252
1 Kings
  3:5 — 122
  3:7 — 122
  3:7-8 — 122
  3:10-12 — 122
  4:5 — 85
  12:28-29 — 241
  18:18 — 12
  18:21 — 246
  19:1-3 — 25
  19:8 — 30
2 Kings
  8:20 — 160
1 Chronicles
  27:33 — 85
2 Chronicles
  7:16 — 242
Job
  1:1 — 207
  2:9 — 14, 30, 203
  2:10 — 206
  28:13 — 215
Psalms
  1:1 — 159
  1:1-2 — 111
  1:3 — 82
  1:4 — 22
  2:2 — 251
  2:7 — 20
  4 — 69
  5:10 — 52
  6:1 — 255
  8:5 — 218
  9:12 — 276
  17:4 — 225
  18 — 338
  18:26 — 336
  21:1 — 145
  23:4 — 355
  25:6 — 170
  27:14 — 56, 131
  30:6 — 23
  30:6-7 — 26
  30:7 — 23, 27
  31:24 — 56
  32:9 — 73, 271
  33:9 — 234
  34:1-2 — 18
  34:2 — 228
  34:7 — 61, 62
  34:9-10 — 144
  34:21 — 52
  37:2 — 144
  37:16 — 66, 369
  37:23-24 — 278
  37:25 — 12, 372
  37:35-36 — 372
  39:6 — 368
  41:1 — 261
  42:6 — 203
  50:13 — 258, 260
  50:15 — 79
  51:4 — 157, 170
  51:7 — 380
  56:8 — 276, 278
  60:6 — 84
  63:11 — 185
  65:6 — 27
  68:35 — 186
  76:11 — 261
  80:10 — 336
  82:6 — 124
  91:11 — 62
  91:15 — 77
  104:4 — 216
  104:8 — 57
  105 — 26
  110:2 — 240
  113:6 — 354
  115:2 — 203
  115:4, 8 — 377
  116:11 — 49
  116:15 — 276, 284
  118:13-14 — 144
  18:22 — 201
  122:8 — 215
  125:3 — 215
  138:6 — 316
  139:8 — 355
  146:3 — 49
  147:11 — 276, 278, 283
Proverbs
  1:24-28 — 170
  3:9 — 264
  4 — 170
  5:18-19 — 34
  8:8 — 338
  12:18 — 180
  13:12 — 203
  14:15 — 120
  16:7 — 81
  25:21-22 — 82
Ecclesiastes
  5:4 — 261
  7:8 — 83
  9:7-9 — 277
Isaiah
  3:5 — 86
  6:1 ff. — 238
  9:6 — 186
  9:13 — 170
  14:13 — 222
  20 — 349
  26:19 — 76
  26:20 — 75
  28:20 — 246
  41:8 — 26
  42:3 — 26, 327, 360, 361
  44:25 — 341
  49:14-15 — 342
  52:3 — 103
  53:3 — 185
  57:2 — 75
  65 — 349
  65:1 — 258
  65:11 — 349

INDEX

65:12-13 — 170
66:12 — 334

Jeremiah
17:2 — 77
46:20-21 — 77
49:12 — 171

Daniel
2:21 — 94
2:29 — 237
7:10 — 216
8:10 — 245
9:23 — 125, 361

Hosea
4:15 — 242
12:4 — 241

Jonah
3:3 — 336

Habakkuk
2:3 — 57
2:4 — 158

Haggai
1:6 — 367, 370

Malachi
3:6 — 43, 135

Matthew
1:2 — 73
4:4 — 54, 61, 137, 144, 202
4:10 — 49
6:9 — 214
6:12 — 22
6:31 — 137
6:33 — 137
6:34 — 195
7:7 — 156, 158
7:7-8 — 361
7:15 — 107
8:25 — 174
9:6 — 140, 233
10:10 — 386
10:28 — 27
10:30 — 276, 283
11:17 — 13
11:28 — 319
12:20 — 26
13:8 — 56
14:28 — 255
16:18 — 25, 130, 143, 231, 234
16:19 — 251
16:23 — 348
17:5 — 45, 348
18:10 — 221
18:20 — 247, 250
19:6 — 33
19:12 — 355
21:42 — 201
22:32 — 73, 224
23:23 — 267
25:11 — 158
25:40 — 261, 282
26:11 — 261
26:41 — 320

Mark
4:8 — 56
16:16 — 45

Luke
1:25 — 362
1:36 — 363
1:39 — 272
1:48 — 270, 316, 320
1:52 — 94
2:10-1 — 220
2:14 — 218
6:30 — 264
6:38 — 305
7:4 — 125
9:58 — 7
10:7 — 137
10:8 — 137
11:13 — 23
12:32 — 226
14:26 — 114
16:29 — 348
17:20 — 20
18:2 ff. — 361
21:19 — 146
22:45 — 211
22:61 — 342

John
1:1 — 130
1:18 — 50
1:47 — 217
1:50 — 217
1:51 — 217, 218
3:36 — 50
6:44 — 47
6:65 — 44
8:56 — 18
10:27 — 47
10:27, 5 — 115
10:28 — 47
11:9 — 174
11:12 — 75
12:24 — 146
12:35-36 — 157
14:1 — 18
14:6 — 44, 48
14:9 — 45, 46, 47
14:10 — 223
14:12 — 132, 142
14:19 — 18
14:20 — 223
14:23 — 245
15:3 — 213
15:7, 8, 6 — 284
15:8 — 274
15:16 — 85
16:1, 4 — 235
16:11 — 227, 240
16:33 — 18
17:17 — 213
17:21 — 223

Acts
1:6 — 44
1:7 — 44, 47
5:12 — 357
5:29 — 115
7:5 — 224
9:15 — 254
10:10 — 116
10:26 — 27, 130
10:34-35 — 51
13:18 — 34
13:22 — 255, 268
14:17 — 138, 236
14:22 — 145
14:23 — 89
28:5 — 310

Romans
1:16 — 130
1:17 — 158
1:19 — 258
1:21 — 259
4:15 — 113
4:25 — 196
6:2 — 274
7:14 — 131
7:19 — 22, 208, 327

7:22-23 — 22
7:23 — 24, 62, 132, 230, 248, 326, 327
7:24 — 23, 24
7:25 — 328
8:19 — 196
8:20 — 38
8:26 — 132, 320, 359
8:27 — 108, 132
8:28 — 117, 276, 304
8:30 — 256
8:31 — 16
9:5 — 19
11:29 — 43, 135
12:1 — 266
12:8 — 6
12:20 — 82
12:21 — 85
13:1-4 — 6
14:1 — 230
14:7-8 — 88
15:4 — 12, 27, 67, 192, 275, 278

1 Corinthians
1:19 — 341
1:30 — 18
2:3 — 254
2:8 — 303
3:12 — 238, 347
4:13 — 52
5:10 — 208
7:1 — 33
7:1 ff. — 33
7:1-2 — 37
7:2 — 326
9:13 — 265
10:9 — 178
13:7 — 172
15:19 — 317
15:32 — 43

2 Corinthians
4:4 — 227, 240, 313
4:6 — 205
4:11 — 341
6:1-2 — 156
6:8 — 57
6:15 — **246**
7:5 — 27, 254
9:6 — 368
9:15 — 230
10:4 — 227

12:7 — 131, 145, 255, 271
12:9 — 28, 196, 227, 256

Galatians
1:20 — 40
3:18 — 105
4:6 — 361
5:17 — 129
6:6 — 264

Ephesians
2:6 — 278
3:20 — 359
4:9 — 218
4:14 — 71
6:12 — 230
6:16 — 16, 48, 203, 210, 215

Philippians
3:12 — 230
4:13 — 293

Colossians
2:3, 9 — 224
2:15 — 151
2:18 — 71, 329
3:17 — 284
3:23 — 287

1 Thessalonians
4:4 — 38
5:17 — 357

2 Thessalonians
2:10-11 — 71

1 Timothy
1:9 — 164
2:15 — 5, 312
4:1 — 330
4:8 — 192
5:8 — 13, 372
5:17 — 264

2 Timothy
2:13 — 48

Titus
2:12 — 54

Hebrews
1:2 — 142
1:6 — 220

1:14 — 216
4:15 — 205, 312
11:1 — 183
11:14 — 198
11:33 — 235
12:1 — 248
12:16-17 — 151
12:17 — 154, 156
13:4 — 193

1 Peter
1:12 — 218
2:23 — 108
3:7 — 31
3:17 — 381
4:11 — 248, 250
4:17 — 171
5:5 — 104
5:7 — 56
5:8 — 215

2 Peter
1:19 — 186, 255

1 John
3:8 — 47, 49
5:4 — 206, 231

Revelation
14:13 — 272
16:19 — 171
21:2 — 250

APOCRYPHA

1 Esdras
4:38-41 — 144

Tobit
2:14 — 203, 206
2:22 — 77

Judith
9:11 — 315

Wisdom of Solomon
9:4 — 123

Ecclesiasticus
3:22 — 47
10:7 — 377
34:4 — 237
36:25 — 181

1 Maccabees
2:18 — 85